Giorgio Baruchello, Ársæll Már Arnarsson
Humour and Cruelty, Vol. 3/1

De Gruyter Studies in Philosophy of Humor

Edited by
Lydia Amir

Editorial Advisory Board
Noël Carroll, CUNY, New York, NY, USA; Simon Critchley, The New School, New York, NY, USA; Daniel Dennett, Tufts University, Medford, MA, USA; Stephen Halliwell, St. Andrews University, St. Andrews, UK; Kathleen Higgins, University of Texas, Austin, TX, USA; John Lippitt, University of Notre Dame, Sydney, NSW, Australia; John Morreall, The College of William and Mary, Williamsburg, VA, USA; Robert C. Roberts, Baylor University, Waco, TX, USA; Quentin Skinner, Queen Mary University of London, UK.

Volume 3/1

Giorgio Baruchello,
Ársæll Már Arnarsson

Humour and Cruelty

Volume 3: Laughing Matters
Part 1: Prolegomena

DE GRUYTER

ISBN 978-3-11-221624-8
e-ISBN (PDF) 978-3-11-076017-0
e-ISBN (EPUB) 978-3-11-076022-4
ISSN 2699-3481

Library of Congress Control Number: 9783111256108, 9783111256573

Bibliographic information published by the Deutsche Nationalbibliothek
The Deutsche Nationalbibliothek lists this publication in the Deutsche Nationalbibliografie;
detailed bibliographic data are available on the internet at http://dnb.dnb.de.

© 2025 Walter de Gruyter GmbH, Berlin/Boston
This volume is text- and page-identical with the hardback published in 2024.
Printing and binding: CPI books GmbH, Leck

www.degruyter.com

To my co-author.
To our mothers. May they never read this filth.
To our siblings, an endless source of cruelty and humour.
To our descendants, weather permitting.
To Lydia Amir, the instigator of these four books. What a cruel joke to make!
To our readers—the whole masochistic lot of you!

Acknowledgments

Writing an academic book is, normally, neither particularly amusing nor painfully aggravating. Writing several such books, on the contrary, is both a strangely humorous enterprise and a cruelly taxing task. We must therefore thank Professor Lydia Amir, founding president of the *International Association for the Philosophy of Humor*, for inspiring and initiating this scholarly endeavour of ours, which has given us plenty of opportunity to experience and reflect upon the two pivotal and titular issues of our work. Similarly, we must thank De Gruyter's Senior Acquisitions Editor for Philosophy, Christoph Schirmer, who is the person that actually decided to transform the original project, i.e., one scholarly volume, into a considerably bigger one. We mean three such volumes, one of which is divided into two parts, i.e., four physically distinct books! Without him, in short, we would have hardly experienced and reflected upon so much humour and so much cruelty as we did, including their mutual combination.

Not to mention the fact that both Lydia Amir and Christoph Schirmer concurred on the additional need to overhaul the citation and referencing standards of the original single manuscript at a point in time when this massive document was almost complete. What a laugh! The number of hours spent on nitty-gritty editorial changes and written reformulations was beyond belief. Consequently, if the reader finds any wrong citations or poor references in this third volume, these two lovely persons are to be held co-responsible for our mistakes—here's another combination of humour and cruelty, if you were looking for one… And if the reader cannot get the tongue-in-cheek tone of our previous statements, a further combination is also *de facto* instantiated, on the spot.

There are also a few colleagues who, under a great variety of circumstances, were crucial in helping us to establish, debate, and refine specific lines of argument on select philosophical and psychological topics. These are mirrored *pari passu* in the present third volume which, as hinted above, now comprises two parts. As regards Part 1, Chapter 4, we must thank Dr. R.T. Allen, Britain's leading expert on Michael Polanyi's thought. Without Dr. Allen, our knowledge and understanding of the great Hungarian polymath would have remained severely deficient. As regards Chapters 1 and 3 of Part 2, we must thank three Italian philosophers, gifted writers, passionate feminists, and Baroncelli devotees: Athena Barbera, Mirella Pasini, and Paola de Cuzzani. Their sense of humour and their awareness of the struggles within the West's liberal camp were of immense help to us. Analogously, we must thank an Italian archetypal psychologist, G. Roberto Buccola, and a Canadian critical thinker, Christopher DiCarlo, for important insights into some of the thorniest matters pertaining to the fields of, respectively, psychotherapy and informal logic. These insights proved most relevant *vis-à-vis* the same two chapters of Part 2.

Thirdly, there are colleagues whom we should thank indirectly because they did not mean to assist us in our arduous endeavour and yet succeeded in providing us with valuable food for thought and meaningful lived exemplar. As regards especially Chapter 1 of Part 2, we have to mention all those academics that gave us repeated example of both conscious and subconscious *self-censorship*. By this we mean the recurrent avoidance of themes, topics, and/or terms that could translate into public outrage, poorer career prospects, and/or prosaic headaches within university departments and/or professional groups. Sometimes, these individuals avoided these obstacles in full cognizance of the obstacles themselves *and* their own decision not to express what they had come to think about certain themes, topics, and/or terms—not even when their conclusions and usages would have been methodologically justified and/or buttressed by empirical evidence and logical reasoning. Other times, instead, the affective import of these themes, topics and/or terms had been internalised to the point of producing unthinking reactions of avoidance. The devil was just too scary to even begin thinking about it, not to mention proffering its name.

As regards Chapter 2 of Part 2, we should thank, also indirectly, the workplace bullies and vicious gossips that we have had the dubious fortune of encountering and enduring in our professional life. Not only have these flesh-and-thorn persons offered us ample and repeated proof of that so-called "Dark Triad" of human personality which keeps being discussed by contemporary psychologists, i.e., narcissism, Machiavellianism, and lack of empathy (aka "psychopathy"). Also, having to suffer their cruel scheming and clever abuses turned out to be an inexhaustible source of bleak jokes without which we would have probably been unable to tolerate the difficulties caused by such obnoxious and, apparently, far-from-rare human beings. Indeed, as John Williams' masterful 1965 novel *Stoner* exemplifies, they can even turn up in the world of fictional universities.

As to much more pleasant individuals, we ought to conclude these acknowledgments by mentioning Raymond Snider and Audrey Matthews-Hill, who helped us with the time-consuming processes of proofreading and editing. Similarly, with special regard to Chapter 1 of Part 2, we must add the brothers James K. and J. Alan Galbraith, both of whom should be acknowledged for their encouragement, as well as for some clever considerations about the consumption of ice cream in very cold climates. Likewise, we must extend our gratitude to our own families who had to put up with us while busy working on three volumes about humour and cruelty. For our spouses and teenage children, these two concepts became a tangible daily reality. The former was called upon by them in order to let their husbands' and/or their fathers' absent-mindedness and mood swings be bearable; the latter was implied by the very same husbands' and/or fathers' absent-mindedness and mood swings. The tome that you have in your hands (or on your screen) is, therefore, yet another demonstration of how humour and cruelty can criss-cross, contaminate mutually, and combat each other.

Akureyri, Iceland, March 2023   Giorgio Baruchello and Ársæll Már Arnarsson

Contents

Acknowledgments —— VII

1 Introduction —— 1
1.1 First Movement: Allegro ma non troppo —— 2
1.2 Second Movement: Grave —— 14
1.3 Third Movement: Scherzo —— 19
1.4 Coda —— 25
1.5 Coda's Coda —— 28

2 Making Sense of Humour —— 29
2.1 An Overview of 'Humour' in the Humanities —— 29
2.2 An Overview of 'Humour' in the Social Sciences —— 60

3 Making Sense of Cruelty —— 87
3.1 An Overview of 'Cruelty' in the Humanities —— 87
3.2 An Overview of 'Cruelty' in the Social Sciences —— 127

4 Making Sense of Polysemy —— 145
4.1 A Theory of Concepts: Michael Polanyi —— 147
4.2 A Theory of Concepts: 'Humour' and 'Cruelty' —— 155
4.3 Two Sets of Family Resemblances —— 164

Bibliography —— 177

Index —— 243

1 Introduction

> A civilization without humor prepares its own funeral.
> —Jacques Maritain[1]

Being intentionally funny is a funny business.[2] Some poor soul may fret about it for years and try in all sorts of creative ways without ever coming close to mastering humour's subtleties or failing miserably on all counts.[3] Another soul, instead, who happens to be in a position of social pre-eminence, can command with the greatest ease the general amusement of all who happen to be surrounding him/her, even if s/he utters the same jokes or performs the same jests as the poor soul with whom we started the present paragraph. A third one, finding him-/herself at a party where most guests are positively inebriated, can make the crowd laugh roaringly with far less apprehension and ingenuity. Aware of such conundrums, it is no big surprise to read that very many thinkers have regarded "humour" proper to be nothing short of a genuine mystery.[4]

---

[1] Maritain (1973b), 62.
[2] On its counterpart, i.e., unintentional humour, see, e.g., the freshmen's blunders in the written compositions tackled by Kristine Hansen (1983). Or consider the unintended comic effect that Nordic-looking actors can have on Italian or Greek audiences watching undubbed Hollywood movies and/or British TV series depicting the classical world. Admittedly, laughing at the actors, perhaps cruelly so, is an alternative to feeling cruelly wounded by any implicit "exploitation and misappropriation of national/cultural mythologies" (Hassapopoulou 2007, 75). The contrast between a comic and a tragic view of life being a central theme in our trilogy's second volume.
[3] This failure, when especially painful, can be listed among the many extant intersections between humour and cruelty. Interestingly, we can retrieve in the writings by the famous Viennese physician and psychoanalyst Alfred Adler (1955, 233) the telling case of a "neurotic ... patient" who "would like to be sarcastic like his aunt", whom the patient resents, but "all he possesses is backstairs humour and he never finds a ready answer". It should be noted that "backstairs humour" refers to the frustrating experience of coming up with a clever rejoinder when it is far too late, figuratively, when one is already in the stairwell, i.e., returning home from the flat or house where the rejoinder should have been uttered. The original and more common phrase among Anglophone speakers is still the French *esprit de l'escalier*, which is said to originate in Diderot's (1994, 1395) writings on comedy. Ironically, the endurance of the French expression in the Anglophone context might be the result of noted English translations (see, e.g., Diderot 1883, 41), which failed to mention any staircases or steps.
[4] Some readers may be under the impression that humour is *not* a serious research topic. The present volume will show them that they are mistaken, especially as regards humour's crucial role in making life more tolerable. Not to mention the fact that the present volume is the third instalment in an academic trilogy (hereafter *H&C1*, *H&C2* and *H&C3*) by one of Europe's leading academic publishers. And let us be explicit on the following point: when writing *"volume"*, we mean

1.1 First Movement: Allegro ma non troppo

> Þegar ég hungraður bið um brauð, / býður mér heimurinn steina.
> —Grétar Ó. Fells[5]

Leslie Stephen, a largely forgotten 19th-century English writer, a pioneering Victorian mountaineer, and the often-neglected father of two much more famous and somewhat less adventurous daughters, wondered, laconically: "What is humour? That is one of the insoluble questions."[6] A hundred years later, Umberto Eco, possibly the most celebrated Italian philosopher, linguist, humorist and novelist of the late 20th century, wrote as follows:

> The greatest thinkers have tripped on the comical. They managed to define thought, being, God, but not why we laugh madly at a gentleman who is walking down the stairs and suddenly trips and falls. When they came to explain this, the greatest thinkers got entangled in a vast net of contradictions, whence they emerged, after huge efforts, with very thin answers.[7]

And at the close of the second decade of the 21st century, two of the world's leading humour scholars, Victor Raskin and Salvatore Attardo, admitted: "we have never really defined humor just as love, life, emotion, society defy concise and universally accepted definitions. So, people proceed on 'common sense' and promptly discover that nothing much is common about it."[8]

"Cruelty", in turn, has been no gentler friend to Western thinkers, whether they were great or small, and were blessed or not with any remarkable offspring of either sex and/or whichever gender.[9] On the one hand, there have certainly flourished countless cases of mundane and hasty linguistic usages of "cruelty"

H&C3 in its entirety, i.e., *both* Parts 1 and 2. When writing *"here"* or *"book"*, instead, we mean a distinct physical tome, i.e., *either* Part 1 *or* Part 2 of *H&C3*.

5 *"When I hunger for bread, / the world offers me stones"* ("Fjallið eina", 1949, 4th stanza, verses 1–2). As the reader will notice, some of the sources for our volume originate outside the Anglophone provinces of the world. Songs, poems and musical compositions, however, are not listed in the closing bibliography.

6 As cited in Figueroa-Dorrego and Larkin-Galiñanes (2009), 540. Virginia Woolf and Vanessa Bell are the sprogs.

7 As cited in Ercoli (2013b), 13. Others' translations being unknown or unavailable, the ones used in this work are ours.

8 Attardo and Raskin (2017), 51. At the same time, some of the most heated human struggles concern such issues.

9 We do not address the *vexata quaestio* of whether sex and gender coincide or not. We simply acknowledge it.

and "cruel".[10] On the other hand, when revising carefully the relevant literature, there seems to have been very few thinkers capable of or interested in addressing 'cruelty' *per se* to any significant level, i.e., such that they did not simply assume and/or apply some tacit and/or common-sense interpretation of the concept.[11]

Candidly, the 20th-century US political theorist Judith Shklar observed:

> [C]ruelty is baffling because we can live neither with nor without it… I suspect that we talk around cruelty because we do not want to talk about it… What we do seem to talk about incessantly is hypocrisy, and not because it hides cowardice, cruelty, or other horrors, but because failures of honesty and of sincerity upset us enormously, and they are vices which we can attack directly and easily. They are easier to bear, and seem less intractable.[12]

Aware of these semantic, pragmatic, theoretical and ethical challenges, we are going to devote the next two short chapters of *H&C3* to retrieving, reconstructing, rearranging, and reviewing succinctly the complex landscape of available conceptions of these two notions.[13] In essence, we endeavour to sketch a basic yet lucid conceptual map for such a hazy and, at times, downright chaotic intellectual landscape, the main elements of which are inevitably based upon our own careful selection of eloquent, eminent, and/or exemplary voices within the canon of the Western humanities and social sciences.[14] Afterwards, in another short chapter, we will explain why the concepts of 'humour' and 'cruelty' must be accepted in their supple and, at times, frustrating polysemy, rather than seeking to cleverly dis-

---

10 Eerily, the same can be said of "ridiculous", which is used extremely often yet never defined (see, e.g., Pareto 1935).
11 In the opening pages of our volume and wherever else we deem it useful and/or necessary, *we highlight concepts or ideas by means of single quotation marks and words by means of double ones*. Whenever no special emphasis or distinction between concepts (or ideas) and words is needed, then no quotation marks appear. Also, single quotation marks can indicate non-literal usages of certain terms or linguistic expressions.
12 Shklar (1984), 3 and 44. As noted in *H&C1*, Shklar's claims are hyperbolic, yet understandable. Even in the subfields where philosophers do talk about "cruelty", e.g., animal ethics, the standard approach is rather superficial, i.e., it either takes a notion of it for granted or fails to acknowledge most alternatives (see, e.g., Tanner 2015).
13 Alliteration aside, each action was needed and duly performed in view of producing the present volume. Readers should never stop at the mere phonetic level with which we play, in line with well-established Anglophone rhetoric.
14 An extensive account lies at the heart of *H&C1*. The potential and actual collaborative character of the two titular concepts lies at the heart of *H&C2*. As to the readers who would have chosen different authoritative sources, they can certainly address them in their own works. Such choices are eminently *personal*. Ideas and arguments, in any case, should come first. People's names, journals' titles, and publishers' logos come a long way after them.

cover and grasp, once and for all, the one and only 'true' meaning of either of them —if not even, boldly, of both concepts.[15]

As to any such selective, conclusive and/or superlative pursuit, we are simply incapable of discounting a caustic yet wise admonition uttered by a noted Italian ethicist and humourist, Flavio Baroncelli.[16] While reflecting on his professional and intellectual experiences among fellow analytic philosophers, Baroncelli remarked bemusedly on how his colleagues would regularly claim with the utmost possible and most palpable sincerity that "toleration is their most widespread and deeply cherished value", while maintaining as well that they were genuinely "respectful" and "democratic ... thinkers", who were fully aware of diversity, doubt and disagreement.[17] At the same time, these tolerant, respectful, and democratic colleagues would also and always be, adamantly when not arrogantly, the sole people in the conference room knowing "what the meaning of a term should be, were only common people not as stupid as they are".[18]

Far more modestly, then, for each of these ambiguous, contested, and, as it will be argued, inexorably contestable concepts, we are going to identify a set of "family resemblances" *à la* Wittgenstein.[19] Hence, we will be focussing upon meaningful connotations that, as the seclusive 20th-century Austrian engineer and philosopher

---

[15] Nor do we seek to define the 'essence' of either "humour" or "cruelty" in an Aristotelian or Thomist sense.
[16] See Karlsson (2019) for an English-language introduction to Baroncelli's life and work.
[17] Baroncelli (2011), 18–19, whose academic work allows us to introduce into our own a pinch of Romantic irony. *As regards the analytic-Continental divide in philosophy, we were trained in both traditions and make use of both.*
[18] Baroncelli (2011), 18. The authors of this volume have frequently observed an analogous perplexing arrogance among adherents to specific disciplines and/or disciplinary schools of thought making claims about what (hence whom) should be deemed 'true' philosophy, 'true' psychology, etc., and, in the process, dismissing major historical contributors to these pre-paradigmatic disciplines, e.g., Boethius, Nietzsche, Freud, Jung, etc. In parallel, a chilling tendency to cultural self-mutilation occurs among colleagues in the social sciences, who disregard huge swaths of human achievement and self-exploration because they are not 'scientific' enough, e.g., ethics, religion, history, drama, analytic psychology. Polanyi (1969a, 42) spoke in this respect of the West's "[s]cientific obscurantism" driven by "false ideals of exactitude" aiming at "reduc[ing all phenomena] to physics and chemistry" and/or turning "consciousness" itself into nothing but "a venerable hypothesis" or "postulate" upon which, however, science relies and depends *qua* conscious activity pursued by conscious persons. See also *H&C1*.
[19] Wittgenstein (1953), par. 67. *Many such terms appear in our volume*, e.g., "socialism", "obscenity", "liberty", "fun". Countless more of these "cluster concepts" exist, also in the legal sphere, where clear definitions or "necessary and sufficient criteria" are of the utmost importance (Shrage 2022, 397). See, e.g., the thorny debates surrounding the possible formulations of "consent" in sexual matters, as covered in Boonin (2022), chaps. 15–23.

depicted them, "overlap and criss-cross" one another and that, as such, should be helpful in highlighting important aspects of their mutual positioning and, above all, their potentially conflictual character.[20] Admittedly, *the possibility of conflicts between humour and cruelty is*, in point of fact, *the main theme of the present volume*, which aims at exploring and explaining

(1) how and why the former concept-*cum*-corresponding phenomenon can lead to the latter, e.g., *qua* rebuke, retaliation or repression; and, conversely,
(2) how the latter pair may elicit the former counterparts, e.g., as means of remonstration, resistance, or repudiation.[21]

The bulky first chapter of Part 2, entitled "Cruelty Against Humour", addresses the various ways in which commonplace humour, whether deliberately malevolent or allegedly civilising, implies targets that, more or less reasonably, can claim to have been the victim/s of "provocative cruelty"—a discerning nomenclature coined by the 20th-century US ethicist Philip Paul Hallie, whom we duly acknowledge and discuss in this volume.[22] These provoked targets can range from specific persons to groupings thereof, including whole societies and/or more or less-easily identifiable communities, e.g., *per* conspicuous pathology, professional occupation, facial type, putative ethnicity, political persuasion, bodily size and shape, erotic appetite, and/or religious creed.[23] Manifestly wronged or not, the targets of commonplace hu-

---

20 Wittgenstein (1953), par. 67. Even this modicum of abstraction may be too much, according to Klepec (2021, 191), who made extensive use of our research on "cruelty" proper, but also described our singling out few key connotations thereof as "a Pandora's box from which everything alive falls out" (his critical target being Baruchello 2017b, which is the basis for our survey of "cruelty" proper). We acknowledge his criticism, but also regard our cautious approach as intellectually necessary, indeed inevitable. A little abstraction is a step towards achieving better *understanding*, which requires gaining some distance from direct lived experience.
21 We must warn the reader that, in this volume, we do *not* discuss the notion of humour *qua* means of *political* rebellion because, in essence, we deem it deeply ineffective. Political satires and pasquinades are as old as Rome, but, *by themselves*, they never caused the fall of any consul, emperor, Pope, king, president, or prime minister (see, e.g., Gilbert 2015). If anything, by reducing the oppressed's sense of awe and humanising the oppressor, humour has regularly made oppression more bearable and less likely to be challenged in ways capable of causing such a fall, which is *our* fundamental criterion to determine whether a means of political rebellion is effective or not, unlike, say, Bhungalia's (2020) one, which focuses on keeping the hope of change alive.
22 Hallie (1969), 80 *et passim*. Readers who are not familiar with *H&C1* and/or *H&C2* should realise that the expression *"commonplace humour"* implies the existence of claims regarding *"true humour"*, which some thinkers have argued to exist and believed to be able to distinguish from the former (see Chapter 2 in this book).
23 By "person", we mean creatures that, either potentially (e.g., infants) or in actuality (e.g., healthy adults), are capable of *coordinated multi-intentionality* at some point in life, on the basis

mour can frankly dislike being cast as the so-called "butt of the joke" or "laughingstock", which the possibly entertaining attempts at issue must mandatorily emplace in order to obtain their mirthful ends and, frequently, ulterior ones too.[24]

The targets' response to this kind of social game can vary to a great extent in its essential quality and, to an even greater degree, in its emotional volatility, which, at times, turns altogether into "responsive cruelty"—another perceptive nomenclature coined by Hallie—aiming at "end[ing] the story" once and for all.[25] In a typically unexpected reversal of their roles, the humourists can then become targets, not merely of humorous retorts, but also of vicious retaliatory actions that, on occasion, can be reasonably and/or legitimately described as "cruel". The 2015 terrorist attack against *Charlie Hebdo*'s headquarters is, under this respect, focussed upon in Part 2 of our volume, for the attack constitutes a recent and conspicuous instance of cruelty, which is to be analysed in some of its most striking ethical and socio-cultural ramifications.[26]

Our volume's chief themes and attendant analyses, and especially those developed in Part II's first chapter, are cast against a background of *liberal* presuppositions, institutions, and praxes that characterise today's Western societies in general and that, as such, are often assumed a-critically, implicitly endorsed, and/or simply taken for granted—not only by the 'right-thinking' man-in-the-street, but also by presumedly thoughtful academicians.[27] Throughout our volume, in-

---

of Prust and Geller's (2019) basic criterion for personal responsibility in moral and legal reasoning. Human beings are such creatures who can do good as well as evil. Please note that when referring to a "person" in our volume, *we then use only the corresponding female pronoun and/or adjective*, insofar as *persona*, in Latin, is a feminine word.

24 Resentful targets need not be the oppressed groups upon which most expert literature rightly focusses today. *Any* thinking and feeling individual can experience his/her becoming a laughingstock as cruel. As for ourselves, let us just note how Icelanders were the regular object of mocking stereotypes in Scandinavia during the Danish Trade Monopoly (1602–1786), and Italians still are in our century's Anglophone countries (see, e.g., Chiaro 2010). The American historian Clifford Rosenberg (2006, 12) noted as well how "[l]ike the Irish in England and the United States, Italians in [19th-century] France were often thought of as black when they first arrived". Poverty, like death, is the cruel source of a bleak equality cutting across genders, ages, cultures, and alleged races.
25 Hallie (1969), 80 *et passim*.
26 For an introduction and first-person witness account, see Lançon (2018).
27 *We broadly use "liberal" in the European sense of markedly 'pro-market', not the American one of moderately 'social democrat'*. In any case, *both senses share considerable ground*, e.g., the primacy of individual freedom, constitutionalism, the separation of powers, due process, the legitimacy of private property and the profit motive, free speech, etc. (see, e.g., Rosenblatt 2018). This shared ground is often forgotten because of, or obfuscated by, the political and cultural struggles *within* the liberal camp, which dominates Western politics and culture. However, it is also easily recovered and immediately grasped when contemplating political stances that lie outside the liberal

stead, a good measure of critical reflection is openly introduced, bringing into the foreground some of the *cruel ironies* and *humorous cruelties* characterising our socio-economic and politico-cultural order.[28] In particular, chapters 1 and 3 of Part 2 identify and investigate the tensions arising in the contexts of economic life and sexual ethics, underscoring some of the most intense tensions that hide therein. Thus, it becomes possible to highlight the conflicts between humour and cruelty emerging thereof, and to explore the psychological, theological, ethical and metaphysical depths that lie underneath such conflicts.[29]

This is done mainly, but not exclusively, *via* direct references to and/or lengthy footnotes on John Stuart Mill, Vilfredo Pareto, G.K. Chesterton, Stephen Leacock, Bertrand Russell, Cornelius Castoriadis, John 'Ken' Galbraith, and the already-cited Flavio Baroncelli.[30] With the exception of Mill, all of these modern thinkers

---

spectrum, e.g., Imam Khomeini's or Alexander Dugin's conservatism on the right, and Rosa Luxemburg's or Ieng Thirith's communism on the left. Some such 'eccentric' views are duly recalled in our volume, so as to retain the awareness of the many and diverse extant provinces in the vast domain of political theory and avoid falling back into the aforementioned forgetfulness and neglect of the common roots of all liberal conceptions. Also, *the presuppositions hereby scrutinised are a few among thousands that any writer-reader exchange tacitly requires.*

28 Our emphasis here is on "reflection", rather than "critical". While we certainly aim at highlighting possible and even grave shortcomings of our socio-economic order, our main goal is, first of all, to lead our readers to *truly* reflect on it, for we have come to believe that this order's 'children' are likely to take liberalism and its many tacit presuppositions for granted to such an extent as to not be able to identify them and/or spell them out in any form or shape, not to mention being able to genuinely fathom and consider any alternative state of affairs. Such an ability, *inter alia*, would involve considering in earnest whether or not the order at issue and its tacit presuppositions are justified, how, what for, and to what extent. As the reader will gather later, *life-value onto-axiology* provides for us the ultimate basis for such a comprehensive assessment and, at times, justification (see McMurtry 2011).

29 The notions of 'free market' and 'free speech' are central to Part 2 of *H&C3*.

30 All of these thinkers agreed with the liberals that there exist individual free will and personal responsibility. Albeit fundamental for Western morality and politico-legal architecture, neither presupposition is obvious. Not only is strict determinism yet to be debunked (see, e.g., List, Caruso, and Clark, 2020). Also, both presuppositions crash against known facts such as addiction, akrasia, self-delusion, *ex-post* insight, psychological hysteresis, bias, copycat behaviour, and luck (see, e.g., Levy 2011). Having no final word, *we accept in principle the plurality of plausible options, while at the same time operate in practice a fiduciary embrace of one or few of them.* Hence, we follow here these authorities and liberals at large in assuming the existence of free will and personal responsibility. Lastly, Mill is representative of both main types of "liberalism" discussed three footnotes before this one. Largely conservative on economic issues, not least in his methodological acceptance the human being *qua* appetitive machine, Mill endorsed many progressive proposals as well, including about taxation and the legal status of private property (see Capaldi 2004). He even called himself a "socialist" (Stafford 1998, title *et passim*).

were well-known for their humour, wit, and/or sarcasm.[31] Three of them, in particular, have frequently been listed among the noteworthy and eponymous "humourists" stemming from the Anglophone provinces of the world.[32] Their prose is an important reminder of the fact that the cruelties of our world can be addressed seriously, yet not unsmilingly, also in the scholarly and scientific domains of Western culture. In other words, their works bear witness to the notion that philosophical studies and, say, psychological investigations can be pursued in earnest while making use of explanatory, expressive, rhetorical, and/or intellectual instruments borrowed from the realms of satire, comedy, wit, and, of course, humour.[33] Our own volume, in point of fact, is built in relevant part also upon the awareness and the conscious use of such communicative and insight-seeking strategies.[34]

Sometimes, in order to disclose more patently the cruel ironies and humorous cruelties of the liberal West, comparisons and contrasts with non-liberal settings and historical experiences are going to be made.[35] Among such settings looms large the vast world of contemporary Islam, which is important in connection with some notorious cases of censorship of comedy as well as with a number of satire-related murders that are duly discussed in Chapter 1 of Part 2. No anti-Muslim sentiment of any sort is implied by this choice. We are most respectful of the Islamic faith, its venerable tradition, and the vast contribution that the historical

---

[31] *Writing philosophically about humour and cruelty means, for us, paying heed to those who did so humorously.* Additionally, the legacy of these authors covers a *broad spectrum of ideological stances*, ranging from Catholic conservatism to libertarian socialism, and can *ipso facto* help our own study to be as broad-minded. In particular, since we are children of a liberal world, the use of non-liberal sources can alert us to our own blind spots. *Far too often, even in academia, plausibility and agreement are obtained by wilful ignorance of dissenting views.*

[32] The celebrated humourists are Chesterton, Leacock, and Galbraith. As to the other cited authors, let us just recall here Femia (1998, 71) writing about "the corrosive sarcasm that made [Pareto] such a formidable polemicist", and Beilharz (1989, 133) stating that, in Castoriadis' critique of revolutionary Marxism, "[t]he humour is significant".

[33] Two noted psychologists loom large in our volume: C.G. Jung and James Hillman. Neither was devoid of a certain sense of humour. Still, the cited list of philosopher-humourists comprises H&C3's chief protagonists.

[34] We do not imply that we can be listed among the great humourists of our culture, or even the lesser ones. However, we do believe that we can make occasional and, hopefully, functional use of humour, not only as done by 'classics' such as Erasmus, Diderot, or Nietzsche, but also by contemporary scholars such as, say, Terry Eagleton and Steve Gimbel.

[35] As we noted in *H&C2, the phenomenon of cruel irony is arguably the most common combination of humour and cruelty* that our research has run into or, at least, led us into acknowledging repeatedly in our volumes.

populations of, say, today's Tunisia and Iran have made to human civilization.[36] Besides, as Chapter 1 of Part 2 makes abundantly clear, there have been cruel responses to unwelcome humour in Western contexts too.[37]

Rather, taken together with the parallel Western examples that we also discuss in our volume, these Islamic tokens of responsive cruelty remind us of a deeper axiological ground for the assessment of that which is to be considered good, bad, or evil.[38] By this we mean the fundamental evaluative principles spelled out, and examined in painstaking detail, by *life-value onto-axiology* (LVOA). LVOA being, at the time of writing, the most lucid and most extensive philosophical theory of value that has been developed in the 21st century. In particular, we rely on the comprehensive presentation of LVOA in the three bulky volumes comprised within the *Encyclopedia of Life Support Systems* (EOLSS) and entitled *Philosophy and World Problems*.[39]

This trilogy, as just said, is part of EOLSS, which is itself the world's largest online repository of information on sustainable development and a growing compendium of encyclopaedias compiled by experts and researchers from all continents. Active and accessible since 2002, EOLSS has been issued by UNESCO, i.e., an international organisation of the highest calibre whose official mission is to protect and promote education, science, and culture across the globe.[40] We urge our philosophically inclined readers to study LVOA, should they be unfamiliar with it.[41] No lengthy and explicit discussion of the theory itself is offered here, given:

---

[36] For the sake of theological balance, we used both Sunni and Shia sources in languages accessible to us.
[37] In *H&C3*, a number of subsections' headings and passages speak of "West", "East", "South" and "North". All of them must be taken by the reader with a modicum of spatial and conceptual flexibility.
[38] Making some use of non-Western sources is also a way for us to be more inclusive. However, as noted already in *H&C2*, criticism can arise in any case, given that *issue can be taken with any act of inclusion as well as of exclusion*. If the reader is sufficiently eager and whatever his/her true motives may be, *reasons for discontent and criticism can always be found*. Let us cite here too a joke that we heard from the Yiddish performer Moni Ovadia back in the 1990s: a proud Jewish mother gives her son two ties as a present for having become officially an adult. From now on, when he goes to visit her, he must dress up fittingly. Also, as soon as he approaches his mother's place, parading a fine jacket and a tie, she can ask him: "why aren't you wearing the other tie?".
[39] See McMurtry (2011).
[40] Concerning any hypothesis of Islamophobia, note that UNESCO was boycotted by the constitutionally liberal US government for alleged pro-Muslim stances. See Beaumont (2017) and Omar and Biçeroğlu (2021).
[41] LVOA's and EOLSS' relevance are all the more significant if we consider that, as even acknowledged by the popular press (see, e.g., Cusick 2020), today's world is moving closer and closer to "runaway greenhouse warming" and "climate flips" that, as stated by Bartels (2001, 232, note 1),

(1) the different focus and the limited scope of our volume which, albeit self-contained, is itself one third of a larger superordinate inquiry into humour and cruelty, as well as some of their many manifestations and mutual relations within interpersonal and intrapersonal existence; and
(2) Giorgio Baruchello's thorough tackling of LVOA in numerous scholarly works of his, including two prior full-length books.[42]

In its most concise expression, though, LVOA can be said to entail three basic tenets:

> (1) "Life-value" is adopted as the only true value on earth. (2) The "ultimate life-coherence principle" (consistency with all conditions that enable life) is the ultimate test of validity across domains. (3) "Life capital" is the substance of all that is of worth on the planet (that is, "life wealth/capacities that create more life wealth/capacities without loss and with cumulative gain through time").[43]

From these three basic tenets ensue the "[p]rimary axiom[s]" of "value" and "disvalue", which can be succinctly expressed as follows:

> X is value if and only if, and to the extent that, x consists in or enables a more coherently inclusive range of thought/feeling/action than without it
> Where these three ultimate fields of value are defined as:
> thought = internal image and concept (T)
> feeling = the felt side of being (F)
> /senses, desires, emotions, moods
> action = animate movement (A)
> across species and organizations
> Conversely:
> x is disvalue if and only if, and to the extent that, x reduces/disables any range of thought/experience/action.
> Symbolically expressed:
> +V = > LR + and −V = < LR where L = Range of T-F-A and / = and/or[44]

While Polanyi's *Gestalt*-based phenomenology and theory of knowledge, which we discuss succinctly here in Chapter 4, provide the epistemological background for our volume, LVOA provides its deeper evaluative framework.[45] As such, LVOA has

---

"would likely involve decimation or extinction of humanity". No laughing matters, then (more on these sober issues is said in Chapter 1 of Part 2).
42 See Baruchello (2018a) and (2018b).
43 McMurtry (2020), 532.
44 McMurtry (2011), vol. 1, par. 6.1.
45 Polanyi's philosophy was tackled extensively in *H&C1*.

guided our own professional choices, not least whether to write or not about 'humour', 'cruelty', and/or other concepts, abstract models, theories, schools of thought, social issues, and philosophical topics.[46] Were we to combine said epistemological and evaluative background into one period capturing both the main objective and the *modus operandi* of the present volume, we could assert that *we attend **to** the conflicts between humour and cruelty by attending **from** the comprehensively life-enabling accumulated wisdom on such conflicts that can be excavated from the Western humanities and the world's social sciences.*[47]

The hefty chapter entitled "Humour Against Cruelty" is going to work in reverse of the first chapter of Part 2. As it happens, in its life-enabling renditions, humour can help single individuals as well as sizeable groups of human beings to stomach, if not even surpass, life's persistent wretchedness, puzzling happenstances, and truly innumerable painful woes.[48] There is indeed much wisdom hidden behind the proverbial notion according to which we laugh in order not to cry.[49] None less than the most renowned champion of the German Enlightenment, Immanuel Kant, remarked emphatically on this point. In his third *Critique*, Kant added *das Lachen* [laughter] to Voltaire's two highly praised springs of spiritual succour for the cruelly troubled and preposterously flawed human race, i.e., hope and sleep.[50]

Albeit frequently called "black", "bleak", "dark", and/or, pertinently, "cruel", when not vocally lambasted as "morose", "miserable", "morbid", "malicious", and/or "mean", gallows humour, humour among oncological patients, funny gags among fellow prisoners, deathbed jokes, and, occasionally, even "debased and degraded ... mockery" of others and/or of oneself are capable of lightening people's

---

[46] As the paragraph above suffices to show, LVOA should not be confused with 'pro-life' sloganeering. Also, it should not be confused with the loose 'school' of so-called "biopolitics" of Foucault (2007) and (2008), Esposito (2008), and Agamben (1998), none of whom could provide a set of well-defined criteria for value assessment, unlike LVOA (see McMurtry 2011).

[47] As was explained in both *H&C1* and *H&C2*, even if our penchant for historical comprehensiveness may seem antiquarian or bookish, we made an extensive use of electronic resources in a conscious continuation of Eco's legacy *qua* "techno-enthusiast" promoting, *inter alia*, free digitised books and archives (Cosenza 2016, par. 3).

[48] We presume our readers to be familiar with life's endless litany of obstacles, struggles, and horrors.

[49] Many variations of this proverb exist, including those stressing one's indecision about whether to laugh or cry. As discussed in *H&C2*, life's paradoxes can be interpreted comically as well as tragically. See also Chapter 3 of Part 2.

[50] Kant (1987), part 1, division 1, book 2, par. 54. *Whenever citing texts of which there exist numerous editions and/or electronic versions, we use or add, if practical, references to chapters, sections and/or paragraphs.*

moods under the most appalling circumstances.⁵¹ Offering our readers a smidgin of optimism, our volume is thus going to gather and examine many tokens of commonplace humour *qua* possible remedy, however partial and provisional, to "cruelty" proper and to many cruel afflictions.⁵²

As ordinary and predictable, the last chapter of our volume covers our own concluding reflections.⁵³ In it, the key information and insights that we will have come across in the volume, both in the main text and its many detailed footnotes, are recollected, rearranged, and recombined so as to enhance and expand upon the extant conceptions of both 'humour' and 'cruelty', paying distinct attention to their mutually conflictual aspects and, as far as possible, tying together the strands inherited from *H&C1* and *H&C2* as well.⁵⁴ In other words, roaming across the conceptual space constructed by our entire philosophical exploration of humour *and* cruelty, we reset the most significant information and insights at a higher level of philosophical awareness and axiological assessment.⁵⁵

Consistently with this approach, some of the thorniest challenges to knowledge and good and/or meaningful personal conduct are identified and discussed in the last chapter of Part 2, while keeping in mind the mutual conflicts between humour and cruelty *qua* centre of gravity.⁵⁶ By so doing, we hope to be able to spur some interesting thoughts within and among our readers, fostering hermeneutical, re-

---

51 Leacock (1935), 12; adding: "Too much of the humor of all ages, and far too much of our own, partakes of it."
52 Given the inherent cruel ingredient of humour that we detected, dissected, and discussed in *H&C2*, we can only endorse an open advocacy of humour that pursues its end with ample self-awareness.
53 *We make very few trenchant statements. Studying humour and cruelty has taught us epistemic humility.* Again, in this as in many other matters, we follow the lead of Baroncelli (1996, 36), who, while tackling Andrea Dworkin's *verbatim* claim that "fucking is entirely a male act designed to affirm the reality and power of the phallus, of masculinity", wondered humorously whether it was possible "for a man and a woman to just make love" (to which he added, as must be noticed, a charitable interpretation of the cultural context whence her claim arose). We too, then, leave room for tolerant doubt and alternative views. *It is when blatant and comprehensive life-disablement may be the case that we become assertive*, turning LVOA into a means of advocacy. Also, more on Dworkin's (1976 and 1981) views and the controversies that they produced among feminists is said in Part 2.
54 *H&C2* was devoted to the mutual assistance that humour and cruelty can mutually provide.
55 As stated, LVOA and Polanyi's epistemology-*cum*-phenomenology lie in the background of the whole effort. The latter, moreover, also provides the key criteria for said "philosophical exploration", as explained in *H&C1*.
56 These twin activities occur within the context of said conceptual space, not in general. Also, our writing "gravity" instantiates a pun. Did you get it? We tried to make use of humour in this volume. But it may not be our forte.

flective, and/or reasoning feats that are typical of Western philosophy.[57] As persistently done throughout our philosophical trilogy, *we seek conclusions that open thought, not close it.*[58]

Implicitly, our present volume aims at contributing to the effective continuation of the art of philosophical reflection, which is, in our view, inherently valuable and, at the same time, commonly marginalised in contemporary Western democracies, academe included.[59] Such an aim is one of the many shapes which scholarly worth can take, alongside, say, creative novelty, problem-solving, problem-positing, theoretical integration, exegetical exactitude, technical excellence, historical synthesis, intuition, meditative depth, moral edification, successful advocacy, analytical acumen, and/or intrinsic intellectual appeal.[60] If we are really lucky, some of these other forms of scholarly worth may also and eventually happen to apply to our volume, i.e., as something that that our work acquires indirectly and unintendedly while pursuing its one declared aim.[61]

Whether it is going to be so, we cannot tell. Nor can our best living colleagues either. Posterity, as normal and inevitable, will be the judge of all such trifles.[62]

---

57 A little more indirectly, *we try to foster the same hermeneutical and reasoning feats by referring chiefly, in the volume's openly philosophical parts, to time-honoured dead authorities*, rather than to living ones, whose fame might be a fragile, fleeting fluke, and whose views, even more importantly, may still change in the most drastic ways.

58 In line with ancient Stoicism, we hope to be able to provide a tad of *logos spermatikos* to our readers, also *via* thought-provoking humour. In this respect, our being *two* authors who disagreed on some issues, proved handy. Also, Since Part 1 and Part 2 belong to the same volume, we write hereby of a "trilogy" and *not* a "tetralogy".

59 Philosophy's fate is worse in many Eastern societies marked by theocracy or autocracy. Yet, despite being its cradle, the West has antagonised philosophy in an almost cyclical way. Instructively, Assereto (2016, 55–72) reported pleas for humanistic studies in 19th-century Genoa that were eerily akin to Nussbaum's (2010) ones in the US of our century.

60 Curiously, funniness is not commonly regarded as one such facet of scholarly worth. Alternatively, Rorty (1993) argued philosophical worth to be chiefly a matter of avoiding "scholasticism", "chauvinism", and "avant-gardism". We sincerely hope to have been able not to fall into any of these three negative '-isms' that Rorty singled out.

61 We must recall here the often-neglected key-role of luck in all human endeavours, as studied, e.g., by Pluchino *et al.* (2018). The reader may also want to ponder upon how contingency determines the most crucial features in a person's life: where on Earth she is born, in which family, which genome she has got, which aptitudes result thereof, etc.

62 *The cruel irony of philosophical in/significance* can take many shapes too. Some thinkers were never satisfied with their work, which successive generations instead found of value. Some others, despite their sense of self-importance, encountered the same generations' favour well after their own death. Others still were bright stars in their academic field, faction, fringe, and/or fiefdom, but vanished from public memory as soon as they could no longer engage in self-promotion. A few got

1.2 Second Movement: Grave

> Somos contos contando contos, nada.
> —Ricardo Reis (Fernando Pessoa)[63]

One additional note is, albeit somewhat tedious, absolutely necessary before pursuing the announced account of the interpretations of "humour" proper in Western thought. The present two-part volume is, as anticipated, the third instalment in a set of three volumes devoted to humour and cruelty that we agreed to complete for De Gruyter's series on the philosophy of humour. In other words, there exist:

(1) H&C1, i.e., *Volume 1: A Philosophical Exploration of the Humanities and Social Sciences;*
(2) H&C2, i.e., *Volume 2: Dangerous Liaisons;* and
(3) H&C3, i.e., *Volume 3: Laughing Matters*, which comprises
(3a) Part 1 – *Prolegomena;* and
(3b) Part 2 – *Theses and Discussions.*

As logically obvious, philosophically reasonable, and, at a more basic level, practically and psychologically inevitable, our reflections and understanding of both "humour" and "cruelty" are rooted in and informed by the protracted research about these two terms that we conducted in our previous two volumes, i.e., *H&C1* and *H&C2*.[64] However, *as far as the reader of the present third volume is concerned,* **no familiarity with either prior publication is needed here.** On the contrary, *H&C3 can be read and, hopefully, appreciated on its own,* i.e., without having to peruse our older two instalments.

Such being the result,
(1) of our contractual obligations. As agreed with the publisher upon breaking up our initial large manuscript into three distinct volumes, *each* of them is expected to be able to stand on its own feet, so to speak, even if all three, taken together, form a linear, cogent, superordinate intellectual endeavour. Clearly, this sort of mandatory contentual independence means that a modicum of overlap

---

consideration and recognition only in their old age. Most, none at all. In this respect, impact factors and bibliometric indexes are one of the most bizarre constructs in today's academe.

63 *"We are tales telling tales, nothing",* as cited in Camões et al. (2022), 168.
64 Once again, *we must highlight the fact that we focussed on sources dealing explicitly and expressly with the terms "humour" and "cruelty"* rather than cognate concepts, e.g., 'laughter', 'fun', 'violence', or 'power'.

occurs across the three volumes, especially as regards a number of foremost authors, powerful quotations, and prominent schools and lines of thought.[65]

(2) The final structure and the actual contents of the same trilogy reflect both the endogenous progression of our laborious research and the exogenous demands that arose in its prolonged editorial development, which began in 2019. Not only were there necessities and prospects pertaining to the historical, theoretical, and exegetical components of our philosophical exploration, but also, there surfaced necessities and prospects pertaining to the rational construction and public presentation of the same.[66]

Let us consider here, however briefly, the five most important aspects concerning said points (1) and (2), not least as regards *H&C3* and its organisation in two distinct parts, which might appear quixotic to some readers, especially those who are familiar with either *H&C1* or *H&C2*.[67]

(1) *Size matters.* The great length of the whole project is the consequence of several concurring factors that could not be underestimated or discounted without compromising the professional quality of our philosophical exploration and the logical sequence of our three volumes, i.e., an intellectual history of humour and cruelty (*H&C1*) followed by the careful study of their mutual combinations (*H&C2*) and mutual conflicts (*H&C3*).

(1a) For one, the humanistic and socio-scientific literature on "humour" and "cruelty" proper is massive, even when cognate notions are downplayed or left aside. A candid and careful account of this literature must be open to addressing a sizeable number of relevant sources, even when these sources are merely representative of the diverse conceptions and divergent lines of thinking that can be deemed to be of substantial import.[68]

(1b) For another, reflecting in an intelligent and insightful way on such relevant sources, diverse conceptions, and divergent lines of thinking calls inevitably for more words, more sentences, more paragraphs, more pages, and more books. Once the pertinent literature has been duly selected and summarised

---

[65] Readers familiar with *H&C1* and *H&C2* will recognise them easily. As to the adjective "contentual", it was listed in the second edition of the *Oxford English Dictionary* (Murray et al. 1989, vol. 3, 818).

[66] To a significant extent, any academic book such as the present one is the brainchild of its author/s as well as of the book series' editor/s and the publisher's expert team.

[67] "We" means here the two authors of this volume.

[68] Determining that which is of substantial import is an eminently *personal* decision (see Chapter 4 here).

and at least *some* of the most important contextual clues have been acknowledged and/or touched upon, ample room is still left for developing one's own theses and discussions.[69]

(1c) Thirdly, the positive expert feedback that we received on *H&C1*, plus the glowing anonymous reports that were returned on the complete drafts of *H&C2* and, above all, *H&C3*, remarked regularly on our three volumes' overall quality and exemplary thoroughness, emphasising unvaryingly their informative comprehensiveness, careful approach to the studied materials, and creative assemblage of plentiful relevant sources. Deleting and ignoring big 'chunks' of the accrued research were not viable or desirable options from a scholarly point of view.[70] Hopefully, after having examined our work in earnest and without malice, our readers will come to concur on this point.[71]

(2) *Similarities arise.* The present book, i.e., Part 1 of *H&C3*, is designed primarily, though not exclusively, in order to make sure that anyone perusing *H&C3* can do so without having to possess any pre-existing knowledge of the contents of *H&C1* and/or *H&C2*. As a result, we do hint here repeatedly at issues, thinkers, and views that were discussed in *H&C1* and/or *H&C2* to a more significant level of depth and in far greater detail.[72]

(2a) Our first volume, in particular, was a much more extensive, encyclopaedic, and in-depth intellectual history of 'humour' and 'cruelty', as well as of the neglected criss-crossing between these two rich, polysemic concepts. In addition, *H&C1* developed a lengthy argument in defence of polysemy itself, based upon the philosophy of Michael Polanyi, who remained an important source of inspiration for us in this third volume as well.[73] Readers that are keen on thorough, comprehensive, context-aware, and detailed *Begriffsgeschichte* can surely find that first volume to their liking.[74]

---

[69] The academic reader may be familiar with the perplexing and unpersuasive sense of vacuous abstractedness and argumentative 'thinness' that affects 'naked' philosophical reasonings, i.e., sorely devoid of *context*.

[70] Luckily, De Gruyter preferred publishing three volumes rather than leaving out potentially valuable material.

[71] Let it be said that we, as authors of these books, are bound to be able spot all kinds of imperfections inside them, most notably when it will be far too late to do anything about it. Authorship's inexorable ironies are very cruel.

[72] Some expert quotes recur across our volumes and, when needed, we repeat some jokes too. Some jokes too.

[73] As the reader going to gather, Polanyi's (1962c) emphasis on personal responsibility is the crux.

[74] Aka "conceptual history", "intellectual history", or "history of ideas".

(2b) While we do not engage here with all of these issues, thinkers, and views to the same extent as we did in our two previous volumes, we neither merely discount them, nor do we always and only refer our readers to the older publications without offering any elucidation whatsoever. Our abundant and fastidious footnotes, in this respect, are an important and useful explanatory tool. This justifies their quantity and their scope.[75]

(2c) The synthesis of relevant sources on "humour" and "cruelty" proper offered in Part 1 can also prove useful to our more 'seasoned' readers. Effectively, it should be a suitable way to recapitulate those crucial theses and critical discussions that were variously acknowledged in our previous two volumes, and that play a considerable role in *H&C3* and/or our multi-volume project as a whole. Our extensive philosophical exploration, which began with *H&C1*, reaches *here* its ultimate conclusion, i.e., in this third volume—starting with Part 1.

(3) *Specificities abound.* In this third volume, including its Part 1, we refer to a number of specific issues, thinkers, and views that we did *not* cover meticulously in our previous two large tomes.[76] We refer chiefly to the *conflicts* between the two titular concepts, the mutual cooperation of which we explored instead in *H&C2*, where we argued, basically, that humour entails cruelty.[77]

(3a) *H&C3*, in other words, *possesses its own distinctive focus* and it has, culinarily speaking, its own unique flavour. As can be learnt in a kitchen or at the dinner table, a creamy risotto with porcini mushrooms and sweet rice pudding share three crucial ingredients and can be served during the same meal, but they are not the same dish by any stretch of the imagination—or of the tongue.[78]

(3b) Were any 'newcomer' to our research interested in approaching *H&C3*'s Part II before Part 1, then s/he should realise that, at some point, Part 1 must be read too, for its contents—hereby styled in a time-honoured, self-ironic, and playfully bookish way as "prolegomena"—establish the historical, conceptual, and exegetical premises whereby the issues tackled in Part 2 acquire their full pertinence, relative prominence, and deeper mean-

---

75 More on our use of footnotes was said in *H&C1*.
76 Thus, the "exploration" that we announced in *H&C1* is enriched a little more—as also done in *H&C2*—in keeping with Polanyi (1962a) and (1962c).
77 As it becomes clear later in this volume, *H&C2*'s chief thesis does not contradict the possibility of conflicts between humour and cruelty. On the contrary, it explains *why* humour can be effective against cruelty.
78 The shared ingredients being rice, milk and salt.

ingfulness. Essentially, the accounts offered in the present book set the stage for and introduce all major theses and discussions of Part 2.

(3c) While the mutual conflicts of humour and cruelty determine the crucial notions, chief phenomena, and central arguments that are tackled throughout *H&C3*, a number of subordinate theses and discussions accompany them as well. These additional paths for philosophical reflections encompass, among others: the cruel costs associated with the gaining and/or guarding of personal liberty; the unnerving shadows cast by the relentless and repressive pursuit of virtue; the rebellious endurance of popular carnivalesque traditions in spite of their unrefined or even dangerous character; the profound mystical and metaphysical mysteries intimated by professedly humorous paradoxes and puzzles; and the gravely misunderstood personal, social, and natural tragedies resulting from commonplace liberal institutions that are often celebrated as the peak of human development or civilisation itself.[79]

(4) *Syncretism applies.* Inter- and multidisciplinary by design, our volume makes use of learned perspectives arising from an ample spectrum of fields of study.[80] As a consequence, the next two chapters in this volume should not only offer a substantial synthesis of many different philosophical, historiographic, literary, psychological, clinical, and socio-scientific conceptions, but also an inevitably selective yet adequately representative variety of entry-points for scholars operating in distinct areas of contemporary academia. Our hope being, of course, that of reaching a wider academic audience than just our fellow philosophers of humour.[81]

(5) *Surprises await.* As we explained in more detail in *H&C2*, at times, in order to identify unseen cruelties and/or disclose humorous facets of reality that would often go unnoticed, we embrace hermeneutical and theoretical perspectives with which our readers may not be familiar and/or comfortable. While we sincerely apologise for any experienced discomfort, we also regard this intentionally mystifying approach as a required means whereby we can hope to 'dislodge', say, platitudes, received views, cognitive bias, unchallenged

---

[79] This list of examples is representative, but not exhaustive.

[80] This multi- and cross-disciplinarity is also reflected in the prosaic tone of much of our prose, which strives to steer away from too insistent a discipline-specific jargon, academe's terminological fads (e.g., "disruption", "woke", "big data", "entitlement"), and current catchphrases (e.g., "rent free", "vibe check", "caught in 4k").

[81] The myth of Pandora should teach us not to hope at all. Regrettably, we are at least as weak as she was.

common sense, conventional wisdom, or groupthink.[82] Besides, as we expound in the remainder of this first chapter, this is not even the *worst* part.

1.3 Third Movement: Scherzo

> The writer who deals with a sexual theme is always in danger of being accused, by those who think that such themes should not be mentioned, of an undue obsession with his subject. It is thought that he would not risk the censure of prudish and prurient persons unless his interest in the subject were out of all proportion to its importance.
> —Bertrand Russell[83]

We must include a warning and a disclaimer. Some particularly nasty horrors are going to be encountered and examined in our study. Any reader who might get negatively affected by harsh imagery and/or vulgar language should better pause and ponder on whether s/he wishes to continue perusing our volume, which builds upon prior publicly available research and presupposes both free speech and academic freedom. Although we wish to offend no one and respect everyone, we also know that an honest examination of humour and cruelty can lead into truly unsettling domains of human history, agency, loquency, and fantasy.[84]

On all such matters and the uncouth language in which they must sometimes be cast, it can be wise to rehash here a specification that the great 20th-century neo-Thomist and existentialist French thinker, Jacques Maritain, made in one of his books, and to which we adhere ourselves in our volumes about the philosophy of humour:

> It may happen that some undignified colloquial expressions will be found here and there in my text. Why did I indulge in this kind of vernacular? I no longer wish (as I did in my youth) to irritate the reader, or even to put his sense of humor to the test. But the fact is that I hate a perpetually and uniformly serious style; it is, to my mind, like those *grandes robes de pedants*

---

[82] As we explained in more detail in *H&C1*, throughout our careers, we have repeatedly been perplexed witnesses of contemporary academe's tendency to disciplinary self-seclusion, wilful blindness, and trained incapacity. See also Chapter 1 of Part 2.
[83] Russell (2009), 327. As we discuss briefly here in Chapter 4, and in greater detail in Chapters 1 and 3 of Part 2, censorial and Puritanical attitudes are still alive and kicking in many a culture and in many a quarter, including Western universities, as lamented by the noted American feminist thinker, Laura Kipnis (2017).
[84] In this context, "loquency" means linguistic self-expression, as in Bearth, Beck, and Döbel (2014) and Anonymous (2003).

of which Pascal spoke and in which people's fancy likes to clothe philosophers. I take truth seriously; I don't take myself seriously.[85]

As is to be shown in this book's Chapters 2 and 3, the concepts of 'humour' and 'cruelty' tap frequently, if not regularly, into two major psychic wells of arousal and discomfort, i.e., aggressiveness and sexuality.[86] *Whoever reads our pages past this point, then, does so to his/her own risk and under his/her own personal responsibility.*[87] Similarly, this volume at large should not be read by anyone who could deem offensive, prejudicial, inimical, violent, degrading, inhumane, inappropriate, and/or disrespectful the correct citing, candid consideration or considered criticism of, and the humorous cogitation about, *controversial* aspects of select human cultures, moral stances, national policies, political ideologies, practical activities, economic praxes, personal preferences, received ideas, and/or cherished traditions.[88]

We know far too well that true controversy is hard to swallow, especially when addressing, affecting, and/or afflicting one's own core values, central beliefs, time-tested reasonings, and/or alleged reasons. Confirmation is comfortable and comforting. Conjecture and confutation are not. Having an open mind is good and well, until something ungainly and/or unsettling starts raining into it. One's guests can be uninvited ones. And some of them can prove terribly obnoxious.[89] 'Critical thinking', in academic life, is not unlike the idea of 'competition' within real capitalist economies.[90] Therein, plenty of people publicly commend and recommend

---

[85] Maritain (1958), 9.
[86] By way of markedly different parodic registers, Pasolini's 1969 surrealist film *Pigsty* and Polanski's 2011 dark comedy *Carnage* did a masterly and unsettling job in showing how vicious aggressiveness and untamed sexuality seethe and simmer under quotidian interpersonal relations, family life, social conventions, and expected civility. Please note also that films and TV series are *not* included in the closing bibliography.
[87] We discussed in detail in *H&C1* Polanyi's (1962c) conception of personal responsibility, to which we must refer our reader, especially insofar as we keep adhering to it in this volume (see also Polanyi 2023). Let us just recall here also Hans Jonas' (1984, 130) basic and "timeless archetype of all responsibility", i.e., "the parental for the child".
[88] This volume's main topic is the conflict between humour and cruelty, i.e., *a dark field littered with dreadful experiences and expressions.* Affectively charged, these experiences and expressions are *normally* controversial.
[89] A number of sentences in our volume start with "And" for reasons of rhetorical emphasis. It is not an error.
[90] Do note that we use the terms "idea" and "concept" as synonyms. No finer distinction is needed at the level of generality at which we address humour, cruelty, their mutual conflicts, and many pertinent attendant phenomena.

"competition" proper, but only as long as it does not actually apply to them, their closest associates, or their vested interests.[91]

But let's not be all gloom and doom. We do have a modicum of optimism and, to some extent, even expect that most of our readers shall be willing and able to agree to disagree, when necessary, and perchance come to appreciate the insights that can be gathered from major classics as well as minor commentators, despite the disturbing insights and the occasional idiocies that they may have spouted—ourselves included (*qua* minor commentators, *ça va sans dire*). We find it lamentable, to be entirely candid, that inquiring minds may decide to stop listening to a speaker, continuing a conversation, or perusing a text simply because the speaker, interlocutor, or author at issue happened to utter one point among many, or develop a single argument in a vast tome, that did not fit with the recipients' worldview and tacit presuppositions.[92]

Not to mention doing the same when there are effectively *more* than just one dubious point and/or there may follow a whole host of disquieting arguments. Engaging with these more extensive intellectual trials is usually more *fun*, in our experience. Yet we are conscious of the fact that some individuals find this sort of challenge unworthy of their attention or even painfully insulting, politically incorrect, patently indecent, and/or personally intolerable.[93] As to those who might so react and yet decide *not* to desist from reading this volume, they must reflect in

---

[91] See Smith (1904), Galbraith and Salinger (1979), and Galbraith (2004) and (2007). *It may well be true that there is no such thing as a free lunch, but all economic agents are most eager to find one and enjoy it, if they can.* Shareholders do not care much about the competitiveness of the enterprises that they formally own if these shareholders make money by way of dividends, speculation, asset inflation, etc. Managers can happily drive an enterprise into the ground as long as they have accrued enough wealth by way of stellar salaries, special bonuses, and/or golden handshakes. Workers would welcome wage increases irrespective of their own productivity, i.e., provided that they can form sufficiently strong unions to obtain such increases. This last *caveat* being necessary insofar as Galbraith's post-war decades of mass-unionised capitalism are gone, and no major recovery from the 20th-century 'union busting' praxes has been recorded in the Western countries. Ironically, trade unions have not yet recovered, despite the 2008 collapse of international finance, even in liberal nations that are famous for having non-Anglo-American forms of capitalism (see, e.g., Dribbusch and Birke 2012, on Germany).
[92] Over the course of many working years, for one, we have witnessed this attitude among the student population. For another, we have observed such immediate, knee-jerk rejections in now-ubiquitous social-media interactions.
[93] Perhaps the authors of the present volume were spoiled in their youth. They were raised in families that thrived on after-dinner debates about contentious topics, especially political ones, and enjoyed the most open-minded and furious classroom discussions in their university years. Somehow, they both came to *favour conversation over condemnation.*

earnest upon the following 22 representative remarks, however bizarre some of them may sound at first.[94]

If we discuss recent cases of terrorism by self-proclaimed heroes of Islam, we are not condoning Islamophobia. If we present analyses of Western military involvements in the Middle East, we are not condoning terrorism. If we mention criticisms of Israeli policies, we are not condoning anti-Semitism. If we cover the religious warfare of different Christian confessions, we are not condoning religious bigotry. If we report a joke involving women, we are not condoning misogyny. If we point towards historical violence occurred in British India, we are condoning neither imperialism nor anarchy. If we hint at the white supremacists' most common offensive slurs, we are not condoning racism. If we talk about animal husbandry or hunting, we are not condoning anthropocentrism. If we observe the marked prevalence of man-made crimes, we are not condoning misandry. If we ponder upon psychopathology, we are not condoning neuronormativity. If we recall a comedy about a lady's sexual promiscuity, we are not condoning slut-shaming. If we evoke a prank played at the expense of an obese gentleman, we are not condoning fat-shaming. If we cite Biblical scriptures and search therein for wisdom or inspiration, we are not condoning dogmatism. If we address philosophical pessimism, we are not condoning misanthropy. If we quote an expert's study of unusual sexual practices among gay men, we are not condoning homophobia. If we convey the words of feminist thinkers or depth psychologists advocating pornography, we are not condoning the sexual abuse of women, men, children, and/or animals. If we focus on Italy's, Germany's, or France's contributions to world culture, we are not condoning Eurocentrism. If we make analogical use of Hindu imagery, we are not condoning Hinduphobia. If we write about marriages between men and women, we are not condoning heteronormativity. If we presuppose knowledge of traditional gender roles, we are not condoning transphobia. And if we pen a flippant remark or two about a stereotypical Catholic nun or a cartoonish Protestant minister—for we are also going to make attempts at humour in this volume—we are nevertheless opposing anticlericalism. The same goes for our tongue-in-cheek remarks about the milieu that we know best, i.e., Western academe. No matter what we write about ourselves, our colleagues,

---

[94] As explained here in Chapter 4, in line with the teachings of *Gestalt* psychology and Polanyi (1962c), an immense plurality of tacit subsidiary details is required in order for any conscious act involving a focal point of attention to take place. Therefore, throughout our volume, *we* intentionally instantiate and indirectly reiterate this important realisation, and *make frequent use of long lists of qualifications, items, and/or examples.*

and the strange circus in which we work and interact, we are not condoning anti-intellectualism.[95]

Following these 22 representative self-reflexive remarks, some of which are already coloured with more than a dash of humour, the name of the game should have become crystal-clear to the reader. Or so we hope. After all, we do not know our readers. Once again, it should be patent that we wish to offend no one and respect everyone. However, we also know that, as it was stated, an honest examination of the concepts of 'humour' and 'cruelty' can lead into truly unsettling domains of human history, agency, loquency, and fantasy.[96] Such domains, which often revolve around the psychologically potent spheres of aggression and sexual *libido*, can be affectively overwhelming and, at times, produce grave misunderstandings at an intellectual level.[97]

These grave misunderstandings, in turn, can generate apprehensions, accusations, and aggravations based upon misinterpretation, exaggeration, indignation, identity-formation, projection, harsh unspoken tribalism, and/or haphazard mental association. All such unhappy consequences being particularly likely to follow whenever the researched ideational processes or phenomena encroach upon some of the reader's identity-centred priorities. These, for their part, can even be rationalised into pseudo-science, conventional wisdom, or inflexible prophetic dogma.[98] That is, when they are not simply held *qua* tacit and potent foundational presuppositions of which the holder has often little direct lucid awareness, if any. To make

---

[95] We discussed in detail in *H&C2* how easily angry accusations of boorish "heresy" can arise whenever a person, who worships a given 'cow' as sacred, meets another person who does not only refuse to worship the same cow, but even pokes fun at it and/or its worship. The former person can find the latter so cruel that s/he responds to the latter's humour with punitive cruelty (see the cases discussed in Chapter 1 of Part 2). Additionally, let us remark on the fact that by using the fairly traditional expression "men and women" we are not tacitly promoting the ascendancy of the former over the latter ('androcentrism') or, for that matter, its opposite ('gynocentrism').

[96] It should also be noted that, were not offending anyone the decisive criterion for publishing or not a book, hardly any scholarly work would ever get published, not least in philosophy and psychology, both of which rely on creative and critical thinking, i.e., thought that is capable of challenging established views, hence coming across as unsettling and, on occasion, offensive, perhaps even *cruelly* so. As the contemporary Romanian philosopher Liviu Cocei (2015, 134) argued with regard to the oldest explicit intellectual methodology ever developed in Western culture, i.e., the Socratic method, making people 'see' things differently than they are used to and/or 'helping' them to realise that they might be wrong are rarely welcome activities, because they "hurt".

[97] Any neat separation between sexual *libido* and aggressiveness is, chiefly if not exclusively, a convenient conceptual abstraction, for our affective reality is probably a mixture of these two energies, at the very least.

[98] For a token of pseudo-science, see Gobineau (1915). More on dogmatism follows in Chapters 1 and 3 of Part 2.

things worse, misunderstandings themselves can be misunderstood, grossly, more than once, and in contradictory ways.[99]

As regards all such mystifying misunderstandings, academia is no blessed oasis. Quite the opposite. It can be a chaotic, confusing, cruel, and somewhat comical and crazy playground for ostensible grownups.[100] As recently stated by a noted American feminist thinker, Laura Kipnis, with regard to the "current climate" on her native country's university campuses:

> Critical distance itself is out of fashion—not exactly a plus when it comes to intellectual life (or education itself.) Feelings are what's in fashion… But this cult of feeling has an authoritarian underbelly: feelings can't be questioned or probed, even while furnishing the rationale for sweeping new policies, which can't be questioned or probed either.[101]

What is more, given our own focus on humorous matters and our own writing style, Kipnis lamented that "[i]rony doesn't sit well in the current climate, especially when it comes to irony about the current climate".[102] Still, Kipnis herself "tend[s] to be ironic—[she] like[s] irony". [103] And for a very good reason: "i[rony] helps you think because it gives you critical distance on a thing".[104]

It is not difficult for us to grasp why the feeling-led spiralling into institutionally rationalised irrationality, about which Kipnis warned her readers, may be par-

---

[99] There has been no lack of Western comedies making fun of this phenomenon, since at least Plautus' *Menaechmi*, whence Shakespeare's *Comedy of Errors* was later derived.

[100] No offence was meant by using "crazy": we were simply testing the reader's readiness to fall off his/her chair.

[101] Kipnis (2017), 2. Laura Kipnis is the first of many female authorities to be encountered by the reader. As far as possible and sensible, *the authors of this volume endeavoured to include expert views arising from historically marginalised and/or minoritarian groups*, whether in the main text or in the extensive and detailed footnotes (e. g., women, working-class intellectuals, European Jews, illegal immigrants, members of crip/queer communities, etc.). Inevitably, some such groups are absent or less represented than others. Their absence or underrepresentation does not imply any prejudice or malice on our part. Rather, it is the result of: (1) the salience of some sources, compared to others; (2) the prior presence of some such sources in *H&C1* and *H&C2*; and (3) our sheer ignorance of others.

[102] Kipnis (2017), 1–2. See also Young (2020) on the sorry state of "irony" proper in today's polarised US.

[103] Kipnis (2017), 1. Another keen and stinging egalitarian ironist, Baroncelli (1996, 29), feared that, "having abandoned the pursuit of any political agency that is capable of changing society at large, the [university] campus is now seen … as a domain where ritual acts of vengeance can be exercised" by left- as well as right-wing "idiots".

[104] Kipnis (2017), 1. As discussed in *H&C1* and *H&C2*, 'distance' is key for humour itself to be effective.

ticularly true of irony and, relatedly, humour. Cruelty, in fact, tends to be, well, cruel. Characteristically, however, it does so in an open, stern, and straightforward manner. Its victims are beaten, blistered, whipped, wounded, disfigured, hacked to pieces, crushed, burnt, and eaten.[105]

Humour, as we argued in *H&C1* and *H&C2*, tends to be cruel too, also *qua* "irony" proper.[106] Generally, though, its distinctive *modus operandi* is far more insidious, indirect, imperceptible, implicit, idiosyncratic, and even innocent—as strange as the last instance may sound.[107] Humour's victims are taunted, ridiculed, teased, poked, irked, or simply invited to play along and expected to engage in the same kind of callous and/or exclusionary behaviour.[108] Whilst the direct and/or indirect effects of a joke, prank, or jest may be experienced as genuine cruelty by the 'butts' of it and/or those who are left 'out' of it, correctly grasping the originator's cruel intentions, if there were any such intentions to begin with, can be a thorny endeavour—if not even an impossible one.[109]

1.4 Coda

> Here comes another one / Here it comes again
> —Monty Python[110]

We must insist once more on the non-academic point that, as members of the academic profession, we presuppose throughout our work both free speech and aca-

---

[105] This list of examples is *not* comprehensive.
[106] How the word "humour" may encompass "irony" is explained here in Chapter 2. For a recent comprehensive survey of the latter term in the philosophical tradition of the West, see Cocei (2022), whose careful and complex approach to this notion is a sort of mirror-like endeavour with respect to our own three-volume take on "humour" proper.
[107] We discussed in *H&C2* the empirical studies showing how most people who claim that they were "only joking" when making some humorous remark that was perceived as cruel would appear to be telling the truth.
[108] We explained in detail in *H&C2* how humour must necessarily entail a modicum of cruelty at the practical level because *at least* it ignores or underplays the potential suffering of those who are left 'out' of the joke.
[109] In *H&C2*, we commented extensively on the opacity of intentions, on which only God or, perhaps, the best psychoanalyst can put their finger with any certainty and precision.
[110] Monty Python, *Contractual Obligation Album* (1980), the other side, song #3, verses 1–2.

demic freedom. Should these legal and moral rights be null and void, there would be hardly any point in activating our creativity, sharpening our intellects, exploring the extant plethora of contradicting views on 'humour' and 'cruelty' that populate Western culture, and writing a scholarly book about these two concepts. Not to mention writing three or four books.

Were such rights actually curtailed, our readership too would be deprived of something important, namely, an authentic opportunity for learning, reflection, and self-examination. Why reading a philosophical text whose authors were not at liberty to discuss philosophical issues that they deemed important, simply because these issues happened to be aesthetically ungainly, morally disquieting, politically tricky, epistemically uncertain, editorially unfashionable, and/or socio-culturally unpleasant? Why bothering at all, really?[111]

Ideally, the academic vocation, not just the philosophical mind, should be free to operate even if such challenges arise or even because *precisely* such irritating yet intriguing challenges have arisen. And by "academic vocation" we mean the sort of *personal* commitment to truth-seeking, deep reflection, and deeper understanding that can be derived from the professional exemplar and the thorough reflexivity that were both demonstrated and defended in our young century by the noted Canadian philosopher and environmentalist, John McMurtry:

> I don't think I have written or attended a paper in over 45 years that this question has not recurred as my wider field of meaning: "What is at stake that this position overlooks? What life capacity of our world does this argument help to release or to repress?" I call this *the life-ground test*. It has taken me on endless journeys into the meta-program of the human condition and its presupposed orders which I still pursue day in and out. But let me be frank. There are endless barriers to such a way of thinking in the actual academy.[112]

---

[111] We deem these questions *not* to be rhetorical.
[112] McMurtry (2008), par. 35; emphasis added. One of these barriers, which we encountered a few times in our careers, is the editor's power to force an author to delete or rephrase humorous remarks that were deemed too scathing, even if they performed the crucial "life-ground test" that McMurtry (2008) wrote about. Another, to which we have not yet succumbed, is the notion whereby only members of a certain group should be allowed to write about issues concerning that group. Thus, jumping immediately into the humorous silliness of this notion, only Icelanders should be allowed to write about Iceland; or left-handed Icelanders about left-handed people in Iceland; or red-haired left-handed Icelanders about red-haired left-handed people in Iceland. By consistent and thorough application of this inane logic, each person ought to write about herself and herself alone and perhaps only as regards their recent or immediate self, which is in a state of flux for as long as she lives.

What is more, as the famous (post)Jungian American psychologist James Hillman observed at the close of the last century, there exists a self-defeating irony inherent to all forms of censorship and, more broadly, censoriousness—however well-meaning they may be in their allegedly sensitive and officially sensible cruelty.[113] Specifically, as the acts of censorship hide an item from public scrutiny, they also make the same hidden item affectively more vibrant than its explicit presentation would be capable of doing.[114] We may call it the perverse logic of "the forbidden fruit".[115] Which also means that the present chapter ends roughly at the Biblical point whence human history began unfolding: Adam and Eve.[116]

---

[113] We write "(post)" because it is hard to determine whether an archetypal psychologist such as Hillman, who also directed the C.G. Jung Institute in Zurich, can ever be said to be 'past' his Jungian background and influences.

[114] *Switching between opposite conditions is a never-ending possibility.* Thus, *neither censorship nor candour can ever satisfy all of one's peers at once.* In this connection, it is instructive and amusing to recall how, while working on our three volumes on humour and cruelty, we were told by a female colleague that we should inject more "feminism" into our project, which she found too "canonical" hence "male-dominated". As we were busy complying with her useful piece of advice and increasing the number of female voices that the reader encounters in *H&C3*, another female colleague told one of the present authors that he should avoid addressing some prurient topics, whence loud controversies arose within the feminist camp, because he happened to be "a middle-class, middle-age, white man", none of which three things he had ever made a conscious effort to become. We were thus left to wonder about what the American novelist Joseph Heller (1961), who authored the famous satire *Catch-22*, would have said on such a strange predicament. In any case, see Chapters 1 and 3 of Part 2.

[115] To be precise, Hillman (1995b, 60) discussed "the tin fig-leaf or small piece of cloth" covering the *pudenda* of statues and crucifixes and "closing off the literal and opening into the imaginable, the implied, sparking the fervour of fantasy". Given our titular concepts, we must mention as well the contemporary US-based philosopher of humour Robert Valgenti (2018), who tackled, *inter alia*, how 'bleeping' profanities in audio-visual media induces the audiences into thinking of which cuss words may be at play and thereby makes the 'bleeps' as such amusing, as patently signalled by the unneeded bleeps now commonly used for comic effect. Instead of simply obliterating vulgar language, censorship obliquely heightens its conversational presence and comedic potential (see also Chapter 3 of Part 2). Truly, *there is nothing that laughter cannot assault* when given a chance, as we discussed in *H&C2*. And such a power explains why so much humour has been cruelly policed, persecuted, prevented, and punished.

[116] We assume our readers to be sufficiently familiar with Biblical sources and Judeo-Christian culture at large.

1.5 Coda's Coda

> Here comes another one / When will it ever end?
> —Monty Python[117]

As to those readers who should find the previous and/or the present subsections annoyingly verbose and possibly superfluous, we salute their faith in contemporary academia's imperviousness to blunt aggressiveness, passive aggressiveness, unfair criticism, knee-jerk reaction, feuding partisanship, Machiavellian scheming, turf war, moral panic, power hunger, fanatical zeal, callous indifference, narrow-mindedness, identity politics, identity posturing, identity crisis, mindlessness, collective paranoia, trained hysteria, self-serving formalism, elitist unfriendliness, rabid factionalism, emotional touchiness, lack of good taste, lack of any taste, lack of patience, lack of scruple, genuine error, and sorely deficient sense of humour. Unfortunately, like Laura Kipnis herself, *we* do not share their faith. Actually, we believe that some readers may already be finding *us* guilty of a number of these professional sins, personal shortcomings, philosophical smirches, and/or stylistic shenanigans.[118]

Lastly, should the reader have failed to grasp the humorous elements injected into the preceding three periods of this supplementary coda, plus those implied by the present chapter's structure and musical headings, s/he is encouraged to abstain from reading the rest of the volume. As Eco himself would have argued, the "*intentio auctoris*" [the author's meanings], "*operis*" [the work's meanings] and, in this particular case, "*lectoris*" [the reader's meanings] are clearly too misaligned to produce any beneficial results.[119] Such is life, at times.[120]

---

[117] Monty Python, *Contractual Obligation Album* (1980), the other side, song #3, verses 3–4.
[118] As noted in our previous volumes, our sense of humour may be perplexingly quaint.
[119] Eco (1988), 154. Stressing further the distinction between the first two sets of meanings, Eco (with Scalfari and Gnoli 2015) jibed: "books are more cunning than their authors". We hope this to be true of our own books, despite their inevitable imperfections.
[120] This is no deep philosophical thought, but a mere practical and prosaic consideration.

2 Making Sense of Humour

2.1 An Overview of 'Humour' in the Humanities

δὶς ἐς τὸν αὐτὸν ποταμὸν οὐκ ἂν ἐμβαίης
—Heraclitus[1]

2.1.1 Semantic Vagaries of Time and Place

The earliest recorded meaning of the term "humour" in Western culture refers to "liquids" or "fluids", especially those of a bodily origin, at least as regards the European languages sharing the Latin etymon *umor*.[2] Indeed, "humour" proper had an established, enduring and explicit technical signification in the natural philosophy of the ancient, medieval, and early-modern times.[3] And it was nothing funny whatsoever. Chiefly, it indicated the four basic liquids found in the human body:
(1) the "chole" or yellow bile;
(2) the "phlegm" or "dirty gray ... mucus";
(3) the one which the Romans called *sanguis* (i.e., our arteries' red blood); and
(4) the "black bile: melancholia".[4]

These primarily chromatic distinctions were first recorded in the 5th century BC by the aptly-named "father of Western medicine", i.e., the Greek empiricist philosopher Hippocrates, who detected and commented upon the most noticeable variances between blood extracted from a healthy individual and blood extracted from someone who had been stricken by a deadly illness.[5]

Hippocrates' experimental observations were corroborated and expanded upon in Roman times by another philosopher and physician, Galen, to whom is owed the firm entrenchment in Western culture of so-called "humourism" or "hu-

---

[1] Proverbially, "you cannot step twice into the same river." As cited in Plato (1903), 402a.
[2] Meaning "moisture" or "humidity", linguists have been debating about which older Greek etymon lies behind the Latin term itself, e.g., whether ὑγρός ("humid", "wet") or χυμός ("juice", "sap") (Pianigiani 1907).
[3] Traditionally, "natural philosophy" deals with changing material entities, unlike "first philosophy".
[4] Kushner (2013), 154. Different humours and numbers thereof were long debated (Jouanna 2012, chap. 16).
[5] Kushner (2013), 154.

moralism".[6] Galen's fundamental stance, which would eventually become *the* standard medico-philosophical tenet of our civilisation for a very long time, linked Hippocrates' four basic liquids with all kinds of causal influences and/or explanatory principles *vis-à-vis* both good and bad health.[7] These included, among the many and most diverse things: sources of nourishment, jobs, times of the year, regular winds and breezes, personal acquaintances, alchemical substances, erotic practices, individual and/or group habits, etc.[8]

The humoral interpretation of humankind meant also that all sorts of psychological phenomena came to be routinely associated, often *via* convenient tetralogies, with the four ultimate fluids that were believed to flow inside our bodies. There were illnesses, of course, but also general mental dispositions, prominent intellectual aptitudes, distinctive inclinations, fleeting tempers, recurring passions, elusive internal energies, obvious personal peculiarities, dominant tastes, discerning perceptions, vivid reminiscences, deeply engrained moods, and/or traits of character. A generally unsmiling person, as a result, would be extremely unlikely to be said to exhibit a "good humour".[9]

At the end of the 16th century, the Galenic medico-philosophical understanding of "humour" was unquestionably present in both spoken and written English, if not unsurprisingly commonplace and ubiquitously common-sensical.[10] This fact can be evinced from a great variety of sources, including literary and theatrical ones, in which the Hippocratic-Galenic liquids and attendant features would describe and, to a large extent, explain the convictions, conducts, clangers, and/or comical characteristics of the people whose artistic portrayal was being realised.[11] In the thespian genre, Ben Jonson is possibly the most famous Renaissance play-

---

6 See, e.g., Rosen (2005), who emphasised the satirical character of much of Galen's writing.
7 Galen's fame and influence have been so prolonged in Western civilisation that his name 'drifted' into 20th-century popular culture *qua* foremost human archaeologist in the long-lived science fiction series *Star Trek*.
8 See Jouanna (2012) on the gradual accruing and variation of causes and principles in ancient times.
9 See, e.g., Kiblansky, Panofsky, and Saxl (1964), focussing on melancholia. As to the recurrence of the number four, numerological compulsions are still a driving force behind much scientific activity such that countless studies keep being published under the aegis of the number 100 (i.e., percentages), even if they may have little or no value.
10 In parallel, traces of humourism can still be found in English (e.g., "choleric", "phlegmatic", "sanguine").
11 H. Miller (1945) showed how the association of Hippocratic humours with theatre is at least as old as Aristophanes.

wright who, in Britain, based his own "Comick ... comedies" on the Hippocratic-Galenic tradition of humoralism, to the point of describing himself as "a Humorist".[12]

According to many pundits, Ben Jonson's theatre was pivotal in creating a closer connection between "humour" proper and the "unbalanced presentation of human qualities and moral infirmities outdoing reason and causing the loss of the self", especially such as to produce amusing on-stage effects.[13] In a rare feat of professional concurrence, today's scholars tend to agree on the notion that the English language changed remarkably in the 17th century, marked by Protestant severity, and that "humour" attained in that period "its modern meaning" *qua* something funny, as "first attested in England in 1682".[14] Anomaly and amusement, both of which can still be described as "funny" in Albion's idiom, were then married together under the umbrella of "humour", conceivably on and/or because of the theatre stage.[15]

Among such contemporary scholars, Brenda Goldberg wrote, at the close of the last century, that the "genealogy" of the modern English interpretation of "humour" as something funny is the result of "the advent of the 'polite society' of the 1600s and 1700s, and a classical redefinition of the arts and theatre into elitist and 'low' forms".[16]

(1) Goldberg claimed that all "unscientific and duplicitous ... 'punning' comedy style, and poetic logic" came then to be seen as "'low bred' ... and summarily relegated ... to 'popular culture'", which became the repository of all things indecent, shameful, obscene, scandalous, vulgar, coarse and uncouth.[17]

(2) Concomitantly, a new "'high' culture" would appear to have developed in parallel, if not in opposition, to the former, "enforcing new regimes of social regulation" on laughing matters, i.e., new recognised means of personal and/or group entertainment, ways of speaking, manners in the company of one's own social peers, and strategies for signalling class membership plus its attendant inner and outer hierarchies.[18]

---

12 As cited in Redwine, Jr. (1961), 317 and 333.
13 Takase (1983–1984), 9. Venet (2002) argued the Hippocratic-Galenic notion of "humour" proper to be central in Shakespeare's works as well.
14 Bremmer and Roodenburg (1997), 1.
15 Theatre having then wide cross-class appeal, rather than being an exclusive playpen for the educated elites.
16 Goldberg (1999), 59 and 63. We cannot stress enough how *our very languages mirror and strengthen class divisions and assumptions*, e.g., the positive tone of "noble" and the negative one of "vulgar" and "common".
17 Goldberg (1999), 63.
18 Goldberg (1999), 63–64. Arguably, *classist rejection of popular humour can be shrouded in academic garb*, thus reflecting the socio-cultural milieu whence most academics originate, i.e., middle-

Relatedly, smiling thoughtfully at an artful "'incongruity' or 'dissonance'" that can only be grasped by a person's educated "reason", hence in a sophisticated display of the high degree of one's own "'inner' awareness of the 'self'", showcases publicly that particular smiling and/or chuckling person's splendid ability for appreciating the new elite's chic "humour", rather than rejoicing in the obstreperous and foulmouthed "laughter" of the bad-mannered plebs.[19]

The late-modern English birth of "humour" *qua* something funny is also validated by the linguistic trend whereby, all over the planet, older words indicating laughter, mirth, fun, comicality *et similia* were not deemed adequate enough in order to translate the Anglophone's new and probably elitist take on "humour".[20] For instance, the Chinese came up with *"youmo"*, i.e., "a loan-word, a neologism dating from interaction with the English language—thus indicative of a novel concept", this novel term "impl[ying] more gentleness than the older indigenous term *huaji* … ('laughable' or 'funny')".[21] Correspondingly, "[t]he same distinction occurs in Japanese terminology, where *yūmoa* … now denotes kindly, gentle laughter in the Dickensian sense, while *kokkei* … (Chinese *huaji*) means comic(al) and another old laughter-related term, *warai* … (Chinese 'laugh'), connotes even broader funniness".[22]

---

and upper-class families. Such being, at least, Kipnis' assessment (1998, 86), who argued that an analogous "class prejudice" explains much of the standard 'sex-negative' character of her country's academic feminism. *In nuce*, the normally upper- and middle-class self-styled "feminists" inhabiting the expensive and rather exclusive American campuses are said to like letting their working-class 'sisters' be mere recipients for the former group's refined, restrained, and reasoned instruction, not self-determining agents choosing far too often the 'wrong' paths in life characterised by poor taste, indecency, and/or apparent adherence to patriarchal standards (see also Kipnis 2006, 124–128). There would be, in short, 'big sisters' who know better and 'little sisters' who are tragically misguided and regularly 'duped' by invariably evil men and their oppressive patriarchal ideology (see also Zakaria 2021 on sisterly hierarchies). See also Chapters 1 and 3 of Part 2.

[19] Goldberg (1999), 63–64. Bakhtin's works are probably the most thorough and influential studies on this British and, more broadly, European process of cultural separation between a high-brow, gentlemanly, conversational, and increasingly private sense of humour, and a low-brow, popular, carnivalesque, and decreasingly public "culture of folk humour"—such being the frequent English translation of the Russian "народная смеховая культура", which, however, refers to "laughter" [смех], not to "humour" [юмор] proper (Bakhtin 1976, 27).

[20] See, e.g., Baldensperger (1907).

[21] Milner Davis (2013), 3 (the spelling of the terms at issue is: "幽默" and "滑稽"). See also Chey (2011). Yet, Russell (2009, 529) deemed traditional Chinese "humour" to be too "sly and delicate" to be grasped by Westerners.

[22] Milner Davis (2013), 3 (the exact Japanese spelling is: "ユーモア"). As to whether "Dickensian" laughter is characteristically "kindly" and "gentle", it is a matter of learned debate (see, e.g., Andrews 2013).

On the European mainland, "in the Dutch Republic, in 1765, English humour was still seen as something 'which they virtually find only on their isle'".[23] "In Germany, too, the word was an English 'import', as Lessing explicitly states".[24] Tellingly, Lessing himself "first translated 'humour' as *'Laune'*, taking it in its older sense [of 'mood' or 'temperament'], although he corrected himself afterwards. And still in 1810 an early German biographer of Joseph Haydn noted that 'a sort of innocent mischievousness, or what the British call humour', had been a principal trait of the composer's character."[25] Who knows? Maybe this cultural mismatch is at the root of the 2020 Brexit—apparently, no laughing matter.[26]

Even the modern French, who knew a thing or two about comedy and hilarity, found it necessary to accept and absorb the novel English notion.[27] None less than Denis Diderot, in an article entitled "Humour" and included in the celebrated *Encyclopédie*, spoke of an "English" derivation for this "original, rare, and rather singular pleasantry", which he sketched along the lines of what today we would dub "cruel" or "black humour", and maintained is exemplified at "its highest point" by the Irish satirist Jonathan Swift.[28] As late as the year 1862, the celebrated French novelist Victor Hugo "still spoke about 'that English thing they call humour'", as though this facet of comicality had not yet become an integral part of the Gallic frame of mind and way of life.[29] Moreover, Hugo noted: "Fun is (like cant, like humour,) an exceptional, untranslatable word."[30] Still today, the world's Francophones distinguish between *humour* as a cause of amusement and *humeur* as a mood, temperament, or trait of character (and a fluid).[31]

At the same time, perhaps as a lasting heritage of the bellicose ethos, adamant austerity, and violent iconoclasm of 17th-century Puritanism, the English were seen

---

23 Bremmer and Roodenburg (1997), 2.
24 Bremmer and Roodenburg (1997), 2–3.
25 Bremmer and Roodenburg (1997), 3.
26 Given the political and bureaucratic chaos accompanying it, Brexit might be a veritable laughing matter instead.
27 We assume our readers to be aware of the vast Francophone contribution to comedy in late-modern times.
28 As translated and cited in Critchley (2000), 6. Diderot was the author of many works that touch on humorous subjects and/or aimed at comicality, e.g., plays, a theory of comedy, essays about visual arts, a philosophical dialogue, and a novel. Contemporary scholars such as Leborgne (2018) and Ibeas-Altamira (2018) had no qualms in using "humour" in connection with him and the French culture of his day, despite Diderot's own claims of this notion's 'Englishness'.
29 Bremmer and Roodenburg (1997), 1.
30 As, ironically, translated by and cited in Vasey (1877), 179.
31 Bremmer and Roodenburg (1997), 1.

in the rest of Europe as a hopelessly disconsolate lot.[32] They were commonly held to be: deadly serious; stubborn to a fault; unbearably low-spirited; generally unfriendly; hostile to dancing, theatre, opera, music, and amiable chats; straitlaced to the point of prudish intolerance; susceptible to bouts of melancholia; unable to grasp non-literal expressions and inventive turns-of-phrase; if not even disastrously incapable of coming across as funny when trying, unless pathetically well-oiled; and completely bereft of any sense of humour, whatever new meaning of this notion they may have happened to spawn and style as such.[33] As it was suggestively written by the noted post-Restoration British playwright, politician, and influential publicist, Joseph Addison: "The English delight in Silence more than any other European Nation, if the Remarks which are made on us by Foreigners are true."[34]

Rather than censuring or carefully qualifying this description, Addison appeared to take pride in it. Indeed, he claimed that the "Genius and natural Temper" of the English nation consists exactly in being "modest, thoughtful and sincere", and in possessing an incomparable "Natural Taciturnity" that no other Continental people can emulate, least of all the French.[35] Ironically—but perhaps reasonably in the face of Britain's Puritanical gloom—the modern notion of 'humour' might have had a Francophone origin, rather than an Anglophone one. As stated by none less than the most celebrated champion of the *philosophes des Lumières*:

> [The English] have a term to signify this natural pleasantry, this true comicality, this gaiety, this urbanity, these jokes that come out without hesitation; and they render this idea with the word "humeur", "humour", that they pronounce *yumor*; they believe that they alone possess this humour and that the other Nations have no term to express this trait of character. However, it is an ancient word of our language, utilised in this sense in many comedies by Corneille.[36]

---

32 Puritanism was tackled in more detail in *H&C2* with respect to Morreall's philosophy. It is also touched on here (Chapter 1 of Part 2) *vis-à-vis* censorship, as well as the personal and social dangers of sexual repression (Chapter 3 of Part 2).
33 See, e.g., Gidal (2003). In today's UK, this stereotype still applies to the Scots. In Scotland, it is attributed to the Highlanders. In the Highlands, to the Wee Frees of the Islands. In the Islands, to those of the Outer Hebrides.
34 Addison *et al.* (1891), editorial #135 (4 August 1711). Much more ensues on *The Spectator* in the present chapter, and *our references to it follow in formulations listing: editor/author* (i.e., Addison, Steele, Budgel, or anonymous), *editorial's number, and publication year.* Therefore, they are not listed as "Addison *et al.* (1891)".
35 Addison, 135 (1711) and 599 (1714).
36 Voltaire's "Lettre à Mr. L'Abbé d'Olivet", dated 20 August 1761 and cited *verbatim* in Robertson (1939), 255.

Voltaire had lived in England at length and observed the English traditions and institutions most attentively—and with no small degree of sincere esteem, if not even with some well-disguised envy.[37] In addition, Voltaire himself was a successful author of comedies and satires, as well as a well-trained public speaker and salons' virtuoso, who excelled in both *jeux d'esprit* and *mots d'esprit*.[38] If correct, then, his statement concerning the real birthplace of the modern notion of 'humour' would run counter to the many later Gallic testimonials to its 'foreign' origins and connotations, not least Hugo's in the second half of the 19th century.[39] Whether Voltaire was right or not, his compatriots would seem to have failed utterly to establish and/or entrench humour's hypothetical and hypothesised French roots, even among themselves, to the point of letting this notion fall into general oblivion.[40]

As to what the English may themselves have understood or may now understand when using the de-medicalised term "humour", it is by no means whatsoever a straightforward and easy matter.[41] Somehow, it keeps flowing. Definitely, many 'foreign' scholars have been studying in remarkable depth the fine semantic and pragmatic distinctions that could explain why so many linguistic communities around the world ended up importing the English word "humour" rather than adapting a prior one from their native tongues.[42] Parallelly, their Anglophone and/or Anglophile counterparts have been surveying the claimed birthplace of "humour" proper and, in the process, given shape to numerous and sorely conflicting accounts which are variously disseminated between two opposite poles.[43]

(1) At one extreme, the term "humour" can mean literally *any*thing that is perceived as somewhat funny by almost *any* one chosen person—insane cachinnators and the pathologically dumb being normally ignored in this context.[44] As written

---

[37] See, in particular, Voltaire (2005).
[38] Why "humour" cannot be rendered as "esprit" is a debated issue. See, e.g., Gifford (1981).
[39] See, e.g., W. Noonan (2011, 94) speaking of "the imported concept of humour" into French high culture.
[40] In the 19th century, D'Ancona (1880, 179) claimed the English word "humour" to derive from the Italian one for "humorist" [*umorista*] in 16th-century literary works. This older alternative too has been obviously forgotten.
[41] The same ambiguity persists also at the level of ostensible behaviour. See, e.g., Warren and McGraw (2016).
[42] See, e.g., Gunawan and Rini (2013), dealing with the Indonesian experience.
[43] See, e.g., Chapman and Foot (1977), covering many such cases.
[44] Pathological laughter has been explained *via* various possible physiological and psychological conditions, as also indicated by the extant terminology: "pseudobulbar effect", "emotional dysregulation", "emotionalism", etc.

in a fictional dialogue by the 20th-century Canadian political economist, literary critic, and humourist, Stephen Leacock: "what one would call a humorous nature" is, flatly, anyone or anything "that would raise a smile, or even a laugh".[45] Wittiness, irony, satire, mockery, horseplay, comic acts, parody, tomfooleries, farce, pranks, burps, farts, etc., would then all be subclasses of the concept of 'humour', in one way or another.[46] This is how, for example, the term is also legitimately approached by one of today's leading philosophers of humour and laughter, Lydia Amir, who was, in 2014, the founding president of the *International Association for the Philosophy of Humor*.[47] As she wrote: "humor [is ...] the contemporary umbrella term we use to refer to the comic and its cognates".[48]

Amir's comprehensive usage of "humour" proper is no novel academic conjecture or wild exaggeration.[49] Historically speaking, whatever elitist form of amusement the proud members of the refined upper echelons of British society may have thought of labelling as "humour" in the 18th century—or in times closer to our own—even a passing examination of the many jestbooks "of wit and humour" that those proud members themselves purchased and relished in their day confirms the view that the word "humour" applies to literally anything that can elicit someone's laughter and/or amusement.[50] This includes odious pranks aimed at the aged and the infirm.[51] Similarly, such a "humour" encompasses the most ill-mannered and "pitiless" jokes which make sport of "[t]he miserable old father, the hunchback, the street vendors, the battered wife, the rape plaintiff: the victims of these jokes [being] as helpless and vulnerable as it is possible".[52]

The adroit, abstract, ahistorical and adaptable definitions of "humour" characteristic of contemporary analytic philosophy would also confirm this realisation—tacitly and indirectly, perhaps, or even unintentionally, yet confirm it nonetheless.[53] For instance, as written in 2019 by the British philosopher Alan Roberts, in-

---

45 Leacock (1913), 176. Leacock's PhD mentor was another economist and humourist: Veblen.
46 How an item is a subclass of another varies: metaphorically, metonymically, exemplarily etc.
47 See the association's website: https://www.philosophyofhumor.org/.
48 Amir (2019), 73. See also Amir (2014), 234, and the father of "humorology", Evan Esar (1954, 10).
49 Whether for the sake of scholarship or sales pitching, academics can produce novel conjectures as well as wild exaggerations, e.g., Isenberg's (2017) subtitle stating: "The 400-Year Untold History of Class in America".
50 Amusement does not necessarily produce laughter, but can lead to smiling and/or arousal.
51 See especially Dickie (2011).
52 Dickie (2003), 2 and 6.
53 Rare are the examples of analytic philosophers of humour accepting openly the most un-PC forms of hilarity as rationally plausible instances of humour, e.g., Gimbel (2017), who seemed to take much delight in being cleverly controversial, while also being at least as insightful and as thought-provoking.

sofar as "humour" requires "amusement" and "funniness", these three key-terms should be understood as follows:

> Theory of Amusement (ToA): Subject S is amused by object O if and only if: (1) S is in the paratelic state. (2) S activates two inconsistent interpretations via unsound reasoning because of O. (3) S's arousal is increased because of (2). [...] Theory of Funniness (ToF): Object O is funny if and only if O merits amusement. Theory of Humour (ToH): Object O is humour if and only if O is intended to elicit amusement.[54]

(2) At the opposite extreme, one of France's leading literary critics of the 20th century, Louis Cazamian, could not make up his mind as to whether "humour" is "a special aesthetic category", which is then to be kept conceptually apart from its many cognates, or "a distinct psychological attitude" that is prototypically British, if not distinctively English.[55] Emblematically, thus reverberating Addison's previous reflections on the same subject, Cazamian could still emphasise in the 1930s the suspected connection between "humour" proper and the *unique* features of "the British" national character: "their faculty of withholding the normal flow of their impressions, their cool-blooded taciturnity, the subdued tone of their outward life, and that reserve which stretches all the way from the captaincy of their souls to pure sluggishness, and to the fear of giving themselves away".[56]

Funnily enough, in Britain, the celebrated 19th-century Romantic poet and pantisocratic philosopher Samuel T. Coleridge had already identified in his day no less than four different national typologies of "humour" proper.[57] They comprised the "thoughtful" one of his fellow Englishmen, of course, but also the "ethereal" one of

---

54 A. Roberts (2019), 116–127. In plain English, if someone is amused by something clever and/or surprising that is said, written, or shown for fun's sake, we can talk of "humour" being the case. Needless to emphasise, *determining whether any such thing is ever done for sheer fun's sake is an impossible task, given our intentions' opacity,* which the daily efforts of many judges, juries, psychoanalysts, confessors, and/or spouses regularly signal. Anscombe's (1963, 11, par. 6) intention-disclosing question, "why are/were you doing that?", is apparently obvious, simple to grasp, and comforts common sense. Psychologically, however, it scratches the surface of human motivation. Motivational complexity applies already to prosaic actions, e.g., turning off the shower at a public swimming pool. While it is certainly true that we do so in order to stop the flow, we may also be compelled by, say, duties with which we want to comply (e.g., civic, environmental, familial), our desire to set a good example, our fear of being reprimanded, etc. (We discussed this matter in H&C2.)
55 Cazamian (1930), vol. 1, 4, in which L'Estrange (1877–1878) was cited as a token of the opposite interpretation of humour. For a long time, English "humour" singled out "the Irish, Scots, and Welsh" as socio-culturally, if not anthropologically, distinct from and possibly inferior to the 'blessed' English race (Snyder 1920, 147).
56 Cazamian (1930), vol. 1, 8.
57 Pantisocracy was an egalitarian social ideal developed by, among others, Robert Southey and Coleridge (1895) himself.

the Spaniards, the "wit[ty]" one of the Italians, and the eminently verbal one of the French.[58] In the early 20th century, however, the great Spanish existentialist and liberal thinker, Miguel de Unamuno, contended: "The entire supply of humor that might have existed in Spain seems to have been exhausted in the telling of Don Quixote's story; today it is not easy to find in the entire world a people more incapable than the Spanish of understanding and feeling humor."[59]

In the face of such pronounced and historically prolonged disagreements among the purported experts, some researchers have simply thrown in the towel.[60] Deeming this "folk category" semantically exasperating, they have preferred dismissing it altogether as "a particularly useful, analytic category" and chosen, instead, controlled and, at times, highly artificial terms and attendant aspects of reality which, at the very least, are easier to isolate, approach, evaluate, and/or quantify.[61] Ironically, humour's own being 'special' and 'distinct' can thus become so pin-pointed and scientifically specific as to do away with "humour" itself.[62]

2.1.2 Semantic Vagaries of Theory and Philosophy

The enduring semantic morass just highlighted is made all the more byzantine by the perplexing fact that even the most extensive and/or most explicit philosophical investigations of late-modern British, or perhaps purely English, "humour" proper have frequently been contradictory.[63] Moreover, some of these investigations have simply avoided defining the key term at issue *ab initio*, hence relying on whatever common-sense understanding of this notion circulated in their social circles and/or

---

[58] As cited in Figueroa-Dorrego and Larkin-Galiñanes (2009), 313–314. Ancient rhetors' distinction between *de re* and *de dicto* looms large behind Coleridge's matrix of national types of humour (see, e.g., Quintilian 1920).
[59] De Unamuno (1967), 245. Interestingly, S. Roberts (2016) connoted him as an underappreciated humourist.
[60] This expression is to be understood metaphorically.
[61] Glenn and Holt (2017), 295. See also Ruch and Köhler (1998, 203). As to the artificiality of scientific concepts, Pareto (1935, par. 115) stated: "the more advanced sciences" give "senses very different … from … everyday usage" even to the most ordinary terms, e.g., "water", "light" and "velocity".
[62] See Chapter 4 (and *H&C1*) on the *Gestalt* relations between a molar entity and its constituent details.
[63] *By suspending and/or scrutinising shared presuppositions, philosophy can complexify as easily as clarify.*

whichever interpretation each reader of theirs would arguably be likely, able, or liable to concoct.[64]

Anthony Ashley Cooper, the third Earl of Shaftesbury, was the first English philosopher to write an entire theoretical essay carrying explicitly in its title the fully de-medicalised, late-modern notion of humour.[65] His 1709 "letter" or "essay on the freedom of wit and humour" does not convey any parallel, precise definition of "humour", however. Instead of stating what it is, Shaftesbury presumed his readers to know what it is, while piling up explicit statements and edifying suggestions about precisely such a "humour" so as to address related moral issues that he considered relevant and foster social praxes that he believed worthwhile.[66]

This term was indeed voiced repeatedly by Shaftesbury in his letter/essay, and it was regularly praised in combination with a vivid and vocal defence of the English gentlemen's unique willingness to "railly with a good grace and humour", i.e., to dispute freely, equitably, and honestly—yet also respectfully, peacefully, and amiably—on *any* topic whatsoever, including the "grave and solemn" ones pertaining to the religious "spirit of bigotry, and false zeal" that had been causing so much death and suffering in 17th-century Britain.[67] Such an "urban[e]" form of crosstalk being, in Shaftesbury's view, an estimable yet extremely trying interpersonal activity to participate in and, *a fortiori*, one calling for much time and effort to "refine it-self", which means making "humour ... agreeable" and devoid of any "scurrilous buffoonery".[68] It is only in this way that, according to Shaftesbury, enlightened individuals can really emerge, who are eager and able to test the "truth" of all things, also by means of "ridicule".[69] Shaftesbury's hope was to be able to witness

---

64 Born during the affirmation of Protestantism, the polysemy of modern "humour" offers an unintended amusing hint at the paradoxical end awaiting Luther's 'universal priesthood': as many Christian creeds as there are heads.
65 In the late 17th century, William Congreve penned the first long essay on "humour" qua funny phenomenon, yet in the field of literary studies, and defined it as "a singular and unavoidable manner of doing or saying anything, peculiar and natural to one man only, by which his speech and actions are distinguished from those of other men" (as cited in Figueroa-Dorrego and Larkin-Galiñanes 2009, 367). His definition remained influential for a long time.
66 Shaftesbury (1732) attends *from* "humour" more than it attends *to* it.
67 Shaftesbury (1732), part 1, sec. 1, par. 2, 3, par. 1 and 5, par. 3.
68 Shaftesbury (1732), part 1, sec. 2, pars. 4–5, 4, par. 8 and 6, par. 1. The notion of *urbanitas* was pivotal in classical Roman rhetoric (see, e.g., Viljamaa 1994, 94), with which Shaftesbury was probably familiar.
69 Shaftesbury (1732), part 1, sec. 1, par. 3, 5, par. 3 and 6. Raillery *qua* means to pursue and test the truth is also an important theme in Shaftesbury (1999), in which "humour" proper is not discussed.

the birth of a nation that can "ridicule folly, and recommend wisdom and virtue ... in a way of pleasantry and mirth".[70]

Having somehow surpassed the religious warfare and the stern Puritan dictatorship of the previous century, Shaftesbury saw his native country as treading already upon this wise path, which promoted gentlemanly humour and penalised unrefined fun. Thus, while in the Italian States of his day, "the only manner in which the poor cramp'd wretches can discharge a free thought" was to resort to "buffoonery and burlesque" or "rustic air[s]", things were different in glorious Albion: "As for us Britons", the third Earl stated, "thank heaven, we have a better sense of government deliver'd to us from our ancestors. We have the notion of a publick, and a constitution; and a legislative, and an executive is model'd."[71] Confirming Shaftesbury's belief, the noted British cultural historian, Quentin Skinner, observed in recent times: "So strongly was mocking or insulting speech debarred that, by the early seventeenth century, the phrase 'to speak in an unparliamentary way' had come to mean (and still means) to speak in just such an insulting way as would never be accepted in Parliament."[72]

Inspired by, *inter alia*, Shaftesbury's seminal essay, Lydia Amir applied today his notion of gradual refinement and unprejudiced truth-testing by means of ridicule to the acquisition of personal "wisdom", which she claimed to be attainable by way of "a systematic exercise of self-referential humor, which aims at disciplining our taste to find pleasure in incongruities that are not immediately funny".[73] Humour, quite aptly, was thus conceived of by Amir as though it were a person's acquired taste, not unlike other liquids, e.g., Italian grappa or Scotch whisky, which cannot be considered a sworn enemy of pleasantry and mirth, in our experience.[74] Besides, Scotch whisky, like humour, can make life's vacuity and horrors a little more bearable, even if at a substantial cost to the same people's livers, brains, and wallets.[75] There is no such thing as a free drink.[76]

Cruel jokes aside, few years after Shaftesbury's essay, Addison and his longtime friend and collaborator, Richard Steele, launched a short-lived but historically significant newspaper, which was called *The Spectator*.[77] In it, all sorts of meanings and facets of "humour", both ancient and late-modern, can be retrieved, especially

---

[70] Shaftesbury (1732), parts 3, sec. 1, note to par. 3 and 4; sec. 2, par. 1.
[71] Shaftesbury (1732), part 3, sec. 1, par. 8.
[72] Skinner (2008), 147.
[73] Amir (2019), 226–227. Amir's philosophy of humour was addressed in detail in *H&C2*.
[74] Given the references to whisky in Leacock's works, we can say that he would agree with us.
[75] We leave it to each reader to choose which pains to prefer and how to cope with them, if at all.
[76] Or maybe there is, but one must be very lucky to have a large supply of it.
[77] The influence of their newspaper can already be gauged in Beattie (1778).

in connection with "Mirth" and "Ridicule".[78] Once again, though, Addison recognised the definitional challenge lying ahead of him, and stated that it is "much easier to describe what is not Humour, than what is".[79]

Even so, Addison found the courage to try to face this plausibly ill-fated definitional challenge and ended up listing those "Qualifications" of an imaginary and imaginative "Genealogy" of "Humour", should this notion be thought of as "a Person", i.e., as though it were a flesh-and-blood individual.[80] "Truth" would then be called "the Founder of the Family", "Good Sense" would be its son, who would in turn give birth to "Wit, who married ... Mirth, by whom he had Issue Humour".[81] Being the offspring of such an "Illustrious Family ..., Humour" should then be able to humour its own very special relatives by conforming to their "different Dispositions", i.e., "sometimes" it must be "grave ... and ... solemn", "sometimes airy ... and fantastick", other times "serious" or "jocular".[82] By being so pliable and compliant, as Addison concluded, humour "never fails to make his Company laugh".[83]

Taking his own fantastic allegory quite seriously, Addison even went so far as to draw two parallel genealogical tables aimed at articulating further his views and contrasting mutually "True Humour", which "generally looks serious, whilst every Body laughs about him", and "False Humour", which "is always laughing, whilst every Body about him looks serious".[84] Hence, in its shortest formulation, "True Humour" would be that sort of "Ridicule" which makes people laugh while feigning seriousness, or "Ridicule ... concealed in Gravity".[85] False humour, on the contrary, would be the one that laughs noisily and incessantly, but does not strike its audience as funny.[86]

Albeit short-lived in its troubled editorial history, *The Spectator* became a paradigm of intelligent progressivism, if not of ingenious publishing, which influenced

---

78 *The Spectator* was intended to bring philosophical debates to the general public, not build a coherent system.
79 Addison, 35 (1711). In the 19th century, Hood (1865, 42–43) rehashed this point by stating as follows: "No doubt, we feel better what humour is than we can describe it", though its "etymological sense" points towards "good humour" and "the incessant play of lively and natural feeling ... which extends its sympathies to all being".
80 Addison, 35 (1711).
81 Addison, 35 (1711).
82 Addison, 35 (1711).
83 Addison, 35 (1711). Arguably, successful commonplace humour could be such a "true humour".
84 Addison, 35 (1711). An additional element is thus inserted, i.e., pretending to be grave or solemn.
85 Anonymous (probably Addison), 616 (1714). This game knows of variations, e.g., something horribly cruel can be uttered ironically, causing laughter in the audience who grasp the speaker's fake seriousness.
86 Anonymous (probably Addison), 616 (1714).

many amongst the declared champions of the European Enlightenment as well as their spiritual heirs. In the 20th century, none less than the founder of the Italian Communist Party, Antonio Gramsci, commended *The Spectator* as a "perfect[ly]" written "moralising" means "for communicating the new [secular] conception of life", as this was then emerging in the Old World, "to the average reader", while also serving as an important precedent, or predecessor, for Gramsci's own day's "humoristic magazines that, in their own way, would like to provide a 'constructive' criticism of social mores".[87]

After Addison, at least four eminent Western humanists tried to define "true humour" and distinguish it from—as either circuitously implied or deliberately avowed—"false humour".[88]

(1)–(2) Two of these intellectuals are to be addressed here in further detail, i.e., the German pessimist thinker and Orientalist philosopher, Arthur Schopenhauer, and the Italian dramatist and Nobel-prize laureate, Luigi Pirandello.[89]

(3) A third, Canada's Leacock, whose name has already been mentioned, provided an interpretation of "true humour" that is, roughly, a reformulation of Pirandello's one.[90] Leacock believed "true humour" to be characterised by bittersweet "kindliness" and, in its "highest stage", capable of "moving from lower to higher forms, from cruelty to horseplay, from horseplay to wit, from wit to the higher 'humor of character' (independent of the single phrase) and beyond that to its highest stage as the humor of life itself. Here tears and laughter are joined, and our little life, incongruous and vain, is rounded with a smile."[91]

---

[87] Gramsci (1977), vol. 3, 2270, Q24, par. 4.

[88] Schopenhauer is the only advocate of "true humour" who denied vocally all remaining humour to be humour. Also, while cursory uses of and brief reflections on "true" or "real humo(u)r" may be abundant (e.g., Carlyle 1835), only a *few thinkers have ever pursued this topic in a thorough way*. It is on these few that we focus here.

[89] Schopenhauer is important in our work also for another reason: he was the first major Western intellectual to make sexuality central for the proper understanding of human and animal reality and discuss sexuality explicitly, expressly, and extensively (see, e.g., Gupta 1975).

[90] We ignore whether Leacock was familiar with Pirandello's work. However, it is certain that many Anglophone intellectuals have been familiar with Leacock's, well into the late 20th century. See, e.g., Simpson (1998).

[91] Leacock (1938), chap. 1, sec. 5, last par. In an involuntary echo of Leacock's stance, the Spanish English Professor Aída Díaz-Bild (2012, 19 and 23) claimed the contemporary Irish novelist Roddy Doyle to have reached "the highest level of humour", which is "the humour of humility and compassion". Suggesting an identical gap in compassion, the ground-breaking Black sociologist and activist, W.E.B. DuBois (1897, par. 12), contrasted white America's "coarse, cruel wit" with the "loving, jovial good humor" of "the light-hearted ... Negro".

(4)   In the 21ˢᵗ century, the English philosopher and Hans Jonas Professor of Philosophy, Simon Critchley, somewhat more timorously than his illustrious predecessors, equated "'true' humour"—the adjective being cautiously placed between quotation marks—with individually and/or collectively "radical" or "critical" humour, i.e., humour that is willing to antagonise the status quo and that is, consequently, the opposite of "reactionary".[92] *In nuce*, Critchley's approach would approve of humour that, as the cliché goes, 'punches up' (e.g., Beaumarchais' Figaro trilogy), whilst disapproving of humour that does the reverse (e.g., the ongoing Canadian TV series *Trailer Park Boys*, which began as a mockumentary in 1999).[93]

Back in the 18ᵗʰ century, the English father of psychological associationism, David Hartley, was the first Western thinker to write explicitly and extensively about "humour" proper in its modern sense, i.e., as something funny.[94] It is true that, in the first part of his lengthy *Observations on Man, His Frame, His Duty, and His Expectations*, Hartley used initially "humour" to refer to the fluids of the body in general, including those that can be found inside the nervous tissues.[95] On that basis, however, he went on to address "the mental ... causes of laughter", among which are listed "wit and humour".[96] Like Shaftesbury before him, Hartley did not provide any crisp definition of the latter kind of "humour", which he not only acknowledged but also discussed under a great variety of respects, anticipating themes and topics that have now become standard issues in the Western humanities and social sciences.[97]

No sharp distinction was made either by Hartley between "humour" and several of its lexical cognates—especially "wit", "ridicule" and "mirth"—with which it has been regularly and repeatedly associated. Such careful defining and keen distinguishing will be the achievements of another 18ᵗʰ-century British scholar,

---

[92] Critchley (2002a), 42 (see also Critchley 2002b, 11). Gramsci (1977, vol. 1, 183, Q2, par. 26) praised Germany's "social democrats" because they had "a humoristic gazette: 'Lachen links' (laughter on the left)".
[93] Recently, the American mathematician Cathy O'Neil (2022) replicated Critchley's approach by praising shame that 'punches up' and blaming shame that 'punches down'. Needless to add, but mockery and ridicule loom large in her account of shaming practices. We addressed the moralisation of humour in much more detail in *H&C2*. As to *the examples used in H&C3: insofar as they are not inside quotation marks, then they are ours*.
[94] D. Hartley (1801).
[95] D. Hartley (1801), vol. 1, 91.
[96] D. Hartley (1801), vol. 1, 437.
[97] A partial list of these issues was provided in *H&C1*.

i.e., the Scottish poet and philosopher James Beattie.[98] First of all, Beattie was to argue that "wit" arises from the "unexpected discovery of resemblance between ideas supposed dissimilar".[99] Further, "humour" was said to arise from the "comic exhibition of singular characters, sentiments, and imagery".[100] While qualifying the latter definition, Beattie would also describe "humour" as the "different arrangements and colourings ... of those ideas of the characters and circumstances of mankind ... form[ing] that species of ludicrous combination".[101]

In the early 19th century, the English painter, renowned essayist, and polyhedric philosopher, William Hazlitt, advanced and enriched Beattie's legacy.[102] In particular, Hazlitt supplied two concordant definitions of "humour" proper, which, adhering to a by-then well-established aesthetic tradition, was contrasted with "wit".[103]

(1) "Humour is the describing of the ludicrous as it is in itself; wit is the exposing it, by comparing or contrasting it with something else."[104]

(2) "Humour, as it is shown in books, is an imitation of the natural and acquired absurdities of mankind, or of the ludicrous in accident, situation, and character; wit is the illustrating and heightening the sense of that absurdity by some sudden and unexpected likeness or opposition of one thing to another, which sets off the quality we laugh at or despise in a still more contemptible or striking point of view."[105]

---

[98] A richer account of his thought was provided in *H&C1*.
[99] Beattie (1778), essay 2, 325.
[100] Beattie (1778), essay 2, 325.
[101] Beattie (1778), essay 2, 464. In *H&C1*, we noted how Beattie, unlike, say, Critchley, argued against humour 'punching' at the ruling elites entrusted with serious, sensitive, and, at times, sacred duties. Tellingly, Galbraith (1975, 259) himself wrote at a time when clownish politicians such as Berlusconi, G.W. Bush, Trump, and Boris Johnson had not yet become the norm: "One of the reasons I dislike government is that it cannot permit itself the luxury of humor. It must comport itself with the deadly seriousness of little boys in a schoolyard."
[102] Hazlitt (1845). No single extant work does justice to Hazlitt's philosophy, which has been tackled by many commentators in connection with specific areas and/or issues, e.g., philosophy of mind, aesthetics, morals, etc. As regards "humour" proper, Hood (1865), emblematically, refereed specifically to Hazlitt's thought.
[103] In the 18th century, wit was understood primarily as the clever pairing of notions, characteristics, or persons that are assumed to be unrelated (e.g., Henry Kissinger and Greta Thunberg, both of whom have alerted the world to the threat of climate change—the former at a largely forgotten address to the UN on 15th April 1974). As of the mid-19th century, such a conceptual characterisation has often been applied *pari passu* to irony, especially when contrasted to humour (see, for a historical overview, Figueroa-Dorrego and Larkin-Galiñanes 2009).
[104] Hazlitt (1845), 13. E.g., humorously, we could describe in keen detail the changed behaviours of a tipsy person. Wittily, we could call plastic and radioactive waste humankind's "eternal legacy".
[105] Hazlitt (1845), 13.

According to Hazlitt, even if "humour" proper is less aggressive than "wit", the capable playwright, comic writer, and/or comedian should always be stressing more "the immediate oddity of the circumstances, and the absurdity or unaccountableness of a foolish action" in order to make sure that "the ludicrous prevails over the pathetic" and "we receive pleasure instead of pain from the farce of life which is played before us", hence avoiding that "comedy" may turn, either suddenly or gradually, into "tragedy".[106]

Equally, at the close of the 19th century, the well-known Spanish-American philosopher, novelist, and essayist, George Santayana, argued that "humour" proper results from the tension between two contrasting drives of this ilk.[107] To begin, there is the "agreeable" yet unkind observation of people's defects and/or foolishness, i.e., "the satirical" component of humour, which "is closely akin to cruelty".[108] On the reverse side, there is "the luxury of imaginative sympathy", i.e., "the expansion into another life" by way of empathic imagination, which can lead to somewhat "painful" experiences.[109]

In order to avoid altogether, or at least reduce, the import of such troubling empathic experiences, Santayana maintained, like Hazlitt, that the "satirical" component of humour must be prevalent so as to cause the "sensuous and merely perceptive stimulation" engendered by that which people find "ridiculous" to be emotionally stronger than any "sympathy", which should therefore add only some "touches of beauty and seriousness" to the rather merciless activity that is unfolding.[110] As Santayana concluded: "the essence of what we call humor is that amusing weakness should be combined with an amicable humanity... We are satirical, and we are friendly at the same time."[111] The renowned 20th-century English novelist and playwright J.B. Priestley, who referred explicitly and specifically to both Hazlitt and Santayana in his writings about "humour" proper, suggested that the

---

106 Hazlitt (1845), 1–2. An apt "dramatist" can turn humorous "absurdity ... stupidity ... paradoxes ... caricatures" and "stereotypes" into something "dramatic", if s/he only wishes to do so (Lippi and Gutiérrez Ortiz Monasterio 2021, 1–4). *Gestalt* switches of this ilk are a rather common feature of literature, drama, and cinema.
107 Though capable of great feats of humour, Santayana (1998, 51–52) doubted its significance for human progress: "humourists" make fun of the "incongruity[ies]" of society, but have "nothing articulate to take its place".
108 Santayana (1896), par. 63.
109 Santayana (1896), par. 63. The inherent painfulness of compassionate imagination might explain satire's prevalence.
110 Santayana (1896), par. 63.
111 Santayana (1896), par. 63.

characteristic English variation of it hangs precisely on the tricky "balance of sympathy and antipathy necessary for the full appreciation of the ludicrous".[112]

Many years later, while commenting on Charlie Chaplin's comedies, the famous German philosopher, musicologist, and social scientist, Theodor Adorno, caught sight therein of a bare modicum of clever, perhaps cynical, and certainly nominal "cruelty", by which the phenomenon of commonplace "laughter" might find "its legitimation and its element of the salvational".[113] As the Marxist Adorno explained in a letter about modern cinema directed to Walter Benjamin, laughter allows the countless poor victims of "bourgeois sadism" to experience some momentary relief and, at the same time, keep on living in their daily sorry condition of persistent liberal manipulation and merciless capitalist exploitation.[114] Whilst generally aggressive and occasionally rebellious, laughter is no full revolutionary act.[115]

For his part, Benjamin characterised Karl Kraus' satirical writings as nothing short of "cruelty" itself.[116] Commenting on Marcel Proust, Benjamin instead contrasted "humour" proper, which "toss[es] the world up", with "comedy", which "flings it down" and "smashe[s it] to pieces, which will then make [Proust] burst into tears".[117] Humour, in this perspective, is somewhat gentler or generally less sharp than satire and comedy, and probably less harmful than "strict" or "cruel jok[ing]".[118] As also penned by the 20th-century American metaphysician and social philosopher, Mary C. Swabey: "if not quieter, humor is more contented" than wit, with which she contrasted it, and other common forms of comicality.[119]

Long before Adorno, Benjamin, or their noted Frankfurt School of social theory and critical philosophy, the Danish existentialist thinker and Lutheran theologian, Søren Kierkegaard, had already found a moderately salvational *quid* in the phenomenon of "humour" proper. The context for this realisation being that of

---

[112] Priestley (1929), 12.
[113] Adorno (1996), 59.
[114] As translated and cited in M. Hansen (1993), 32. Most philosophers and social scientists focus on relief-inducing laughter in connection with negative emotions (e.g., anxiety, fear). However, laughter can also be the result of pent-up energy connected with positive emotions (e.g., joy, gratitude), as exemplified by exuberant toddlers, cheerful personalities, exhilarated mystics, self-satisfied carpenters, and gratified writers.
[115] Hansen (1993) and Adorno (1996) might be said to suggest a timid yet fascinating distinction between comic mass-mediatic entertainment at large and Chaplin's unique comedic artistry, but we leave such fine points to the Adorno specialists.
[116] Benjamin (2007a), 252.
[117] Benjamin (2007b), 207.
[118] Benjamin (1998), 126–127.
[119] Swabey (1961), 89.

Christian belief, however, not any specific socio-political and/or economic reality.[120] In a dense, insightful, yet self-mockingly complex, anti-Hegelian philosophical tome, entitled sardonically *Concluding Unscientific Postscript to Philosophical Fragments*, Kierkegaard posed openly as and declared before his readers to be a "humourist" whose name is "Johannes Climacus", like that of an obscure 7th-century Christian monk.[121]

Under this eccentric guise, Kierkegaard/Climacus remarked on the "humour" needed for "the simple-mindedly religiously aware person" to encounter, embrace, and enjoy, if possible, the Creator's "divine madness", which includes many a baffling "paradox", e.g., the crucified God, Mary mother of God, Christ as man and God, love as God's new law, etc.[122] "Whether humour and speculation are in the right", however, was not firmly validated by Kierkegaard/Climacus in his tome, given that there shall always be a pivotal and petrifying decision to be made by each and every individual believer, i.e., a *salto mortale* or "leap" into religious "faith", the "absurd" characteristics of which do not magically disappear for that same believer, unless s/he is an unreflective "enthusiast" of sorts.[123]

In truth, "[h]umour" can make things far more complicated, rather than simpler and more reassuring, by poking fun at "the religious", its human institutions and its many baffling paradoxes, hence showing "a religious person" the "way out" of Christian belief, "if only [s/]he is willing" to follow it.[124] As Kierkegaard worriedly noted in two short journal glosses, "[h]umour can therefore approach blasphemy" and turn into something "demonic ... that attempts to draw even the divine along into the humoristic 'Go to the devil'".[125] Looked at closely, faith is no easy, exhilarating, and/or exonerating act of ecstatic self-denial, according to Kier-

---

120 An atheist, Adorno (1939) had nonetheless considerable philosophical interest in Kierkegaard's work.
121 Kierkegaard (2009), 520. We then write "Kierkegaard/Climacus" because the former used sobriquets such as the latter in order to explore different and, frequently, contradictory worldviews, approaches and lines of argument.
122 Kierkegaard (2009), 150 and 227. On history of "divine madness", see Jung (2009), 238, note 89.
123 Kierkegaard (2009), 85 and 227, note 1. We pen "religious" because sheer "faith" is *prosaic: most of our beliefs are based on our trusting others, not on our testing hypotheses scientifically* (see Hazlitt 1912 and Polanyi 1962c). More on the necessity of a fiduciary embrace of tacit presuppositions is said here in Chapter 4, and Chapter 3 of Part 2 (see also *H&C1*).
124 Kierkegaard (2009), 437. E.g., in this volume, we come across very different interpretations of that which lies at the bottom of, and/or behind, all significations: nothingness (e.g., Leopardi), a fundamental polymorphous energy of sorts (e.g., Schopenhauer and Nietzsche), God (e.g., Aquinas), monads, events, or singularities (e.g., Deleuze).
125 Kierkegaard (1992), 432 and 444.

kegaard/Climacus, who portrayed the thinking Christian believer as a person "with a sad smile", i.e., the physical manifestation of "the lyrical element in humour".[126]

What "humour" can do, in this intricate existential and theological context, is merely cast some light on "the amusing aspect" of the whole affair that is playing out, especially the puzzling "paradoxes ... of faith", rather than allowing "the suffering side" to be the sole character on stage: "[f]or it is suffering, a faith's martyrdom even in times of peace, to have the eternal happiness of one's soul related to something over which the understanding despairs".[127] Casting some light on "the amusing aspect" of the Christian faith can thus offer a modicum of "relief" to the thinking and feeling believer, not unlike slapstick comedies should be able to do, according to Adorno, to the victims of liberal institutions.[128]

In any case, according to Kierkegaard/Climacus, the daunting issue of whether to accept or reject "faith" will have to be faced, in the end, by each discerning and sensing religious person: "Humour is not faith but is prior to faith; it is not after faith or a development of faith."[129]

While Kierkegaard was churning out Christian writings in Denmark, Schopenhauer developed in Germany a proudly and openly atheistic anti-Hegelian project of his own, inside which, almost as an onerous aside, the latter thinker offers a brief philosophy of "humour" proper as well.[130] Like Kierkegaard, Schopenhauer did so while contrasting "humour" with "irony", rather than "wit": "if ... the joke is concealed behind seriousness, then we have irony. [...] The converse of irony is accordingly seriousness concealed behind a joke, and this is humour. It might be called the double counterpoint of irony."[131] Addison's older remarks about "True Humour" were therefore turned upside-down by the in/famous Ger-

---

[126] Kierkegaard (2009), 227, note 1. Kierkegaard (1992, 426) hinted even at a cynical mode of "humour", i.e., "one's not giving two hoots for [the world]", which "irony", instead, is still "trying to influence" constructively.

[127] Kierkegaard (2009), 244. Thus does Kierkegaard (1992, 446) find "humour" in Tertullian's claim "*credo quia absurdum*". More on the limits of understanding in the face of the numinous is said in Chapter 3 of Part 2.

[128] We are suggesting an analogy, not an identity, between the two stances, both of which aim at relief *via* humour.

[129] Kierkegaard (2009), 244. Acknowledging our cognitive and biological limitations, while stressing their concomitant hinting at the Unlimited, led Marmysz (2003, 102) to write that Kierkegaard casts "the problem [of nihilism] in a manner that empowers rather than destroys, and elevates rather than belittles the individual". Whether the thoroughly secular Western readers of our volume can grasp the sort of personal inner drama entailed by Kierkegaard and admired by Marmysz is, however, something that we cannot gauge and, at times, doubt.

[130] While disagreeing on almost everything, both Kierkegaard and Schopenhauer loathed Hegel's idealism.

[131] Schopenhauer (1909), vol. 2, chap. 8, 276.

man pessimist.¹³² It was now irony that seeks levity by feigning gravity. Humour, this time, was gravity feigning levity.¹³³

Harking back to the early-modern characterisation of "humour" proper, Schopenhauer also claimed that he could spot a "true humourist" from a distance, so to speak, insofar as "humour depends on a special kind of mood or temper (German *Laune*, probably from *Luna*) through which conception in all its modifications, a decided predominance of the subjective over the objective in the apprehension of the external world is thought".¹³⁴ Schopenhauer admitted that "at the present day the word humorous [*humoristisch*] is generally used in German literature in the sense of comical [*komisch*]".¹³⁵ However, he was also of the opinion that "humour is borrowed from the English to denote a quite peculiar species of the ludicrous" i.e., one that "is related to the sublime, and which was first remarked by them".¹³⁶ In Schopenhauer's view, "it is not intended to be used as the title for all kinds of jokes and buffoonery, as is now universally the case in Germany, without opposition from men of letters and scholars".¹³⁷

Concerning one of the most famous men of letters and scholars in turn-of-the-century France, the Nobel-laureate philosopher Henri Bergson, "irony" was said to arise from "enunciating that which ought to be the case while pretending to believe that it is precisely that which is"; whereas humour should arise from "describing meticulously that which is the case while pretending to believe that it is how things ought to be".¹³⁸ These two "directions" being the only and inevitably opposite ways in which the comically effective "transposition" between reality and

---

132 Shunned by his contemporaries for a dismal worldview of the human being *qua* suffering animal that is tricked by its unconscious instincts into perpetuating life in a godless and cruel universe, much of Schopenhauer's thought has now become *de facto* the standard Western *Weltanschauung*, especially in educated circles, which sometimes 'rediscover' his insights and believe them entirely original (e.g., Richard Dawkins' idea of the 'selfish gene').
133 As we commented in further detail in *H&C1*, Schopenhauer's stance was rooted in the German Romantic aesthetics of his day, e.g., Jean Paul Friedrich Richter's theory of the sublime. Whilst the metaphysical character of humour was more pronounced in this particular tradition, it too had Anglophone roots (see Stewart 1968).
134 Schopenhauer (1909), vol. 2, chap. 8, 277. The likely lunar association persists in "lunatic" and in the Italian phrases about a "twisted moon" [*luna storta*], which causes persons to exhibit an ill or odd "humour".
135 Schopenhauer (1909), vol. 2, chap. 8, 278.
136 Schopenhauer (1909), vol. 2, chap. 8, 278. See also Kierkegaard (1992, 435) on "genius".
137 Schopenhauer (1909), vol. 2, chap. 8, 278.
138 Bergson (1959), chap. 2, sec. 2, par. 2, 38. The translation is ours.

ideality can be pursued: either by moving from the "ideal" to the "real"; or from the "real" to the "ideal".[139]

Bergson added as well that "humour feigns a concrete terminology, technical details, exact facts"; this is "the essence itself" of "humour", in point of fact.[140] As Bergson wrote, the "humourist is a moralist who disguises himself [or herself] as a [wo/]man of learning" in his or her works, analogously to "an anatomist who would not dissect if not to disgust us", hence "transposing" the ideas that s/he expresses from a "moral" tone to a "scientific" one.[141] Consistently with this picture, Bergson submitted that "irony" has an "oratory nature", whereas "humour" has a "more scientific" one.[142]

Both "irony" and "humour" can engender "forms of satire", according to Bergson, but whereas "irony" aims at "the idea of the good that ought to be" and, in so doing, steps "higher and higher", "humour" steps "lower and lower, inside the evil that is the case, noticing all the details with a colder indifference".[143] Accordingly, parodies, lampoons and spoofs, if ironic, can make us dream and experience a sense of hopefulness.[144] Humorous ones, instead, are much more likely to cause us to recoil and feel resentful.[145]

Yet, never so much as to transform a comical work into a tragic one—Hazlitt's and Santayana's fundamental insight into this matter endures.[146] In order for "the comical" to occur, as famously stated by Bergson, all attempts at mirth or joviality must entail "a momentary *anaesthesia of the heart*", i.e., an effective reduction or wholesale cancelling of our sympathetic feelings.[147] As such, humour and its cognates can all work very efficiently in criticising individuals deviating from the social norm.[148]

A few years after Bergson, Luigi Pirandello, whose name too was already mentioned, argued that, commonly, "humour" refers to the "the comical in its var-

---

139 Bergson (1959), chap. 2, sec. 2, par. 2, 38. The great 19th-century Bostonian poet and essayist, Ralph Waldo Emerson (1904, 158), took it as *the* root of all "comic" phenomena proper.
140 Bergson (1959), chap. 2, sec. 2, par. 2, 38.
141 Bergson (1959), chap. 2, sec. 2, par. 2, 38.
142 Bergson (1959), chap. 2, sec. 2, par. 2, 38.
143 Bergson (1959), chap. 2, sec. 2, par. 2, 38.
144 E.g., Thomas More's *Utopia*.
145 E.g., Jonathan Swift's *Modest Proposal*.
146 Naturally, we dealt with their work in finer detail in *H&C1*.
147 Bergson (1959), chap. 1, sec. 1, par. 2; emphasis added. Intriguingly, while tackling "cruelty" in politics and religion, Meister (2011, 38) noted that both operate by way of strategies that "desensitize us to the cruelties that might be committed in their name".
148 We discussed in detail this aspect of Bergson (1959) in *H&C1*.

ious expressions".¹⁴⁹ As such, "humour" is as "ineffable" and as "hard to define" as "good taste".¹⁵⁰ That said, however, there can exist "true humour", as Addison and Schopenhauer had already suggested.¹⁵¹ Specifically, Pirandello argued that "true humour" occurs whenever "[w]e commiserate while laughing, or laugh while commiserating".¹⁵² "[T]rue humour", then, would consist in "the feeling of the contrary", i.e., in sensing "how every ridiculous event ... is followed by deep bitterness, like shadows follow each and every one of our steps".¹⁵³

While "summing up" his reflections on the last point, Pirandello declared:

> Humour consists in the feeling of the contrary, induced by the special activity of reflecting [on a prior feeling] without hiding from view and becoming, as commonplace in the arts, a formal expression of that [prior] feeling; but rather becoming its opposite, though following at the same time the [prior] feeling like a shadow follows the body. The ordinary artist cares only about the body. The humourist cares about both; sometimes, he cares more about the shadow than the body, noticing all the insolence of this shadow, which becomes longer or shorter, as though mocking the body, which ignores the shadow all the while.¹⁵⁴

About a decade later, the illustrious German philosopher and Jewish liberal thinker, Ernst Cassirer, claimed that "humour" is actually a "fundamental power of the soul and ... an objective criterion of truth", hence recovering Shaftesbury's much-older observations on this issue.¹⁵⁵ As Cassirer explained: "By a masterly swordsman's trick [Shaftesbury] knows how to exchange weapons in this conflict. Humour need not justify itself before religion, but religion before humour."¹⁵⁶ Gorgias' ancient rhetorical advice "to spoil the seriousness of opponents by jest and their jest by seriousness" was thus rediscovered in a new context.¹⁵⁷ As Amir

---

149 Pirandello (1920), 33. The translation is ours.
150 Pirandello (1920), 11.
151 Pirandello (1920), 115. Educated in Germany, the Sicilian playwright was more indebted to the latter than to the former in both his worldview at large and his studies on "humour" proper in particular. Teutonic intellectuals were primary sources, e.g., Lipps (1898), who pioneered the psychology of humour *qua* means of empathic union and emotional release, and the Romantic humourist K.J. Weber (1838, 36), who had already written of "the true humourist [*der wahre Humorist*]" as opposed to the satirist that has no such *"Menschenliebe* [love of humankind]".
152 Pirandello (1920), 107–108.
153 Pirandello (1920), 113 and 115.
154 Pirandello (1920), 180.
155 Cassirer (1953), 168.
156 Cassirer (1953), 169–170.
157 As translated and cited in Amir (2014), 63. For a recent example of seriousness snuffing humour, see Soucy-Humphreys, Judd, and Jürgens (2023) on, *inter alia*, how the TV cartoons *Spongebob Squarepants* did too poor a job in adequately and respectfully representing modern science and female scientists. As we explained at length in *H&C2*, if an issue is taken to be of paramount

also postulated in years much closer to ours, Shaftesbury "transforms the sophist's rhetorical advice into a statement with philosophic import".[158]

Unlike Voltaire and many other Enlightenment thinkers, Shaftesbury was no militant enemy of the Christian faith.[159] Even so, he did reject "religious revelation and ecstasy" that cannot withstand being put before "the comic mirror".[160] In this context, Cassirer put forth the idea that the modern English notion of "humour" is not reducible to earlier forms of barbed "sarcasm and jest, ... satire and irony, ... polemic and invective".[161] Instead, this novel creation was "that strange mixture of gentleness and energy, of cautious scepticism and of fiery reforming enthusiasm" which can be retrieved already in the "new humanistic ideal" expressed by the clever satires penned by learned Christian humanists such as "Erasmus and Thomas More" in the early 16th century.[162]

This peculiar "mixture" can certainly utilise ancient and medieval comic strategies, such as "coarseness and burlesque", but "it never loses its distinctive dignity, freedom, and intellectual superiority [...,] purity and depth".[163] Modern English humour, in other words, is inherently refined, just like Shaftesbury proposed and aimed at, while also capable of original stylistic syncretism at the same time.[164] Echoing Pirandello's "feeling of contrary", Cassirer detected inside its studied object the presence of a "twofold feeling" that is, emblematically, "characteristic of Shakespearean humour".[165] The "humour" utilised therein being neither "purely intellectual sarcasm", nor "purely intellectual irony", but

> a liberating, life-giving, and life-forming power of the soul ... directed against a mistaken seriousness and an arrogated dignity, against pedantry and bigotry. To the pedant, as to the zealot, freedom of thought is an abomination; for the former takes shelter from it behind the dignity of knowledge, the latter behind the sanctified authority of religion.[166]

---

importance, any humour directed at said issue will be condemned, for only humour that the assessor/s would permit, *if any*, is then viable and 'real', according to the same person/s.

158 Amir (2014), 63.
159 Cassirer (1953), 170–171.
160 Cassirer (1953), 170.
161 Cassirer (1953), 172.
162 Cassirer (1953), 172. These authors' intentionally ambiguous mixture of levity and gravity means also that it is difficult to identify which points of theirs are to be taken seriously and which are not, e.g., which features of More's 1516 *Utopia* should be pursued in reality and which, instead, belong to his chosen literary genre, i.e., satire.
163 Cassirer (1953), 173.
164 Arguably, Cassirer's stance implies that alleged "humour" that is unrefined is not, in fact, 'real' English humour.
165 Cassirer (1953), 178.
166 Cassirer (1953), 183–184.

In May 1928, Gilbert Keith Chesterton authored a theoretical entry on "humour" for the *Encyclopedia Britannica*.[167] In it, he acknowledged:
(1) humour's "being indefinable";
(2) its regular utilisation of "incongruity" for comic effects;
(3) its sympathetic "humility" in the face of "human weakness"; and
(4) its recurrent focus upon "eccentricity", the recognition of which comprises "stages of ... development, which are rather slow and subtle, [and] correspond to the various degrees in which the eccentric has become conscious of his eccentricity".[168]

A masterful writer of detective stories, celebrated humourist, and committed Catholic apologist steeped in Scholastic philosophy, Chesterton claimed the "wit" of "irony" to be the potential expression of the Christian virtue of "justice" in clever bantering and comic works of art, while attributing an even more benevolent one to "humour" as such: "Humour corresponds to the human virtue of humility and is only more divine because it has, for the moment, more sense of the mysteries."[169]

While Pirandello believed "true humour" to be exceptional, Chesterton found this humble and enigmatic literary device to be the mainstream expression of European mores in general:

> [T]he history of humour is simply the history of literature. It is especially the history of European literature; for this sane sense of the incongruous is one of the highest qualities balancing the European spirit. It would be easy to go through the rich records of every nation and note this element in almost every novel or play, and in not a few poems or philosophical works.[170]

Dickens, whose "humour" is claimed to be so deeply rooted in his psyche as to be part of his "unconscious", was also said to have been able to imbue with this

---

167 The Latin title "*Encyclopædia Britannica*" lasted from 1768 to 1901, when US-based publishers took over.
168 Chesterton (1929–1973), par. 1. Possibly, this "humility" results from the "gentleness" noted earlier by Cassirer.
169 Chesterton (1929–1973), par. 2.
170 Chesterton (1929–1973), par. 6. Given that tragicomic elements are as old as Sophoclean irony and abound in today's so-called TV "dramedies", Chesterton's assertion sounds plausible. At the same time, however, it may be true that only a select part of these are genuine examples of "true humour" à la Pirandello, i.e., *ex animo* felt and spontaneously created tokens of the "feeling of the contrary". Bierce (1911, 101), on his part, claimed "humor [to be] everywhere a *patois* not 'understanded of the people' over the province border. The best part of it ... is indigenous, and will not flourish in a foreign soil". Disagreement is rife. Our readers may judge as they please.

peculiar European feature many of his most famous characters, including Mr. Scrooge, whom Chesterton contended to be "not really inhuman at the beginning any more than he is at the end. There is a heartiness in his inhospitable sentiments that is akin to humour and therefore to humanity; he is only a crusty old bachelor, and had (I strongly suspect) given away turkeys secretly all his life."[171]

Outside the realm of drama, poetry, novels and literary creativity at large, Chesterton recognised also a noteworthy philosophical aspect pertaining to humour, i.e., its *sui generis* ability to reveal the conventionality and/or inner limits of all forms of signification and, ultimately, of all coherent thought:

> It is not children who ought to read the words of Lewis Carroll; they are far better employed making mud-pies; it is rather sages and grey-haired philosophers who ought to sit up all night reading *Alice in Wonderland* in order to study that darkest problem of metaphysics, the borderland between reason and unreason, and the nature of the most erratic of spiritual forces, humour, which eternally dances between the two.[172]

In the second half of the 20th century, a French grey-haired philosopher, Gilles Deleuze, did explore painstakingly the borderland identified by Chesterton in Carroll's playful nonsense and enticing paradoxes.[173]

Specifically, Deleuze wrote of the "adventure of humor", i.e., the "twofold dismissal of height and depth to the advantage of the surface".[174] Casting logico-linguistic operations in topological terms, Deleuze asserted "humour" to roam

> across the abolished significations and the lost denotations, the void is the site of sense or of the event which harmonizes with its own nonsense, in the place where the place only takes place *(la ou on n'a plus lieu que lieu)*. The void is itself the paradoxical element, the surface nonsense, or the always displaced aleatory point whence the event bursts forth as sense.[175]

---

[171] Chesterton (1998–1999), chap. 7, par. 16, and chap. 10, par. 8 (referring to Dickens' 1843 *Christmas Carol*). A much-debated turn-of-the-century notion, the "unconscious" was firmly established as a basic category in psychology by Jung's (1910) empirical studies on word association.

[172] Chesterton (1958), 26. By disrupting the trilateral correspondence among interpersonal language, private thinking, and referential being, humour founders the very bases of our rational pictures of the universe.

[173] Deleuze (1990, 93) stated unequivocally: "Carroll remains the master and the surveyor of surfaces."

[174] Deleuze (1990), 136.

[175] Deleuze (1990), 139. Deleuze (1990) added a third dimension whereby words can be said to acquire, possess, and/or make sense i.e., "manifestation", which is basically the *affective* side of a person's utterings, especially as her self-expressive aims are concerned. Analogous awareness of this triple root of linguistic meaningfulness can be found also in Cassirer (1980) and, going further back in time, Frege (1892). Additionally, Kristeva (1984) built her psychoanalytic approach on the distinction between language's subjective-affective and objective-abstractive components. As to the many

Humour exploits shrewdly the seemingly adamantine laws of logical thought and the conventional rules of language to reveal the chaotic origin of all thought and all languages—*eo ipso* making light of those very adamantine laws and conventional rules:

> [Humor] overturns the law by descending towards the consequences, to which one submits with a too-perfect attention to detail. By adopting the law, a falsely submissive soul manages to evade it and to taste pleasures it was supposed to forbid... [Humor] is an art of consequences and descents, of suspensions and falls... [I]t is by nature transgression or exception, always revealing a singularity opposed to the particulars subsumed under laws.[176]

Every law has exemptions and gaps; every model, anomalies and abstractions; every principle, counterexamples and countervailing influences. Humour can annihilate anything and everything. And given that logic and language are not only essential tools whereby we establish any viable notion of 'reality' for ourselves, but also require reality for their own existence, their utter pulverisation has ontological implications too. As also Swabey tellingly admitted in her careful analyses of "the comic as nonsense, sadism, or incongruity ... the deepest source of knowledge involved in the perception of the ludicrous we would venture to call *metaphysical* as having to do with the structure of truth and reality".[177]

Significantly, Deleuze declared: "The art of the aesthetic is humor, a physical art of signals and signs determining the partial solutions or cases of solution".[178] His definition of humour is thus as far removed from any mere "attempt to stimulate amusement" as there could be.[179] Humour is no longer taken to be an issue belonging solely to aesthetics, literary criticism, or even linguistic philosophy. Also and above all, it is seen as an issue appropriately belonging to logic and metaphysics, perchance in one of their most obscure and most difficult incarnations.[180]

Another, less abstract, yet similarly unfunny context in which Deleuze addressed the issue of humour is available too: Freud's *libido*-centred theory of sado-

---

further differences that may apply to means of sense-giving or sense-making, we do not pursue them here, e.g., the distinctive characteristics of 'symbols', 'signs', 'syntagms', 'paradigms', etc.
176 Deleuze (1994), 5. The spatial metaphors of Deleuze (1990) and (1994) differ, but the central idea persists, i.e., the different directions of humour and irony.
177 Swabey (1958), 819 and 822–823; emphasis added. See also *H&C2*.
178 Deleuze (1994), 245. In the hard sciences themselves, formalisable uniformities are possible only by way of conventional abstraction from the empirical cases, and geometrical representations by convenient approximation.
179 Jauregui (1998), 325.
180 Thanks to or because of Deleuze too, postmodernism enjoys an equivocal reputation for obscurity. As to "obscure" and "obscurity", they do not mean solely 'unknown' or 'unimportant', but also 'mysterious' or 'unclear'.

masochism.[181] Therein, according to Deleuze, "humour" proper can be seen to be at work as a clever means of disjointedness and disintegration:

> [T]he very law which forbids the satisfaction of a desire under threat of subsequent punishment is converted into one which demands the punishment first and then orders that the satisfaction of the desire should necessary follow upon the punishment... [M]asochism is not pleasure in pain, nor even in punishment; at most, the masochist gets a preliminary pleasure from punishment or discomfort; his real pleasure is obtained subsequently, in that which is made possible by the punishment... What else but a demonstration of absurdity is aimed at, when the punishment for forbidden pleasure brings about the very same pleasure?... The masochist is insolent in his obsequiousness, rebellious in his submission; in short, he is a humorist, a logician of consequences.[182]

Humour's *modus operandi* becomes a little clearer when it is contrasted with that of "irony":

> There are two known ways to overturn moral law. One is by ascending towards the principles: challenging the law as secondary, derived, borrowed or 'general'; denouncing it as involving a second-hand principle which diverts an original force or usurps an original power. The other way, by contrast, is to overturn the law by descending towards the consequences. [...] The first way of overturning the law is ironic, where irony appears as an art of principles, of ascent towards the principles and of overturning principles. The second is humor.[183]

---

[181] An admirer of Freud's work, Deleuze collaborated for many years with a psychotherapist, Félix Guattari. In our own research, we refer mostly to Freud and, secondarily, to Jung, as our key psychodynamic sources. The latter clinician, in particular, serves here as a reminder of the methodological limits inherent to standard empirical psychology *vis-à-vis* probing and understanding, in an existentially meaningful way, the human psyche and its inner experiences. While Jung himself acknowledged repeatedly that he, by the 1920s, had basically abandoned both mainstream science and mainstream psychoanalysis, his commitment to his own introspective, humanistic, and cross-cultural approach produced not only a psychotherapeutic tradition that is still alive today, but also a sophisticated philosophy of the mind that keeps attracting the attention of numerous theologians, anthropologists, humanists, humanistic psychologists, psychiatrists and neuroscientists, *in spite of*: (1) a veritable "fear of Jung" among 'self-respecting' academicians and 'serious' scientists (Cope 2006, title *et passim*); (2) the difficulties resulting from the frequently obscure and scholarly demanding "intellectual baggage" characterising Jung's later research (e.g., medieval and Renaissance alchemy; Segal 2012, 351); and (3) Jung's 'rediscovery' by the Toronto-based best-selling psychologist-turned-public-intellectual, or classic-liberal guru, Jordan Peterson (1999).

[182] Deleuze (1989), 88–89. Thus construed, masochism recalls the classical rhetorical figure of *accismus*. (Listed in the bibliography as *Masochism*, the book contains Deleuze's essay "Coldness and Cruelty" and Sacher-Masoch's *Venus in Furs*.) More on Freud follows in this chapter and the next one. See also *H&C1*.

[183] Deleuze (1994), 5. The British feminist thinker Anita Phillips (1998, 112) wrote that "[n]othing guarantees an upsurge so much as a preliminary defeat", while describing the male masochist as "a consummate strategist".

As Deleuze maintained: "Humor is the art of the surface, which is opposed to the old irony, the art of depths and heights."[184] While the former art explodes the law or the moral principles by driving them into a "paradox", the latter art attacks them directly by way of contradiction.[185]

Whether anything funny is left in the picture, however, it is very hard to detect.[186] Perhaps, given the 19th-century birth of "masochism" in psychiatry, we have somehow marched all the way back to the serious technical use of "humour" proper *qua* pathology-related fluid that could be found in the medical works of Hippocrates and Galen.[187] So-called "sick humour" might well intimate much more than just a variation on the common theme of 'cruel humour'.[188]

2.1.3 A First Set of Reflections

> One thing is a 'resistance' causing us to change our beliefs; another is a 'resistance' telling us how to change our beliefs. *We* talk. The world has never been heard talking.
> —Richard Rorty[189]

Deleuze's equation of humour with paradoxicality reminds us of the fact that any set of fundamental values, logical axioms, and/or rational principles, if shrewdly reinterpreted and sufficiently reconceptualised, can lead to nothing less than ab-

---

184 Deleuze (1990), 9.
185 Deleuze (1990), 9. 'Humorously', then, in today's France, Becker's (as interviewed in Mastrantonio and Becker 2021, pars. 7–13) experience as a free and "happy prostitute" led "[s]ome feminists" who were not "intersectional" to balk at the idea of "self-empowerment" that they had championed. And as she further jibed: "[I]n the brothel I was given 55% of my money... As a writer you can get up to 10, 12% of the earnings, and you must work more." Naturally, no such humour could work, were prostitution not mired in the cruelties of trafficking noted in *H&C2*.
186 We cannot be certain that no reader would ever find Deleuze's accounts of aesthetics or masochism humorous, especially if inebriated. As far as we are concerned, however, we cannot retrieve anything amusing in them.
187 The words "sadism" and "masochism" are the 'brainchildren' of Richard von Kraft-Ebing (1892), whose 1886 *Psychopathia Sexualis* included many terms that became standard in later medicine and psychiatry. The latter term owes its name to the 1870 novel *Venus in Furs* by Leopold von Sacher-Masoch (1989). While the book's heroine is often labelled "cruel" and the hero's predilections for humiliation and flagellation are vividly depicted, no lengthy explicit discussion of "cruelty" is present in the novel as such, unlike Sade's much more cerebral works, which lie behind "sadism". As to the subsequent history of the word "sadism", see Bourke (2020).
188 See also *H&C2*.
189 Baruchello and Rorty (1998), 468. As to *talking* as such, Rorty was a follower of the noted 20th-century British thinker Michael Oakeshott (2004, 198), who believed that the "conversation" distinguishing a "'civilized' manner of living" from an uncivilised one should continue indefinitely.

surdity. Tellingly, in Western culture, whether in a serious tone or in a satirical one, historical cases as well as fictional ones (e.g., literary dystopias) have been used repeatedly to show how the noblest aims (e.g., equality, liberty, purity, kindness) and the most intelligent creations (e.g., mechanical inventions, industrial efficiency, artificial intelligence, synthetic chemicals) can give birth to veritable monstrosities. This being the case because, fundamentally, actual human beings are incapable of anticipating, recognising and/or controlling all the relevant factors, both at the individual and at the collective level, in the present and in the future.[190]

Paradoxical outcomes contradicting much-cherished tacit assumptions lying beneath the explicitly stated theses and arguments have then been brought to the surface, again and again, in literary and scholarly games of clever dissection and cultured deconstruction.[191] Countless parodies, lampoons, exposés, and critical attacks have been built on such argute forms of denouement, whether all of us would deem them "humorous" or only Deleuze and his disciples.[192] No one is safe from this sort of challenge, whether right or left on the ideological spectrum. Humour's scathing touch can burn and blister anything and anyone, for paradoxical and troubling consequences, not least of the cruel sort, can be brought to the surface from within *any* stance or project, no matter how well-meaning or well-designed it may be.

Historically, for one, the noble ideals of national independence and national glory have been lambasted by means of satire as an inexhaustible engine of pillaging, raping, and butchering.[193] The much-extolled virtues of loyalty and honour

---

190 The reader may want to ponder on the *ceteris paribus* [all other things being equal] assumptions of standard economic models, which fail regularly to predict the future, given the incessant pressure of mutating factors that were conveniently 'frozen' *ab ovo* in the model and/or the appearance of other factors that had not been considered. Thus, for one, crises and crashes are always 'unexpected', even if the actual history of our concrete economies is rife with them. (More on the bizarre world of mainstream economics follows in Chapter 1 of Part 2.)

191 This *denouement can be pursued in stately and sombre ways too*. Think, say, of how the verb "to be", which has been used since the start of this volume and quite assuredly tacitly grasped by our readers, can be dissected, distinguished and defined, almost *ad infinitum*, by grammarians, logicians, and specialists in ontology.

192 Insofar as each person, in accordance with her unique psycho-physical make-up and hermeneutical framework, reacts to and assesses any given phenomenon as being humorous or not, we dare not make sweeping claims in this regard. The same applies to each denouement's being deemed convincing or not. Consistently with Polanyi's (1962c) approach, which we tackle here in Chapter 4, a specific socialised individual must make a reasoned and responsible personal call, in the end, under unique socio-cultural and temporal circumstances.

193 See, e.g., Voltaire (1912) and (1918). No anti-patriotic spirit is implied by the example. Rather, we are reminded of LVOA's criteria to distinguish, at least in principle, between good and bad (see Chapter 1 in this book).

have been similarly ridiculed, e. g., when an incredulous solitary soldier, hidden in the deep of the tropical jungle, continues to fight a war that has long ceased to be fought everywhere else.[194] The brave and long struggles for gay rights, for their part, have been shown to produce, on occasion, attendant troubling acceptance of man-boy love, if not outright paedophilia.[195] Similarly, the cosmopolitan, pluralistic, Rousseauvian embrace of exotic and 'uncorrupted' pagan cultures has later caused some Western persons to balk perplexedly at not-so-idyllic practices such as human sacrifices, ceremonial cannibalism, female circumcisions, child marriages, widow burnings, and ritual pederasty.[196] Fictionally, the best and most sophisticated computer systems have been turned into the craftiest and cruellest foe.[197]

Many, if not all, of the farcical tragedies and tragic farces engendered by the inherently limited human abilities are, in this perspective, tokens of Deleuze's conception of 'humour', yet seen this time from a rather sombre angle. This being also the angle whence a person's subtle attempts at leading another into error or causing offence can be read as attempts at enjoying an eventual sense of moral superiority; or a person's passivity causing another to tell her what to do as the former's channel whereby to enjoy being resentful for being told what to do. "Masochism", in these twisted ways, remains somewhat paradoxical, results perchance humorous on select occasions, and clearly does not mean exclusively a psycho-sexual phenomenon.[198] Rather, *via* the convoluted machinations of the masochist, human values, lucid reasonings, and logical cogency are exploded and exposed by this quintessentially Deleuzian humour for what they are: expedi-

---

[194] See, e.g., the Australia-based comic podcast "Do Go On" (2017) about Hiroo Onoda, a Japanese soldier who went on fighting for decades after 1945. No Nipponophobia is implied by the example. Rather, we are reminded of LVOA's criteria to distinguish, at least in principle, between good and bad (see Chapter 1 in this book).
[195] See Cleves (2020), Maasen (2010), and Johansson (1990). No homophobia is implied by the examples. Rather, we are reminded of LVOA's criteria to distinguish, at least in principle, between good and bad (see Chapter 1 in this book).
[196] See, e.g., Canetti (1966, 261, citing Humboldt) and Ezzo (2008) on cannibalism and Herdt (1984) on mandatory fellatio and sodomy among Melanesian tribes. No Eurocentrism is implied by the example. Rather, we are reminded of LVOA's criteria to distinguish, at least in principle, between good and bad (see Chapter 1 in this book).
[197] See, e.g., the computer HAL 9000 in Stanley Kubrick's 1968 film *2001: A Space Odyssey*. No Luddism is implied by the example. Rather, we are reminded of LVOA's criteria to distinguish, at least in principle, between good and bad (see Chapter 1 in this book).
[198] See also the US-based humour scholar Beau Shaw (2015, 31 and 44), who argued that "masochism" is central for the phenomenon of "humor" and its recurrent "cruelty" because, by joking, we enjoy the lesser "suffering" of "humiliation" in *lieu* of the worse one of "guilt", in a sort of algolagnic psychic trade.

ent yet exhaustible resources for human self-direction, both individual and collective.[199]

Humour itself and some of its theories can thus become the target of the same corrosive spirit. Exemplarily, in recent years, the Australian comedian Hannah Gadsby built an entire show around the analysis of the limitations of humour, especially of the self-deprecating kind, particularly as regards dealing conscientiously with personal trauma, negative prejudice, and unrelenting social cruelty.[200] If, in accordance with ancient myth, Chronos was capable of devouring his own children, then Gelos and Comus would appear to be able to eat each other, when not themselves.[201]

2.2 An Overview of 'Humour' in the Social Sciences

> [W]hat makes us laugh ultimately defies analysis.
> —James A. Simpson[202]

The historically young social sciences offer as cacophonic a conceptual interpretation of 'humour' *qua* something funny as the much-older Western humanities have been doing for a considerably longer stretch of time. As the 20th-century American psychologist Harry Harlow acknowledged:

> Humour is difficult to define but easily understood. At a common-sense level, everyone comprehends the meaning of humour, and almost everyone uses it. Indeed, humour is a common criterion of social acceptability. It is a high compliment to ascribe to an individual a "good

---

199 See Kozintsev (2010) on this paradoxical aspect of "humour" proper, as discussed in *H&C2*.
200 See the *Netflix* version of her show, *Nanette* (2018), directed by Madaleine Parry and John Oib. No misogelasm is implied by the chosen example. Rather, we are reminded of LVOA's key criteria to distinguish, at least in principle, between good and bad (see Chapter 1 in this book). *As to the terms "misogelasm" and "agelasm", or their nominal and adjectival forms "misogelast/ic" and "agelast/ic", they refer, respectively, to a condemnation of laughter and/or merriment, or a refusal to engage in it/them* (see Billig 2005, 14, on George Meredith).
201 In Greek mythology, Chronos was the personification of time. Gelos and Comus, instead, were the gods of, respectively, laughter and revelry, which we extend here to comedy. Interestingly, both Gelos and Comus were in the retinue of Dionysus, the god of wine, fertility, festivity, and madness. Ironically, scholarly debates abound today on their exact mythological roles, socio-psycho-religious function, and distinctive degree of divinity (see, e.g., Antal 2016, 5). The past is past, the present moves fast, and much that was known gets lost.
202 Simpson (1998), 80.

sense of humour" and an insult to characterize an individual as being a person "with no sense of humour".[203]

The lack of expert agreement on the exact understanding of this key-notion, or on how exactly it differs from its many cognates and related phenomena (e.g., laughter, smiling, joking, playfulness, clown behaviour, etc.), is possibly the outcome of the modern social sciences being, as Thomas Kuhn famously explained in *The Structure of Scientific Revolutions*, in a pre-paradigmatic state.[204] There are, in other words, no univocal definitions, standard criteria, and/or universally endorsed sets of protocols applying within each individual discipline, not to mention across the social sciences at large.

Nevertheless, social scientists have not abandoned investigating humour, in one way or another. Indeed, three ways seem particularly pronounced:

(1) Building on the uneven yet vast knowledge amassed by the Western humanities, social scientists have frequently reduced the overall ambiguity at play by referring regularly, if not constantly, to three main conceptions of humour.
(2) A number of psychologists, sociologists, business pundits, and, to a lesser degree, anthropologists and political scientists have directed their attention towards select and specific observable aspects pertaining to the concept of 'humour' that could be mustered, monitored, measured, and/or managed with satisfactory precision, and would therefore comply with the expected and/or established methodologies characterising these disciplines.[205]
(3) Many social scientists have kept presuming common-sense renditions and/or interpretations of the concept of 'humour', discussing them in connection with generally allowed approaches and/or favourite theoretical perspectives, i.e., invested with enough clout and/or consideration in their fields of inquiry, e.g., evolutionary elucidations of human behaviours, operational parallels with information technologies, and Darwinian mechanisms for sexual selection.[206]

---

203 Harlow (1969), 227. See Blum (2002) on Harlow's legacy.
204 See Kuhn (1970), 187.
205 Once again, behind the alliteration lurk crucial activities in which extant specialists engage in earnest.
206 In one of life's many *cruel ironies*, most scientists never depart too much from the accepted orthodoxy of their day and professional community, whose approval the former need to be: acknowledged as 'peers', given occupational opportunities, publish their own research, etc. As centuries go by, and long-ostracised notions become the new norm (e.g., atomism), most of their time's conventional wisdom is cast aside and, eventually, forgotten.

In line with these three explanatory strategies, we select, systematise, and summarise in the following subsections some representative conceptualisations and/or theories of "humour" proper that have been advanced in the social sciences.[207]

2.2.1 Explanatory Strategies of Authority and Persistence

One way in which the conceptual-linguistic disagreements and difficulties about "humour" proper have been coped with in the modern social sciences—to a non-indifferent degree of practical expediency, we must add—has been to acknowledge and focus upon three overarching theories of humour and/or laughter, all of which enjoy a venerable theoretical pedigree in the Western humanities and constitute basic knowledge among humour scholars today.[208]

(1) The first one is known as the theory of *superiority*, which claims that humour and any attendant laughter are, fundamentally, expressions of dominance, i.e., of triumph over others, however variedly and self-deludingly concrete this 'triumph' may be perceived to be by the involved parties.[209] By making the target look inferior, wrong, and/or defeated, the humourist builds his/her own confidence and self-esteem and/or that of the group to which s/he belongs.[210] This school of thought can be traced back to Plato and, to a lesser extent, Aristotle, who was, after all, one of Plato's students. Still, there can be no doubt that this view has never been formulated more unapologetically than by Thomas Hobbes—albeit regarding nominal "laughter", not "humour" proper. As he stated: "Laughter is nothing else but sud-

---

[207] Once again, *the reader finds here the sources that the present authors selected, not those that the reader might have wanted them to select.* As discussed here in Chapter 4, Polanyi's (1962c) phenomenology-*cum*-epistemology explains why such differences exist and, more often than not, do so in a justifiable manner. See also *H&C1*.

[208] In our professional experience, much modern social science has been busy rediscovering and/or re-examining, through novel methodological lenses, themes, topics, ideas, and/or intuitions that philosophers, theologians, jurists, playwrights, and many other intellectuals had already been discussing in earlier stages of our civilisation. This phenomenon is all the likelier when disciplines and/or schools of thought engage in wilful indifference to others.

[209] *Gestalt* switches can sometimes alter dramatically the established hierarchy, e.g., causing a 'superior' party to become 'inferior' by denying the funniness of his/her jest, or by showing its immorality and/or inappropriateness.

[210] See Buijzen and Valkenburg (2004), 149. As we write these lines, an English football fan, a Lewis Holden of Oldham became the object of worldwide kidding for getting a tattoo celebrating England's victory at the Europe 2020 football championship ahead of the final game, which was won by Italy (Wilkinson 2021).

den glory arising from some sudden conception of some eminency in ourselves, by comparison with the infirmity of others, or with our own formerly."[211]

In modern psychology, Harlow himself laid out this realisation in the 20th century:

> Most forms of humour relate to social acts, and the primary function of humour is to maintain or elevate the self-image of the person initiating the humour. A person's self-image or social status is, by definition, relative and therefore may be improved either by social degradation of some other individual or social group or by the elevation, real or imputed, of the status of the individual or social group to which the person initiating the comic thrust belongs.[212]

(2) The second main theory is the *incongruity* theory, which assumes that we humans laugh at things that are mismatched and, *a fortiori*, unusual, unexpected, puzzling, and/or surprising. Our readers may recall how the quote that was selected from A. Roberts's 2019 *Philosophy of Humour* speaks exemplarily of "two inconsistent interpretations *via* unsound reasoning". Beattie and Hazlitt had already remarked on this notion, respectively, in the mid-18th and early-19th century.[213] Farther still in time, Cicero and Quintilian had commented on the inconsistencies and/or funny contrasts that can elicit laughter.[214]

In essence, funny is what is funny, as also Leacock had noted, in times closer to ours, with regard to a broken umbrella: "We can appreciate this by remembering that a broken umbrella looks 'funny'. This broadened into a general notion of contrast, of incongruity, of a disharmony between a thing and its setting, between its present and its usual accompaniment, like a naked savage in a silk hat."[215]

Consistently with this approach, paradox, nonsense, amazement, and bewilderment are often considered to be the building blocks of humour.[216] The crucial incongruity happens when we, as adequately functioning and socialised human beings, start to process information and interpret it in a way that is most salient for

---

211 As cited in Morreall (1987), 20. Superiority does not imply refinement. E. g., individuals and/or groups may experience superiority by defying accepted norms or standards and laugh at those who abide by them instead.
212 Harlow (1969), 226. *H&C2* focussed on this first theory much more than we do here.
213 For a detailed discussion, we must refer our readers to *H&C1*.
214 See, e. g., the historical accounts in Morreall (1987) and Figueroa-Dorrego and Larkin-Galiñanes (2009).
215 Leacock (1935), 11.
216 See Buijzen and Valkenburg (2004), 149.

us, only to be hindered by a conceptual obstacle that forces us to come up with a completely different and previously unrecognised explanation for the original information. The renewed understanding is then accompanied and/or followed by emotions of surprise and/or satisfaction, often causing physically detectable reactions such as smiling and/or laughter.[217]

Possibly because of its emphasis on cognitive aspects of reality, the US-based humour scholar Noël Carroll indicated this theory to have become the most relevant one among 21st-century philosophers, linguists, psychologists, and social scientists in general.[218] Writing in 2019, the UK-based literary and cultural theorist Terry Eagleton went as far as to reduce to it most other 'original' and 'ground-breaking' theories circulating among contemporary experts: "the play theory, the conflict theory, the ambivalence theory, the dispositional theory, the mastery theory, the Gestalt theory, the Piagetian theory and the configurational theory".[219] Not, however, the superiority theory of humour; and neither, as it appears below, the *relief* theory.

(3) The dominant theme of the third theory is probably obvious from its name. The reason why we humans laugh is, in essence, to rid ourselves of excessive nervous tension and/or pent-up psychic energy.[220] Shaftesbury, in the 18th century, and Spencer, in the 19th, are commonly regarded as its earliest proponents, although the emotionally relieving function of laughter had already been touched on in earlier times by Quintilian and Aquinas.[221] In the social sciences, it was Freud's psychoanalysis that made this third theory central and widely debated.[222]

Freud's own understanding of 'relief' borrowed heavily from physiology, especially from the concept of 'homeostasis' that was set forth by Walter Bradford Cannon in 1926.[223] Originally, this notion referred to the tendency of bodily systems to reach equilibrium. In humour studies, clearly, the build-up of nervous tension is more psychological than physiological in nature, and it gets released by a positive emotion originating from our thought that, crucially, is typically transformed into

---

[217] See Krikmann (2006), 27. No finer distinctions of "emotion" from "affect", "feeling", "passion", etc., are needed here, as drawn instead by Heller (2005), pitting basic natural affects against socially aware and culturally shaped emotions.
[218] Carroll (2014), 2.
[219] Eagleton (2019), 67. We should add to this list the "Dismissal Theory of Humor" discussed in Olin (2020, 61).
[220] What exactly "nervous energy" is and how best to approach it scientifically have been major neuropsychological concerns since at least Cabanis' day. For a recent research token, see, e.g., Wang and Wang (2015).
[221] See, once again, the rich historical survey by Figueroa-Dorrego and Larkin-Galiñanes (2009).
[222] Freud's stance was discussed in detail in *H&C1*.
[223] See Cannon (1932), 177–201. As to Freud's reception of his work, see Symington (2018), 208.

laughter.[224] Interestingly, Eagleton compared the discharge granted by humour and, in particular, its attendant laughter with the one that is experienced in orgasms.[225]

Albeit much of Freud's oeuvre has been subjected to scathing and sometimes superficial criticism, his reflections on this particular topic are still relevant insofar as the discharge of psychic tension continues to be thought of as having a cardinal role with regard to laughter and, relatedly, humour.[226] For instance, in our century, the US-based humour expert Daniel D. Perlmutter highlighted the short-term 'conspiracy' that the joker and the listeners enter into for their reciprocal pleasure.[227] While 'conspiring' in this tacit pact, both parties agree to suspend at least two standard rules of communication:

(1) The first rule-breaking involves the speaker no longer claiming to be telling the truth. Jokes, very often, are sheer fabrications or fictions, and so is in actual practice the entire realm of comedy.[228]
(2) The second is that the listeners decide to stay clear of critical evaluation of what is being said. In that way, ethnic, sexist, and all kinds of cruel jokes—which we do realise are sometimes terribly hostile towards their targets—are still able to unite the conspirators, even though just momentarily.[229]

The wilful deferment of a listener's ethico-political values is, *inter alia*, a sign of a profound and potent need for the pleasure proper to humorous release.[230] As the influential Soviet linguist, philosopher, and literary theorist, Mikhail Bakhtin, ex-

---

[224] The seemingly obvious relationship between humour and laughter has also been debated for a very long time.
[225] Eagleton (2019, 19), as also mentioned by Woode Amissah-Arthur (2022, 215), who offered a rare glimpse into visual sexual humour in contemporary Ghana.
[226] Lothane (1999, 151) claimed "Freud bashing" to be no longer "*à la mode*, in certain circles", but "*de rigueur*". Fittingly, modern psychologists hate their famous father.
[227] See Perlmutter (2002), 158–159. The factual claims following in the same paragraph are based on this text.
[228] Comedies can be inspired by true events but are essentially the creations of one or more artists. Historically, such a fictional tone was emphasised by satirists to avoid censorship. Today, it can still protect artistic freedom. See also Chapter 1 of Part 2.
[229] We find it most interesting to read about rule-breaking in the context of the superiority theory, insofar as many contemporary linguists and most philosophers defend and/or describe the incongruity theory as a matter of "violation" of one or more modalities of Grice's "principle of cooperation" (i.e., between speaker and audience), which consists, essentially, in saying as much as is needed of that which is believed to be true and relevant, while avoiding "obscurity ... ambiguity ... prolixity" and/or disorder (Attardo 2017, 175–176). See also Dynel (2018) for a more recent and staunchly 'Gricean' account of humour.
[230] More on this point follows in Chapter 3 of Part 2.

plained it, such a pleasure-filled 'conspiracy' is the signal of a deep-rooted psychic need for rule-breaking that all civilisations have recognised, in one way or another, and unvaryingly integrated in their comedic materials and popular traditions, especially carnivalesque ones.[231] Then, the line separating, on the one hand, making merry and carousing and, on the other hand, going berserk and descending into anarchy is thinned to a potentially risky level.[232]

Nonetheless, such a thinning has been commonplace throughout history, which is rife with carnivals, whether in the West or in the East. This simple human fact hints further at the necessary character of occasional behavioural deviance, the dubious phenomenon of humour included, without which our psychic wellbeing and social stability would be compromised.[233] If wisdom consists in moderation, as it has often been argued in the history of philosophy, this principle applies to moderation itself. At times, as the Roman poet Horace suggested, "*dulce est desipere in loco*" [sweet is to be silly on the right occasion].[234]

Occasionally, then, order may call for disorder; rules for exceptions; expectations for surprises; equilibria for volatility; self-restraint for inconsistencies.[235]

---

[231] See, e.g., Bakhtin (1976) and (2014). Think, e.g., of today's so-called "hen" and "stag" nights (see also Chapter 3 of Part 2).

[232] Tellingly, popular events such as rave parties, rock concerts, and football games are often heavily policed. Thus, in all likelihood, the wildest carnivalesque festivals occur in shared fantasies rather than concrete reality. As Okabe and Pelletier-Gagnon (2019, 37–41 and 50) elucidated, some of the most gruesome erotic creations in the fictional realm of *anime* conform to "Japanese feminist forms of *asobi* (play)", i.e., the so-called "*asobigokoro* ... flesh[ing] out, quite literally, scenes of rape, sex, and torture and ... bombarding the player with hard-core pornographic images", while also exhibiting "witticism, lightheartedness ... mischief ... intersect[ing] the boundaries of play and parody". On *anime*, including its *hentai* [kink, perversion] variety, see Chateau Canguilhem (2014), Dekimpe (2020), Diogo de Sousa (2020), Klar (2013), Napier (2007), Pelletier-Gagnon (2011), and Weiss (2014) (some of these sources being degree theses written by, presumably, young scholars). More on wild partying, football-related frenzies, eroticism, and seemingly cruel Oriental 'carnivals' follows in Chapters 1 and 3 of Part 2.

[233] See, e.g., Armstrong and Young (2000, title *et passim*) on "fanatical football chants". See also Chapter 3 of Part 2.

[234] Horace (n.d.a), book 4, ode 12, verse 28. A traditional Roman adage about carnivalesque festivities recited: "*semel in anno licet insanire*" [once a year it is permissible to go mad].

[235] We should not be overly surprised by the presence of contradictory longings, wants, and needs within the human breast. As two diametrically opposite thinkers such as the positivist Pareto (1935) and the occultist Jung (1960–1990) concluded, the fundamental motives of human action that they described, respectively, as "non-logical" and "unconscious", are often contradictory: making new 'things', keeping 'things' as they are, doing something, fitting in the group, remaining oneself, and living out freely one's own socially controlled sexuality (see Baruchello forthcoming; we write "things" between single quotation marks because such 'things' can be nearly anything, e.g., ideas, imaginings, feelings, mental associations, physical structures, modes of behaviour, etc.).

Farts and burps may be rude, yet they too contribute to the physiological balance. Moreover, they have been the fodder of countless ludicrous jests, however uncouth. Perhaps such chaos, mayhem, and unruliness, rather than sheer disorder, are part of a superordinate harmony. As Eagleton wrote, on this subject:

> Social order is shrewd enough to encourage us to disrupt it from time to time. The traditional name for this in medieval Europe was carnival. The common people tumble into the streets wearing monstrous papier-mâché phalluses and vaginas and hump merrily away in defiance of the state. A wave of travesty and inversion – nose/phallus, face/buttocks, mouth/anus, high/low – sweeps through social life. Absolutely nothing escapes this great spasm of satire. Nothing is too solemn or sacred to be blasphemed. People dress up as Cardinals and piss in the streets. All this calls the established social order into question, but it is also a way of protecting it, a collective blow-off after which the sun will rise on myriad empty wine flagons and gnawed chicken legs and the populace will return obediently to work.[236]

Humour, as a carnivalesque phenomenon, may then help people to stay sane, even if it costs some embarrassment and/or nuisance.[237] Overall stability is a dynamic game which, to come about successfully, requires roundabout solutions and apt imbalances, analogously to the way in which effective lawn bowling calls for the curved trajectories of cambered balls. As the Irish-Italian philosopher Liberato Santoro-Brienza asserted: "[I]nsofar as, to be 'normal', we all need to be a little neurotic and a little psychotic, by the same token—and consequently—we are all in need of laughter, now and again."[238]

Another fascinating 20th-century testimony was provided in psychology by Harlow, whose interpretation of relief theory focusses more on anxiety, seeing commonplace humour as a relief-inducing reaction to stress-inducing situations, in what constitutes a much-simpler version than the one typically offered by Freud and the Freudians:

> Observational, anecdotal, and experimental data support the position that an anxiety-producing situation is perceived as humorous by the perturbed person after and only after the anxiety has been alleviated. Presumably every heroine who was tied to the railroad tracks and

---

Moreover, Jungian psychology has long established the concept of 'enantiodromia', i.e., the unconscious tendency to bring about the opposite of any conscious determination. Once we consciously establish A, in other words, we not only tacitly and logically imply non-A, but we also start longing for non-A in some way.

236 Eagleton (2022), par. 16. In their impressive survey of French poststructuralist thought, Blake and Christiansen (2011, 4) showed, perchance inadvertently, how little thorough social change the much-glorified "transgression" of Western artists has been able to engender in our modern history.
237 More on these matters follows in Chapter 3 of Part 2. See also *H&C2*.
238 Santoro-Brienza (2004), 84. Freudian slips too are thought to signal our unmet psychic libidinal desires.

saved at the last second saw the situation as humorous after, but not before, the sight of the engine receded over the terrain.[239]

Harlow identified this form of humour as perhaps the most basic kind, since it is brought forth by social and/or environmental situations and, therefore, may not have to depend entirely on language.[240] Insofar as anxiety demonstrates to ourselves our own repressed personal inadequacy, so it carries with it a grave threat to a person's *ego* due to feelings of individual helplessness, as well as to the attendant possibility and threat of social degradation.[241]

There is absolutely no way to claim that these three foremost theoretical approaches form definite schools of thought in either psychology or the social sciences as a whole, or that they cover all relevant aspects of humour and/or cognate notions. Each theory has its own focus, but a single humorous jest eliciting laughter may, in many cases, be explained by more than one theory, each of which highlights some significant components of the studied phenomena.[242] Moreover, the three theories are by no means mutually exclusive.[243] Indeed, they have been continuously mingled together by various writers in all extant disciplinary fields, as exemplified already by Hartley in the 18th century or, with regard to *ludus* [play] and *risus* [laughter], by Aquinas in the 13th.[244]

2.2.2 Explanatory Strategies of Aspect and Precision

In the 19th century, Charles Darwin utilised an intentionally provoking physiological metaphor when tackling linguistic-conceptual humour, e.g., ordinary jokes, which he described as the *tickling* of the human mind.[245] A champion of modern science, Darwin's approach starts from that which actual people can observe, record, possibly measure, and eventually reflect upon. Thus, as he approached the issue of humour, Darwin noted how unrestrainedly children tend to laugh and their very bodies shake when they are tickled. As he added, the same kind of be-

---

239 Harlow (1969), 226.
240 Harlow (1969), 226.
241 Harlow (1969), 226.
242 As we discussed in *H&C1*, each main theory can actually be used to explain the other two.
243 *H&C2* stresses superiority as crucial, whereas *H&C3* emphasises relief (see Part 2).
244 See our account of Hartley's views in *H&C1*, and Roszak (2013) on Aquinas.
245 Darwin (1872), 199.

havioural response can be seen in anthropoid apes when tickled, especially under their armpits.[246]

Darwin admitted that the laughter caused by comical ideas cannot be claimed to be a strictly reflex action, even if it is an involuntary one.[247] For one, in both cases (i.e., the tickling of a body and the mental jokes), we must also be in an adequately amenable disposition.[248] If a child were tickled by a total stranger, it would probably cry or scream in terror. Moreover, Darwin added: "[t]he touch must be light, and an idea or event, to be ludicrous, must not be of grave import".[249]

In keeping with his starting metaphor, Darwin also made the point that nobody is able to tickle him-/herself and posits as well that the bodily place that is going to be touched must not be known in advance. And this is pretty much what happens in our minds when coming across something humorous—it is largely an unanticipated, new, and/or incongruous notion that interrupts our habitual train of thought.[250]

Darwin cited the research of the French electrophysiologist and neurologist, Guillaume-Benjamin-Amand Duchenne, who first described in detail the phenomenon of human smiling as an anatomical issue. As is still studied in medical schools, a so-called "Duchenne smile" is the one capable of reaching our eyes, causing the corners to wrinkle up, and making 'crow's feet' appear on our faces. It is the kind of smile that most of us would recognise as the most authentic and/or most patent expression of human joy.

Probably we all have been guilty of producing false, non-Duchenne smiles, whether out of politeness or unease, but such smiles are quite easy to identify, insofar as our lower eyelids and other facial muscle groups do not contract in the same exact way as they do instead when our joy is sincere and unaffected.[251] Professional actors and seasoned conmen aside, our general incapacity to fake our own emotional expressions may be a sore limitation for us *qua* specific individuals

---

246 Darwin (1872), 199.
247 Darwin (1872), 199.
248 Darwin (1872), 199.
249 Darwin (1872), 199.
250 See Darwin (1872), 200.
251 Darwin (1872), 200–206. "We all" is used here for the sake of emphasis. There can be exceptional outliers.

under particular circumstances, but it is likely to have been beneficial for our species, i.e., in terms of evolutionary selection.[252]

In the 20th century, Harlow engaged in a thorough study of observable public sources of laughter and, especially, verbal jokes which, unlike a person's inner sense of humour, can be easily recorded and reviewed. Specifically, Harlow identified eight categories, which he lists and elucidates in an article entitled "The Anatomy of Humour":

(1) "Massacres, mutilations, torments and tortures have all been considered humorous by various people on various occasions. These acts are the extreme forms of personal degradation, but they provide examples of behaviours that fall within any comprehensive definition of humour".[253]

(2) Physical degradation.[254]

(3) The bulk of verbal humour: acts of degradation, e.g., when we joke about the haves and the have-nots, virtues and vices, etc.[255]

(4) Vulgar and/or sexual jokes (no sharp line of separation is drawn between them).[256]

(5) Ethnic, racial, and/or socio-cultural humour (largely reliant upon shared stereotypes and common prejudices).[257]

(6) Children's and/or childish jokes, e.g., "Why did the chicken cross the road? (To get to the other side.)"[258]

(7) "[T]ransitional abstract wit", i.e., jokes in which "elements of abstract or harmless wit can be found as components", insofar as "pure examples of harmless wit with no connected elements of degradation" are "difficult to find".[259]

---

[252] Being able to know what people around us feel is, practically, an important precondition for planning our next action, fitting within the family or clan, and avoiding or reducing the danger of harmful confrontation.

[253] Harlow (1969), 230. We addressed this work in more detail in *H&C2*.

[254] Harlow (1969), 230–232.

[255] Freud (1960), loc 1060.

[256] Harlow (1969), 235. By discussing vulgarity and sex together, Harlow confirms the 'sex-negative' and elitist character of the Western search for cultured and 'refined' fun. Yet there may be a loss in this move. As Phillips (1998, 78) wrote: "Dirt … is composed of all the residues of our own bodies, the murky depths of our memories, the opaque things that escape our ideals, everything that is corrupt and mixed", but it "is a very productive medium, which sustains all forms of life" (more on her work follows in Chapter 3 of Part 2). See also Deotto (2021, 367, *et passim*) on the theoretical re-evaluations of "junk".

[257] Harlow (1969), 235.

[258] Harlow (1969), 237.

[259] Harlow (1969), 237.

(8) The "ideal or abstract comic".²⁶⁰ Pristine and innocent, this last category of "humour" is, regrettably, also a mere academic construct, in all probability:

> Whether or not there does exist a type of harmless wit meriting the name of abstract ideal comic, it is obvious that it is easier to achieve tendency wit, which is founded on debasement, than harmless wit. No easy explanation exists to account for the overwhelming preponderance of tendency wit. It cannot be a question of a language's vocabulary since there is an equal population of words to express adoration and animosity. However, it is true that statements of positive feeling towards others may be openly and directly revealed. It is only the more aggressive impulses escaping repression through wit-work that need to be cloaked in the social garment of humour. Life provides few men the circumstance or the status that our very nature and upbringing tell us we deserve. Humour is born as we bare our teeth in laughter to ease the accumulating burdens we bear. Thus humour may be viewed as one means of rectifying the grievous error of existence.²⁶¹

Focussing upon jokes and verbal humour in general, cognitive theories of laughter and humour have also been regularly espoused for quite some time.²⁶² For example, in the 1970s, the US psychologist Jerry Suls developed a theory of the humour-appreciation process based upon information-processing models.²⁶³ Additionally, also in the 1970s, the script-based semantic theory of humour was made public by Raskin.²⁶⁴ Once again, only the verbal part of humour was dealt with.²⁶⁵ The special, when not exclusive, research emphasis being set firmly upon jokes, which are understood by Raskin as relying on ambiguities caused by the vague nature of most of our vocabulary, e.g., "The paralyzed bachelor hit the colourful ball."²⁶⁶

As of the 1990s, Raskin began collaborating with Attardo and produced the "general theory of verbal humour", integrating Raskin's script-based semantic theory with a five-level representation model that Attardo had worked out independently in prior studies of his. ²⁶⁷ The eventual result was a revised, six-level

---

260 Harlow (1969), 238.
261 Harlow (1969), 239. Harlow's quote reminds us also of the fact that the price to be paid for civilised life comprises not only taxes, but also thorough and continued repression of our natural drives, leading to all sorts of neuroses and psychoses, as well as to feats of sublimation and occasional relief. More on these mechanisms of psychological self-protection will be said in Chapters 1 and 3 of Part 2 (see also *H&C2*).
262 See, e.g., Feng *et al.* (2014), 60.
263 See Suls (1972), 81–82.
264 Raskin (1979). A further elaboration of his central ideas can be found in Raskin (1985).
265 As our frequent mentions of pranks indicate, there exists plenty of commonplace humour that is not linguistic.
266 Raskin (1979), 330.
267 Attardo and Raskin (1991), 293.

model of verbal jokes comprising the following structural conditions for humour to be able to arise:
(1) Script oppositions.
(2) Logical mechanisms.
(3) Situations.
(4) Targets.
(5) Narrative strategies.
(6) Linguistic parameters (e. g., wording, placement, etc.).[268]

Attardo and Ruskin are still continuing their joint endeavours at the time of our writing.[269] Empirical studies, however, have only been partially successful in showing the validity of their models.[270] Also, as seen in Chapter 1, despite spending decades researching it, they admitted that the task of defining "humour" proper, once and for all, is still awaiting completion.[271]

In the beginning of our century, the US-based communication expert John C. Meyer separated and discussed four distinct functions of "humour" proper, which he did not attempt to define in detail.[272] Rather, endorsing a common-sense understanding of it, he described it as a double-edged sword, i.e., capable of uniting people in jovial fellowship as well as of dividing them into in- and outgroups, or high- and low-status groups.[273] The four functions are:

(1) Reducing tensions and/or making the joker come across as part of the group, i.e., increasing group cohesiveness.[274]

(2) Clarifying the meaning of a message, often in a succinct manner:[275]

> A short, humorous line, as modern politicians have learned, gets more play on radio and television newscasts than does a thorough presentation of policy positions. Humorous lines often serve to express one's views creatively and memorably because they are presented incongru-

---

[268] The synoptic list is based on Krikmann (2006), 36.
[269] See, e.g., Attardo (2020, ix, *et passim*), where an echo of Polanyi's possibly infinite "subsidiary details" (see Chapter 4 in this book and *H&C1*) is given to the reader when discussing the countless "markers of humour" in Part 3.
[270] See, e.g., Ruch *et al.* (1993).
[271] We explain in this book (Chapter 4) why such a completion may never be attained.
[272] See Meyer (2000).
[273] A contemporary Cypriot student of "gelotology" described this duality as "a paradox" (Eker 2017, 49 and 59), arguing as well that "cruelty" [*acımasızlık*] is one of the most common sources of "humour" [*mizah*].
[274] Meyer (2000), 318–319.
[275] Meyer (2000), 319.

ously or unexpectedly. For the same reason, such lines are more likely to be picked up by the media.[276]

(3) Clarifying social norms without engaging in severe censorship: "Social norms are illuminated while the stress is on the expected norm rather than the seriousness of the violation."[277]

(4) Enforcing social norms, more or less delicately, by criticising select individuals and/or groups, e.g., attorneys:

> Several collections of lawyer jokes make the rounds, including comments such as this: Q: Why don't snakes bite attorneys? A: Professional courtesy. Even more cruel is the one that asks: How can you tell that an attorney is about to lie? A: His lips begin to move. Both of the above are as insulting and venomous as they are humorous–a superiority theorist's touchstone. Another dart at the legal system noted that "a jury is a collection of people banded together to decide who hired the better lawyer". Here was a shot at those who were swayed by "good lawyers" instead of by the socially desired norms of truth and justice. Finally, one asked: What do lawyers use for birth control? A: Their personalities.[278]

Fifteen years later, two experts in business studies and marketing psychology, Caleb Warren and Peter McGraw, devised a "Benign Violation Theory" (BVT) of humour, which has gained considerable traction in recent years. BVT is based on the idea that humour requires some positive emotion to be at work and, typically, is accompanied by laughter.[279] The latter is important, in their view, because it tells the other persons that everything is, more or less, all right.[280] (Clearly, Harlow's first category of humour does not register in their apprehension of laughter.) Under most circumstances, such a message has no real value *per se*.[281]

There can be situations in which an initial threat, i.e., the theory's titular "violation", was perceived in reality, but the danger of which was also assessed to be nil or negligible—hence the "benign" character of the violation at issue.[282] Warren's and McGraw's notion of 'violation' is very broad, for it can refer to anything that may be perceived as threatening someone's expectations and beliefs *vis-à-vis* how things are meant to be like.[283] What matters in relation to humour is

---

[276] Meyer (2000), 319.
[277] Meyer (2000), 319.
[278] Meyer (2000), 322.
[279] Warren and McGraw (2015), 75.
[280] See Warren and McGraw (2015), 75.
[281] Warren and McGraw (2015), 75.
[282] Warren and McGraw (2015), 75.
[283] Warren and McGraw (2015), 75.

that, whatever this violation may consist in, it is also perceived as sufficiently unharmful.[284]

As regards having a "sense of humour", a team of contemporary psychologists led by Rod A. Martin produced an instructive list of characteristics. According to them, such a sense involves:

(1) specific cognitive abilities (e.g., to generate and grasp verbal jokes);
(2) appropriate aesthetic responses (e.g., appreciating and enjoying such jokes);
(3) a set of habitual behaviours (e.g., guffawing often, telling jokes to amuse others);
(4) a fundamental emotion-related trait of character (e.g., a cheerful disposition);
(5) a related general attitude (e.g., a charitable outlook with respect to the world's incongruities, a positive attitude towards humorous attempts made by other people);
(6) and an underlying coping strategy or defence mechanism (e.g., a propensity to sustain a humorous perspective, even in the face of misfortunes and/or adversities).[285]

To gauge at least some of these characteristics, Martin and his team of social scientists utilised a number of tools for the measurement of humour.[286] Purportedly, they assessed:

(1) to which degree the studied individuals smile and laugh in a variety of settings;[287]
(2) the rate of recurrence of these individuals' use of humour as a coping strategy;[288] and
(3) whether such individuals are capable of discerning other people's humour and/or enjoying it.[289]

Despite all this, Martin and his colleagues acknowledged openly humour's intrinsic multi-dimensionality and the resulting difficulty with regard to grasping it in a sat-

---

[284] Once again, BVT too has very old roots. Moderation in laughter-inducing stimuli had already been observed and commented upon many times in Western culture, notably by Aristotle in the fifth chapter of his *Poetics*, in which the "mistake or unseemliness" that is meant to come across as "ridiculous" is said to have to be "not painful or destructive", e.g., "[t]he comic mask" of the ancient actors (as translated and cited in Morreall 1987, 14).
[285] See Martin et al. (2003), 49.
[286] Martin et al. (2003), 49.
[287] See, e.g., the Situational Humor Response Questionnaire (SHRQ) in Martin and Lefcourt (1984).
[288] See, e.g., the Coping Humor Scale (CHS) in Martin and Lefcourt (1983).
[289] See, e.g., the Sense of Humor Questionnaire (SHQ-6) in Svebak (1996).

2.2.3 Explanatory Strategies of Approach and Perspective

According to the father of psychoanalysis, "[t]he essential kinship between the two is so little open to doubt that an attempt at explaining the comic is bound to make at least some contribution to an understanding of humour".[291] Echoing many predecessors' reflections on the subject, Freud stated that, for something to be perceived as comical, it must outweigh the hindrances posed by any accompanying stressful affects: "As soon as the aimless movement does damage, or the stupidity leads to mischief, or the disappointment causes pain, the possibility of a comic effect is at an end."[292]

Humour, in Freud's mind, was a means to experiencing pleasure despite all these negative emotions, and it was said to arise because of an underlying economy of psychic expenditure.[293] The emotion that is economised can vary: it may be empathy, rage, sorrow, gentleness, etc.[294] The forms in which this economisation can occur vary as well, but they all require two fundamental factors:
(1) an external combination with a joke or some other type of comic agency; and
(2) the internal countering of an opposing psychic influence standing in the way of experiencing pleasure.[295]

Humour is therefore yet another defensive process of the psyche, such as projection, reaction-formation, regression, displacement, and repression.[296] As Freud wrote, these are: "the psychical correlative of the flight reflex and perform the task of preventing the generation of unpleasure from internal sources. In fulfilling this task, they serve mental events as an automatic regulation, which in the end, incidentally, turns out to be detrimental and has to be subjected to conscious thinking".[297]

---

290 Kuiper and Martin (1998), 160.
291 Freud (1960), loc 3710.
292 Freud (1960), loc 3715.
293 Freud (1960), loc 3719.
294 Freud (1960), loc 3772.
295 Freud (1960), loc 3777.
296 We addressed Freud's psychoanalysis in finer detail in *H&C1*.
297 Freud (1960), loc 3792–3795.

In his 1928 article on "humour" proper, Freud added to the mix the key-elements of his original theory of the human psychical structure.[298] Thus, the defence mechanism at issue becomes contingent upon the person's *super-ego*, which conflicts with the *ego*. The latter, in a humorous event, engages in a temporary narcissistic refusal to accept the limitations and vulnerability imposed by the *super-ego*, turning them into amusing occurrences.[299]

As Freud stated: "Humour is not resigned; it is rebellious. It signifies not only the triumph of the *ego* but also of the pleasure-principle, which is able here to assert itself against the unkindness of real circumstances."[300] For example, the convict who is about to be executed on a Monday can get some consolation, i.e., experience some pleasure, by opposing the reality-principle with a gallows joke: "Well, the week's beginning nicely."[301] As Freudian psychoanalysis entails: "The inevitable is coming, and at least he cannot make the situation any worse by joking."[302]

The emotions being economised upon define each type of ludicrous phenomena, among which "humour" is one common case:

> The pleasure in jokes has seemed to us to arise from an economy in expenditure upon inhibition, the pleasure in the comic from an economy in expenditure upon ideation (upon cathexis) and the pleasure in humour from an economy in expenditure upon feeling. In all three modes of working of our mental apparatus the pleasure is derived from an economy. All three are agreed in representing methods of regaining from mental activity a pleasure which has in fact been lost through the development of that activity. For the euphoria which we endeavour to reach by these means is nothing other than the mood of a period of life in which we were accustomed to deal with our psychical work in general with a small expenditure of energy – the mood of our childhood, when we were ignorant of the comic, when we were incapable of jokes and when we had no need of humour to make us feel happy in our life.[303]

---

[298] Freud (1928), 3. This structure has been debated and modified endlessly, not least by Jung himself. We believe depth psychology's picture of the psyche as a composite structure to offer a plausible way out from many circularities, puzzles, and paradoxes that too monolithic a conception of the mind can engender (see, e.g., Corvino 2022, 525, *et passim*, on the curious topic of "naughty fantasies", which we address in Chapter 3 of Part 2).

[299] Freud (1928), 2.

[300] Freud (1928), 2.

[301] Freud (1928), 1.

[302] Hietalahti (2015), 123. Claiming "corruption" to be inevitable in today's Russian society, and despite being the target of "hatred, impotent rage and hyperbolic cruelty", Vorkachev (2021, 118) followed the Freudian line of understanding and argued that common Russian citizens have been led to develop many forms of "humour" about such a predicament because of humour's "cathartic-therapeutic function, aimed at relieving a psychological stress caused by the prevalence of bribery, and the aggression function, specified in the outrage by corruption".

[303] Freud (1960), loc 3824–3830.

After Freud, the Hungarian polymath Arthur Koestler briefly yet influentially addressed the topic of humour, which he regarded as one of the three ultimate grounds of human creativity, i.e., in addition to scientific discovery and art.[304] All three activities were said to be based upon "bisociation", i.e., each of them possesses a two-planed nature, which consists in a mental oscillation between different frames of reference.[305]

(1) When this "bisociation" affects linguistic-conceptual meanings, humour occurs.
(2) When it affects objective analogies, we have originality in the sciences.
(3) When, instead, it affects thought-images, we have creativity in the arts.[306]

Correspondingly, Koestler identified three chief types of human creators as well: the jester, sage, and artist.[307] In parallel, he also listed three chief emotional states: the aggressive one in the case of humour; neutral objectivity in the case of scientific discovery; and sympathetic, admiring, or tragic ones in the case of the arts.[308]

Koestler took it as evident and uncontentious that humour is rooted in aggression. This attitude can be explained by the fact that the cultural repression of natural aggressive tendencies is a standard theme in Freud's works and among all Freudians, including Koestler himself. To give a measure of this phenomenon, we can quote the contemporary Colombian psychologist Juan G. Uribe, who felt justified in stating that "Freud places *cruelty* at the center of human drives."[309]

At any rate, the pivotal "bisociation" at play in humour was best exemplified by Koestler by way of a joke:

> Two women meet while shopping at the supermarket in the Bronx. One looks cheerful, the other depressed. The cheerful one inquires:
> "What's eating you?"
> "Nothing's eating me."
> "Death in the family?"
> "No, God forbid!"
> "Worried about money?"
> "No... nothing like that."
> "Trouble with the kids?"
> "Well, if you must know, it's my little Jimmy".

---

304 See Scammell (2009) on Koestler's considerable fame in the 20th century, especially outside mere academia.
305 Koestler (1964), 35–36.
306 Koestler (1964), 26.
307 Koestler (1964), 27.
308 Koestler (1964), 27. See also Krikmann (2006), 28.
309 Uribe (2010), par. 1; emphasis added.

> "What's wrong with him, then?"
> "Nothing is wrong. His teacher said he must see a psychiatrist."
> Pause. "Well, well, what's wrong with seeing a psychiatrist?"
> "Nothing is wrong. The psychiatrist said he's got an Oedipus complex."
> Pause. "Well, well, Oedipus or Shmoedipus, I wouldn't worry so long as he's a good boy and loves his mamma."[310]

The chosen joke brings us back to Freud but, for Koestler, it also explains the meaning of "bisociation". In the jolly woman's prosaic logic, nothing at all is wrong if Jimmy is a good boy who loves his dear mother.[311] However, within the specialistic context of Freudian psychoanalysis, the same words acquire a whole new meaning.[312] The joke's bisociation entails entertaining in our mind two largely coherent but also mutually exclusive frames of reference, which Koestler said "vibrate simultaneously on two different wavelengths".[313]

Psychologically, Koestler added that all these humorous events can be turned easily into tragic ones or into emotionally neutral objective facts, depending on the viewer's emotional disposition.[314] The cruel schoolboy may crack up roaringly at the pained victim of a sudden fall on the ice, while the pious old lady may cry aloud, worry, call for help, or shed tears.[315] If humour is chosen and laughter duly ensues, it can serve the Freudian function of producing "a disposal of redundant emotions".[316]

Evolutionarily, humour left Koestler sincerely perplexed: "What is the survival value of the involuntary, simultaneous contraction of fifteen facial muscles associated with certain noises that are often irrepressible?"[317] Paradoxically, the one and only strictly utilitarian purpose that Koestler could discover for the phenomenon of humour is that it grants us a transitory break from utilitarian concerns themselves:

---

310 Koestler (1964), 3.
311 We do not imply that women alone are capable of such a jolly prosaic logic. Besides, if Jung's teachings are to be taken seriously, drawing too sharp a distinction between the sexes is unadvisable, for all men have a variously strong female component (i.e., their *anima*) and all women a variously strong male one (i.e., their *animus*).
312 Koestler (1964), 35.
313 Koestler (1964), 35.
314 Koestler (1964), 45–46.
315 We are pandering to trite stereotypes, of course. In reality, schoolboys can be sensitive and old ladies cruel.
316 Koestler (1964), 62. See also Borisova (2019), 48.
317 Koestler (1964), 31.

Laughter, as the cliché has it, is "liberating", i.e., tension-relieving. Relief from stress is always pleasurable, regardless of whether it was caused by hunger, sex, anger, or anxiety. Under ordinary circumstances such relief is obtained by some purposeful activity which is appropriate to the nature of the tension. When we laugh, however, the pleasurable relief does not derive from a consummatory act which satisfies some specific need. On the contrary: laughter prevents the satisfaction of biological drives, it makes a man equally incapable of killing or copulating; it deflates anger, apprehension, and pride. The tension is not consummated—it is frittered away in an apparently purposeless reflex, in facial grimaces, accompanied by overexertion of the breathing mechanism and aimless gestures. To put it the other way round: the sole function of this luxury reflex seems to be the disposal of excitations which have become redundant, which cannot be consummated in any purposeful manner.[318]

According to Koestler, a Freudian measure of psychic apprehension and/or hostility was also at work in the realm of humorous occurrences.[319] It may present itself openly as spite, scorn, superciliousness, or utter lack of any sympathy whatsoever, i.e., a Bergsonian 'anaesthesia of the heart' of the amplest sort. As such, in sociopsychological terms, it should be understood as an aggressive-defensive or self-asserting tendency, both of which have broad and deep social ramifications.[320] The unkind character of humour was described by Koestler as a necessary ingredient of all types of humour, very much "like the presence of salt in a well-prepared dish—which, however, would be tasteless without it".[321] Indeed we might say that finding a new viewpoint *via* Koestler's biosociation translates into advance in science, appreciation in the arts, but indifference in humour.

Uniting Darwin's evolutionary legacy and Freud's focus on the pleasure-principle, a number of contemporary social scientists have tried to explain the origins and the functions of humour from the perspective of sexual selection.[322] According to these researchers, a sense of humour, which is commonly and conveniently left un- or underdefined by the very same researchers, is a sexually alluring attribute insofar as it displays intelligence, mental dynamism, and/or impressive creativity. Perhaps this Darwinian insight was the deeper meaning of Georges Simenon's playful statement about the "croupe" (i.e., rump, hips) of his lover, Josephine Baker: "that croupe has a sense of humor".[323]

---

[318] Koestler (1964), 51.
[319] Koestler (1964), 51–52.
[320] Koestler (1964), 51–52.
[321] Koestler (1964), 52.
[322] See an overview of such studies in Greengross and Miller (2011), 188.
[323] As translated and cited in Baker and Chase (2001), 154. We expect most of our readers to have grasped the several ironies entailed in the sentence above.

In the 21st century, Greengross and Miller confirmed a set of three predictions that they inferred from Miller's older sexual-selection model of commonplace humour:
(1) that intelligence predicts humour skills,
(2) humour predicts mating success, and
(3) males surpass females in this specific ability.[324]

Greengross and Miller also recorded that humour skills correlate significantly with the positive effects of intelligence on mating success and interpreted this empirical result as suggesting that intelligence may be erotically appealing primarily *via* verbal humour.[325] If true, humour, whether commonplace or true, should be a crucial trait of character with regard to mating success.[326]

Such a conclusion is likely to sound anomalous and unconvincing to some of our readers who may actually be able to recall with ease vast cohorts of truly amusing, yet also hopelessly ugly or unappealing, operatic *buffi* and cinematic comedians.[327] Nevertheless, evolutionary psychology, overall, has been describing humour quite consistently as a formidable tool in the never-ending competition for successful breeding, as well as a reliable avenue for instituting allegiances, testing beliefs, and even increasing a person's social capital.[328]

As noted, defining "humour" as such has not been a prime concern for the involved researchers, whose works have also insisted on the notion that, phylogenetically, the human smile is likely to have originated from aggressive displays of bared teeth and/or the submissive/fearful grin that can still be seen among simians.[329] Theirs and our laugh-like vocalisations, moreover, are found almost exclusively in the context of play, particularly in social games involving tickling, mock fights, and/or hunt-like chases.[330] We can still experience this primeval ambiguity of laughter in our daily life, e.g., whenever we are having a heated argument with our partner, and an undesirable stupid grin and/or a nervous burst of laughter suddenly come to pass.[331]

---

[324] Greengross and Miller (2011), 188.
[325] Greengross and Miller (2011), 188.
[326] Greengross and Miller (2011), 188.
[327] One of this volume's authors had some experience as an operatic *buffo* and is no credible Casanova or Don Juan.
[328] See, e.g., Hurley *et al.* (2011), 21.
[329] See, e.g., Storey (2003), 320.
[330] Storey (2003), 320.
[331] It is unlikely that the two authors of this volume should be the only human beings who have had this experience.

The American evolutionary psychologist Geoffrey Miller claimed, on this point, that humour would have had no evolutionary value whatsoever among the early humans who populated the prehistoric savannas of Africa.[332] Instead, he argued that some traits leading to what we call today "humour" must have evolved *via* mechanisms of sexual selection because of these traits' value *qua* indicators of other, more basic, more crucial traits, such as creativity and/or intelligence: "A capacity for comedy, reveals a capacity for creativity" and creativity, indicates intelligence, energy, youth, and suggests proteanism.[333] In other words, humour is attractive, and that is why it was passed on, in our species, through sexual selection.[334]

Evolutionary psychologists have also regularly associated the observable phenomenon of laughter among primates with humour.[335] Upon this empirical basis, the self-styled American "gelotologist" William F. Fry theorised that such a laughter arises in social games involving a bizarre paradox: "This is an attack that is not really an attack."[336] Furthermore, as stated by his fellow-national Paul E. McGhee: "Humor is the logical result of an extension of playful forms of behavior to the more abstract intellectual sphere of ideas."[337] As such, these psychologists have concluded that humour must have, or must have had, a decisive adaptive role in the historical evolution of social primates such as ourselves, who may now enjoy it without specific mating- and/or survival-related ends in mind.[338]

Combining evolutionary and cognitive psychology with the philosophy of mind, Matthew Hurley, Daniel C. Dennett, and Reginald Adams tried to show how humour must have evolved out of a computational problem that occurred when our prehistoric ancestors developed the peculiar art of open-ended thinking. Specifically, they argued that insofar as emotions direct all our cognitive processes, humour can offer valuable insights into the mechanism of our own minds.[339] As they claimed, humour "cannot be just a happy accident of our biology", but must have evolved in order to provide solutions to authentic human problems, primitive versions of which can be observed in species that are evolutionarily close to

---

332 See G. Miller (2000).
333 G. Miller (2000), 415–416.
334 G. Miller (2000), 415–416.
335 See, e.g., Storey (2003), 323–324, and Gaspar, Esteves, and Arriaga (2014), 110–111. Given evolutionary psychology's prominence in today's social sciences, we have granted it ample room in our own account.
336 As cited in Storey (2003), 321.
337 McGhee (1979), 103.
338 McGhee (1979), 103.
339 Their case is interesting because, albeit originating in a cognitive context, it casts the same in evolutionary terms.

ours.[340] Albeit emotions do play a big role in it, humour is not a pure reflexive response to a stimulus, but is dependent upon fundamental thought processes too, such as recollection, inference, and semantic integration.[341]

Hurley and associates highlighted the similarities between the joys of problem-solving and humorous exchanges.[342] In addition to recognising the patent delights of *Schadenfreude*, they also emphasised how humour involves a false belief that flags how someone must have made an error of judgement and, consequently, that can open the path to its solution.[343] Funnily enough, the error-maker is frequently also the one who laughs at the error-making: "the mistake-discoverer is also the mistake-maker".[344] Instead of feeling humiliated, upset or irritated, we often celebrate our discovery of the error.[345] The mistake-discoverer can thus experience a significant degree of Hobbesian superiority over the prior version of him-/herself, who was responsible for the mistake: "One has discovered a bug and repaired it; one is suddenly a little bit better, a little bit wiser, a little bit more in the know."[346]

In contemporary neuropsychology, the Indian-American V.S. Ramachandran endorsed an evolutionary ethological approach to humour as signalled by laughter, which he interpreted as a stereotyped vocalisation whereby an individual organism tries to communicate something to other individual organisms belonging to the former's social cluster.[347] Laughter would be, in short, one among the animal "voices" that can still be heard in the human domain, alongside screams of fear and moans of pleasure.[348]

Ramachandran maintained that laughter is still used to signal the laughing individual's close companions that an anomaly was detected and, fortunately, it was a benign and/or inconsequential one, i.e., a false alarm.[349] This, as Ramachandran

---

340 Hurley et al. (2011), 10–11. While we are cautious about endorsing any biological reductionism, we are also aware of the crucial role played by biological factors in human life, both evolutionarily and individually. Anyone who has experienced puberty, pregnancy, menopause, and/or glandular disorders is unlikely to disagree with us. Not to mention the indirect wisdom that can be gauged from having pets or farm animals neutered, whether callously so or with genuine concerns for their stress-levels and well-being (see, e.g., Klintip et al. 2022).
341 Hurley et al. (2011), 19.
342 See Hurley et al. (2011), 49.
343 Hurley et al. (2011), 49.
344 Hurley et al. (2011), 49.
345 Hurley et al. (2011), 49.
346 Hurley et al. (2011), 50.
347 See Ramachandran (1998), 352.
348 Ramachandran (1998), 352.
349 Ramachandran (1998), 352.

wrote, explains as well why laughter is so contagious, inasmuch as it serves the group's survival interests to convey this information as promptly and as rapidly as possible.[350] Such a line of reasoning can also explain why we feel far more comfortable when laughing in the company of our closer friends and relatives than we do when we are in the company of strangers.[351]

2.2.4 A Second Set of Reflections

> Humour dilates over a subject with alternate tears and smiles; its eye is not wanting in a certain roguish twinkle—nay, it sometimes winks at an absurdity, but laughs on.
> —Edwin P. Hood[352]

As interesting as the ethological premises of these theories are, the evolutionary step from the "I am clever", "thank God it's an error" or "a false alarm", to the mental and emotional gymnastics of Western humour as may be displayed in the works of Shakespeare, Swift, Shaw, or Leacock is not only a very big step, but seems over-conveniently contrived and/or not fully thought through. Our bodily, mental, and communicative abilities have certainly evolved through the aeons, but there may be major qualitative differences between the evolutionary selection of physical skills and the cultural election of creative ones.

G.K. Chesterton had already remarked on this point, in the heyday of Western socio-cultural Darwinism:

> The speculations on the nature of any reaction to the risible belong to the larger and more elementary subject of Laughter and are for the department of psychology; according to some, almost for that of physiology. Whatever be their value touching the primitive function of laughter, they throw very little light on the highly civilized product of humour. It may well be questioned whether some of the explanations are not too crude even for the crudest origins; that they hardly apply even to the savage and certainly do not apply to the child. It has been suggested, for example, that all laughter had its origin in a sort of *cruelty*, in an exultation over the pain or ignominy of an enemy; but it is very hard even for the most imaginative psychologist to believe that, when a baby bursts out laughing at the image of the cow jumping over the moon, he is really finding pleasure in the probability of the cow breaking her leg when she comes down again. The truth is that all these primitive and prehistoric origins are largely unknown and possibly unknowable; and like all the unknown and unknowable are a field for furious wars of religion. Such primary human causes will always be interpreted differently according to different philosophies of human life. Another philosophy would say,

---

350 Ramachandran (1998), 352.
351 Ramachandran (1998), 352.
352 Hood (1865), 46. More on him was said in *H&C1*.

for instance, that laughter is due not to an animal cruelty but to a purely human realization of the contrast between man's spiritual immensity within and his littleness and restriction without, for it is itself a joke that a house should be larger inside than out. According to such a view, the very incompatibility between the sense of human dignity and the perpetual possibility of incidental indignities, produces the primary or archetypal joke of the old gentleman sitting down suddenly on the ice. We do not laugh thus when a tree or a rock tumbles down; because we do not know the sense of self-esteem or serious importance within. But such speculations in psychology, especially in primitive psychology, have very little to do with the actual history of comedy as an artistic creation.[353]

Interestingly, the so-called "mother of psychoanalysis", Karen Horney, observed a parallel distance between the far more "complicated ... sadistic trends" of socialised adults and the "elementary cruelty" of children towards animals that, as we are going to see in the next chapter, shocked Locke and seduced Sade.[354] Somehow, the civilisational gap that Chesterton remarked upon endures also in much 'darker' phenomena than just those of humour or laughter alone.[355]

At the same time, moreover, Horney's own research revealed a shared aetiological root for all forms of cruel behaviour, i.e., the person's sense of unworthiness, e.g., in the child's "feeling oppressed and humiliated", and in the adult's "profound feeling of futility as regards his own life"—as was already identified by "[p]oets" and philosophers such as "Nietzsche" and "Dostoevski ... long before we were able to dig it out with our prodding clinical scrutiny".[356] Insofar as the studied beings are human, humanists and the humanities may plausibly provide insight into, as well as knowledge and understanding of, these beings' nature, motives, attitudes, and behaviours.[357]

---

[353] Chesterton (1929–1973), par. 3; emphasis added. The quotation is long but, given its relevance for the point being made in our paragraph, worth citing in full, considering the pointed remark on "cruelty" proper that the passage contains.

[354] Horney (1945), 200. See also *H&C1*.

[355] No offense is meant at any point of our books by the metaphorical use of "dark" as meaning 'evil' or 'scary'.

[356] Horney (1945), 200–202. Today's famous French economic historian, Thomas Piketty (2014, introduction, par. 4), was therefore not the first or the only social scientist to recognise how "[f]ilm and literature, nineteenth-century novels ... the novels of Jane Austen and Honoré de Balzac", or even "the intuitive knowledge that everyone acquires", if alert enough, can grasp important aspects of reality, sometimes "with a verisimilitude and evocative power that no statistical or theoretical analysis can match".

[357] See also Polanyi (1962c) and *H&C1*. "Humanist" meaning here someone who works in the humanities, e.g., historians and dramatists, i.e., neither the sole early-modern Christian philologists and philosophers discussed by Cassirer (1953), nor today's militant atheists who, as of the 1960s, started using this term to describe themselves.

Humanistic psychological theories, for their part, have emphasised how humour, the precise meaning of which is also and always presupposed and/or left conveniently undefined, possesses a built-in face-saving device, insofar as it is a relatively safe channel whereby to unveil taboo interests and/or values, and initiate positive interpersonal relationships, especially with those who happen to have more power than we do.[358] In this perspective, humour could then work as a convenient tool that allows a person to assert her worthiness in the face of unfriendly or unhelpful circumstances. As written by Robert Storey in our century: "Humor seems to have evolved as a potent instrument for at once forging indispensable social bonds and permitting the individual a great deal of (self-serving) manoeuvrability within them."[359]

In the 20th century, Abraham Maslow's self-actualising psychology concluded that a person's "sense of humour" is not necessarily revealed by clever sallies, funny ripostes, and/or entertaining jocularity, but by "thoughtful, philosophical humor that elicits a smile more usually than a laugh".[360] Indeed, back in the 19th century, Thomas Carlyle had already penned in an obituary commemorating the passing of the Romantic German humourist, Jean Paul: "True humour springs not more from the head than from the heart … it issues not in laughter, but in still smiles, which lie far deeper."[361] In our century, Robert Storey went as far as stating that: "[t]o have a sense of humor, in other words, is to show a readiness and skill for bonding", rather than exhibiting clownish behaviour or making other people laugh all the time, as it is frequently argued and generally presumed.[362] Paradoxically, a person endowed with such a true sense of humour could be quiet, clearheaded, and pensive, most of the time.[363]

"Humour" proper, then, comes to describe, once more, very different personal attitudes and behaviours. True to its original conception as a fluid, its meanings infiltrate and transpire throughout the greatest variety of contexts, characterisations, and comportments.[364] Semantic separators and pragmatic barriers are moistened and weakened by it, leading to an unstable yet ever-flowing course of surprising lived experiences, both individual and collective. We are thus reminded of Wittgenstein's very brief, hopelessly sketchy, yet intriguing reflections on the ideas of "sense of humour" and "humour" as such, which he understood "not

---

[358] See McGhee (1979), 30–31.
[359] Storey (2003), 323.
[360] Maslow (1954), 222–223.
[361] Carlyle (1835), 454.
[362] Storey (2003), 327–328.
[363] We use "true" here in a commendatory sense.
[364] See Crowther (2021) for a study of humour going full circle: bodily fluids *qua* comic trope.

[as] a mood" but "a way of looking at the world" peculiar to each person, historical period, and analogous to the equally shifty notion of "taste":

> The concept of 'festivity'. We connect it with merrymaking; in another age it may have connected with fear and dread. What we call "wit" and "humour" doubtless did not exist in other ages. And both are constantly changing.
> [...]
> What is it like for people not to have the same sense of humour? They do not react properly to each other. It's as though there were a custom amongst certain people for one person to throw another a ball which he is supposed to catch and throw back; but some people, instead of throwing it back, put it in their pocket. Or what is it like for somebody to be unable to fathom someone else's taste?[365]

In yet another demonstration of the incredibly wide semantic and theoretical range of "humour" proper, social scientists have thus explored and corroborated its applicability not solely to the seemingly obvious realm of laughter—whether only among humans or a great number of primates too—but also to the far more obscure domain of measured conversation, subtle smiling, and inaudible thinking.[366] Personal attitudes, presuppositions, moods, and quirks have been identified, repeatedly when not consistently, to various degrees of centrality and/or significance, as key-players in laughing matters.

Whether the resulting broad space for divergence and diversity is amusing or not, it remains to be seen. Perhaps it is a case of understated cruelty against the many keen minds in our midst that still seek neat unequivocal definitions or clear-cut universal truths.[367]

---

[365] Wittgenstein (1984), 78e and 83e.
[366] Other social animals have been studied in connection with laughter, e.g., rats (see, e.g., Pankseep 2007). Indeed, since as early as 1876, there have been claims of nothing less than "animal humor", e.g., mammals such as dogs, porpoises and monkeys (Lockwood 1876, 257).
[367] As noted in H&C2, an even deeper challenge exists, i.e., the things that we do not fully understand may actually be significant, or even paramount, to *us* as individuals or as humankind, e.g., love, friendship, faith or art.

3 Making Sense of Cruelty

> It seems the psyche itself insists on pathologizing the strong ego and all its supportive models, disintegrating the 'I' with images of psychopathic hollowness in public life, fragmentation and depersonalization in music and painting, hallucinations and pornographies in private visions, violence, cruelty, and the absurd surrealisms of urban wars, racisms, causes, freakishness in dress and speech. These images, like the pathologized metaphorica in the memory art, alchemy, and myth, twist and shock the 'I' out of its integrative identity, out of its innocence and its idealization of human being, opening it to the underworld of psychic being.
> —James Hillman[1]

As explained in this book's first chapter, we are going to provide a parallel, synoptical, and succinct account of those few works in the Western humanities and social sciences that have been capable of and interested in examining "cruelty" declaredly and directly, i.e., burrowing deeper into its presumed meanings and/or acknowledged occurrences so as to excavate valuable insights, especially as regards the possible conflicts between humour and cruelty. Cognate concepts such as 'evil', 'aggression', 'discipline', 'totalitarianism', 'punishment', 'violence', 'oppression', or 'alienation' are thematically related to 'cruelty', sometimes inseparably so, but they are also nominally distinct. Hence, these cognates are not included or, at the very least, not prioritised in the literature that was carefully examined, enquired into, and expounded upon here, unless "cruelty" as such was also prominently present —and/or "cruelties", "cruel", "crueller", "cruellest", "most cruel" and "cruelly".[2]

3.1 An Overview of 'Cruelty' in the Humanities

3.1.1 Cruelty as a Vice

> Every time transcendence falls back into immanence, stagnation, there is a degradation of existence into the '*en-soi*' – the brutish life of subjection to given conditions – and of liberty into constraint and contingency. This downfall represents a moral fault if the subject consents to it; if it is inflicted upon him, it spells frustration and oppression. In both cases it is an absolute evil. Every individual concerned to justify his existence feels that his existence involves

---

[1] Hillman (1975), 109. More on Hillman's reflections on intra-psychical cruelty follows in Chapters 1 and 3 of Part 2.
[2] The last sentence applies primarily to English, Latin, and the Romance and Germanic languages. Unfortunately, we are fluent in only some of them and can work on a few more with some effort. It is a sorely limited, probably imperfect, and philologically uneven landscape.

an undefined need to transcend himself, to engage in freely chosen projects.
—Simone de Beauvoir[3]

As mentioned, there is no univocal conception of 'cruelty' to be retrieved in Western culture, but it is possible to identify a handful of recurrent interpretations and attendant emphases. One arises from the first expressed and extensive Western study of cruelty, penned by Lucius Annaeus Seneca, to whom we owe as well one of the earliest written sets of observations about self-mockery as an instrument for psychosocial self-defence.[4]

Tackling *crudelitas* [cruelty] as such, Seneca claims it to be "hardness" or "harshness in exacting punishments", "intemperance of the soul in exacting punishments", "the inclination of the soul towards more severity", or, in a typically Roman manner of speaking, "towards more severe things".[5] As argued in his *De clementia* [On Clemency], cruelty is a personal vice of excess, which characterises "those who have a reason for punishing, but no moderation in it".[6] Cruel individuals are therefore not to be confused with those men and women who are affected by "bestiality" [*feritas*], which is the personal vice exhibited by people "who find pleasure in violence" [*cui voluptati saevitia est*], i.e., a fundamentally irrational disposition that, as Seneca affirms, "we may even call madness" [*insania*].[7]

Albeit distinguishing sharply between *crudelitas* and *feritas*, Seneca admits that too much of the former can eventually lead to the latter, so that "crossing first the common boundaries, then those of humanity itself, ... cruelty turns into a pleasure and thus revels in the killing of people".[8] Additionally, he distinguishes between "private" (e.g., vendettas) and "public" cruelties (e.g., wars).[9] It is Seneca's belief that "public cruelty" is a worse version of this evil, insofar as "a cruel rule" causes much more harm than "private cruelty", given that only the former can: plunge entire countries into "war"; "increase the number of enemies by eliminating them"; provide the worst possible "examples" of leadership to the citizens; and

---

[3] De Beauvoir (1956), 27.
[4] See, e.g., Haugh (2017), 204–205. Seneca should also be regarded as the first Western intellectual to provide an extensive portrait of a patent "libertine", i.e., "Ostio Quadra in *Naturales Quaestiones*", who, driven by "libidinous fury ... tries to exceed the limits imposed by nature upon the human being" like "the characters in the works by the Marquis de Sade" (Migliardi 2015, 29).
[5] Seneca (1900), book 2, chap. 4, pars. 1 and 3. The translation is ours. *In this chapter, we switch to historical present tense* so as to change the tempo of our prose and, hopefully, make the reading experience more pleasant.
[6] Seneca (1900), book 2, chap. 4, par. 2.
[7] Seneca (1900), book 2, chap. 4, par. 2.
[8] Seneca (1900), book 1, chap. 25, par. 2.
[9] Seneca (1900), book 1 chap. 5, par. 2; chap. 26, pars. 1 and 3.

turn "kings" into "tyrants", who "have to guard their many crimes with ever more crimes".[10]

Incidentally, there can also be too much clemency, since a "cruelty" is, for Seneca, also "forgiving everybody".[11] In such a case, "clemency" mutates into "pity" [*misericordia*], which is yet another "vice of the soul" [*vitium animi*].[12] This claim, and many others, will reverberate through the ages. In medieval times, Seneca's understanding of this notion can be found, explicated briefly and essentially unchanged, in the works of Archbishop Hincmar of Laon (9th century), Peter Damian (11th century), Alan of Lille (12th century), and Frère Laurent (13th century).[13] Above all, it resonates in the immortal *Summa Theologiae* of Thomas Aquinas, which defines cruelty as "hardness of the heart in exacting punishment" and distinguishes it starkly from "mercilessness", i.e., failing to display mercy when mercy ought to be displayed.[14] A 'cardiac slumber' *à la* Bergson might then be a key to cruelty too.[15]

Aquinas acknowledges as well that "mercy" resembles "clemency" in "that both shun and recoil from another's unhappiness"; however, mercy and clemency do so in different ways: the former accomplishes it by "relieve[ing] another's unhappiness by a beneficent action"; the latter accomplishes it by "mitigat[ing] another's unhappiness by the cessation of punishment".[16] Like Seneca, Aquinas condemns cruelty as "human wickedness" which includes an element of considerate deliberation.[17] It is therefore not to be identified with "savagery or brutality", i.e., cases of utterly irrational "bestiality" caused by "the pleasure [that some people] derive from a [wo/]man's torture".[18] Unlike "cruelty", "bestiality" is the lamentable result of "either ... evil custom, or ... a corrupt nature, as do other bestial emo-

---

[10] Seneca (1900), book 1, chap. 5, par. 2; chap. 7, par. 3; chap. 8, par. 7; chap. 12, par. 1; chap. 13, par. 2; chap. 15, par. 3.
[11] Seneca (1900), book 2, chap. 2, par. 2. Further cases of ethical "messiness" arising from "cruel mercy" were discussed by Bolduc (2008, 36 and 39), who did briefly address Seneca's reflections.
[12] Seneca (1900), book 2, chap. 4, par. 4.
[13] Baraz (2003), 18–19 and 75.
[14] Aquinas (1920), part 2 of part 2, question 159, art. 1.
[15] We discussed at length in *H&C2* the extensive criss-crossing of brutal cruelty and humour.
[16] Aquinas (1920), part 2 of part 2, question 159, art. 1.
[17] Aquinas (1920), part 2 of part 2, question 159, art. 2. As Bernard Williams (1976, 73–74) states in times closer to us: "For if it is a mark of a man to employ intelligence and tools in modifying his environment, it is equally a mark of him to employ intelligence and tools in destroying others. If it is a mark of a man to have a conceptualized and fully conscious awareness of himself as one among others, aware that others have feelings like himself, this is a preconception not only of benevolence but ... of cruelty as well."
[18] Aquinas (1920), part 2 of part 2, question 159, art. 2.

tions", driving people into losing control over their actions and, in the most extreme cases, their minds.[19]

Expanding on the earlier works of Isidore of Seville, Aquinas reflects also on the etymology of the word "cruelty":

> Cruelty apparently takes its name from "cruditas" [rawness]. Now just as things when cooked and prepared are wont to have an agreeable and sweet savor, so when raw they have a disagreeable and bitter taste. Now it has been stated above ... that clemency denotes a certain smoothness or sweetness of soul, whereby one is inclined to mitigate punishment. Hence cruelty is directly opposed to clemency.[20]

Modern linguists agree with Isidore and Aquinas, at least as regards Indo-European languages.[21] Besides, Seneca's and Aquinas' conception of 'cruelty' still echoes in the context of contemporary jurisprudence, where the Brazilian legal expert Paulo Barrozo has recently identified "four distinct conceptions of cruelty found in underdeveloped form in domestic and international criminal law sources", i.e.,

(1) "Agent-objective" (e.g., lawful punishments exceeding in severity those that are commonly bestowed);
(2) "Agent-subjective" (e.g., commonly bestowed punishments leaving room for exceedingly severe impositions);
(3) "Victim-subjective" (e.g., lawful punishments that prove excessive in that they are unbearable for specific victims); and
(4) "Victim-objective and agent-independent" (e.g., lawful punishments that are so severe as to exceed the common boundaries of human decency and/or dignity, or are culpably blind to the institutional aetiology of the punished crimes).[22]

Within the Christian context of the European Middle Ages, it should be noted how, in its early centuries, none less than Augustine of Hippo mentions "cruelty" several times and used "cruel" in many of his influential works, although in a far less detailed, systematic, and analytical way than Aquinas.[23] According to Augustine, "cruelty" is to be listed among the many sins "originating from the root of error and misdirected love with which every child of Adam is born", and he therefore dubs "cruel" all sorts of sinful actions imperilling the otherworldly salvation of our souls.[24]

---

19 Aquinas (1920), part 2 of part 2, question 159, art. 2.
20 Aquinas (1920), part 2 of part 2, question 159, art. 1.
21 See, e.g., Trubacheva (1981), vol. 8, 178 and 192 on Slavic languages.
22 Barrozo (2015), 1026 and 1031–1035. Barrozo (2008) establishes already this framework.
23 See Baraz (1998), 204–207.
24 Augustine (1877), book 22, chap. 22, par. 1.

At the close of the Medieval period—hence, at the concomitant dawn of the European Renaissance—the French Catholic Pyrrhonian philosopher Michel de Montaigne unprecedentedly devotes two whole essays to the subject of "cruelty" as such (i.e., chaps. 11 and 27 in book 2 of his *Essays*).[25] Once again, "cruelty" is said to belong to the long list of "vices" that a person can exhibit, while "cowardice" is singled out as "the mother of cruelty".[26] The more "inhuman" our behaviours are, the more "cruelty" seems apt a term for Montaigne to employ.[27]

Graphically, with regard to the dreadful reality of warfare, Montaigne writes:

> I could hardly persuade myself, before I saw it with my eyes, that there could be found souls so cruel and fell, who, for the sole pleasure of murder, would commit it; would hack and lop off the limbs of others; sharpen their wits to invent unusual torments and new kinds of death, without hatred, without profit, and for no other end but only to enjoy the pleasant spectacle of the gestures and motions, the lamentable groans and cries of a man dying in anguish. For this is the utmost point to which cruelty can arrive.[28]

Despite Montaigne's familiarity with the literary and philosophical works of Seneca, the latter thinker's distinction between "cruelty" and "bestiality" is totally disregarded by the former.[29] Perhaps this vice is just too crass and ugly to spend any time drawing fine distinctions.[30] As Montaigne states: "Amongst other vices, I mortally hate cruelty, both by nature and judgment, as the very extreme of all vices: nay, with so much tenderness that I cannot see a chicken's neck pulled off without trouble, and cannot without impatience endure the cry of a hare in my dog's teeth, though the chase be a violent pleasure."[31]

The even earlier examples of compassion and moderation—also with regard to 'lowly' creatures—that can be found amid the "Egyptians", in the ancient biographies of "Pythagoras", in the pagan beliefs of the "Druids", and among the "Gauls" of old are, instead, emphatically recalled by Montaigne, who argues that "there is … a certain respect, a general duty of humanity, not only to beasts that have life and sense, but even to trees, and plants. We owe justice to men, and gra-

---

25 Montaigne (1877).
26 Montaigne (1877), book 2, chap. 27, pars. 1 and 10. In the 20th century, Russell (2009, 70) also notes: "Fear generates impulses of cruelty, and therefore promotes such superstitious beliefs as seem to justify cruelty."
27 See, e.g., Montaigne (1877), book 2, chap. 11, pars. 17 and 20; book 3, chap. 6, par. 25.
28 Montaigne (1877), book 2, chap. 11, par. 20.
29 Montaigne (1877), book 2, chap. 11, par. 20.
30 Hair-splitting distinctions are commonly associated with medieval thought, after all, not with modern thinkers.
31 Montaigne (1877), book 2, chap. 11, par. 13.

ciousness and benignity to other creatures that are capable of it; there is a certain commerce and mutual obligation betwixt them and us."[32]

As Montaigne reflects, repeated cruelty towards our animal fellow creatures can lead to cruelty towards other human beings: "Those natures that are sanguinary towards beasts discover a natural proneness to cruelty" that can be brought to further frightful fruition by way of pedagogical and social cultivations of the "instinct to inhumanity", which most of us seem to possess from childhood.[33] For example, Montaigne abhors the gruesome "spectacles ... at Rome", whether in the guise of ancient gladiatorial combats or modern public executions which he witnessed while visiting to the Papal kingdoms.[34]

It is therefore of the greatest importance, according to Montaigne, to ponder carefully on what sort of examples are prioritised, prepared, and presented "in the education of children" and, in particular, on how we teach them to manage their "anger", e.g., whether or not to instruct them in "the art of boxing ... and that of wrestling", the martial art of "fencing", the then-common practice of military or aristocratic "duels", and/or other potentially misguiding "vices and follies".[35] Advocating pedagogical reform, Montaigne blames all those educators who "present nothing before [their pupils] but rods and ferules, horror and cruelty. Away with this violence!"[36]

Long before Barrozo, Montaigne condemns already all the lawful punishments exhibiting too much severity, such that they can be judged cruel: "even in justice itself, all that exceeds a simple death appears to me pure cruelty; especially in us who ought, having regard to their souls, to dismiss them in a good and calm condition; which cannot be, when we have agitated them by insufferable torments".[37] The ways in which the allegedly 'civilised' European nations "torment and persecute the living" are, in Montaigne's opinion, far more contemptible than Amerindian "savages ... roasting and eating the bodies of the dead".[38]

---

32 Montaigne (1877), book 2, chap. 11, pars. 22–23.
33 Montaigne (1877), book 2, chap. 11, par. 22.
34 Montaigne (1877), book 2, chap. 11, par. 22. Chesterton (1997, part 1, chap. 7, par. 16) reminds us of a perplexing fact related to the Romans' notorious cruelty: in the pagan world that they inhabited and, to a great extent, conquered, there existed several other major civilisations, the institutional cruelty of which was even worse than the Romans', e.g., the Carthaginians, whose archaeological legacy is epitomised by "hundreds of little skeletons", representing "the holy relics of ... Carthage" and its gory worship of "Moloch" by human sacrifices.
35 Montaigne (1877), book 2, chap. 27, pars. 7–10; chap. 31, par. 1.
36 Montaigne (1877), book 1, chap. 25, par. 43.
37 Montaigne (1877), book 2, chap. 11, par. 15.
38 Montaigne (1877), book 2, chap. 11, par. 14.

In the 17th century, John Locke recovers some of Montaigne's concerns, specifically *vis-à-vis* the education of children born in "gentlemen's families", so that their social "inferiors, and the meaner sort of people"—especially domestic "servants"—may be treated humanely by the well-off youth.[39] Outside this specific setting, the lowest social orders can be dealt with far less kindly, as long as this is done for the socially paramount sake of making such people economically productive, whether they are *de jure* African slaves, 'lazy' savages, or 'mere' British paupers.[40] Confident in the notion that no cruelty was thus being advocated, "[i]n his 1697 *Report of the Board of Trade*, … Locke recommends the separation of mothers from infants so that both can earn their daily bread, commended the whipping of children above the age of two who fail to earn their subsistence, advocated the mutilation of the idle able bodied, and the flogging of cripples who refuse to work".[41]

Locke observes as well how some children, even within the well-off families with whom he regularly associated, take visible "delight" in "tormenting and killing" innocent creatures.[42] However, unlike Christian thinkers such as Montaigne and Aquinas—not to mention the older pagan Seneca—the staunchly Protestant Locke is not willing to accept the idea that such a worrying behaviour should be the result of a natural propensity towards evil. A radical notion of this ilk, however sensible it may have seemed to so many educated minds in the course of Western history, would resemble far too closely the principle of the Original Sin endorsed by the Church of Rome, which Locke loathes intensely:

> I cannot persuade myself to be any other than a foreign and introduced disposition, a habit borrowed from custom and conversation. People teach children to strike, and laugh when they hurt, or see harm come to others; and they have the examples of most about them to confirm them in it. All the entertainment of talk and history is of nothing almost but fighting and killing; and the honour and renown that is bestowed on conquerors (who for the most part are but the great butchers of mankind) farther mislead growing youths, who by this means come to think slaughter the laudable business of mankind, and the most heroic of vir-

---

39 Locke (1824), vol. 8, par. 117.
40 Racism and callousness abound in Locke, and traces can be found in Kant (see, e.g., Bernasconi 2003).
41 Andrew (1995), 35. Locke's callousness is all the more shocking insofar as he enjoys great fame *qua* noble father of liberalism. However, we must remind our readers of the enormous semantic flexibility of all political and cultural '-isms' (e.g., socialism, feminism), which are internally diverse and identifiable chiefly on the basis of a single major focus point (e.g., universal economic security, women's empowerment) rather than many stable traits. See also Chapters 1 and 3 of Part 2.
42 Locke (1824), vol. 8, par. 116.

tues. By these steps unnatural cruelty is planted in us; and what humanity abhors, custom reconciles and recommends to us, by laying it in the way to honour.[43]

Locke concludes that it ought to be the supreme aim and paramount duty of all well-meaning pedagogues to teach their pupils to be "compassionate" and "benign".[44] Echoing once again Montaigne, Locke instructs all educators to avoid "[a]ll the entertainment of talk and history" referring to "fighting and killing", as well as "the beating of children", for this physical violence is precisely a grave token of the sort of "cruelty" that ought to be stopped.[45] As Locke states, the use of physical violence is "tyranny over" and "not correction" of the supervised children, for it consists in "put[ting] their bodies in pain, without doing their minds any good".[46]

In 18th-century Scotland, the Ulster-born Francis Hutcheson will also echo Montaigne, this time with regard to "Cruelty" resulting primarily from fear—as the former asserts, it is nothing but a "common attendant" to "Pusillanimity and Cowardice".[47] Hutcheson adds as well that "cruel actions" are the consequence of excessive "malice" causing people to lose sight of their real "interest", fuelled as they are instead by misdirected "Sensations and Passions", e.g., "the Imaginations of the Amorous", "Anger or Hatred", "[s]ome Point of Honour, or Fear of Reproach".[48] "Cruelty" is thus said to emerge from such misguided "Tendenc[ies]" which, should a person's self-control by habitual "Reluctance" and/or mulled "Remorse" go amiss, the only apparently "cruel and inhuman ... Correction of a Child, or ... Execution of a Criminal" can and must keep under control, in view of that which is deemed "publickly useful".[49]

Hutcheson's conclusions are straightforward. All socially manageable circumstances engendering cruelty must be avoided (e.g., bad education, gladiatorial sports, "frequent spectacles of tortures") if and whenever possible, while each person's inherent "natural kindness" must be cultivated.[50] Above all, "useless" cruelty,

---

[43] Locke (1824), vol. 8, par. 116. Awareness of religious history and bigotry can help us understand Locke's work.
[44] Locke (1824), vol. 8, par. 116.
[45] Locke (1824), vol. 8, pars. 112 and 116.
[46] Locke (1824), vol. 8, par. 112.
[47] Hutcheson (2007), 72. Hutcheson (1973) is also pivotal in the philosophical discussion of laughter, particularly as a means of mutual tolerance and solidarity. Though often cited in studies about humour, Hutcheson (1973, 107) focusses on "laughter" proper, speaking also of "humourists", yet not of "humour", and once only.
[48] Hutcheson (2002), 53–54, 95–96, and 113.
[49] Hutcheson (2002), 55 and 148–150.
[50] Hutcheson (2007), 133 and 274.

which displays no concern for the "interests of others", should be prevented and/or curbed most thoroughly:

> That violence alone is just which is necessary, or naturally conducive, to repell the injury, repair the damage, or obtain security for the future. Any cruelty not requisite for these ends is plainly criminal and detestable; as it occasions grievous sufferings to some of our fellows, without any necessity for the interests of others; and is a precedent to like cruelties on other occasions, even towards those who have a just cause in war.[51]

As to the apparent "cruelty towards [animals]" caused by human hunting and/or husbandry, Hutcheson argues that it is actually a necessary instrument for human "lives" not to become "exceedingly toilsome and uneasy".[52] Moreover, hunting and husbandry are also an unrecognised form of mercy, insofar as the animals at issue "perish with less pain" than if they had been left "a more miserable prey to lions, wolves, bears, dogs, or vultures".[53]

Unlike Montaigne, Hutcheson's reliance on sympathetic feelings is consciously and cautiously limited. Reasoning coldly about the animals' condition can thus change the erroneous path of action that we would follow, were we to listen solely to our "natural kindness and sense of pity".[54] As also a team of contemporary animal ethicists have recently recognised, all living creatures are condemned to face and, at times, operate as the very instruments of an awfully "cruel nature", the pitilessness of which must be pondered upon at length and with intellectual candour before passing any trenchant judgement about animal rights and/or our own duties towards them.[55]

Concerning the most extreme expressions of cruelty as a personal vice, i.e., downright sadism, some thinkers have doubted that it can truly exist. If it does, or if it seems to exist, it must be some kind of misunderstood madness. Even the notoriously cynical Hobbes states: "contempt, or little sense of the calamity of others, is that which men call cruelty; proceeding from security of their own

---

51 Hutcheson (2007), 93 and 200.
52 Hutcheson (2007), 133.
53 Hutcheson (2007), 134–135. Having grown up in the countryside, the comedic artist Terry Gilliam (2015, 6) notes that the "youthful farmyard experiences" of predation, hunting, butchering, and death "don't make you callous" necessarily, but rather "give you a respectful understanding of how cruel nature can be".
54 Hutcheson (2007), 133.
55 Piazza, Landy, and Goodwin (2014), 108. These ethicists note also how such natural kindness and sense of pity are generally absent vis-à-vis beings that are harmful to us, irrespective of their sentience and/or intelligence. *Primum vivere.*

fortune. For, that any man should take pleasure in other men's great harms, without other end of his own, I do not conceive it possible."[56] As Hobbes insists:

> Revenge without respect to the example, and profit to come, is a triumph, or glorying in the hurt of another, tending to no end; (for the end is always somewhat to come) and glorying to no end, is vain-glory, and contrary to reason; and to hurt without reason, tendeth to the introduction of warre, which is against the law of nature, and is commonly styled by the name of cruelty.[57]

In the 18th century, the equally notorious yet enormously influential Scottish champion of scepticism and atheism, David Hume, will affirm: "Absolute, unprovoked, disinterested malice has never, perhaps, had place in any human breast."[58] Not even "the cruelty of Nero be allowed entirely voluntary, and not rather the effect of constant fear and resentment".[59]

3.1.2 Cruelty as a Malfunction

> Eu hoje estou cruel, frenético, exigente;
> Nem posso tolerar os livros mais bizarros.
> Incrível! Já fumei três maços de cigarros
> Consecutivamente.
> —Cesário Verde[60]

As partially anticipated by many thinkers, Montaigne included, cruelty should be best understood as the result of faulty pedagogical, cultural, environmental, and/or legal structures, praxes, and traditions. As such, it might go away if we modify intelligently said structures, praxes, and traditions.[61] Although anti-cruelty institutional reforms may have been advocated since at least Seneca's dedication of *De clementia* to emperor Nero, the *philosophes* of the Continental Enlightenment are probably the most representative members of this approach, which essentially

---

56 Hobbes (1985), part 1, chap. 6, par. 28.
57 Hobbes (1985), part 1, chap. 15, par. 76.
58 As cited in Raphael (1991), vol. 2, 72. See Beam (1996) on Hume's staunchly antireligious stance.
59 As cited in Raphael (1991), vol. 2, 72.
60 "*Today I'm cruel, frenetic, exacting / I can't tolerate the most bizarre books / Crazy! I have already smoked three packs of cigarettes / consecutively.*" As cited in Camões et al. (2022), 42.
61 Much disagreement keeps surrounding the issues of which modifications of what and by whom are 'intelligent'.

conceives of cruelty as a malfunction to be fixed or cured, depending on the analogy at play being mechanical or medical.[62]

In France, Montesquieu condemns as "cruel" the use of "torture" and gruesome "punishments", the debtors' indentured labour and attendant supplementary penalties, knee-jerk legislation, the centuries-old institution of "slavery", religious enthusiasm, the States' regular reliance upon warfare to settle their disputes, antisemitic prejudice, child marriages, and armed conquest, e.g., the European colonialism of his day and age.[63] Similarly, Voltaire opposes as "cruel" religious fanaticism and all attendant wars of religion, whilst condemning as equally "cruel" rape, corporal punishments, and ritual mutilations, even when lawful.[64] For Condorcet, "cruel" is the institutional neglect for "the progress of education", which delivers men and women into the hands of "ignorance" and "prejudices", which are "an overly fecund source of injustices and cruelties and crimes".[65]

In Italy, Pietro Verri writes that "[r]eason can show what is unjust, extremely dangerous, and immensely cruel", i.e., the then-revered official use of judicial "torture".[66] Cesare Beccaria, the single most influential penal reformer of all times, rejects torture as "cruel", whilst adding, in yet another echo of Montaigne's wisdom: "man is only cruel in proportion to his interest to be so, to his hatred or to his fear".[67] Therefore, it should be any sensible legislator's aim to "[c]ause men to fear the laws and the laws alone. Salutary is the fear of the law, but

---

[62] See Delon (1997) for an extensive overview of the Enlightenment.
[63] Montesquieu (2001), 77, 101, 220–221, 261–265, 270–271, 307, 337, 468, 518, 606, 617, and 672.
[64] Voltaire (1912) and (1918).
[65] Condorcet (1998), epoch 10, pars. 270 and 294. The translation is ours. The negative connotation of 'prejudice', which was originally a legal concept concerning precedent, took root in Descartes' day. A minority of intellectuals have defended a positive connotation of 'prejudice' *qua* inevitable and/or important received opinion on nature, society, morals, and/or religion making science, peaceful coexistence, good behaviour, and/or spiritual growth possible: Voltaire, Swift, Fontenelle, Duclos, Burke, Hazlitt, and Gadamer (see Hoffmann and Baruchello, 2020). In an unintentionally ironic manner, contemporary economics and business practice keep alive the notion of 'good prejudice' (i.e., 'pre-judgment') insofar as so-called "brands" and "signposts" are regarded as commercial boons, given how consumers 'trust' (i.e., spend their money on) already-seen and/or heard logos (e.g., Nike's or Adidas'), institutions' names (e.g., "Oxford" or "Harvard University"), corporate denominations, *et similia*, without really ever appraising (i.e., 'judging') the quality of their 'products', their underlying methods for production and dissemination, and/or comparing them with those provided by less famous 'competitors'. Thus, we find yet another sign of the "pseudorational" spirit of capitalism satirised by Castoriadis (2005, 146) and tackled in Chapter 1 of Part 2.
[66] Verri (1994), 18. The translation is ours.
[67] Beccaria (1880), 140–141. On Beccaria's influence, see, e.g., Todaro and Miller (2014), vol. 1, A–K, 43–45.

fatal and fertile in crime is the fear of one man of another. Men as slaves are more sensual, more immoral, more cruel than free men."[68]

In Germany, Kant disparages as "most cruel" [*allergrausamsten*] the very profitable and very common institution of "slavery", especially as exemplified by the Dutch "Sugar Islands".[69] Merely "cruel" [*grausam*], instead, are "duels" being fought for the allegedly virtuous sake of "military honour", which, like "Maternal Infanticide", causes people to be guilty of "Homicide" as distinct from "Murder".[70] As to the controversial Swiss genius of that era, Jean-Jacques Rousseau, his posthumous *Confessions* list as "cruel" and/or "cruelties" all kinds of painfully arresting and/or disquieting phenomena—in all sorts of literal, metaphorical, or metonymical ways. The list includes reminiscences, anguishes, misgivings, separations, lost loves, sicknesses, people's hands, defeats, blunders, invectives, defamations, demises, dreams, malfeasances, and even mere idleness.[71]

In the early 19th century, the Italian poet and philosopher, Giacomo Leopardi, continues the tradition and the sworn mission of the European Enlightenment, this time by dubbing "cruelty" [*crudeltà*] the countless musings and venerable teachings of philosophers and clerics concerning our souls and the afterlife. Whether "healthy or sick", these musings and teachings are, in his view, "childish illusions", born out of "cowardice" in the face of "the absence of any hope, … the desert of life, … men's infelicity[,] … and destiny's cruelty".[72] Life is a valley of tears, and this valley is the desolate and only place that we will ever inhabit.

Mother Nature, whom Leopardi sketches allegorically as a "beautiful and terrible" dark-haired giantess, has no concern whatsoever for "human happiness or unhappiness", and "were the whole species [of humans] to go extinct", she "would not notice it", since "this universe is a perpetual cycle of production and

---

[68] Beccaria (1880), 243.
[69] Kant (1977), 216. The translation is ours.
[70] Kant (1887), part 2, sec. 1, chap. 49, art. E, par. 7. Defending one's personal honour was, in Kant's view, a mitigating factor, for it was equivalent to preserving one's own dignity, about which he had rather clear and adamant views. Albeit somewhat hidden behind a wall of abstract rationalism, if not even outright formalism, Kant's day-to-day views were largely (i.e., often) consistent with the mores and the morals of his day's Protestant Prussia. As such, they were inclusive of open "racism" directed at Blacks, Jews and the Romani (Hund 2011, 69), the acceptance of capital punishment as a means of just retribution (see, e.g., Ataner 2006), and categorically strait-laced sexual ethics (see, e.g., Kerstein 2008 and Denis 1999). More on his prudishness ensues in Chapter 3 of Part 2.
[71] Rousseau (1889). Superficially, Keats' Romantic heroine Isabella, whom he adapted from Boccaccio's medieval *Decameron*, would seem to deem cruel the loss of so prosaic an object as a pot of basil (Peksen Yakar and Demirtepe Saygili 2018). (The truth being that she hid in it the severed head of her dead lover.)
[72] Leopardi (n.d.a. [1835]), 226–227. The translation is ours.

destruction", the "conservation" of which requires "nothing to be free from suffering".[73] As also held by the ascetic Russian existentialist philosopher, Lev Shestov: "No despot, not the greatest villain on earth, has ever wielded power with the cruelty and heartlessness of nature. The least violation of her laws—and the severest punishment follows. Disease, deformity, madness, death—what has not our common mother contrived to keep us in subjection?"[74]

Leopardi claims that the main path towards any significant consolation is for "the strong man", who is personified in his works by the mythical Tristan, "to see, with stoical gratification, all of destiny's cruel and hidden cloaks being stripped off".[75] Another path, which Leopardi mentions only *en passant* in his personal notebooks, consists in acknowledging the erasure of all religious and metaphysical fantasies, and *then* devoting oneself to the worthiest endeavours known to our frail and sorry race: the sciences, the arts, and "laughter".[76] As Leopardi quips: "All is foolish in this world but fooling around. All is worth laughing about but laughing about everything. All is vanity but beautiful illusions and pleasing frivolities."[77] Likewise, in the 20th century, the Romanian pessimist and existentialist thinker, Emil Cioran, remarks: "We are all mistaken, except for the humourists. They alone have perceived how to amuse oneself with the inanity of all that is serious and, equally, of all that is frivolous."[78]

As regards the most famous pessimist of the West's philosophical canon, Schopenhauer, he never pursued any special study of "cruelty" as such.[79] Nevertheless, he does frequently apply its adjectival formulation to a vast and sometimes puzzling assortment of experiences and events, such as: "mock[ing]" the mediocrity of German philosophy; the "customs of priests of different religions"; "wild-beast fights"; "the refusal to help another in great need, the quiet contemplation of the death of another from starvation while we ourselves have more than

---

73 Leopardi (n.d.a. [1835]), 86–88. Two hundred years later, the Italian philosopher Galimberti (as interviewed in Alba and Galimberti 2021, par. 18) speaks of nature's "innocent cruelty" and states: "[w]e must stop believing that Nature is good".
74 Shestov (1920), part 2, par. 14.
75 Leopardi (n.d.a. [1835]), 227.
76 Leopardi (n.d.a. [1898]), 785. See also Sigurðsson (2010).
77 Leopardi (n.d.a. [1898]), 2528. A lesser-known, later 19th-century pessimist, Julius Bahnsen, concurs (Beiser 2018). If correct, writing this volume and engaging in countless other common activities to which value is ascribed (e.g., starting a family, raising children, pursuing a career, seeking truth, etc.), are a misguided waste of our time.
78 As cited in Demont (2017), par. 32. It is not known whether Cioran influenced another great 20th-century Romanian pessimist, i.e., Nicholas Georgescu-Roegen (*né* Georgescu), the father of bioeconomics.
79 Nominally, "pain" and "suffering" are more central to Schopenhauer's (1909) system of thought.

enough"; violent acts of "revenge" as distinguished from judicially approved acts of "punishment"; the "disinterested ... delight in the suffering of others"; "bloodthirstiness", aka "pure cruelty"; the abuse of "brutes" and "beasts of burden and dogs ... in the chase" or in their otherwise morally acceptable uses for human well-being; and scientific "vivisection".[80]

In 19th-century Ireland, the historian and Unionist politician, William Edward Hartpole Lecky, explains how human beings, were they left to nature, would not always be sufficiently "repelled by cruelty".[81] Hence, as he concludes, humane institutions and enlightened "art and literature" must be fostered in the name of civilisation.[82] Instead of doing like the ancient Romans, whose "gladiatorial games" turned "the carnage of men [into] their habitual amusement", Lecky contends that it would be wiser to promote a better "education" of the masses, capable of softening their hearts, refining their customs and institutions, and making their minds capable of tolerating ways of life that are very different from their own, rather than perceiving them immediately, instinctively perhaps, as alien, and therefore condemning them as promptly as vile, immoral, unnatural, perverse, irreligious or obscene.[83]

"To an uneducated man", as Lecky elucidates, "all classes, nations, modes of thought and existence foreign to his own are unrealised, while every increase in knowledge brings with it an increase of insight, and therefore sympathy".[84] Such an increase in sympathy is therefore the key to any moral, legal, social, political and cultural progress of lasting significance:

> Every book he reads, every intellectual exercise in which he engages, accustoms him to rise above the objects immediately present to his senses, to extend his realisations into new spheres, and reproduce in his imagination the thoughts, feelings, and characters of others, with a vividness inconceivable to the savage [whose lack of ...] sensitive humanity [stops them from ... recoiling] from cruelty.[85]

Were we to apply contemporary categories of understanding, Lecky's approach reminds us of the fact that knowledge spurs the imagination; the imagination spurs sympathy; sympathy spurs compassion; compassion spurs tolerance; toler-

---

80 Schopenhauer (1909), vol. 1, 15, 68, 427, 434, 446, 453, 465, 467, and 477, note 81 (see also *H&C1* and *H&C2*). The famed English champion of children's and animals' protection against the terrible scourge of cruelty, Stephen Coleridge (1918, title), dubs the last item "scientific cruelty".
81 Lecky (1890), vol. 1, 83.
82 Lecky (1890), vol. 1, 138, note 143; and 231.
83 Lecky (1890), vol. 1, 274.
84 Lecky (1890), vol. 1, 139.
85 Lecky (1890), vol. 1, 139.

ance spurs social cohesion; and social cohesion, in turn, averts cruelty. According to Lecky, moreover, there is "an important distinction to draw... Under the name of cruelty are comprised two kinds of vice, altogether different in their causes and in most of their consequences."[86]
(1) On the one hand, there is cruelty that "springs from callousness and brutality";
(2) on the other hand, there is "the cruelty of vindictiveness".[87]

Lecky's distinction is, in all likelihood, derived from Jean Bodin's 16th-century most celebrated political treatise, known in English as *The Six Books of the Commonwealth*, whereby differences in predominant "humour" between "northern" and "southern" peoples—and, in parallel, "western" and "eastern" too—lead the former peoples to behave like "irrational animals", and the latter like "fox[es] who savour [their] revenge".[88]

As Lecky clarifies his distinction, the former type of human cruelty "belongs chiefly to hard, dull, and somewhat lethargic characters" and "appears most frequently in strong and conquering nations and in temperate climates".[89] This type of cruelty "is due in very great degree to [the] defective [faculty of] realisation".[90] The "strong and conquering nations" are, for their greatest part, made up of "insensitive" people, who are then very well-suited for wars and colonial expansion.[91] The latter type of human cruelty, instead, is characterised by "delight" and is "usually displayed in oppressed and suffering communities, in passionate natures, and in hot climates".[92] "Great vindictiveness", as Lecky observes, "is often united with great tenderness, and great callousness with great magnanimity".[93] Inversely, "a vindictive nature is rarely magnanimous, and a brutal nature is more rarely tender".[94]

Lecky puts forward that both types of cruelty can be "diminished with advancing civilization", which affects them "by different forms and in different degrees".[95] As Lecky states: "callous cruelty is diminished before the sensitiveness

---

[86] Lecky (1890), vol. 1, 139.
[87] Lecky (1890), vol. 1, 139.
[88] Bodin (1955), book V, chap. 1. Lecky cites Bodin, yet not in clear connection with the two types of cruelty.
[89] Lecky (1890), vol. 1, 139. It is implied that there can be deviations from the geographic norm.
[90] Lecky (1890), vol. 1, 139.
[91] Lecky (1890), vol. 1, 139.
[92] Lecky (1890), vol. 1, 139.
[93] Lecky (1890), vol. 1, 139.
[94] Lecky (1890), vol. 1, 139.
[95] Lecky (1890), vol. 1, 139.

of a cultivated imagination", whereas "vindictive cruelty is diminished by the substitution of a penal system for private revenge".[96] Progress, then, can be attained.

Lecky was a self-styled "liberal" thinker and an active politician in the British Empire whose example has been followed by many other self-declared "liberal" enemies of "cruelty" proper, notwithstanding the ambiguities of both terms.[97] Thus, in the 20th century, the Canadian-born economist, diplomat, civil servant, and humourist, John 'Ken' Galbraith, penned, pursued, and promoted vast political projects for educational and socio-economic reform that could secure, in his intentions, "a good standard of living equitably distributed ... that eliminates the terrible cruelty of poverty".[98]

No tougher indictment would be possible for such self-styled "liberals" than calling something a "cruelty". As the liberal American philosopher, Hilary Putnam, remarks in a 1992 essay, any "attempt of non-cognitivists to split words like 'cruel' into a 'descriptive meaning component' and a 'prescriptive meaning component' founders on the impossibility of saying what the 'descriptive meaning' is without using the word 'cruel' itself, or a synonym".[99] And as the British philosopher Eve Garrard writes in our century: "cruelty ... is always a *wrong*-making feature of an action".[100]

Judith Shklar and Richard Rorty, the proud 20th-century promoters of the so-called "liberalism of fear", should then be added to the US-based lot to which Galbraith and Putnam belong.[101] Crucially, Shklar offers as well two crisp definitions of "cruelty":

(1) "Cruelty is ... the wilful inflicting of physical pain on a weaker being in order to cause anguish and fear ... horror ... [it] repels instantly because it is 'ugly' ... [and] disfigures human character."[102]

---

96 Lecky (1890), vol. 1, 139–140.
97 As noted here in Chapter 1, the European and the American interpretations of "liberal" are not identical. Despite sharing much ground (e.g., on the desirability of private property, entrepreneurship and individualism), the former is much more conservative and anti-State. For a historical account of this divergence, see Rosenblatt (2018).
98 Pal and Galbraith (2000), par. 25. See also Gardiner *et al.* (2023), indicating that poverty reduces people's abilities to develop, engage in, and/or appreciate humour. Could there be anything crueller?
99 Putnam (1992), chap. 5, par. 17. See also Stade (2016, 8) on conflict- and ethnographic studies, who states: "Unsatisfying as it may be, we, as researchers of suffering and perpetration, are in all likelihood condemned to enduring the absurdity of, at the same time, trying to make sense of cruelty and being abhorred by it."
100 Garrard (2006), 124; emphasis removed and added.
101 Shklar (1989), title *et passim.*
102 Shklar (1984), 8–9.

(2) "Cruelty is the deliberate infliction of physical, and secondarily emotional, pain upon a weaker person or group by stronger ones in order to achieve some end, tangible or intangible, of the latter."[103]

In Shklar's view, modern liberalism is a broad institutional scheme aimed at reducing cruelty in the public sphere: "the first right is to be protected against the fear of cruelty. People have rights as a shield against this greatest of human vices. This is the evil, the threat to be avoided at all costs. Justice itself is only a web of legal arrangements required to keep cruelty in check."[104]

Inspired by Shklar's work, Rorty states incisively that "liberals ... think that cruelty is the worst thing we do".[105] Echoing earlier suggestions by Montaigne, Locke, and Lecky, Rorty argues as well that liberal societies, if they want to reduce cruelty in the public sphere, should cultivate the knowledge of the greatest humanising "poets" of our civilisation, i.e., geniuses such as Tolstoy, Kundera, Nabokov, or Orwell, whose most distinctive characteristic was, according to Rorty, "the fear of being, or having been, cruel ... not having noticed the suffering of someone with whom one had been in contact".[106]

Literary-poetic imagination backs love and toleration, for the humanities help us to understand the great many ways to be human.[107] Whereas direct experience can open our hearts and minds to just a few such ways, historical accounts, philosophical speculations, and, above all, artistic fictions can let us envision, entertain, and, hopefully, empathise with the cosmic kaleidoscope of existences and experiences that the members of our imaginative species had, might have, or can have.[108]

Another US-based voice can be added to this list of relatively recent liberals, i.e., the noted animal ethicist Tom Regan's, who drafts a carefully designed taxonomy of cruelty:

---

103 Shklar (1989), 29.
104 Shklar (1984), 237.
105 Rorty (1989), xv and 74.
106 Rorty (1989), 157. Penelas (2019, 325) adds Marx too, who "redescribes certain practices in terms of cruelty".
107 We write "understand" [*verstehen*], i.e., to put oneself into someone else's shoes, not "explain" [*erklären*], i.e., to reduce to general principle or abstract law (Nardin 2001, 102–110). See also Jung (1989) and Nussbaum (2010).
108 Rorty (1989) is most aware of the fact that some life-paths may also be life-destructive. While it may be useful and enlightening to know of them, he did not recommend playing them out in concrete reality. Besides, in his estimate, concrete reality needs no help in this direction: "I don't think there's any nation that's really far from totalitarianism. Wherever you go, whenever things go bad, there's always a fascist party ready to seize power" (Baruchello and Rorty 1998, 480).

> People can rightly be judged cruel either for what they do or for what they fail to do, and either for what they feel or for what they fail to feel. The central case of cruelty appears to be the case where, in Locke's apt phrase, one takes "a seeming kind of Pleasure" in causing another to suffer. Sadistic torturers provide perhaps the clearest example of cruelty in this sense: they are cruel not just because they cause suffering (so do dentists and doctors, for example) but because they enjoy doing so. Let us term this sadistic cruelty... Not all cruel people are cruel in this sense. Some cruel people do not feel pleasure in making others suffer. Indeed they seem not to feel anything. Their cruelty is manifested by a lack of what is judged appropriate feeling, as pity or mercy, for the plight of the individual whose suffering they cause, rather than pleasure in causing it... The sense of cruelty that involves indifference to, rather than enjoyment of, suffering caused to others we shall call brutal cruelty... Cruelty admits of at least four possible classifications: (1) active sadistic cruelty; (2) passive sadistic cruelty; (3) active brutal cruelty; (4) passive brutal cruelty.[109]

Whichever actual "cruelty" we may encounter in our life and whether its types are clearly distinguishable or ambiguously enmeshed, Regan wants us to try to oppose it.[110] In particular, Regan is most critical of (3) and (4), which he argues to be distinctive of the treatment of reared animals in contemporary agro-industrial societies.[111] Legal reform, the strict monitoring of businesses, vast educational plans, and eventually, the ancient practice of vegetarianism can make much cruelty disappear, according to Regan.[112]

3.1.3 Cruelty as a Paradox

> Everyone has felt (at least in fantasy) the erotic glamour of physical cruelty and an erotic lure in things that are vile and repulsive.
> —Susan Sontag[113]

---

[109] Regan (1983), 197–198.
[110] Kekes (1996), 843, and (1997), 186, produce a neat definition, synthesising much of Regan's wisdom: "cruelty is the disposition of human agents to take delight in or be indifferent to the serious and unjustified suffering their actions cause to victims". The crux here being the determination of cruelty's seriousness and lack of justification; plus, at a deeper level, the claim itself of "cruelty". Who decides it? Is it the self-declared victim, or a third party? Perpetrators rarely claim that they are "cruel", as noted in Baruchello and Hamblet (2004, 33–38 and 56).
[111] Regan (1983), 197–198. Chesterton (1922, 297–308) argues that all liberal campaigns for humane conduct can be easily demolished by questioning their contingent secular theoretical foundation, i.e., *why* ought we to be humane?
[112] See especially Regan (1975) on vegetarianism.
[113] As cited in Maes and Levinson (2012), 218. Ironically, Jarvie (2013, 134) lambasted the wide scholarly acceptance of such bold statements, irrespective of the authoritative 'ring' of the utterer: "This rises to the level of bullshit. The a priori method licenses such pontification; any kind of external check would be empiricist (boo!)."

As Shklar had to admit, cruelty has not disappeared, despite the application of many of the remedies advocated for several centuries by variously self-declared "liberals" and by other humanitarians, at least in the Western nations.[114] Cruelty, as Shklar holds, is "baffling".[115] Also, as Rorty acknowledges, while liberal institutions may reduce cruelty in the public sphere, they may not be able to attain the same result in the private one. As he elucidates, "private perfection" and/or aesthetic "self-creation" are not one and the same thing as enlightened "justice" and "human solidarity".[116] In other words, "there is no synthesis of ecstasy and kindness", even if some individuals may laudably try to achieve it.[117]

As already noted by Chesterton, gross "positive cruelty" manifesting itself "in acts" can be thwarted by sensible public institutions, but smaller forms of "negative cruelty" manifesting themselves "in words" may still go on unabated in ordinary, private, interpersonal contexts.[118] The life-disabling effects of such negative cruelties are not negligible. Quite the opposite, they can be devastating. Think, for instance, of the mental exhaustion and social exclusion suffered by the victims of malicious gossip, relentless mocking, and/or workplace bullying that are perpetrated, sometimes for many years, by horrible bosses, envious colleagues, narrow-minded neighbours, small-town chatterboxes, misguided do-gooders, and/or particularly unsavoury characters veering towards the sociopathic end of the behavioural spectrum.[119]

The private sphere, which all streaks of liberalism avowedly protect and aim at widening, is the place where the latter kind of cruelty can prosper the most.[120] Intimate and/or domestic relations may be particularly apt settings, in this regard, as prosaically exemplified by cruelties among siblings, close relatives, long-time partners, lifelong friends, and/or married couples. Intimacy, by lowering the extant emotional barriers and increasing the involved persons' knowledge of one another, can open the floodgates to some of the most exquisite, excruciating, and extended cruelties that any Mr. and Mrs. Doe may be capable of in their lives.

---

114 Effective Western humanitarianism may be as old as Stoicism' cosmopolitan worldview or the recognition of slaves' legal personhood in Roman law, under the influence of Stoic philosophy (see Berger 1953 and Ishay 2004).
115 Shklar (1984), 3.
116 Rorty (1989), xiv.
117 Rorty (1989), 160.
118 Chesterton (1919a), chap. 15, par. 12.
119 Psychopathy may explain some such incidents, but not all of them. Probably not even the vast majority.
120 A committed US conservative, Kekes (1996 and 1997) insists on this inherent contradiction of liberalism. See also *H&C1*.

Such prosaic cruelties are then dressed as stern instruction, benevolent advice, obnoxious mansplaining, oblique moralism, interminable nagging, racing on high horses, repeated lying, scornful silent expressions of total disbelief, and/or seemingly 'innocent' and 'friendly' humorous remarks.[121] As the Dutch thinker, Baruch de Spinoza, had already stated in the 17th century, "[c]ruelty, or [s]everity" can be "a [d]esire by which someone is roused to do evil to one whom we love or pity".[122] Conceivably, such cruelty or severity is precisely that which Spinoza's own family, together with the rest of Amsterdam's Jewish community, had unleashed onto him. Spinoza was, in fact, expelled from their midst because of his suspicious familiarity with many Dutch Christians—to say nothing of his publicly professed heretical views about the authenticity of the Torah, the validity of Talmudic hermeneutics, and the onto-logical plausibility of a transcendent personal God to whom Spinoza's relatives were devoted, just like Jews at large have been for countless generations.[123]

Humour, in the private sphere, can even become the ideal accomplice for such an anticathectic "negative cruelty".[124] As Leacock discusses:

> The original devil of malice was not so easily exorcized. It still survives. The development of humor was not always and exclusively of a refining character. One is tempted to think that perhaps the original source parted into two streams. In one direction flowed, clear and undefiled, the humor of human kindliness. In the other, the polluted waters of mockery and sarcasm, the "humor" that turned to the cruel sports of rough ages, the infliction of pain as a perverted source of pleasure, and even the rough horseplay, the practical jokes and the impish malice of the schoolboy. Here belongs 'sarcasm'—that scrapes the flesh of human feeling with a hoe—the sardonic laugh (by derivation a sort of rictus of the mouth from a poison weed), the sneer of the scoffer, and the snarl of the literary critic as opposed to the kindly tolerance of the humorist. Not even death, if we may believe the spiritualists, terminates the evil career of the practical joker. He survives as the thing called a "poltergeist" in Ger-

---

121 We assume our married and otherwise partnered readers to be familiar with these prosaic phenomena which countless Western works of fiction have depicted—tragically of course, but also comically (see, e.g., the 1975–1985 US sitcom *The Jeffersons*, or the 1988–2007 Italian one *Casa Vianello*).
122 Spinoza (1985), vol. 1, 540.
123 Uttered in his youth, Spinoza (1985) confirms his heretical arguments in favour of an intellectually sophisticated pantheism in his mature years too. Not only did Spinoza suffer excommunication, but he was also targeted for murder by a fellow Jew who, however, failed in his attempt. A thorough account of Spinoza's *horribile dictu* leading to his excommunication can be found in Nadler (2002).
124 "Anticathexis" is psychology's term for the phenomenon captured by Catullus' most famous poem: *odi et amo*.

man—or a something or other in English—a malicious noisy spirit, haunting for haunting's sake, and unfortunately beyond the grasp of the law."[125]

Adding scorn to injury, it was Rorty's realisation that the same well-meaning "liberal" progressives like himself, who aim at overhauling the world's cruel institutions and cultures, can do so chiefly, if not solely, by means of "the power of redescription" which will have to be deployed even if "most people do not want to be redescribed".[126] Quite the reverse:

> [Most people] want to be taken on their own terms – taken seriously just as they are as they talk. The ironist tells them that the language they speak is up for grabs by her and her kind. There is something potentially very cruel about this claim. For the best way to cause people long-lasting pain is to humiliate them by making the things that seemed most important to them look futile, obsolete, and powerless.[127]

Writing about Shklar and Rorty, a noted 20th-century US conservative ethicist and Montaigne scholar, John Kekes, comments: "benevolence can lead to great cruelty ... routinely justified by the belief that they are necessary for the prevention of even greater cruelties".[128] Besides, as Kekes observes, by seeking to give more liberty to private agents, liberalism increases rather than decreases the actual opportunity for cruelty in human societies.[129]

Ironically, the liberals' very weapon of "redescription", as advocated and utilised by Rorty, if "sufficiently nimble, ... transforms ... [c]ruelty ... [into] the reluctant administration of deserved punishment, hatred ... into righteous indignation ... envy ... [into] opposition to elitism, jealousy ... into principled objections to one's rival, and resentment... [into] skepticism about the dubious ventures of some objectionable people".[130] As Bertrand Russell notes on the "vindictive feeling" associated with phenomenon of "moral indignation": it "is merely a form of cruelty".[131] And as the French poet Charles Baudelaire had already observed: "Dear brothers,

---

125 Leacock (1938), chap. 1, sec. 5, par. 20.
126 Rorty (1989), 89. Redescription may occur publicly as well as "in the private forum" (Penelas 2019, 320).
127 Rorty (1989), 89.
128 Kekes (1996), 841–842. At the same time, Kekes (1997, 185) insists that "surgeons" and "dentists" are not liable of "cruelty", hence neglecting the historically common charges levied against them (see, e.g., Davis 2020).
129 Kekes (1996), 836.
130 Kekes (1990), 82.
131 Russell (2009), 358.

when you will hear someone boast the progress of the Enlightenment, do never forget that the finest trick by the devil is to persuade you that he does not exist."[132]

In the history of liberalism, great cruelty for the sake of preventing greater cruelty was identified by none less than Beccaria, who, in *Dei delitti e delle pene* [Of Crimes and Punishments], states as follows about the common yet terrible crime of "theft":

> This is usually the crime of wretchedness and desolation, the crime of that unfortunate part of men to whom {the appalling, and perhaps unnecessary right to} property has allowed nothing but a basic existence, {and given that fines only increase the number of criminals above the original number of crimes, and take bread from the innocent in order to take it from the rogues} the most appropriate punishment will be the only kind of slavery that can be termed just, namely the provisional enslavement of the labour and person of the criminal to society, so that he may atone his unfair tyranny *vis-à-vis* the social contract by way of a period of total personal subjugation.[133]

According to Beccaria, the lawful "punishments" ordinarily imposed by the judiciary are inherently "atrocious" and their "public and solemn cruelty" can only be reduced, not eliminated, by making them "useful ... necessary ... fair", and consistent with "the goal of the laws".[134] This is true even of the abolition of capital punishment, i.e., "the right [of people ...] to slaughter their kin".[135] Life-long imprisonment is, according to Beccaria, a better alternative, but not because of its clemency or mercifulness, given that "permanent penal bondage is as grievous as death, and consequently as cruel".[136]

Life-long imprisonment may actually be a worse chastisement for the suffering criminal: if anyone "said that perpetual bondage is as painful as death, and therefore equally cruel, I shall reply that the sum of all the unhappy moments of bondage may be even more so".[137] However, and crucially, life-long imprisonment is capable of greater deterrence than the death penalty.[138] *That* is why it should be utilised.

---

[132] Baudelaire (1988), poem 29.
[133] Beccaria (1994), 42. The significance of this quote required us to go back to the original Italian edition, in which passages expunged in later editions are signalled between brackets. Perhaps Beccaria was trying to diminish the controversial conclusions to which too dispassionate and rational an aetiology of theft had led him at first. We do not know for sure.
[134] Beccaria (1994), 22 and 30.
[135] Beccaria (1994), 47.
[136] Beccaria (1994), 49.
[137] Beccaria (1994), 49.
[138] Beccaria (1994), 49.

Beccaria's aetiology of "theft" reveals also how a commonplace and crucial liberal legal, political, economic, and socio-cultural institution lies behind theft itself: "private property".[139] By allowing some people to own privately a conspicuous part of society's collectively generated wealth, countless others are condemned to endure "nothing but a basic existence".[140] It is among the latter masses of have-nots that those who are chiefly responsible for "theft" arise.[141]

Yet, rather than touching the paramount institution of private property, which is dearest to Western liberals as well as to Western conservatives, Beccaria concludes that penal cruelty should be maintained insofar as it can serve the interests of both the non-thieving individuals (e.g., "the happiness of this mortal life") and, above all, society *qua* aggregate thereof (i.e., "the greatest happiness for the greatest number").[142]

Beccaria's logically perplexing point will be corroborated some years later by another noted 18th-century liberal thinker, Adam Smith of Kirkcaldy, who writes: "Civil government, so far as it is instituted for the security of property, is in reality instituted for the defence of the rich against the poor, or of those who have some property against those who have none at all."[143] Consistently with this assessment, any liberal society's general opposition to "cruelty" proper must be moderate and considerate, according to Smith, given that the free-trade economic order which best provides for "the wealth of nations" is structured in such a way that "[t]he order of proprietors may, perhaps, gain more by the prosperity of the society, than that of labourers: but there is no order that suffers so cruelly ... as the race of labourers" whenever a business cycle enters a recessive phase.[144]

Sometimes, the cruel suffering of some individuals, families, and/or communities must be accepted for the sake of greater collective prosperity, which is never universal.[145] For instance, as regards the violent colonisation and forced modernisation of the Americas, Smith argues that, "in spite of the cruel destruction of the natives", the lands that the indigenous once inhabited have been successfully transformed into pastures for profitable herds of "European cattle" and the home for a "more populous" breed of considerably more productive labourers: "we must

---

139 Beccaria (1994), 42.
140 Beccaria (1994), 42.
141 Beccaria (1994), 42.
142 Beccaria (1994), 19.
143 Smith (1904), book 5, chap. 1, part 3, par. 12.
144 Smith (1904), title page and book 1, chap. 11, par. 263. Smith (1790, part 2, sec. 2, chap. 3, par. 21) claims, *à la* Seneca, that penal moderation must be moderate too, for "mercy to the guilty is cruelty to the innocent".
145 Classical political economists have long taught that there is no such thing as a free lunch.

acknowledge, I apprehend, that the Spanish creoles are in many respects superior to the ancient Indians".[146] In *Liberalism*, the 20th-century political thinker and Austrian economist, Ludwig von Mises, essentially rehashes Smith's reasoning: although recent European colonialism was marked by despicable "cruelty", it made it possible for "Africa and large parts of Asia" to join and, eventually, benefit from "the gradual development of the world economy".[147]

The baffling persistence of cruelty is tackled in unsurpassed detail by the liberal US ethicist and Montaigne scholar, Philip Paul Hallie, in the second half of the 20th century. To this day, no other Western thinker has been so prolific on this particular topic, which he focussed upon after his traumatic personal experiences as a soldier fighting in World War II.[148] Hallie chose this specific term and topic because he believed "cruelty" to convey the full force of the "empirical evil" that he had witnessed in person, i.e., the *horribile visu* that alternative medical, legal, academic, and/or institutional notions (e.g., 'psychopathy', 'malice', 'evil', 'crime') would abate, abstract away, or avoid entirely.[149]

In his rich philosophical oeuvre, Hallie offers at least three definitions of "cruelty":
(1) "the infliction of ruin, whatever the motives";[150]
(2) "the activity of hurting sentient beings";[151] and
(3) "the slow crushing and grinding of a human being by other human beings".[152]

---

[146] Smith (1904), book 4, chap. 7, part 2, par. 7. The noticeable centrality of the theme of Divine Providence in Smith (1790) might provide an explanation for Smith's (1904) *prima-facie* unchristian callousness which, apart from the obvious time-lag at play in his case, is sinisterly akin to the unashamed profit-centred attitude of the pirate, the profiteer, or the mafioso, all of whom can spot lucrative opportunity and thereby provide economically 'rational' justifications for their actions under otherwise unbearably inhumane circumstances, such as civil wars, human trafficking, forced migration, and/or the destruction of Earth's life support systems (see McMurtry 2011).

[147] Von Mises (1978), 126–128, where he also establishes a spurious rift between the 'bad' colonial "cruelties" and the 'good' market-based "development", as though the two trends were neatly separable from each other. See also Chapter 1 of Part 2.

[148] See, in particular, Hallie (2001).

[149] Hallie (1988), 119. *This is also the main reason behind why and how we use "cruelty" in our own volumes.*

[150] Hallie (1969), 14. Additional ones could be extrapolated from Hallie (1969), but this one is the first, most explicit, and overarching definition.

[151] Hallie (1992), 229.

[152] Hallie (1985b), 2. As discussed in *H&C1*, Hallie's focus is set primarily upon human suffering.

On the basis of these definitions, Hallie produces a noteworthy classification of "cruelty" proper.[153] His taxonomy can be reconstructed as follows:

(1) "[C]ruelty upon humans" subdivides into:
(1a) "fatal cruelties", which are caused by nature (or fate, the gods, etc.), and
(1b) "human ... cruelties", which are caused by people in
(1bi) "violent" ways (e.g., corporal punishments) or
(1bii) via "indifference or distraction" (e.g., child marriages).[154]
(2) "Human ... cruelties" can be:
(2a) "explicit", aka "direct" (i.e., caused by a manifest "intention to hurt"), or
(2b) "implicit", aka "indirect", hence capable of transforming from
(2bi) "episodic" acts of "personal" callousness into
(2bii) "institutionalized cruelty", by way of protracted practice and collective habituation.[155] As such, this type of cruelty may even go unnoticed *qua* "cruelty" in the very eyes and minds of both its victims and its perpetrators, hence looking "covert ... peaceful ... commonsensical".[156]
(3) "Human ... cruelties" can be further subdivided into:
(3a) "sadistic" (i.e., "violent" and "self-gratifying") and
(3b) "practical", i.e., the many and ever-varied forms of instrumental cruelty (e.g., violent police repression of peaceful demonstrations, factory discipline, the so-called "collateral damage" of "peacekeeping" aerial bombings,

---

[153] Unlike the other liberal thinkers cited in this chapter, Hallie seemed more concerned with capturing each and every case of cruelty, rather than producing sharp definitions that were not at odds with today's common sense.

[154] Hallie (1969), 5–6 and 13–14. In depth psychology, Viktor Frankl (1984, 113) writes of "fate" being "so cruel". On her part, Karen Horney (2000, 319) speaks of the "cruel world" inhabited by "neurotic[s]" obsessing about their being "pure and fine". More on such ascetic and Puritanical neuroses follows in Chapters 1 and 3 of Part 2.

[155] Hallie (1969), 13–14, 29–31, 63, and 163–166. Time is of the essence. As Galbraith (1980, 56–57) observes: "Poverty is cruel. A continuing struggle to escape that is continuously frustrated is more cruel. It is more civilized, more intelligent, as well as more plausible, that people, out of the experience of centuries, should reconcile themselves to what has for so long been the inevitable" and therefore fall into "the grip of the poverty equilibrium".

[156] Hallie (1985a), 11. Von Mises (1978, 21) recalls the "astonishing" case of "slaves ... declar[ing] themselves in opposition" to their own "emancipation". Conditioning runs deep. As to domestic servants, Galbraith (1973, 31) notes: "Nothing reflected more admirably on a person than diligent and enduring service to another. The phrase 'old family retainer' suggested merit only slightly below that of 'wise and loving parent'. The phrase 'good and faithful servant' had recognizable scriptural benediction. In England a large and comparatively deft literature associated humor, conversational aptitude, social perception and great caste pride with a servant class."

post-crisis austerity policies afflicting people who had nothing to do with causing and/or worsening the 2008 financial crisis, etc.)[157]

Hallie's classification is further enriched by a parallel nomenclature of cases of cruelty *qua* "paradox" (which, as seen, is also a term frequently associated with "humour" proper).[158]

(1) There can be cruelty resulting from no patent "intention to hurt"; as Hallie avers, "substantial maiming" can follow from "wanting the best and doing the worst".[159]

(2) Conversely, there can be cruelty exhibiting a patent "intention to hurt" which is, however, a means to avoid worse cruelties, e.g., shocking drink-driving adverts and *in terrorem* literary techniques.[160]

(3) "[T]he *fascinosum*" of "cruelty" is also a paradoxical manifestation, i.e.,

(3a) the enigmatic lure that violent, gruesome and even clearly sadistic thrills possess, not least over cruelty's victims themselves, at times.[161]

(3b) In addition, Hallie acknowledges how this fascination relates to a variety of boons that people can obtain through cruel means and, perhaps, through them alone:

(3bi) "erotic stimulation";[162]

---

[157] Hallie (1969), 22–24. Balibar (2001) and (2008) essentially rediscover independently Hallie's 3b and 2bii. As for our examples, see, e.g., Hinton (2021), Melossi and Pavarini (1977), Cerna (2002), and Mavridis (2018).

[158] As discussed in *H&C1*, additional cases of paradoxical cruelty can be retrieved as well.

[159] Hallie (1969), 14–20. Polanyi (1969a, 14–15) addresses the telling issue of "moral inversion" among 19th- and 20th-century Russian revolutionaries, who "were morally dedicated to commit any act of treachery, blackmail, or cruelty in the service of a programme of universal destruction" to create a good new world. As Clara Zetkin (1926, pars. 2 and 13) writes: "the Bolsheviks cannot escape the necessity of sacrificing, as a transient measure, the rights of certain individuals and of certain social groups", for "the path of the soviet dominion will lead from the harsh and cruel reality of dictatorship to the beautiful and realised dream of democracy" promised by Lenin.

[160] Hallie (1969), 20–22. We kept writing "manifest" and "patent" because people's "intention to hurt" can be subtle and ambiguous. See, e.g., the genuinely painful and self-loathing effect on an older dancing couple by a younger, handsome and alluring couple in Sartre's *Age of Reason* (1973, 191–192): "[T]hey were cruel, but quite unconsciously so. Or perhaps they were faintly aware of being so."

[161] Hallie (1969), 70–75. E.g., the Stockholm syndrome affecting victims of spousal abuse. In vicarious settings, viewers can be led into identifying alternatively with victims and perpetrators (see, e.g., Picart and Frank 2006).

[162] Hallie (1969), 41 and 46. E.g., BDSM practices leading to orgasm. Those that do not, instead, belong to (3biv).

(3bii) deeper, higher or broader "awareness";[163]
(3biii) sensuous and/or creative "imagination";[164] and
(3biv) the "pleasure" of "masochism".[165]
(4)   There are then the cruelties involved in the processes of "growth" and maturation of real living persons who must endure painful experiences to attain full "individualis[ation]" and/or authentic "subjectivity" (e.g., humiliating defeats, heartbreaks, burdensome griefs).[166]
(5)   Hallie also lists paradoxical cruelties that are
(5a)   "responsive", i.e., enacted in reaction to
(5b)   "provocative" cruelty.[167]

Lawful penal chastisements, social rebellions, patriotic fights, and just wars are examples of such a responsive type of paradoxical cruelty, although Hallie recommended avoiding cruelties that would "escalate" hence "creating new victims".[168]

3.1.4 Cruelty as a Tool

> Dura lex sed lex
> —Roman legal maxim[169]

Pace much common sense and as much recent scholarship, cruelty might not be bad in and by itself. On the contrary, it might merely possess instrumental value. Such being, at least, the conclusion reached in the early 16th century by the famous Italian politician, historian, and playwright, Niccolò Machiavelli, to whom we indirectly owe the pejorative terms "Machiavellian" and "Machiavellianism" that we too have been using in this volume.[170]

---

163 Hallie (1969), 39–47. E.g., Catholic nuns' mutual whipping and self-flagellations, as reported in Scott (1996).
164 Hallie (1969), 52–55.
165 Hallie (1969), 48–49. Arguably, the intensity of experience of endurance- and contact sports belongs here.
166 Hallie (1969), 55–58 and 60–62.
167 Hallie (1969), 80 *et passim*. These two types of cruelty play a key role in Chapter 1 of Part 2.
168 Hallie (1969), 79–82 and 166. Penal abolitionist Hanna (2009, 232) argues against all "reactive attitudes".
169 "The law is harsh, but it is the law." Arguably, this principle applies also to natural laws and the moral law.
170 See, in particular, Meinecke (1998). Contemporary psychology combines Machiavellianism with narcissism, psychopathy, and/or sadism into the so-called "Dark Triad" or "Tetrad" characterising

As Machiavelli writes, it may be wise to distinguish between "cruelties being badly or properly used ... and the possibility of evil ... to speak well ... [i.e.,] of those [cruelties] that are applied at one blow and are necessary to one's security, and that are not persisted in afterwards unless they can be turned to the advantage of the subjects".[171] For example, Hannibal's "inhuman cruelty" complemented "his other virtues" as a capable military leader.[172] Similarly, Machiavelli notes:

> Every prince ought to desire to be considered clement and not cruel. Nevertheless he ought to take care not to misuse this clemency. Cesare Borgia was considered cruel; notwithstanding, his cruelty reconciled the Romagna, unified it, and restored it to peace and loyalty. And if this be rightly considered, he will be seen to have been much more merciful than the Florentine people, who, to avoid a reputation for cruelty, permitted Pistoia to be destroyed [by the rioting between the Cancellieri and Panciatichi factions in 1502 and 1503].[173]

In our century, none less than the French postmodernist thinker *par excellence*, Jacques Derrida, writes: "Politics can only domesticate [cruelty], differ and defer it, learn to negotiate, compromise indirectly but without illusion with it ... the cruelty drive is irreducible."[174] In the real life of historical communities, as Derrida

---

dangerous sociopaths (see, e.g., Thomas and Egan 2022). Bizarrely, Stacey Vanek Smith (2021) advises contemporary Western women to adopt Machiavelli's strategies in order to succeed in today's *business world*, thus confirming indirectly that there is therein something psychopathological which is taken for granted, if not cultivated and commended as clever or even egalitarian and emancipatory. (More on these matters follows in Chapter 1 of Part 2.)

171 Machiavelli (1908), chap. 8, par. 7.
172 Machiavelli (1908), chap. 17, par. 4.
173 Machiavelli (1908), chap. 17, par. 1. Ironically, Maritain (1952, 139) claims that Machiavelli wrote his 'scandalous' treaty while presuming an underlying socio-culturally well-established Christian tradition of virtue and humaneness that disappeared with secularisation: "he would pale at the sight of modern Machiavellianism".
174 Derrida (2002), 252. Having a drive, however, does not mean *per se* to be bound to express it in some standard manner, and even less to act on it in a deliberate standard manner. As the British psychologist Joseph Schwartz (2001, 200) writes with regard to "violence" proper: "human beings have a demonstrable and fundamental capacity for violence analogous to the demonstrable and fundamental capacity for language. A capacity is, of course, very different from the fundamental or instinctual expression of violence. The many forms of expression of violence we can point to are no more fundamental to the biological organism than the exact language that we end up speaking. The origin of the precise expression of the universal human capacity for violence is social-developmental: a neonate is no more programmed to be born expressing envy than it is programmed to be born expressing English." In keeping with this analogy, it is perhaps perplexing to realise that a neonate who should never learn to express at least one language would be regarded as developmentally deficient. Therefore, in order to avoid a parallel deficiency, each person would seem to be advised to try to find one or few socially and personally suitable ways to express their drive to violence, e.g., by means of contact sports, satirical writings, and artistic performances (whether

argues, we are more likely "to oppose various sorts of violence to one another than oppose violence to nonviolence".[175]

Analogously, Deleuze and his long-time intellectual partner, the French Trotskyist psychoanalyst Félix Guattari, recognise the necessity of at least *some* cruelty in the formation of basic social principles, mores, and habits in each new person's psyche: "Cruelty is the movement of culture that is realized in bodies and inscribed on them, belabouring them."[176] Acquiring all these necessary psychosocial elements implied, in our distant past, "a system of cruelty, a terrible alphabet [of ...] blood, torture, and sacrifices".[177] Today, this "terrible alphabet" persists in compulsory schooling and the forced socialisation of young people: "we give children language, pens, and notebooks as we give workers shovels and pickaxes".[178]

Along a similar Freudian line of thinking, there emerges also the psychological phenomenon of "[s]elf-hatred", at least according to Castoriadis, for whom this bleak mental element cannot but be:

> "[A] component of every human being". It results from the psychical monad's rejection of the individual into which it has been transformed through its painful encounter with alterity and the world. The individual is the socially fabricated product of an irreducible tension between the singular dimension of the human being rooted in the psyche and the social historical anonymous collective.[179]

The 20th-century French existentialist philosopher and Schopenhauer scholar, Clément Rosset, claims that cruelty cannot be avoided if we aim at living a meaningful life of any sort. As he states: "[C]ruelty [is] not ... pleasure in cultivating suffering but ... a refusal of complacency towards an object, whatever it may be."[180]

---

acted, scripted, facilitated, sponsored, or attended). Warfare, persistent nagging, and physical assaults seem far less suitable pathways, in comparison. LVOA would agree (see Chapter 1 in this book). See also Chapter 3 of Part 2.
175 As translated and cited in Gasché (2020), 1. As the Trinidadian historian C.L.R. James (1979, 43) writes: "there is a lot of talk about violence... When was there no violence? ... [V]iolence is there whether you want it or not." The inevitability and importance of "cruelty" as one of our fundamental "drives" for the sake of individual and collective "survival" was derived by Derrida not from Caribbean history, however, but a close study of Nietzsche and Freud (Senatore 2018, 58 and 75).
176 Deleuze and Guattari (2004), 144.
177 Deleuze and Guattari (2004), 144–145.
178 Deleuze and Guattari (1987), 84.
179 As translated, cited and discussed in Nicolacopulos and Vassilacopoulos (2020), 8. Castoriadis did not tackle "cruelty" as such in detail, although Rundell (2012, 4) argues that this term can be understood in line with the former's philosophy, i.e., as "a mode of one-sidedness, of an interaction without regard for and recognition of, the other. It is thus a created 'interaction' with neither the possibilities of power or autonomy".
180 Rosset (1993), 18.

This means, also and above all, avoiding complacency with regard to "the 'cruelty' of the real", i.e., "the intrinsically painful and tragic nature of reality" in which we are condemned to live.[181]

If we want to be able to obtain any satisfaction from and in such a "painful and tragic" condition, no matter how minimal and/or irregular this satisfaction may be, then we must understand and accept that "joy is necessarily cruel".[182] Living is, *au fond*, a necessary evil. As Cioran also attests:

> Passion is also cruelty towards others and towards oneself, for one cannot experience it without torturing, without torturing oneself. Outside of insensibility and, perhaps, of scorn, everything is pain, even pleasure, pleasure especially, whose function does not consist in dispelling pain but in preparing it. Even admitting that it does not aim so high and that it merely leads to disappointment, what better proof of its inadequacies, of its lack of intensity, its lack of existence![183]

The celebrated joys of romantic love are no exception, in Rosset's view:

> [T]he cruelty of love (like that of reality) resides in the paradox or the contradiction which consists in loving without loving, affirming as lasting that which is ephemeral – paradox of which the most rudimentary vision would be to say that something simultaneously exists and does not exist. The essence of love is to claim to love forever but in reality to love only for a time. So the truth of love does not correspond to the experience of love.[184]

The 20th-century French playwright and essayist, Antonin Artaud, can be said to have anticipated Rosset's existentialist philosophy of cruelty to some extent, whilst focussing on the shocking aesthetics of his aptly-christened "theatre of cruelty".[185] As Artaud asserts: "Death is cruelty, resurrection is cruelty, transfiguration is cruelty… Everything that acts is a cruelty."[186] The art of "theatre" itself, as a consequence, will have to be cruel: "in the sense of continuous creation, a wholly magical action, [it] obeys this necessity" of "permanent … evil".[187] Artaud's aesthetics are thus consonant with Adorno's ones, who states: "[A]rt's own gesture is cruel. In aesthetic forms, cruelty becomes imagination: Something is excised from the liv-

---

181 Rosset (1993), 76 f.
182 Rosset (1993), 17 f (hence also the book's title).
183 Cioran (1970), 137; emphases removed.
184 Rosset (1993), 121.
185 Artaud (1958), 89. Ercoli (2013a) bases her study of "cruelty" proper on Artaud's approach.
186 Artaud (1958), 101–103 and 85.
187 Artaud (1958), 103.

ing, from the body of language, from tones, from visual experience. The purer the form and the higher the autonomy of the works, the more cruel they are."[188]

At the same time, as also argued by Rosset, "[c]ruelty is not just a matter of either sadism or bloodshed, at least not in any exclusive way... ['Cruelty'] must be taken in a broad sense, and not in the rapacious physical sense that is customarily given to it."[189] In Artaud's innovative conception and practice of theatre, cruelty is therefore to be understood, represented, and experienced as a powerful and painful means of sensory hyperstimulation and profound self-enlightenment: "All this culminates in consciousness and torment, and in consciousness in torment."[190]

Curiously, Artaud's and Rosset's secular concerns echo older religious ones, as summarily yet exemplarily expressed in the late 15th century by Caterina Fieschi Adorno, aka Saint Catherine of Genoa, who acknowledges, in her introspective *Treatise on Purgatory*, the usefulness of exerting psychological "cruelty" onto oneself, whereby "the soul" of the penitent Christian tries "to get rid of every hindrance to its perfection".[191] Even in the afterlife, then, we may have to be cruel to ourselves in order to attain full awareness and, eventually, true joy.[192] Eternal bliss, *a fortiori*, cannot be said to be a laughing matter, at least as far as the so-called "Seraph of Genoa" is concerned.[193]

---

[188] Adorno (1997), 50, whose philosophical 'inspirer' on this aesthetic point is Nietzsche.
[189] Artaud (1958), 101–103.
[190] Artaud (1958), 114. Tellingly, while describing many painful events as "cruel", Jung (1989, 62) speaks of "utmost cruelty" in relation to his childhood's "certain and immediate experience" of God's existence and agency. Similarly, Maritain (1957, 151) describes as "almost cruel" the sense of "intoxication with the object" that "the philosopher" can experience *via* "decisive intuitions and illuminating certainties". At the same time, in a creative mix of art commentary and unabashed ranting, the US poet Maggie Nelson (2011, title *et passim*) reminds her readers that there is no guarantee that the "cruelty" so commonly exploited by artists of all stripes should always lead to some kind of enlightenment. Sometimes, it merely shocks us and/or titillates our animal affects.
[191] Fieschi Adorno (1858), viii and 46–47. The word *crudeltà* reads as "severity" in the 1858 English translation.
[192] Most Christian confessions have maintained that real *beatitudo* can be attained only in the afterlife.
[193] Born and married in two of Genoa's wealthiest families, Caterina became a mystic and ran its biggest hospital.

3.1.5 Cruelty as a Virtue

> [C]ruelty to the defeated enemy, the abuse of victory, etc. were virtues, i. e., strength of patriotic love
> —Giacomo Leopardi[194]

Touching instead upon the outlandish notion of "satanic beings", the 20th-century Jewish-Hungarian philosopher and Chesterton devotee, Aurel Kolnai, styles such creatures as individuals who are willing to asseverate: "Evil be thou my Good."[195] Sade, the notorious 18th-century Enlightenment thinker, playwright, and pornographer, is perhaps one of these beings.[196] His works offer, very much *inter alia*, a reasoned and lengthy paean for "cruelty" as such.[197] For instance, one of his in/famous libertines states: "Cruelty is imprinted within the animals ... that can read the laws of Nature much more energetically than we do; [cruelty] is more strongly enacted by Nature among the savages than it is among civilized men: it would be absurd to establish that it is a kind of depravity."[198]

Sade claims that "cruelty" is "nothing but the human energy that civilization has not yet corrupted... Cruelty, far from being a vice, is the first sentiment that Nature has imprinted within ourselves. The child breaks his toy, bites his nurse's nipple, strangles his pet bird, long before he has reached the age of reason."[199] As can be witnessed in wartime "sieges", people are more than able to "devour each other" most readily, and without reluctance or repentance.[200] Whenever the purely

---

[194] Leopardi (n.d.a. [1898]), 785, hence "Homer creating his Heroes ... merciless and unrelenting to the defeated enemy." See Dahlkvist (2007) for an account of Leopardi's influence on Nietzsche.
[195] Kolnai (1978), 181. As to modern Satanism, it seems to be an insignificant phenomenon (see, e. g., Oliver 2001).
[196] Following established conventions, *we attribute the claims made by Sade's libertines to Sade himself*, who might have just been fooling around, however (see H&C1). Similarly, we take Sade's claims at face value, although we do acknowledge that "whatever the cruel bondage or degradation displayed by porn, these images of exploitation are all *images*... All are such stuff as dreams are made on ... as archetypal functions of the natural psyche" (Hillman 1995b, 56–57 emphasis in the original). More on the distinction between signified and signifier follows in Chapters 1 and 3 of Part 2.
[197] Between a daily quickie with the stable boy and a monthly orgy in the countess' alcove, Sade's novels present the reader with lengthy philosophical dialogues that are as carefully crafted as those of any other Enlightenment thinker wishing to make use of Plato's venerable literary form, e. g., Hume, Diderot, and Voltaire. (See Hösle 2013.)
[198] Sade (2010), 74. The translation is ours.
[199] Sade (2010), 74. Interestingly, another Frenchman, Merleau-Ponty (1964b, 143–144), later describes jealous children's "cruelty" as a potent cathectic mixture of pain and pleasure, i. e., "sado-masochism".
[200] Sade (1999), part 1, chap. 17. The translation is ours.

conventional and inevitably provisional social norms disintegrate, we can see clearly, according to Sade, how "fear", not moral or religious virtue, and fear's even deeper fountainhead, "selfishness", are the true basic psychic drives of all humankind.[201]

A self-appointed 18th-century agent of the modernising and scientific European Enlightenment, Sade rejects the "odious chimera" of "a fantastic God", whether Jewish, Christian, Muslim, or else, and all those "imbecilic", "ridiculous", "absurd", and "vulgar prejudices" that have been based upon it, e.g., the idea of a "conscience" within us that guides or conduct along ethical lines, the Catholic Church, and the whole of organised religions, and all the "grand principles … laws … and morals" of reputedly 'civilised' societies, not least the French one of his day.[202]

The apparent "moral crimes" of "libertinage", which embraces "sacrilegious fantasies and cruel predilections" promoting "prostitution, adultery, rape and sodomy", are nothing but a rediscovery of our true nature, in Sade's view.[203] No negative moral judgement should be passed about them:

> Our constitution, our organs, the flows of the humours, the energy of the animal spirits, here are the physical causes that make us be … Titus or Nero, Messalina or Chantal; one should not be proud for virtue and contrite for vice, nor should one accuse nature for having generated

---

[201] Sade (1999), part 1, chap. 23. We cannot fail to notice how the disintegration of social norms may also be at work, to a more limited extent, within carnivals and commonplace humour, and therefore explain, to a degree at least, the outpourings of aggressiveness that, as seen here in Chapter 2, many commentators have identified therein. See also Chapter 3 of Part 2.

[202] Sade (1999), part 1, chap. 11. Sade's peculiar mix of pornography with self-aware anti-authoritarian and anti-conventional stances found several later echoes, whether more or less philosophically articulate as his own, e.g., Jeannie Pepper's self-perception *qua* agent of black women's empowerment (Miller-Young 2016), Japanese young women's self-assertive appropriation of their country's *anime* imagery (Kinsella 2014), or Nina Hartley's (2018, 176–177) "confessions" on her own being a "feminist porno star" as "satisfying on a number of levels". Not to mention the early and much-debated feminist defence of Sade's work by Angela Carter (1978), who praised the notorious French thinker for establishing forcefully in modern Western culture the notion that women could be proactive sexual beings, rather than the passive and meek creatures that traditional Judeo-Christian patriarchy presupposed. Thus, she called Sade a "moral pornographer" (Carter 1978, 19). Curiously, as Rubinson (2000, 717) wrote in a later essay on Carter's literary career, "despite wide-ranging critiques of the anti-pornography dominance of feminist agendas (see Ellis, Strossen, Segal and Macintosh, Williams), the false equation of feminism, antiporn agendas, and 'male-bashing' is so common that Carter's early proposal of pornography's potential to be critical of gender relations seems even more radical than when it was first published in 1978". More on these topics and possible false equations follows in Chapters 1 and 3 of Part 2.

[203] Sade (2010), 68 and 135.

us good or evil; she has acted according to her views, her plans and needs: let us surrender to her.[204]

Even Bertrand Russell admits, in the 20th century, that "science alone ... cannot prove that it is bad to enjoy the infliction of cruelty".[205] Possibly, then, murderous types such as Titus, Nero, Messalina, and Chantal were, in point of fact, as innocent as Calverley's poetic cat, about which we read: *"They call me cruel. Do I know if a mouse or songbird feels? / I only know they make me light and salutary meals: / And if, as 'tis my nature to, ere I devour I tease 'em, / Why should a low-bred gardener's boy pursue me with a besom?"*[206]

Sade's stuffing is no light-hearted balladry aimed at children and teenagers, however. His copious porno-philosophical prose is meant for adults, their strong stomachs, thick skins, and hard looks.[207] Still, the core wisdom is the same. Putative 'monsters' such as Gilles de Rais, Countess Báthory, Irma Grese, Idi Amin, and Gertrude Baniszewski were just being themselves. They were Mother Nature's sons and daughters, like their own victims; but, unlike the latter group, they got a myopic, narrow-minded, and hypocritical bad rap for pursuing their natural dispositions.[208]

At the same time, there may even be a need for a deliberate, 'civilised' rediscovery of cruelty. As Sade writes:

> We distinguish two types of cruelty ... [the former] originates from stupidity and, involving no reason or analysis, makes the individual that was born like this similar to a wild beast... [It] does not provide any pleasure, for the one who is prone to it does not search for any refinement... [The latter] is the result of the sensitivity of the organs ... known only to extremely delicate beings, and the excesses it generates are nothing else than refinements of their del-

---

[204] Sade (2010), 75.
[205] Russell (2009), 282.
[206] Calverley (1959), 66, 4th stanza.
[207] Whenever discussing sexually explicit materials, we presume their restriction to adult audiences. We do *not* address the issue of minors' exposure to them. In any case, LVOA can help explain, at least in principle, whether, when, why, and which restrictions should be warranted (see Chapter 1 in this book).
[208] As outrageous as Sade's stance comes across, it nevertheless makes his readers reflect upon the limits of individual self-control and the fact that we never decide what to want or long for, but only whether to pursue it or not. All kinds of urges animate our life and, in some individuals, these urges seek objects that their society, at that point in history, abhors and/or forbids (e.g., homosexual love, premarital sex, alcoholic beverages, wearing short skirts, erotic art, tobacco, dog fights, chewing gums, Kinder eggs). Life's *cruelty prospers also under such mutable socio-cultural and legal conditions*. More on these matters follows in Chapter 3 of Part 2 (see also *H&C2*).

icateness; it is this delicateness that employs all the resources of cruelty to alert itself, as it vanishes too easily because of its fineness.[209]

If we want any goodness or joy to arise, as Sade maintains, our cruel nature must be allowed to rule: "Cruelty is in nature; we are all born with a dose of cruelty that is up to education to modify; but education is not in nature, and it is as damaging to the sacred effects of nature as cultivation is to trees ... the tree abandoned to the whims of nature is more beautiful and produces better fruits."[210] Deep down, as Sade argues, even the seemingly 'civilised' human domains cannot but recall this fundamental natural logic of cruelty in some way or another, and Beccaria's thorny theme of theft is thus brought back into the spotlight:

> [T]he mighty has taken possession of everything, hence the defect in nature's balance; the weak defends himself and robs the mighty: here are the crimes that establish the necessary equilibrium of nature... If the mighty seems to be causing disorder by stealing to the one who is beneath him, the weak re-establishes it by stealing to his superiors, and both serve nature.
> [...]
> When going back to the origin of the right to property, one reaches necessarily usurpation. In this case theft is not punished as it establishes the right to property; but the right itself is originally nothing but a theft itself: as a consequence the law punishes the theft of that which is itself a theft, the weak who tries to regain his due, and the mighty who wants to found or increase his own, taking advantage of that which he has received from nature.[211]

In the 20th century, the social-democratic German psychoanalyst and sociologist, Erich Fromm, further corroborates this association between cruelty and liberalism by claiming that Sade was merely one of the many Enlightenment "thinkers who lived in the age of the bourgeois class's final victory", such that "the unphilosophical practices of aristocrats became the practice and theory of the bourgeoisie", which Sade's libertines embody most emphatically in their selfish and efficient pursuit of "the satisfaction of cruel impulses".[212]

Also in the 20th century, an influential Russian-born US-based actress, novelist and conservative philosopher, Ayn Rand, selects the "boastful and self-confident" child murderer "[William Edward] Hickman" *qua* real-life "model" for a new liter-

---

209 Sade (2010), 75.
210 Sade (2010), 74.
211 Sade (1999), part 1, chap. 12.
212 Fromm (1985), 14. See also Horkheimer's and Adorno's (1989, excursus 2) earlier and extensive reflections on Sade's *Juliette* as announcing the bourgeoning 'new order' of the West's bourgeoisie: secular, amoral, efficient, murderous, and cruel. More on corporate capitalism is said in Chapter 1 of Part 2 (in today's parlance, "corporate" replaced "bourgeois"). See also *H&C1*.

ary hero of hers—the declared personification of the "Superman".[213] Hickman is lauded by Rand for rejecting "the criminal, inconsistent, ludicrous, tragic nonsense of Christianity", as well as society's "established morals" and "laws".[214] In her view, Hickman's lived example refutes "that civilization is sympathy, i.e., a great sympathetic understanding and co-feeling with others", and the merciless way in which "mob cruelty" targeted Hickman after having been caught by the police unveils, in her judgement, the "bloodthirsty, blind, carnivorous beast that is hidden beneath the polished surface of our 'civilized', religious, respectable citizens!"[215]

Rand's philosopher of reference is not Sade, however, but the great German thinker, classical philologist, and musical composer, Friedrich Nietzsche, who argues cruelty is or has been nothing short of a human virtue.[216] Specifically, Nietzsche states that he is be able to

> empathise with those tremendous eras of "morality of custom" which precede "world history" as the actual and decisive eras of history which determined the character of mankind: the eras in which suffering counted as virtue, cruelty counted as virtue, dissembling counted as virtue, revenge counted as virtue, denial of reason counted as virtue, while on the other hand well-being was accounted a danger, desire for knowledge was accounted a danger, peace was accounted a danger, pity was accounted a danger, being pitied was accounted an affront, work was accounted an affront, madness was accounted godliness, and change was accounted immoral and pregnant with disaster![217]

Nietzsche defines "cruelty ... as one of the oldest and most unrationalizable cultural substrata ... the psychology of conscience is not, as is generally believed, 'the voice of God in man'— but the instinct of cruelty turned back upon itself after it can no longer discharge itself outside".[218] In Nietzsche's opinion, "almost everything we call 'higher culture' is based on the spiritualization and deepening of cruelty. The 'wild animal' has not been killed off at all; it is alive and well, it has just – become divine."[219] In the language of psychology, it could be said that Nietzsche identifies a mechanism of thorough affective repression and indicates some tokens of its ensuing cohort of psychopathological effects.[220]

According to Nietzsche, the most significant difference is that, in 'civilised' times, cruelty is not played out openly as the virtuous expression of the human

---

213 Rand (1997), 22–27.
214 Rand (1997), 36–38.
215 Rand (1997), 42–44.
216 See Nietzsche (1997a), pars. 18 and 30.
217 Nietzsche (1997a), par. 18.
218 Nietzsche (2004), "Genealogy of Morals – A Polemic", 81.
219 Nietzsche (2002), par. 229.
220 More on the psychological accounts of this phenomenon is said in Part 2.

will that it was and perhaps still should be, but lies concealed in all sorts of seemingly innocent activities:

> Cruelty is what constitutes the painful sensuality of tragedy. And what pleases us in so-called tragic pity as well as in everything sublime, up to the highest and most delicate of metaphysical tremblings, derives its sweetness exclusively from the intervening component of cruelty. Consider the Roman in the arena, Christ in the rapture of the cross, the Spaniard at the sight of the stake or the bullfight, the present-day Japanese flocking to tragedies, the Parisian suburban laborer who is homesick for bloody revolutions, the Wagnerienne who unfastens her will and lets Tristan und Isolde "wash over her" – what they all enjoy and crave with a mysterious thirst to pour down their throats is "cruelty", the spiced drink of the great Circe.[221]

As Nietzsche states: "Cruelty is one of the oldest festive joys of mankind ... for to practise cruelty is to enjoy the highest gratification of the feeling of power", which, in Nietzsche's opinion, is the fundamental energy permeating all things.[222] Cruelty is, therefore, a candid reflection of the "'sorry scheme' of things" that the universe consists in: an endless succession of "begetting, living and murdering".[223] As Nietzsche intimates, nature is "profligate without measure, indifferent without measure, without purpose and regard, without mercy and justice, fertile and barren and uncertain at the same time".[224]

Nietzsche finds cruelty hiding even in the most pious and declaredly moral endeavours to which persons may commit themselves. We should "not think too highly", he writes, of "a morality which rests entirely on the drive to distinction".[225] What kind of psychology "lies behind it", in reality?[226] Nietzsche's answer is that, in seeking distinction, we wish to make others suffer—even if we would never admit it, perhaps not to even to ourselves. In working hard to "do our best", we are really trying "to make the sight of us painful to another and to awaken in him the feeling of envy and of his own impotence and degradation".[227] Find a person, he says, who "has become humble and is now perfect in his humility" and then "seek for those whom he has long wished to torture with it!"[228] "[Y]ou will find them soon enough!", Nietzsche concludes.[229]

---

221 Nietzsche (2002), par. 229.
222 Nietzsche (1997a), par. 18.
223 Nietzsche (1911a), vol. 2, 8.
224 Nietzsche (2002), par. 9.
225 Nietzsche (1997a), par. 30.
226 Nietzsche (1997a), par. 30.
227 Nietzsche (1997a), par. 30.
228 Nietzsche (1997a), par. 30.
229 Nietzsche (1997a), par. 30.

Montaigne's Druids or ancient Egyptians may be far less praiseworthy than the great 16th-century Frenchman takes them to be. Nietzsche claims that if someone is "kind to animals and is admired on account of it", there must inevitably be "certain people on whom he wants to vent his cruelty by this means".[230] The "great artist" is another such example, according to Nietzsche, because his/her work is motivated by "the pleasure he anticipated in the envy of his defeated rivals … [and] allowed his powers no rest until he had become great… [H]ow many bitter moments has his becoming great not cost the souls of others!"[231]

Nietzsche detects cruelty also inside all those socio-cultural institutions that we now presume to be pure and virtuous, such as philosophical ethics and institutional codes of conduct:

> In conditions obtaining before the existence of the state the individual can act harshly and cruelly for the purpose of frightening other creatures: to secure his existence through such fear-inspiring tests of his power. Thus does the man of violence, of power, the original founder of states, act when he subjugates the weaker… Morality is preceded by compulsion, indeed it is for a time itself still compulsion, to which one accommodates oneself for the avoidance of what one regards as unpleasurable. Later it becomes custom, later still voluntary obedience, finally almost instinct: then, like all that has for a long time been habitual and natural, it is associated with pleasure – and is now called virtue.[232]

Inevitably, the original cruelty drive cannot but keep lurking, according to Nietzsche, and it re-emerges whenever these pure and virtuous institutions are under threat: "political sectarians are treated harshly and cruelly, but because one has learned to believe in the necessity of the state one is not as sensible of the cruelty as one is in the former case, where we repudiate the ideas behind it".[233] As Hallie himself will later observe, many vicious forms of cruelty hide behind "the self-deception and often the hypocrisy that seek to hide harm-doing under justifications".[234] And as Hallie soberly concludes: "To a large extent the history of mankind is the history of hurting and killing with a clear conscience, and often in the name of conscience."[235]

Christianity is, under this perspective, singled out by Nietzsche as a major example of this kind of hypocrisy, which is said to generate perverse ascetic forms of self-directed cruelty:

---

230 Nietzsche (1997a), par. 30.
231 Nietzsche (1997a), par. 30.
232 Nietzsche (2005), par. 99.
233 Nietzsche (2005), par. 101.
234 Hallie (1971a), 248.
235 Hallie (1971b), 579.

> [I]t is imagined that the gods too are refreshed and in festive mood when they are offered the spectacle of cruelty – and thus there creeps into the world the idea that voluntary suffering, self-chosen torture, is meaningful and valuable... All those spiritual leaders of the peoples who were able to stir something into motion within the inert but fertile mud of their customs have, in addition to madness, also had need of voluntary torture if they were to inspire belief – and first and foremost, as always, their own belief in themselves! The more their spirit ventured on to new paths and was as a consequence tormented by pangs of conscience and spasms of anxiety, the more cruelly did they rage against their own flesh, their own appetites and their own health – as though to offer the divinity a substitute pleasure in case he might perhaps be provoked by this neglect of and opposition to established usages and by the new goals these paths led to.[236]

The West's Judeo-Christian culture, but also the Buddhist and Taoist traditions of the East for that matter, teach "the ways of self-narcotization", according to Nietzsche, such as "intoxication as cruelty in the tragic enjoyment of the destruction of the noblest... Attempt to work blindly as an instrument of science ... resignation to generalizing about oneself, a pathos; mysticism, the voluptuous enjoyment of eternal emptiness."[237] Modern, secular versions of this kind of cruel self-deceit exist as well, e.g., the positivistic "worship" of modern science, "rocks, stupidity, gravity, fate, or nothingness out of [people's] sheer cruelty to themselves", who "sacrifice God for nothingness" and enact a "final cruelty" that had begun in prehistory with gruesome "human sacrifices".[238]

Nietzsche's paradigm of human excellence is very different:

> [T]he magnificent blond beast avidly prowling round for spoil and victory ... Roman, Arabian, Germanic, Japanese nobility, Homeric heroes, Scandinavian Vikings ... their unconcern and scorn for safety, body, life, comfort, their shocking cheerfulness and depth of delight in all destruction, in all the debauches of victory and cruelty ... [and] the magnificent but at the same time so shockingly violent world of Homer.[239]

Like Sade, Nietzsche aims at teaching us to accept human nature for what he claims it to be like: "Do I counsel you to slay your instincts? I counsel you the in-

---

[236] Nietzsche (1997a), par. 18.
[237] Nietzsche (1968), par. 29.
[238] Nietzsche (2002), par. 55, who implied that having great knowledge may not save a person from being stupid or fall for the masochistic pleasure of nihilistic self-loathing, e.g., by reducing humankind to sheer animals, cosmic insignificance, and/or self-replicating selfish genes.
[239] Nietzsche (2006), 1st essay, par. 11. It is a *cruel irony* of recorded history, old as well as new, that the collapse of the oppressive, hypocritical, and frequently cruel State should bring back the equally far-from-pleasant individual glorified by Nietzsche, e.g., the Chinese, Somali, and Afghani warlords, or the Haitian criminal kingpins.

nocence in your instincts."[240] As he adds, poetically: "Not when the truth is filthy, but when it is shallow, doth the discerning one go unwillingly into its waters."[241] The end result could be sadism, in point of fact: "As far as our nervous system extends we guard ourselves against pain: if it extended further, namely into our fellow men, we would never do harm to another (except in such cases as when we do it to ourselves, that is to say when we cut ourselves for the purpose of a cure, exert and weary ourselves for the sake of our health)."[242] Yet, as universally recognised, we are able to do harm onto other persons, whose "degree of pain ... is in any event unknown to us".[243]

Nietzsche's appreciation for "the magnificent blond beast" means also, for him, that "[w]e must accept this cruel sounding truth, that slavery is of the essence of Culture... This truth is the vulture, that gnaws at the liver of the Promethean promoter of Culture... The misery of toiling men must still increase in order to make the production of the world of art possible to a small number of Olympian men."[244] If we want to have any culture worthy of this name, strict hierarchical power and merciless exploitation must be accepted.[245]

Consistently with this precipitous vertical chain of command and its assumed necessity for the glory of civilisation, Nietzsche fears "the secret wrath nourished by Communists and Socialists of all times, and by their feebler descendants, the white race of the 'Liberals', not only against the arts, but also against classical antiquity".[246] In Nietzsche's view, these modern ideologies are secular forms of religious belief, especially Judaism and Christianity, that, were they left unopposed, "would be the cry of compassion tearing down the walls of Culture".[247] Thus, even the phenomenon of "laughter" is, for Nietzsche, a strict and telling hierarchical matter: it is either a superior expression "of the height" or a lowly utterance

---

[240] Nietzsche (1911b), part 1, par. 13.
[241] Nietzsche (1911b), part 1, par. 13.
[242] Nietzsche (2005), par. 104.
[243] Nietzsche (2005), par. 104.
[244] Nietzsche (1911a), 7.
[245] If aero-spatial engineering counts as significant culture, the oft-reported poor wages and bad working conditions at Amazon may be needed to allow the US oligarch Jeff Bezos to launch his New Shepard rocket into space.
[246] Nietzsche (1911a), 7. We leave it to each reader to ponder on the fate of 'high culture' in mass democracies. See also Chapter 3 of Part 2.
[247] Nietzsche (1911a), 7. Ideologies, which Tagore (1918, 110–111) claimed to be epitomised in his times by "the Nation" created by the modern West, may be such that "men who are naturally just can be cruelly unjust both in their act and their thought, accompanied by a feeling that they are helping the world to receive its deserts".

"of the herd".²⁴⁸ We do not need to explain at which end of the hierarchy Nietzsche himself believed to belong.²⁴⁹

3.2 An Overview of 'Cruelty' in the Social Sciences

> We have often seen how certain customs, originally cruel or obscene, became mere vestiges in the course of time.
> —Carl Gustav Jung²⁵⁰

Victor Nell is the only contemporary social researcher who, while studying in detail nominally "cruel" phenomena, has also articulated an attendant, concise, and poignant definition of "cruelty", which he understands as "the deliberate infliction of physical or psychological pain on other living creatures, sometimes indifferently, but often with delight".²⁵¹ Needless to say, Bodin, Lecky, Hallie, Regan, Kekes, and Shklar, whose earlier works are never cited by Nell in his writings, would certainly agree with him.²⁵²

For the greatest part, however, the world's social scientists have followed the example set by most Western humanists over a longer stretch of time. Routinely, they have been assuming some common-sense interpretation of "cruelty" and applying it a-critically. Along with that, they have been talking of cruelty's many lexical cognates and related phenomena, e.g., "narcissism", "callous personality", "psychopathy", "Machiavellianism", "sadism", "spite", "maladaptive risk taking", "destructiveness", "authoritarianism", "negative affectivity", "fearless dominance", "sensations seeking", "distractability", "inability to ignore", "perfectionism", "overconfidence", "emotional lability", "anxiousness", "depressivity and anhedonia", and "high and low self-esteem".²⁵³ Some of these notions, compared to "cruelty" proper, are methodologically more amenable to dispassionate empirical observation, plausible quantification, and standard modelling praxes.²⁵⁴

---

248 Lippitt (1992), 39.
249 A tad jokingly, Nietzsche sometimes boasts his lineage as a Polish nobleman, e.g., Nietzsche (2004), chap. 3, par. 3.
250 Jung (1960–1990), vol. 9.1, 265, par. 474.
251 Nell (2006), 211.
252 As often noticed in the course of our research, much alleged originality is pursued in today's social sciences by ignoring vast swaths of prior knowledge in the humanities. Ignorance of the past is neophilia's best ally.
253 Zeigler-Hill and Marcus (2016) cover all such cases.
254 As such, many of these notions were addressed to a major extent in *H&C1*.

Frequently, behaviours that we would describe as "cruel" have also been thoroughly medicalised and treated exclusively as pathological, including the historically well-established use of torture by judicial authorities. Yet, as an expert in social work has recently observed:

> [T]o consider torture as anything but antisocial behavior or the exclusive provenance of uncivilized cultures distances it to a narrow but certainly more comfortable domain of inquiry. There is no dearth of psychological theorizing on the motives driving inhuman behaviors, but relegating torture to the realm of pathology or cultural idiosyncrasy turns a blind eye to exploring more discomforting possibilities, including that of torture as a reasoned, social act– one grounded in morals and driven by commitment.[255]

Occasionally, behaviours that we would describe as "cruel" have been facilitated, enacted, and studied in notorious experiments that, however, did not focus on "cruelty" *per se*, e.g., the 1961 "Milgram Experiment", designed by Stanley Milgram at Yale University, and the 1971 "Stanford Prison Experiment", designed by Philip Zimbardo of Stanford University.[256] As such, these experiments can be regarded as capable of providing insights about the concept of 'cruelty', even if indirectly.[257] For instance, Haslam and his associates state, *vis-à-vis* the latter experiment: "Framing cruelty as essential for the achievement of noble collective goals thus appears to be a critical strategy for mobilizing people to hate and harm others in theatres of conflict both small and large."[258]

At any rate, some rare studies did take an explicit stab at "cruelty" proper, expressively and extensively so. Therefore, they deserve being summarised in the remaining pages of this short chapter.

---

[255] Moio (2006), 2. Here too, we must refer our readers to *H&C1*. Let us merely add a *cruel irony* noticed by the famed 20th-century Jewish-Dutch clinician and psychoanalyst, Joost Meerloo (2015, chap. 4, secs. 4–6), i.e., the sense of affection that victims can develop for their tormentors *qua* substitute parental figures and/or sources of companionship. 'Sociality' would then play a pivotal role in torture too, psychologically speaking.

[256] *Ditto*. The declared focus of both studies was the idea of 'obedience', not "cruelty" proper.

[257] Again, these studies were addressed in detail in *H&C1*. Let us just add here that Zimbardo's interests in experimental psychology ironically moved from how to make 'monsters' into how to make "heroes" who "serve as powerful reminders that people are capable of resisting evil" (as cited in Franco *et al.* 2016, 385). Thus, whether intentionally or not, Zimbardo reintroduced in social and humanistic psychology some of the wisdom of "Freudian psychoanalytic theory" and, above all, of "Jung's theory of archetypes", which lists the Hero as a key motif of the unconscious (Goethals and Allison 2012, 197).

[258] Haslam *et al.* (2019), 824

3.2.1 Sigmund Freud

> [T]he second sexual revolution was built on the ideas initiated by psychologists, scientists and feminist philosophers such as Wilhelm Reich, Alfred Kinsey and Sigmund Freud, who believed that sexual repression could cause long-term harmful consequences.
> —Anne-May Smits[259]

Freud uses "cruelty" several times in his seminal work, *Three Essays on the Theory of Sexuality*.[260] While discussing the issues of sadism and masochism, Freud refers to the desires to cause and/or experience pain in the sexual context, on the basis of Krafft-Ebing's earlier studies in psychiatry. In the same pages, Freud acknowledges the narrower technical term "algolagnia", which emphasises the pleasure derived from pain and notably "cruelty", while also distinguishing this medical category from Krafft-Ebing's one of "masochism", which covers instead all kinds of extreme acts involving humiliation and submission.[261]

Freud states that active algolagnia, i.e., sadism, can be found in medically normal individuals, who merely express through it the remnants of biologically inherent proclivities towards functional aggression in mating behaviour, i.e., a tendency towards subduing the sexual partner and thereby secure reproductive success: "Sadism would then correspond to an aggressive component of the sexual impulse which has become independent and exaggerated and has been brought to the foreground by displacement."[262]

Cruelty, in Freud's rather masculine *libido*-centred psychosexual model, is what psychoanalysis would call a "partial impulse".[263] Freud and his disciples maintain that all children begin, from a very early age, to perceive other people as sexual objects, independently of the absent or limited physical development of their own erogenous zones, which vary during the early years of human life

---

259 Smits (2020), 12, where we also read that while "the second sexual revolution" refers to the 1960s, "the first" one refers to the "early-twentieth century ... 'flapper girl'". A rather tame version of Sade's Juliette, then. Also, it is interesting that a contemporary scholar *in fieri* should describe these 'classics' as "feminist philosophers".
260 Freud (2018).
261 Today's understanding of 'sadism' in psychology and the social sciences at large is still wider and widely debated. Under this category, e.g., Burris and Leitch (2016, 87–93) mention: "Sexual sadism disorder ... Animal cruelty ... Sadistic personality disorder ... Internet trolling ... Organizational hazing ... Pranking ... [and] Vicarious sadism ... [e.g.,] MTV's/BET's *Punk'd* ... violent video games ... [and] 'crush' videos". See also Bourke (2020). More on select such examples is said in Chapter 3 of Part 2. See also *H&C2*.
262 Freud (2018), 25.
263 One of Jung's (1989, 286) innovations was to address feminine *libido* too, also within men, i.e., in their "anima".

and only later mature into bodily channels for the experience and/or discharge of "full impulses".²⁶⁴ Instead, partial impulses present themselves in behaviours such as looking intensely at the desired persons and/or showing off in front of the very same:

> Under the influence of seduction the looking perversion may attain great importance for the sexual life of the child. Still, from my investigations of the childhood years of normal and neurotic patients, I must conclude that the impulse for looking can appear in the child as a spontaneous sexual manifestation. Small children, whose attention has once been directed to their own genitals—usually by masturbation—are wont to progress in this direction without outside interference, and to develop a vivid interest in the genitals of their playmates. As the occasion for the gratification of such curiosity is generally afforded during the gratification of both excrementitious needs, such children become voyeurs and are zealous spectators at the voiding of urine and feces of others. After this tendency has been repressed, the curiosity to see the genitals of others (one's own or those of the other sex) remains as a tormenting desire which in some neurotic cases furnishes the strongest motive power for the formation of symptoms.²⁶⁵

While most sexual *libido* is eventually, and normally, fully developed and truly experienced *via* the erogenous zones centring upon the physical organs for pleasure, partial impulses can nevertheless find their avenue towards pleasure in other, more indirect ways, cruelty included.²⁶⁶

Although Freud admits that he cannot provide a satisfactory psychoanalysis of this phenomenon, he believes that it originates in the impulse for sexual mastery and that it comes into play long before the genitals have taken their well-known and thoroughly studied role in people's sexual life.²⁶⁷ If the psychic barrier of sympathy does not develop properly during the years of sexual bodily maturation, the early links between cruelty and erogenous impulses will follow the individual into

---

264 Freud (2018), 50–55.
265 Freud (2018), 55. Castoriadis' (2005, 373) relentless sarcasm comes eventually to deride a too faithfully Freudian understanding of the psyche: "When we read psychoanalytic texts, we have the impression that the sole model of sublimation is the one in which the child, instead of playing with its feces, plays with colors and has become a painter. That's entirely ridiculous. The truth is that, as soon as the child begins to speak, the child is carrying out a sublimated activity and is in the process of sublimating. The child doesn't seek any organ pleasure; he is seeking to communicate and, in order to do this, he has cathected—and he uses—a social object, language."
266 Rican (1999) offers a psychoanalytic study of the wish to make another living being suffer *and* derive pleasure from it. More motives are thus identified than in most other studies, such as algolagnia, lust for power, compensation of inferiority feelings, curiosity, desire for intense experience, and the need to overcome loneliness.
267 Freud (2018), 51–52.

adulthood.²⁶⁸ Thus, in an indirect yet interesting medical variation on the centuries-old theme of pedagogical reform, Freud writes:

> An erogenous source of the passive impulse for cruelty (masochism) is found in the painful irritation of the gluteal region which is familiar to all educators since the confessions of J.J. Rousseau. This has justly caused them to demand that physical punishment, which usually concerns this part of the body, should be withheld from all children in whom the libido might be forced into collateral roads by the later demands of cultural education.²⁶⁹

Children who suffer repeatedly acts of cruelty while growing up, as Freud observes, end up having great difficulties in appreciating and/or accepting themselves, also as adults.²⁷⁰ Rather than examining and exculpating the neurotic and psychotic parts of our own psyche, most of us are likely to project them onto other individuals.²⁷¹ Relatedly, these children are likely to become particularly preoccupied with affirming their own value relative to other people, also by means of cruelty, which socio-cultural conditions can enable further by means of institutions such as the military or myths such as the inherent desirability of strong and stoical men.²⁷²

Some years later, in *Instincts and their Vicissitudes*, Freud comes back to the topic of sadism, arguing that the aim of the instinct for sadism is not merely to initiate dominance, but to inflict pain as such.²⁷³ Freud does not cast away his earlier reflections on the psychic origins of this instinct. As he submits: at first, a "sadistic child takes no account of whether or not he inflicts pains, nor does he intend to do so".²⁷⁴ However, Freud adds the pleasure-seeking component of sexuality to the biologically inherited instinctual propensity to subdue the sexual partner and copulate, so that the former may end up absorbing the seemingly contradictory element of pain, first in a masochistic fashion and then in a sadistic one. In a telling deviation from Nell's later use of "cruelty", Freud distinguishes between this term and

---

268 Worse barriers, based on shame, guilt or fear, produce sexual neuroses and psychoses (see, e.g., Hillman 1989).
269 Freud (2018), 51–52.
270 Psychoanalysis acknowledges different degrees of suffered cruelty, the most common being the culturally sanctioned repression of "lust" that "psychopathologizes" our most potent natural drive and, as a result, engenders "the neurotic or the psychopathic", for "the repressed always return, said Freud" (Hillman 1995b, 56 and 62–64).
271 Staub (1999), 188.
272 Staub (1999), 188.
273 Freud (1957a), 127.
274 Freud (1957a), 128.

"sadism" proper: cruel people are indifferent to other people's pain, whereas sadists derive sexual pleasure from it.[275]

In the same period, Freud's "Thoughts on War and Death" present a curious echo of Sadean and Nietzschean themes concerning amorality, the illusions of civilised life, and self-directed cruelty.[276] According to Freud, basically, there exists no real evil, but only variously chthonic instinctual impulses which all human beings share, aimed at satisfying their primal needs. These impulses are neither good nor bad, but acquire these evaluative 'labels' in the symbolic context of human societies, which oblige their members to learn how to restrain their natural drives and, *ipso facto*, develop all kinds of neuroses and/or psychoses:[277] "Civilization has been attained through the renunciation of instinctual satisfaction, and it demands the same renunciation from each newcomer in turn."[278]

As the Viennese sage explains, for societies to be able to function, our most potent and deepest individual psychic drives "are inhibited, directed towards other aims and fields, become commingled, alter their objects, and are to some extent turned back on their possessor".[279] Ironically, Freud observes how many individuals who had vigorous tendencies towards 'bad' conduct in childhood seem to be inclined towards 'good' conduct in adulthood, and *vice versa:* "Those who as children have been most pronounced egoists may well become the most helpful and self-sacrificing members of the community; most of our sentimentalists, friends of humanity and protectors of animals have been evolved from little sadists and animal-tormentors."[280]

Later in his career, Freud will also add to the mix the notion of an instinctive drive towards death, insofar as all life would seem to be seeking the restoration of its former inorganic form, in an analogy to the physical principle of entropy.[281] As Freud asserts:

---

[275] Freud (1957a), 128.
[276] Freud's private correspondence proves that he had read Nietzsche (see Chapman and Chapman-Santana 1995).
[277] In depth psychology, the aetiological crux is the repression of psychic contents, which later irrupt into a person's conscious existence and make it problematic. The irruptions of unconscious contents into a person's conscious existence are not problematic *per se*. They are a mere fact of life and, at times, they can be very healthy and very helpful, e.g., imaginings, inspirations, intuitions, insights, and ecstasies.
[278] Freud (1957b), 282. Freud's readers may wonder whether trying to cure patients is *really* good.
[279] Freud (1957b), 281. This necessary cruelty thus explains neuroses, psychoses, and prosaic lapses.
[280] Freud (1957b), 282
[281] As mentioned in *H&C1*, entropy has been associated with Sade's understanding of life and sex.

> In (multicellular) organism the libido meets the instinct of death, or destruction, which is dominant in them, and which seeks to disintegrate the cellular organism and to conduct each separate unicellular organism [composing it] into a state of inorganic stability (relative though this may be). The libido has the task of making the destroying instinct innocuous, and it fulfils the task by diverting that instinct to a greater extent outwards—soon with the help of a special organic system, the muscular apparatus—towards objects in the external world. The instinct is then called the destructive instinct, the instinct for mastery, or the will to power. A portion of the instinct is placed directly in the service of the sexual function, where it has an important part to play. This is sadism proper. Another portion does not share in this transposition outwards; it remains inside the organism and, with the help of accompanying sexual excitation described above, becomes libidinally bound there. It is in this portion we have to recognize the original, erotogenic masochism.[282]

So dismal reads Freud's understanding of human life that Bertrand Russell includes "what the Freudians call the death wish" among "the things that [our age] must avoid", i.e., "envy, greed, competitiveness, search for irrational subjective certainty" and, of course, "cruelty".[283]

3.2.2 Randall Collins

> When a savage is made prisoner of war, and receives, as is usual, the sentence of death from his conquerors, he hears it without expressing any emotion, and afterwards submits to the most dreadful torments, without ever bemoaning himself, or discovering any other passion but contempt of his enemies.
> —Adam Smith[284]

In sociology, Randall Collins published in 1974 a largely forgotten essay entitled "Three Faces of Cruelty: Towards a Comparative Sociology of Violence", in which he offers a thoroughly articulated study of 'cruelty' on the basis of Marxist Conflict Theory.[285] While ignoring the possible cruelties of nature or fate, Collins identifies three dimensions of human cruelty:

---

[282] Freud (1995), 279.
[283] Russell (2009), 626. Overall, Freud's depiction of an endless and hopeless struggle between desire and reality can be said to constitute yet another token of dim cosmic irony, akin to the tragic outlook of Western pessimism.
[284] Smith (1790), part 5, chap. 2, par. 9.
[285] Collins (1974).

(1) "ferociousness" or "overt brutality";
(2) "callousness"; and
(3) "asceticism".[286]

(1) Cases of "ferociousness" or "overt brutality" refer to mutilation, amputations of feet and hands, gouging out eyes, and the many types of maiming that have been used throughout history so as to impose a "punishment not by death, but by life at its lowest level".[287] Similarly, Collins points also to the regular use of torture, which he describes as the careful use, lengthening, and augmentation of human pain so as to maximise not only the victims' terror, but also attendant deterrent effect, which can therefore be most helpful in preserving the existent class structure and social hierarchy.[288] Ritual war-hunts fall under this category, and so do peremptory executions and human sacrifices: "These cruelties are not only deliberate, they are ceremonially recurrent defences of the structure of group domination."[289]

(2) "Ferocity" is not a major feature in modern societies.[290] Public tortures and executions, ritual mutilations and humiliations, and so many other macabre carnivals of history are no longer commonplace in most nations, although they may still be carried out behind closed doors in at least some of them.[291] This remarkable change Collins credits to philosophical rationalism, the European Enlightenment, the anti-slavery campaigns, British utilitarianism, and progressive movements.[292] In its place, "callousness and bureaucratization" have become the new norm, i.e., cruelty devoid of strong passions.[293] This is cruelty that is routinely inflicted without any open intention to hurt the victims. Albeit not a modern invention, this cold, calculating, functional cruelty has thrived in modern societies because of their advanced level of economic development, institutional organisation, and technological advancement.[294]

---

[286] Collins (1974), 419.
[287] Collins (1974), 419.
[288] Collins (1974), 419–422. Beccaria's notes about life-imprisonment may reveal it to be the 'best' of tortures.
[289] Collins (1974), 422.
[290] Collins (1974), 431.
[291] Leacock (1942, chap. 1, par. 4) reminds us also of the fact that *regress* into cruelty is a historical possibility: "[T]ill just a short time ago this almost world-wide freedom seemed to be a permanent achievement and advance of humanity. Then came the war... Human kindliness is replaced by cruelties unknown for centuries."
[292] Collins (1974), 431.
[293] Collins (1974), 432.
[294] Collins (1974), 432.

(3) "Asceticism" is, à la Nietzsche, cruelty towards the self.[295] Again, this is not a modern reality, but the age-old tradition of painful self-denial in the name of mystical rewards. While apparently a very private affair, Collins claims it to be a most potent social activity.[296] Not only does it elevate the status of its most successful practitioners, but it also reinforces the notion of non-interference into the affairs and decisions of the ruling elites.[297] Moreover, insofar as asceticism concentrates the psychic energies of the individual, it can successfully motivate legions of well-meaning persons to take part in all sorts of life-destructive crusades, whether religious or secular, old or new, and always somewhat paradoxical, for they aspire to do paramount good by means of palpable evil.[298] Repression can pervert expression, but it cannot entirely prevent the latter. As a result, questionable cruelty often accompanies and mirrors these persons' quest for purity.[299]

Psychologically, Collins' study is important, for its forays into the realm of "ferocity" provide a well-documented denial of the widespread pathologising notion whereby cruelty is to be understood as the result of an empathy deficit and/or cognitive misery, i.e., as an abnormal deficiency in recognising other persons' thoughts and feelings:

> The torturer or the mutilator, however, could not even attempt his arts without a capacity to for taking the role of the other. The torturer does not kill and eat; he concentrates instead on inflicting pain, and above all, in conveying to his victim his intentions and powers for inflicting this pain. For the animal, terror is only an incident in the combat; for the torturer, it is the prime target. Torture and mutilation, then, are distinctively human acts; they are indeed advanced human acts. The boundaries between groups are involved, making possible the detachment that allows (and motivates) a free use of cruelty; but there is a skill at empathizing across the boundary, enough to be able to gauge the effect of cruelty on the victim. This distinctively human violence becomes symbolic; torture and mutilation are above all forms of communication usable as threats and supports for claims of complete domination. "I can get inside your mind", the torturer boasts: "don't even think of resistance".[300]

---

295 Collins (1974), 434.
296 Collins (1974), 433–436.
297 Collins (1974), 433–437.
298 Collins (1974), 433–437.
299 Collins (1974), 433–437.
300 Collins (1974), 422. For a recent example of a conception of "cruelty" proper as "the worst thing that can be done to a human being" resulting from "empathy erosion", see Baron-Cohen (2012, 6–10). As to the mental connection between torturer and victim, Kathryn Bigelow's 1995 sci-fi crime thriller *Strange Days* twists and toys with it artistically in the cruellest manner. The film depicts a serial rapist who, by means of a neural device, causes his victims to experience the former's pleasures while raping them, yet without suppressing their pain either.

Should this truly count as madness, there would still be a conscious, chilling, considered, and calculating method to it.

3.2.3 Caputo, Kemp, and Brodsky

> I am not surprised ... that a multitude of persons whom I do not at all suspect of barbarism and of cruelty consider, on the faith of opinions commonly received, capital punishment and the guillotine as things normal and necessary: just as in Middle Ages one considered as things normal and necessary the stake,—and torture.
> —Jacques Maritain[301]

At the close of the 20th century, three social psychologists tackle straightforwardly the only seemingly "simple question, what is cruelty?"[302] Admittedly, "despite its wide descriptive use", which is duly recorded by lexicographers and linguists, this notion remains "elusive" and, perhaps unsurprisingly, their own research confirms this point.[303]

(1) The extant dictionaries of the English language depict very many interpretations of this term, which is further complicated by its adverbial usage as meaning "'very' or 'exceedingly'", as well by its being synonymic, in Oceania's English, with "'to spoil', as 'to cruel a chance' at winning a hand in a card game".[304]

(2) A survey of how the notion itself, its acceptance, and/or its condemnation have changed in the course of history presents a most diverse picture too. While referring to Aristotle's reflections on "calculated acts of outrage" as a possible germinal take on "cruelty" proper, the oldest and most significant source on the subject is said to be, predictably, Seneca, whose "distinction between cruelty and savagery" is duly recalled and emphasised.[305]

(3) As to the motives for cruel agency, two standard explanations are reconstructed:

(3a) "revenge", whether fairly immediate and well-targeted or mutated into generalised cruel behaviour in a person's adulthood; and,

---

301 Maritain (1973b), 283 note 19, is also a reminder to all empirical scientists: institutionalised cruelty can go unseen.
302 Caputo, Brodsky, and Kemp (2000), 649. Their earlier study appeared as Kemp, Brodsky, and Caputo (1997) but, in order to facilitate their association, our bibliography lists the two articles as in the former list of authors. Playfully, our heading matches neither.
303 Caputo, Brodsky, and Kemp (2000), 649.
304 Caputo, Brodsky, and Kemp (2000), 650.
305 Caputo, Brodsky, and Kemp (2000), 650.

(3b) pretty much *à la* Sade or Nietzsche, a "natural urge" to wreak havoc.[306]

(4) While considering the previous literature on "sadistic offenders" and "psychopathy" that corroborate and/or falsify these two standard explanations, the three social scientists state that "one possible way to define cruelty may be as awareness and enjoyment of the pain intentionally inflicted on others".[307] Logically, then, "simple brutality and mindless aggression" would not constitute "cruelty" from this perspective, nor would sexual or other kinds of assault on "comatose victims" and "corpses" or the consensual paedophilia practices "by the members of the National Man-Boy Love Association".[308] Such a conclusion, they imply, is highly perplexing and, ultimately, unconvincing.[309]

(5) Merging new empirical evidence with the results of earlier studies, which were conducted in New Zealand and the US, the three social psychologists end up identifying "four common themes" that, unequivocally, give rise to claims of "cruelty": "murder and physical assault … sexual assault … societal harm … and ordinary or minor acts of cruelty".[310] Thus, "cruelty" would apply to homicide, battery, "molestation … torture … religious, racial, and ethnic persecution … prank telephone calls … throwing eggs at houses … gossip, teasing, and ridicule".[311] Less common, yet also mentioned and, in their view, most plausible, are cases referring to "confinement, kidnapping, mental abuse, and attempted suicide as an act of revenge".[312]

While "male participants were more likely … to cite murder of physical assault as the cruelest acts … the female participants were more likely … to cite societal cruelty or miscellaneous acts as most cruel".[313] The latter typology includes "the

---

[306] Caputo, Brodsky, and Kemp (2000), 650–651.
[307] Caputo, Brodsky, and Kemp (2000), 652.
[308] Caputo, Brodsky, and Kemp (2000), 652.
[309] We expect most of our readers to agree with the three social psychologists on this point.
[310] Caputo, Brodsky, and Kemp (2000), 654.
[311] Caputo, Brodsky, and Kemp (2000), 654.
[312] Caputo, Brodsky, and Kemp (2000), 654. Ironically, the great 20th-century Polish philosopher Roman Ingarden (1983, 21) retrieved a redeeming feature for suicide that relates to cruelty: "Man is capable of frightful, cruel and inhumane deeds, but at the same time he is the sole creature to feel humiliated by his evil deeds, and to try to atone for his sins. In the limit, he is prepared to kill himself in order to salvage his honour, and he is surely the only creature for whom honour, and the denigration of this honour, exists at all."
[313] Caputo, Brodsky, and Kemp (2000), 655. What we grasp as 'murder' depends on our ethico-/onto-/cosmo-/logical assumptions and tacit socio-cultural standards. For example, a controversial US cultural critic and self-styled "dissident feminist", Camille Paglia (2008, pars. 11 and 23–24), states: "[N]ature has a master plan pushing every species toward procreation and … it is our right and even obligation as rational human beings to defy nature's fascism… Hence, I have always frankly admitted that abortion is murder, the extermination of the powerless by the powerful. Lib-

crucifixion of Christ, the Nazi killings of Jews in concentration camps, and the assassination of Martin Luther King, Jr.".[314] Most of the reported cruelty is "vicarious" rather than personally committed and/or experienced, although more than 60 % of the respondents admit to being guilty of "ordinary cruelty", especially "sexual victimization" among "male participants".[315] As to the reasons why the respondents characterise certain actions as "cruel", the features of the offense (e.g., "slowness", "painfulness", "longevity of damage"), victim (e.g., "innocence", "disabilities", "helplessness"), and perpetrator (e.g., "sadism") are regularly taken into account too.[316]

Summa summarum, as far as their studies in social psychology are concerned: the overall statistical differences relate to the respondents' gender; old and new data are mutually consonant; and, above all, they are very 'ecumenical', since the recorded usages of "cruelty" proper cover an immense array of occurrences, from the rare personal accounts of criminal sadism to the much more prosaic reported wounds of unrequited love among adolescents.[317] However, a general tendency to underplay personal cruelty and instead emphasise vicarious cruelty emerges as well.[318]

Perhaps the world seems crueller when it is seen from a distance, perchance through "popular films or television programs"; or else, deep-seated self-defence psychic mechanisms kick in (e.g., "a social desirability effect") whenever dealing with one's own cruel experiences, whether as a victim or as a perpetrator (e.g., "verbal degradation and lying").[319] In any case, studying what "cruelty" means in daily language results, in the end, in acknowledging a vast and diverse plethora of loosely associated phenomena which may yet fail to include those cruelties that,

---

erals for the most part have shrunk from facing the ethical consequences of their embrace of abortion, which results in the annihilation of concrete individuals and not just clumps of insensate tissue."

314 Caputo, Brodsky, and Kemp (2000), 656.
315 Caputo, Brodsky, and Kemp (2000), 657. Studying vicarious cruelty among university students, Park and Kim (2019, 733) report that "the majority of the students identified as both victim and perpetrator". Perhaps our propensity for 'toying' with and possibly revelling in *both* roles in our imagination is what makes violence so commonplace in fictional scenarios (more on this matter is discussed in Chapter 3 of Part 2).
316 Caputo, Brodsky, and Kemp (2000), 658.
317 We do not mean to belittle teenage romances and heartbreaks, which can scar deeply and still echo in old age.
318 Caputo, Brodsky, and Kemp (2000), 659.
319 Caputo, Brodsky, and Kemp (2000), 659.

3.2.4 Victor Nell

> Fucking is entirely a male act designed to affirm the reality and power of the phallus, of masculinity. For women, the pleasure in being fucked is the masochistic pleasure of experiencing self-negation.
> —Andrea Dworkin[321]

In a 2006 article, Nell proposes that the reinforcement value of exacting pain and instigating carnage derive from animal predatory adaptation processes, the beginnings of which can be retrieved in the Middle Cambrian period, i.e., about 500 million years ago.[322] Nell puts forth five hypotheses as relevant research topics in the bio-social sciences.[323] Echoing in part Sade's and Nietzsche's worldview, his hypotheses are as follows:

(1) Cruelty is a behavioural derivative of animal predation.
(2) Cruelty is driven by reinforcers springing from this adaptation processes.
(3) Given that cruelty presupposes the intention to inflict pain and is, in all likelihood, exclusively a hominid behaviour, it cannot pre-date *homo erectus*, i.e., it may have begun emerging around 1.5 million years ago.
(4) Cruelty provides evolutionary benefits with regard to survival and reproduction.
(5) The enjoyment of cruelty is a culturally expanded indicator of the older evolutionary process of predatory adaptation.[324]

Nell proposes three stages in the evolutionary history of human cruelty.[325]

---

320 See also *H&C1*.
321 Dworkin (1976), 108. Male-female sexual relations might be an example of institutionalised cruelty—or not (see Baroncelli 1996, 36, as mentioned in Chapter 1). Masochism itself can be interpreted in different ways (see also Chapter 3 of Part 2).
322 Nell (2006). A more extensive account was given in *H&C1*.
323 Nell (2006), 211.
324 Nell (2006), 211. After Sade and Nietzsche, the depiction of the human being as "a gorgeous, bold, cunning and cruel beast of prey" reverberates in many varieties of Darwinism (Kolnai 1938, 204, citing Oswald Spengler).
325 Nell (2006), 212–217. All ensuing quotes and statements are based on these pages, until noted otherwise.

(1) *Predation* and aggression are, in his view, closely intertwined. Mere aggression does not necessitate complex neural networks and/or effector organs. It can be observed in the most primitive organisms. From a Darwinian standpoint, moreover, all species are assumed to be constantly competing for resources, both inter- and intra-specially. Competitive aggression is therefore the likeliest precursor to predation, which gave select animals an evolutionary advantage *vis-à-vis* self-preservation, procreation, protection of the offspring, and access to vital resources. In the Cambrian period, this precursor may have fully matured into the existence of predators, which are reinforced by conditioned stimuli that scientists call "the pain-blood-death (PBD) complex".[326]

(1a) PBD refers to the prey's terrible struggle to flee which, if unsuccessful, leads to the shedding of its blood and its screaming while being devoured. Studies of mammalian predation show unequivocally the co-occurrence of increased levels of arousal, major sensory feedback, and the presence of the search-swoop-kill-feed cycle, which involves all kinds of auditory, visual, olfactory, tactile, gustatory, and visceral stimuli.

During both mammalian and hominid evolution, the prey's flight, and pain, and then the sight, smell, and taste of blood, were prominent among the reinforcers that shaped the predatory and hunting adaptations. For predators, pain and blood signal satiation; for humans, they are the harbingers not only of impending satiation or sexual access, but also of the animal's death, which was bound up with the precarious survival of Pleistocene hunters. A great variety of anticipatory and consummatory reinforcers are equally activated, and neurobiological studies suggest that this process is driven by dopamine, a neurotransmitter related to our pleasure centres, and which is not the same as those accompanying observed instances of rage.

(1b) Predatory animals appear to be extremely tense when involved in the search-swoop-kill-feed cycle, both physically and mentally. Also, predators become greatly aroused in the presence of prey, and although the former may look ever-so-patiently approaching the latter, the autonomic nervous system is fully activated in anticipation of the likely chase and attendant infliction of pain, release of the prey's blood, and stimuli signalling its imminent death. Nell suggests that it is quite possible that, in predatory species, blood turned eventually into the reward

---

[326] As noted by Horkheimer and Adorno (1989, 113): "[Z]oology tells us that, in the male and female, 'love' or sexual attraction were originally and essentially 'sadistic', and ... associated with pain; love is as cruel as hunger."

system driving this kind of behaviour. Later, through unknown processes that Nell does not dare address, it may have become a symbolic-cultural icon.[327]

(2) Nutritional killing by our hominid ancestors was also a demanding endeavour which was driven by the same reinforcers of the PBD complex. *Hunting*, it should be noted, is not only deadly to the prey, but it also presents critical dangers to the predator. The prey, for instance, can fight back, sometimes with grave consequences, and even when the hunting deed is successfully completed, the predator may have to fight off dangerous scavengers. It is therefore not particularly surprising, at least from a neurochemical point of view, that, along with a boost of pleasure-enhancing dopamine, the search-swoop-kill-feed cycle is also accompanied with endogenous opioid production which guards against and/or prepares for the pains of injury.

(3) Cruelty is, however, a human mental activity which requires cognitive and social functions allowing for intentionality and discipline. Once these fundamental abilities evolved, various adventitious socio-cultural elaborations concerning retribution, gratification, and dominance followed—though how and when they did so are questions to which we may never be able to find an answer. Each of these elaborations further confirmed the *power* of the perpetrator of cruelty, whether at an individual level or a collective one. For the individual, cruelty can translate into evolutionary advantage *vis-à-vis* survival, status, and sexual access. For collective entities, cruelty can translate into power-bolstering entertainments, ritualised displays of dominance, and/or means of conquest and further hierarchical entrenchment.

Nell links a wide array of human behaviours to the pain-blood-death complex. In his view, everything on this hypothetical axis, from the vicarious enjoyment of media violence to the vicious participation in acts of torture and abuse, is reinforced by primeval neuronal pathways channelling powerful emotive responses. This hidden animal basis would explain, in his view, the universality of these emotions, "which erupt as powerfully in the educated and morally exemplary citizens of the twenty-first century as in the monsters of history".[328]

Given the social character of the human animal, cruelty has not evolved in directions threatening our own very survival as a species. Rather, it has morphed and developed into a variety of ways making human communities more likely to survive and, at the same time, eminently cruel. For example, as Nell argues, "pub-

---

[327] How exactly the animal and physiological phenomena investigated by evolutionary psychology turn into human and psychosocial phenomena is a gap that no discipline has been able to fill.
[328] Nell (2006), 223.

lic punishment would have been strongly adaptive by contributing to effective hunting, defence, mate guarding, and stable food sharing".[329]

Militarism, oppressive social control, disciplinarian pedagogies, vicious moralism, sadistic mockery, and subtler forms of violence and oppression, in an evolutionary perspective, are neither 'good' nor 'bad', but a matter of fitness and survival. Echoing the seemingly amoral neutrality reached by Freud in his mature years, Nell concludes: "Whether a cultural innovation spreads or becomes extinct will be determined by its social utility and its contribution to individual fitness."[330]

3.2.5 George Ainslie

> Discipline was cruel enough in all the eighteenth-century armies, created long after the decay of any faith or hope that could hold men together. But the state that was first in Germany was first in ferocity. Frederick the Great had to forbid his English admirers to follow his regiments during the campaign, lest they should discover that the most enlightened of kings had only excluded torture from law to impose it without law.
> —G.K. Chesterton[331]

George Ainslie, a contemporary US psychiatrist, behavioural economist and psychologist, has recently tried to explain "cruelty" proper as a self-control device against sympathy; i.e., as a form of self-protection.[332] Insofar as sympathy, as a mental response, is promptly rewarded by positive emotions, it is inherently difficult to subject it to voluntary control. A person's sympathy, as Ainslie argues, can easily be abused by plenty of people around us.[333] When other options fail or are unavailable, cruelty may be an effective shield against such people.[334] In other words, to protect ourselves, we counter our sympathies by means of negative empathy.[335]

Ainslie rejects Nell's idea that only humans can be cruel because of their ability to see themselves acting cruelly. Quite the opposite, Ainslie refers to animal ex-

---

329 Nell (2006), 218.
330 Nell (2006), 219.
331 Chesterton (1916), chap. 4, par. 8. Instrumental cruelty has always been of the essence in military life.
332 Ainslie (2006), 225.
333 Ainslie (2006), 225.
334 Ainslie (2006), 225.
335 Ainslie (2006), 225.

amples of cruelty that make no use of such sophisticated cognitive faculties.[336] In doing so, he also indulges in a little humorous wordplay:

> It is not clear whether a cat plays with a mouse partially in order to savor the distress of the victim, or merely because it is an optimally challenging game. The common human projection onto this activity certainly includes the savoring, as in *Tom & Jerry*, but since a real Tom has no TOM he is presumably not imagining his victim's suffering, much less trying to induce it.[337]

Ainslie claims that most human hunters have never been elated by watching their prey agonise and die.[338] Some deviant, truly sadistic individuals may have always existed, but the traditions of many 'primitive' cultures show a marked propensity towards ceremonial apologies to their prey, customary displays of gratitude, and sacred means of shortening the victims' agony.[339] At the same time, Ainslie acknowledges that the same pious cultures can ritualise and enjoy torturing their prisoners of war. In this respect, as Ainslie argues, "the urge to do injurious things while disregarding or actively avoiding attention to the suffering of victims is different from the urge to seek out and even enhance this suffering—although the disregarding might sometimes be a reaction against the latter urge".[340]

Ainslie is well aware of cruelty's life-disabling and potentially detrimental effects, but he is willing to acknowledge its redeeming qualities too. Sometimes, as a form of individual and/or collective "negative empathy", cruelty can facilitate and/ or protect the good, however construed this axiological notion may be:

> As with anger, there are people who cultivate cruelty habitually, presumably in default of richer sources of reward, but occasional cruelty seems to be common to everyone. It is the commonplace examples that best differentiate negative empathy from Nell's examples of predation: the pleasures of seeing the boor get his comeuppance, the driver who cut us off stopped by the police, and the pretensions of the poseur punctured, as well as less respectable examples like schadenfreude and our minor persecution of people whom we hope we do not resemble.[341]

This is commonly seen in popular entertainment, as most of us would be terribly disappointed if the James Bond villain did not suffer a terrible fate at the end of

---

336 Whether or not animals possess such faculties, or how much, is open to debate and ongoing research.
337 Ainslie (2006), 224. "TOM" standing for "theory of mind", i.e., the ascription of mental states to others.
338 Ainslie (2006), 224.
339 Ainslie (2006), 224.
340 Ainslie (2006), 225.
341 Ainslie (2006), 225.

the movie.³⁴² We need to get our dose of cruelty, however vicarious and seemingly innocent, to leave the theatre pleased. As perplexing as it may appear, at least *prima facie*, Ainslie's account buttresses further this cautious yet reasoned positive appraisal of cruelty, especially of the vicarious sort, and suggests that life-enabling cruelty can prove to be, in ultimate analysis, effectively *good.*³⁴³

Instrumentally, positive value may, can, and, reasonably, should be attributed to cruelty, at least under special circumstances, i.e., when it broadens and/or deepens compossible and comprehensive life-ranges much more thoroughly than avoiding it reduces them. Perhaps it even ought to. As seen, this counterintuitive approach was already defended during the Italian Renaissance by Niccolò Machiavelli, about whom the great 20th-century child psychologist and phenomenologist, Maurice Merleau-Ponty, states: "in historical action, goodness is sometimes catastrophic and cruelty less cruel than the easy-going mood".³⁴⁴ Proverbial wisdom agrees. On occasion, according to the grapevine, "you've got to be cruel to be kind".³⁴⁵

---

342 We discuss in more detail the cruel joys of popular entertainments in *H&C2*.
343 We remind our readers that LVOA offers solid coordinates for distinguishing between good and bad. Given that LVOA cuts underneath and through all received dichotomies (e.g., individualism vs. collectivism, paternalism vs. egotism, conservatism vs. revolutionism), our reader might feel uncertain about our moral and political stances. The uncertainty may also be increased by our repeated attempts at presenting the same phenomena from a variety of perspectives, so as to reveal cruelties or forms of humour that could easily go unnoticed. Then, the reader must ask him-/herself: *What leads to the deepest and broadest ranges of comprehensive and compossible action/felt being/thought?* Answering this question may not be easy and/or possible, yet *that* is the ultimate criterion of good and evil in morals and politics.
344 Merleau-Ponty (1964a), 216.
345 If, when, how, by whom, and why the necessary determinations are made are all thorny context-specific issues. See Chapter 3 of Part 2.

4 Making Sense of Polysemy

> All thought is incarnate; it lives by the body and by the favour of society. But it is not *thought* unless it strives for truth, a striving which leaves it free to act on its own responsibility, with universal intent.
> —Michael Polanyi[1]

Whether one charts the main usages of a word, devotes him-/herself to conceptual and/or linguistic analyses, reconstructs the history of the notions under scrutiny, or investigates the insights provided by common sense and/or shared idioms, variances and/or discrepancies are bound to surface. Normally, unless some ingenious, expedient, and restricting stipulation has been actuated beforehand, most people offer neither regularly nor exactly the same interpretations of a certain concept. Not only are these people likely to disagree mutually, but given enough time, they may end up disagreeing with themselves too—and even call it "wisdom".[2]

Wiser or not, univocity is *not* the norm whenever a concept belongs to people's natural languages, as opposed to the ever more artificial languages of, say, administrative law, formal logic, chemistry, or algebra. Certainly, people's uses of any ordinary concept are bound to display sizeable areas of conspicuous and helpful overlap, but also frequent eccentricities, deviating rhetorical goals, and enthymemic reasonings, as well as ample arrays of regional and/or individual peculiarities. Were these eccentricities, deviations, and peculiarities never to occur, not even once, all misunderstandings would simply disappear.[3]

Yet, differences and misunderstandings persist, even among people who have lived very close to one another for extremely long periods of time, sometimes since birth. Blunders, yes, but also new uses of an old term, exploits of personal creativity, emergent linguistic-conceptual drifts, shrewd in-group jargon, variously credible substitutions, suggestive anomalies, solving new problems with old tools, and, maybe, the budding new normality, which a yet-unknown future can alone prove or disprove to be so—provided, of course, that the linguistic community does not vanish suddenly because of war, cataclysm, environmental collapse, and/or any other fatal event of adequately tragic magnitude.[4]

---

[1] Polanyi (1969a), 134; emphasis in the original.
[2] We explained our own take on the term "wisdom" in *H&C1*, with reference to the Icelandic philosopher Páll Skúlason.
[3] See Richards (1965), lecture 1.
[4] The gravity of the ongoing climate crisis, which we tackle briefly in Chapter 1 of Part 2, makes such an end likely. Any reader thinking that this crisis is a matter of opinion, a political baseball, or

Artificial, fundamentally stipulative, and painstakingly agreed-upon meanings have been commonplace among scholars, academicians, professionals, and all sorts of experts for a very long time. Consistency of signification has been regarded, quite reasonably, as extremely desirable and, *au contraire*, ambiguity has been generally presumed to be negative.[5] Nevertheless, there may exist valid reasons why ambiguity endures in all languages, including within specialised and/or truly paramount socio-cultural and interpersonal contexts, such as literature (e.g., poetical allusion), psychotherapy (e.g., mental associations), diplomacy (e.g., peace-keeping flexibility), legal hermeneutics (e.g., constructive equivocation), pedagogy (e.g., suggestive analogies), fire-fighting (e.g., context-dependant standards of danger), married life (e.g., charitable interpretation), and the hard sciences (e.g., insight-generating "models").[6]

Basically, we just can't help it. Concepts and conceptions vary. Meanings are, both diachronically and synchronically, supple, if not fluid. They are like a river, its banks, and its bed; or like a seafaring vessel that, over time, gets rebuilt, again and again, with new planks, new sails, and new materials, until nothing of the original ship is left, not even the initial structure.[7] This simple truth may be unsatisfactory to some well-meaning and very intelligent people, who aim at carving nature at its joints and/or at promulgating laws *sub specie aeternitatis*, whether consciously or subconsciously. Nevertheless, it is true.[8]

It would be enough to consider and ponder upon the differences and misunderstandings arising from translations and/or textual exegeses.[9] Polysemy, if not, at times, ultimate indefinability and/or pronounced obscurity, can affect the most commonplace concepts as well as the most uncommon ones.[10] And there may be

---

worse, a hoax, is sincerely invited to read Armstrong McKay *et al.* (2022). It is a *cruel irony* that the ongoing climate crisis, by unfolding at a somewhat slower pace than human everyday perception allows each person to grasp with immediacy, fails to arouse the same sense of patent threat and attendant instinct for survival as, say, a burning house or a physical assault in the middle of a street would be generally capable of producing.

5 See, e.g., Cole (2019). Lately, Brogaard and Gatzia (2021, title *et passim*) covered some analogous issues under the umbrella-term of "ambivalence". Curiously, none of the collected essays deals with "humour" proper in any form.

6 On the last example, see Agazzi (2014), par. 6.3.3.

7 See, respectively, Wittgenstein (1975, propositions 96–97 and 99) and Neurath in Zolo (1989, 22f.).

8 We warned the reader that we would make few trenchant statements in our volume. This is one of them.

9 See, e.g., Hemmat (2021, 4), who stressed the importance of "being playful" when translating.

10 It is frustrating, but also rather funny, to come across academic peers who behave as if their understanding of terms such as "liberalism", "humour", "political correctness", "justice", etc., were the one and only one of any genuine and reliable significance. And yet, ironically, "humour" itself has both meant and been 'fluid'.

good reasons for accepting things the way they are, as we are going to illustrate in the rest of this short chapter.[11]

4.1 A Theory of Concepts: Michael Polanyi

> The soul is only an abstraction until we meet its courageous will to live or its judicious decision or its humor.
> —James Hillman[12]

The noted 20th-century Hungarian polymath Michael Polanyi, for one, observed how any lexicon, in order to be beneficial, has to be finite, so that its constituent terms can be acquired, assessed, and applied to the potentially infinite circumstances awaiting that lexicon's users. Confronting unusual circumstances, new terms are certainly created, yet never as a matter of course. No language, whether ordinary or specialistic, can allow its lexicon to grow without end, lest the lexicon stops being useful. This is akin to the way in which too detailed a map would eventually lose any value for its per-users: "A map is the more accurate the nearer its scale approaches unity, but if it were to reach unity and represent the features of a landscape in their natural size, it would become useless, since it would be about as difficult to find one's way on the map as in the region represented by it."[13]

4.1.1 Gestaltpsychologie

Without addressing the fascinating and, on occasion, intricate details of Polanyi's account of scientific knowledge whence most of his reflections about language and ambiguity unfolded, we can nevertheless derive from it the key-idea that concepts are *Gestalten* [forms, structures]. This term refers to the 20th-century *Gestalt* school of thought in psychology that Polanyi described as a decisive source of inspiration for his work.[14] He was far from being unconventional or alone in embracing this influence. None less than Bertrand Russell, one of the noble fathers of analytic philosophy, wrote:

---

11 The acceptance at issue is a token of personal responsibility in a socio-epistemic context.
12 Hillman (1999), 11. Concepts come alive for a person when they are *cathected* by her.
13 Polanyi (1962c), 84. The wisdom of this passage was also central to *H&C1* and *H&C2*.
14 Polanyi (1962c), preface and 158. Mixing equally philosophy and psychology, his angle appeals greatly to us.

> There are three matters to be considered in beginning the study of language. First: what words are, regarded as physical occurrences; secondly, what are the circumstances that lead us to use a given word; thirdly, what are the effects of our hearing or seeing a given word. But as regards the second and third of these questions, we shall find ourselves led on from words to sentences and thus confronted with fresh problems, perhaps demanding rather the methods of *Gestaltpsychologie*.[15]

By this specific German term, *Gestalt*, which we ourselves adopt hereby, Polanyi intended to signify *organised molar structures of personal cognition uniting in a meaningful way a plurality of diverse facets of reality* that, without such structuring concepts, would be either meaningless or merely partially integrated within other concepts.[16] Let us expand on this definition a little and explain it further.

According to Polanyi, each concept or, to be exact, each thinking individual's conception of a concept, when deliberately considered, becomes *ipso facto* a personally private yet socially rooted "focal" object.[17] This object being that *to* which we attend by attending *from* the uncountable and often undefinable "subsidiary details" that we cannot but entertain too—not least a plethora of appurtenant concepts upon which we are not focussing at that point, but rather relying upon *tacitly* as a legacy of our mental make-up and acculturation.[18]

This intentional 'from-to' phenomenological order combines together:
(1) ourselves *qua* the specific psychophysical actions' chief 'subject/s';
(2) whatever central 'object/s' may be at issue (e.g., 'humour' or 'cruelty' *qua* concepts); and
(3) the innumerable secondary ones—concepts included—residing inside and around us (e.g., the rules of grammar allowing the reader to grasp the meaning of these sentences, the light that makes the printed markings visible).

As such, in Polanyi's estimate, it is at work in *all* cognitive operations of which we are capable, e.g., perception, recollection, problem-solving, pattern-recognition, etc.[19] In other words, all inputs for any person's *Gestalt*-based cognitive apprehen-

---

[15] Russell (2009), 80. See, e.g., S. Schwartz (2012) on Russell's being among the founders of analytic philosophy.
[16] The term "personal" was Polanyi's pointed choice, especially as distinguished from "subjective", which carries strong sceptical implications in the imaginary of modern Western philosophy. Therefore, when using "subject/ive" and "object/ive" in this section, we cast each term between single quotation marks, so as to stress its non-literal and analogical use. We use it here for the sake of theoretical explanation, not of textual exactitude.
[17] Polanyi (1962c), 57.
[18] Polanyi (1962c), 57–58.
[19] That the subsidiary details (SD) lead to (1) a person's perceptual and/or cognitive *phenomenon* is, probably, the most obvious description of the relationship between SD and their focal point (FP).

sion at any level (i.e., Polanyi's "subsidiary details")—whether known, unknown, knowable, and/or unknowable to the specific person—originate from:
(1) the item that the person tackles attentively (e.g., a painting), which may not yet be known in an exact way (e.g., the yet-unresolved solution to a riddle);
(2) the item's surroundings (e.g., the frame and wall around the painting, the ground on which the wall stands, etc.); and
(3) the physical and psychological inner worlds to which that very same person, if healthy and socialised, may have access (e.g., her cervical and ocular muscles, kinaesthetic sense, recollections of earlier visits to art galleries, tacit assumptions and/or expectations about frames and walls, socio-culturally inherited "comprehensive … interpretative framework[s]" that have not been forgotten and are being applied tacitly, etc.)[20]

This fundamental phenomenology of mental activity is exemplified and elucidated by Polanyi by reflecting on the way in which we attend thoughtfully *to* the head of a "nail" by attending, less thoughtfully, *from* a "hammer" whereby we plan to strike the head of that nail.[21] If we did not have any "awareness" whatsoever of the hammer, its weight, our distributed muscular tension, our memory of former similar actions, the wall in front of us, etc., to at least *some* degree—albeit a lesser one than that at which we are currently focussing on the nail's head—we would not be able to hold the hammer effectively in our hand, move it in the correct way, and, essentially, perform the planned task well or well enough.[22]

Indeed, this fact could also explain why Polanyi's epistemology is often dubbed a "phenomenology". However, in his oeuvre, Polanyi describes, more or less clearly, at least three more: (2) FP is the *function* of SD (e.g., a machine's propulsion is the function of its parts and processes); (3) FP is the *meaning* of SD (e.g., the reader's understanding of what we have just written; the mind *qua* meaning of the body); (4) FP is an inexhaustible and genuine *aspect* of reality presented to us by SD (e.g., humour and cruelty as reported and investigated in our volume) (Baruchello 2017a, 228).

20 Polanyi (1969b), 82–84. The comprehensive character of cognitive apprehension is highlighted by another 20th-century phenomenologist and psychologist inspired by the *Gestalt* school, i.e., Merleau-Ponty (see , e.g., Nilsen 2008).

21 Polanyi (1962c), 57. Concepts are like hammers, which we use subsidiarily and efficiently for an indeterminate number of ends. When our attention turns onto the hammer itself, *defining* "hammer" shows immediately the complexity of this different task, for, *inter alia*, we may have been holding in our hand a mallet, rock or shoe.

22 Polanyi (1962c), 57. Although part of the subsidiary details at play may be admittedly subliminal, subconscious, or even "unconscious", Polanyi's (1962c, 64) epistemological curiosity pivots around all those physical and mental details requiring a lower yet conscious level of awareness, e.g., our muscular tension in holding the hammer, the sense of its weight, the perception of its distance from the nail, our memory of previous hammerings, etc.

4.1.2 Excursus

As a matter of common experience, plenty of black fingernails and swollen thumbs go to show that we do not always hit the nail on the head. As stated, *all* cognitive apprehensions fall under the scope of Polanyi's *from-to* phenomenology, which therefore applies as well to cognitions that are erroneous, misguided, and even psychopathological.[23] Upon their eventually unhelpful basis, failures, blunders, accidents, mishaps, and all sorts of unintended consequences can and do ensue, sorrily and prosaically, when not cruelly. Indeed, even specialists and professionals, at times, can make serious mistakes, whether individually or as a group.[24]

In contemporary psychology, David J. Ley presented a curiously 'Polanyian' or, perhaps more aptly, unintentionally '*Polanyiesque*' depiction of the *foregrounded* category of "sex addiction" as resting upon a wide-ranging *background* of tacitly assumed notions.[25] These, in turn, make such a controversial clinical category acceptable and accepted among many alleged experts because a suitable plethora of tacitly assumed notions are conveniently and consistently left unquestioned, in spite of the "vagueness and lack of clarity" transpiring thereof whenever these background notions are actually foregrounded and actively examined *in se*.[26]

"Sex addiction" can then make sense and be taken seriously, according to Ley's critical account, as long as an adequate number of vague and unclear background notions are accepted on fiduciary grounds and/or used accessorily with sufficient insistence and persistence, hence "confusing rhetoric and poor science".[27] Thus far, according to Ley, these accessory notions have already included: "hypersexuality, nymphomania, satyriasis, Don Juanism, erotomania, hypereroticism, hyperlibido, hyperaesthenia, sexual compulsivity, perversion, dysregulated sexuality, hyperphylia, pseudohypersexuality ... and atypical impulse control disorder".[28] As Ley mockingly concluded: "Sex addiction is a *moral panic*, and sex addictionologists are in

---

[23] More on these themes follows in Chapters 1 and 3 of Part 2.
[24] Our expert readers, of course, must be the exception.
[25] Ley (2012), title *et passim*. Polanyi (1962c, 27 *et passim*) tackled already the existence of scientific "cranks".
[26] Ley (2012), title *et passim* and 28. No direct reference to Polanyi appears in this volume. "In se" is used to mean 'in itself', though not in the exacting ways of Scholastic philosophy or Christian theology.
[27] Ley (2012), 28. See also Clarkson and Kopaczewski (2013, 128) on the "science of pornography addiction".
[28] Ley (2012), 15. As is to be stressed in Chapter 3 of Part 2, expert disagreements add to life's many sore cruelties.

league with the media as moral entrepreneurs. The field of sex addiction is *a belief system*, not a scientific or medical school of thought."[29]

4.1.3 The Tacit Dimension

Something considerably more 'normal', i.e., far less technical and psychopathological, such as seeing a painting as a painting, calls equally for the use of innumerable and, to a significant extent, immeasurable bodily and mental competences and presuppositions on our part.[30] Of these, only some we could explain in any detail, i.e., if required to do so by other people or by some special circumstances.[31] While we might be able to recall the very first time that we heard someone uttering the word "painting" or saw an item that was subsumable under the concept of 'painting', we would be at a loss explaining how much we are straining our ocular muscles and/or directing our conscious will so as to see the painting as a painting and/or entertaining it as a concept in our mind.[32]

Even if we know that we can perform all of these crucial actions and even if we can show other people that we can do them and how so, we still cannot articulate them through our language, whether at all or to any major extent. These actions exemplify that "tacit knowing" or, following much of today's academic literature, "tacit knowledge", for which Polanyi's work is still famous.[33]

We should recall how Polanyi argued that only a small part of our tacit knowledge is transformable into explicit knowledge (e.g., dictionary entries, mathemat-

---

29 Ley (2012), 211; emphases added. As the reader will gather, psychiatric and psychodynamic concepts such as 'panic', 'hysteria', 'phobia' *et similia* recur, if not abound, in the extant literature *outside* the sole clinical context, thus pointing towards deeper and broader psychosocial forces and phenomena. "Belief" proper may be crucial too. For instance, Blinka *et al.* (2022), Grubbs and Perry (2019), and Grubbs, Grant, and Engelman (2019) noted how *religious* belief plays a key role in people's likelihood of self-identifying as 'addicts'.
30 A person's belief system is at play behind all of her cognitive apprehensions, whether or not *she* knows it. See also *H&C1*.
31 As was noted in *H&C1*, we do not normally reflect on our presuppositions unless something has gone amiss.
32 As anticipated in Chapter 1, *the immense plurality of the subsidiary details required in any* cognitive act involving a *Gestalt has been intentionally exemplified in our volume by making frequent use of lists of qualifications, items, and/or examples*. Moreover, as Eco (1980, 81) recalled in a fictional context, such lists make effective rhetorical hypotyposes.
33 Polanyi (1962c), 278. See also Polanyi (2009), dedicated entirely to this notion, which is so commonplace in today's social sciences as to be used at times without any reference to its origin (see, e.g., Yakhlef 2022). Perhaps no greater success for a philosophical notion can be thought of than its becoming part of the world's furniture.

ical formulas, explicit verbal stipulations, textbooks, databases, etc.) and that, when so transformed, the knowledge at issue mutates in both overall quality and noticeable characteristics. For example, the reader may want to compare our biologically inherited and ordinarily enacted capacity for recognising faces with an explicit technical account of it.[34] Or, as regards the titular concept of 'humour', s/he may want to reflect on the peculiar notion advanced by three contemporary computer scientists, according to whom, in order to avoid any *faux pas* when making a joke, we should be "selecting an item that satisfies" the following explicit function:

$f_{p,n}(S_p(I)) \cap f_{CH}(S_{CH}(I)) \cap f_{FC}(S_{FC}(I)) \cap f_{LB}(S_{LB}(I)) \cap f_{AS}(S_{AS}(I)) \cap f_{PD}(S_{PD}(I))[,]$ where I is an item, $S_{k \in \{p,n,CH,FC,LB,AS,PD\}}()$ is a scoring function (i.e., applying softmax to the cell state), and $f()$ is a thresholding function that returns 1, when above/below the threshold $T_{upper,lower}$. Note that p, n, CH, FC, LB, AS, and PD represent positive, negative, Care-Harm, Fairness-Cheating, Loyalty-Betrayal, Authority-Subversion, and Purity-Degradation, respectively.[35]

It is hard to see how a stand-up comedian could make use of such a function which ignores how successful "humour", as the late Canadian feminist philosopher Jean Harvey stated, must be "sparkling, quick witted, born on the moment".[36] As her US colleague, Noël Carroll, also affirmed: "what makes for successful comic timing depends on the context of delivery and the comic's assessment of her audience", i.e., a snap-judgement of sorts that must be passed on the spot, in a very short time.[37] What is needed, then, is not careful computation, but the "tacit integration of the particulars" that we are capable of *qua* members of our animal species.[38] "A good comedian", as the American business ethicist Edwin Hartman wrote while discussing Aristotle's moral philosophy, "cannot reduce humor to a series of propositions about what makes people laugh and what does not".[39]

---

34 See, e.g., the technical account by Li and Wen (2019).
35 Yamane, Mori, and Harada (2021), 6. Given their technical focus, they were probably unaware of the comical interpretation that can be given of their study. We hope they will not get offended by our humorous take.
36 Harvey (1999), 15. As seen in *H&C2*, she was willing to sacrifice this kind of success for kindliness' sake. *Primum respectare.*
37 Carroll (2020), 11.
38 Polanyi (1962c), 93. See also Kahneman (2012), who revamped this issue *qua* "slow-" *versus* "fast thinking". As to the animal character and evolutionary advantage of such vast tacit integrations, see Lorenz (1962).
39 Hartman (2013), 74.

4.1.4 Personal Knowledge

Tacit abilities, "skills[,] and connoisseurship" that cannot be fully articulated and explicated are at work in all cognitive contexts, not just humour-related ones.[40] According to Polanyi, for instance, whenever "we use a word for denoting something", we are nothing short of "perform[ing]".[41] And as is usually the case in all human performances, different persons are bound to give them well, badly, efficiently, chaotically, in better and/or worse ways than other persons do, and under ever-varying circumstances, however slight the variations may be. Here lies the most profound root of linguistic-conceptual polysemy: "into every act of knowing there enters a tacit and passionate contribution of the person knowing what is being known, and that this coefficient is no mere imperfection, but a necessary component of all knowledge".[42]

All knowledge is, ultimately, *personal knowledge*.[43] As some degree of abstract explicitness can be reached with regard to all forms and types of human cognition —e.g., even the ineffable can be styled, however unsatisfactorily, as "ineffable"— so does a "personal coefficient" play a role in it too, for someone must be thinking of the ineffable as 'ineffable'.[44] A chemist, a man of faith, and a philosopher, Polanyi resisted the "rationalistic cult of the explicit" characterising modern Western culture, which regularly neglects or underplays the ineffable and indefinable aspects of reality that are required for science itself to operate.[45] Artists are—typically and, perhaps, understandably—more open to acknowledging such a largely intractable domain than scientists tend to be. For example, the late Italian composer of spaghetti-Western fame, Ennio Morricone, argued that the language of music "does not actually stimulate rational understanding, which is a more prosaic aspect of the human being, but a higher sentiment, insofar as consciousness can reach domains where logic cannot get".[46]

---

[40] Polanyi (1962c), 17. The reader who looks at the markings in this footnote and makes sense of them is engaging in a huge host of tacit activities which allow him/her to grasp the explicit knowledge transmitted by such markings: seeing them, attaching sounds to them, grasping words, applying rules of grammar, sensing the authors' tone, etc.

[41] Polanyi (1962c), 57.

[42] Polanyi (1962c), 329. Then, when using artificial stipulative terms, persons' tacit skills are still called upon.

[43] Polanyi (1962c), title *et passim*.

[44] Polanyi (1962c), 329.

[45] Pareyson (2013), 20.

[46] Morricone (2020), par. 8. Funnily, the atheist Marcuse expressed analogous considerations about the uniqueness of aesthetics (Marcuse and Magee 1977). As to those who have never fathomed this aspect of music, there is nothing that we can write that could change their situation.

Rejecting the widespread yet erroneous positivist ideal of complete neutral 'objectivity', while also trying to steer away from self-defeating relativistic 'subjectivism', Polanyi stated: "Nomothetic and idiographic ... [are] parts of all knowledge."[47] And he added: "deprived of their tacit coefficients, all spoken words, all formulae, all maps and graphs, are strictly meaningless... The ideal of a strictly explicit knowledge is ... self-contradictory."[48] Therefore, even the "formula of laughter" concocted in our century by the Ukrainian-born engineer Igor Krichtafovitch needs interpreted by *someone*. Not to mention the deeper implicit requirement whereby the formula must be brought to bear upon a specific context in which attempts at humour are then made by a person.[49] In and by itself, "EH = PE*C/Tp + BM" says, and does, nothing at all.[50]

To corroborate his stance, Polanyi made use of the mathematical logic of Gottlob Frege, i.e., yet another noble father of 20th-century analytic philosophy.[51] As the former wrote: "The significance of my writing down ' $\vdash.p$' [i.e., 'that p', namely, that the proposition p is the case, i.e., 'p is true'] is not that I make an assertion but that I commit myself to it... I believe what the sentence p says".[52] Unless some definite 'I' commits him-/herself to asserting the sentence p as a true proposition about the world, whether internal or external, thus signalling a tacit personal belief in its being true for all humankind, all the cognitive-linguistic load which p conveys is that it is a possible proposition among countless others.

In his works about the logical features of human thought, Frege confirmed Polanyi's stance by distinguishing clearly between p *qua* "content of a possible judgment" and the propositional "recognition" that such a sentence is true, which is "manifest[ed]" formally in the assertion " $\vdash.p$", i.e., that p is—which means, in

---

Certain realities must be experienced for someone to make sense of them. As to the derogatory use of "spaghetti", the present authors mean no offense—one of them being Italian to boot.
47 Polanyi (1969a), 100. Historically, this issue has been recognised in ethics with regard to *phronesis* and wisdom.
48 Polanyi (1969a), 195, his target being the enduring influence of positivism in today's science's (self-)image. At a deeper level, it is also implied that "[r]eality is an anthropomorphism", as Jung's (1973, 214) put it. While an independent universe is presumed and believed in, each and every person copes with it *via* her take on the available semiotic tools, which in turn embody a long-lived legacy of personal creativity and inter-personal interaction.
49 Krichtafovitch (2006), title *et passim*. Distinguishing 'propositional' and 'procedural' knowledge reissues the point, for grasping propositions requires procedural knowledge, only part of which can be abstracted into propositions. More was said on this point in *H&C1*.
50 "PE" is "Personal Empathy", "C" is the "complexity" of a "riddle", "Tp" is the time for "its solution", "BM" is "the background mood" of the audience, and "EH" is "the effect of humor" (Krichtafovitch 2006, 83–100).
51 See, e.g., A. Kenny (1995).
52 Polanyi (1962c), 28.

short, that a particular person believes p to be true for all of us.[53] The freedom and responsibility of the person stating p apply at all levels of communicative complexity: from discovery to interpretation, and from ordinary observations to scientific theories. Instructively, Merleau-Ponty styled "Einstein['s] conception of the world" as "humour [*qua*] mode of risky certainties", i.e., "the creative physicist's paradoxical and irrepressible consciousness of having access to a reality through an invention which was nevertheless free".[54]

4.2 A Theory of Concepts: 'Humour' and 'Cruelty'

> The psyche creates reality every day.
> —Carl Gustav Jung[55]

The understanding that Polanyi extrapolated from Frege's technical reflections is pregnant with epistemic, moral, social, and personal implications. Let us consider a mere two of them. [56]

---

53 Frege (1956), 294. Recall this chapter's opening quote. Polanyi (1962c) steered a middle course between the opposite poles of sceptical solipsism and absolute certainty, as also pursued in the same decades by Perelman and Olbrechts-Tyteca (1969) and, in recent years, by Avaliani (2018, title *et passim*), who was the champion of the "pseudoabsolute", i.e., we think and act *as though* we had absolute certainty, while we know that we do not.
54 Merleau-Ponty (1964a), 193.
55 Jung (1960–1990), vol. 6, 52, par. 78. It is not only the healthy individual psyche that accomplishes this marvellous feat every morning, i.e., after awakening from sleep, which is an effective state of unconsciousness. If taken seriously, Jung's notion of the 'collective unconscious' knocks the bottom out of the individualistic conception of the psyche, since it establishes a direct and deep link between each person and the fund of instincts, imaginings, and irreducible archetypes that we are likely to share *qua* members of our species and long-lived civilisations, i.e., the psychic deep-well that analytic psychology retrieves in the first-person experiences of our genetic and epigenetic legacies, which are standardly retrieved instead by the third-person accounts favoured by experimental psychology. This is no wild hypothesis. It was taken seriously by many students of Jung, such as Barbara Hannah or Marie-Louise von Franz. Besides, the absence of a clear end to the psychic field can be experienced in our lives, such as when lovers complete each other's sentences, psychiatric patients share identical delusions (e.g., *folie à deux*), mothers anticipate their new-born's needs (e.g., by beginning to lactate moments before their children wake up in a separate bedroom), or people's affects and agency are captured by those of the "group psyche" (Hughes 2009, 245 *et passim*) or "mass psychology" (Budi and Widyaningsih 2021, title *et passim*) where they find themselves immersed. We can suppose, e.g., at football games, an on-campus "moral panic" (Kipnis 2017, 1), or during those private clubs' "mass sexual orgies" reviving in modern times the far more public "Komastic dance[s]" of the ancient "Corinthian, Attic, Beotian, Laconian and Etruscan" cultures

(1) Polanyi's understanding implies that each living and thinking person may have, at some point, to decide whether to pay heed to certain concepts and/or conceptions or not, however commonplace or unusual they may seem *prima facie*.[57]

(2) In addition, it implies that any major abstraction of our culture (e.g., the laws of science, theorems of geometry, ethical principles of our cultural community, maxims regulating social etiquette, received notions making up common knowledge, etc.) is liable to having to be re/considered and/or applied by each responsible person, who can then do so more or less effectively.[58]

While the former implication tells us that it is up to each reader to decide whether to deem the conceptions of 'humour' and/or 'cruelty' presented in our work adequately warranted or not, the latter implication tells us that s/he may be mistaken in his/her judgement—and so could we *qua* authors of this volume.[59] Ironically, reflecting a little on human fallibility, which has been the bountifully fertile ground for innumerable feats of hilarity and humour (e.g., slapstick comedy), is also a terribly serious matter.[60]

4.2.1 Toxicity and Buggery

Cognitive, logical, and/or epistemic mistakes are the birthplace of countless human cruelties. Such cruelties encompass those of the paradoxical sort that were studied

---

(Csapo and Miller 2007, 16). More on football fandom, furious panics, and potentially scandalous sex follows in Chapters 1 and 3 of Part 2.

56 The implications at issue can be really enormous, e.g., when ruling elites happened to believe in the truthfulness of the ethnocentric, racial, or eugenic claims of noted sources such as the *Bhagavad Gita*, Moses' *Deuteronomy*, Aristotle's *Politics*, Ibn Khaldun's *Book of Lessons*, Bernard of Clairvaux's *Liber de laude*, Ibn Taymiyyah's anti-Mongol fatwas, Hume's essay "Of National Characters", Kant's *Anthropology*, Gobineau's *Essay*, Ploetz's *Basics*, Stopes' *Radiant Motherhood*, or Dugin's *Foundations*—this last entry being cruelly topical at the time of writing.

57 While reasoning cannot but be part of the evaluative process, once it is started, the parallel import of habitation, imagination, and/or intuition cannot be stressed enough *vis-à-vis* such possible processes and decisions. Polanyi (1962c) shows how easy it is to fall into scepticism *in abstracto*, while relying on some faithful dogma *in concreto*.

58 "Kant says that no system of rules can prescribe the procedure by which the rules themselves are to be applied. There is an ultimate agency which, unfettered by any explicit rules, decides on the subsumption of a particular instance under any general rule or a general concept" (Polanyi 1962b, 171). Such an ultimate agency is *personal*.

59 *Knowing our prior record and that of the human race, we are positive that there must be plenty of mistakes.*

60 Effectively, any attempt at explaining error fully means pursuing a fundamental epistemology *via negativa*.

and classified by Hallie and that, on occasion, may stem from the agency of highly educated and ostensibly moral individuals.[61] These people too, after all, may simply display the thoroughly common, yet also commonly thorny, phenomenon of "immorality" which, according to Hallie, entails enormous motivational "complexities", akin to "a mass of intricately intertwined pipes", including "the ferocious ugliness" exhibited by cruel behaviours.[62]

We can make use of an example arising from the field of clinical therapy which allows us to combine together, once again, philosophy and psychology.[63] Specifically, the contemporary British psychologist John Barry noted how, in his clinical and academic experience, the mental ill-being of "white heterosexual men" is often dismissed by many well-meaning colleagues as routine cases of "toxic masculinity", who "don't really need – or even deserve – our help".[64] As Barry explained, under "[t]he prevailing narrative", it has become a widespread and common-sense belief that "men have all the power", which these well-meaning colleagues of his wrongly interpret, however, as entailing that all men have all the power, while in fact only some men have any appreciable power and, additionally, of such a type and/or degree that it should make such fortunate men immune from "depression" and other mental pathologies.[65]

In the hope of forcing his well-meaning colleagues out of their complacent and conventional "blind spot", which causes these colleagues to (1) assume that "white heterosexual men" as such are intolerably privileged and (2) "feel justified in re-

---

61 See the preceding Chapter 3. *Whether and how far moral people really are so is largely a known unknown.* God alone, according to Biblical wisdom, can really grasp people's true intentions (see, e.g., 1 Kings 8:39, Rom 2:1–11).
62 Hallie (1985c), 42.
63 As explained in Chapter 1, these are the disciplinary fields to which the present two authors belong.
64 Barry (2019), pars. 10–11. We refer here to a contemporary issue. As to Polanyi himself, he had to deal in his lifetime with the dogmatic Stalinism of communist Europe and the dogmatic *laissez-faire* liberalism of several members of the Mont Pelerin Society of which he was a co-founder (see Polanyi 1962c and Beddeleem 2019). Hence, he encountered the phenomena of so-called "parallel universes", "epistemic bubbles", and "echo chambers", albeit *ante litteram*, that are now so common, e.g., Qanon votaries, partisan news, and climate-change denialists. Such experiences might explain, at least in part, his insistence on the centrality of the Western cultural canon, which ensures that enough conceptual ground is shared so as to allow for rational debate, disagreement, and resolution.
65 Barry (2019), pars. 7 and 10. Having encountered scores of utterly destitute, ill, suffering, and/or generally powerless men, we cannot but sympathise with Barry's criticism, which Baroncelli (1996, 27) echoed in his typical humorous manner, i.e., by way of an ironic hyperbole: "Luckily, we have ready at hand the winner of all winners, the greatest oppressor among all oppressors: the European male."

jecting them or even punishing them rather than helping them", Barry wittily contrasted the ordinary term "toxic masculinity" with "'toxic femininity', 'toxic blackness', and 'toxic Jewishness'".[66] As Barry humorously and committedly contended, such uncommon terms "make your toes curl", and so should "toxic masculinity", by implication.[67]

Applying Polanyi's understanding of concepts to 'humour' and 'cruelty' and analysing their import in light of current ethical and social issues constitutes no act of intellectual violence towards Polanyi's broader philosophical project. We, the authors of this volume, are not engaging in wilful deeds of conceptual "experiment[ation]", philosophical "buggery" and/or the exultantly perverse procreation of "monstrous children", as intentionally performed and amusingly styled by Deleuze in his creative rendition of other thinkers' views.[68]

Far more prosaically, Polanyi was a dedicated student of socio-political and economic matters, and his logico-semantic reflections were and, in our view, *are* still meaningful and relevant, well beyond the realm of scientific concepts alone.[69] This point applies, even if these scientific concepts are those which were of special interest to him, at least initially, *qua* philosopher of science and, above all, *qua* foremost expert in physical chemistry.[70] Emblematically, as Polanyi himself acknowledged, speaking an "ordinary language applying to matters of experience" means having already "a theory of the universe", in which we live, think, and act.[71]

'Humour' and 'cruelty', in short, are *Gestalten*, each of which is, at the same time, *one*—i.e., the concept and/or chosen conception—and *many*—i.e., the structured or united facets thereof, which can then extend as well into ethically and so-

---

[66] Barry (2019), pars. 7 and 11. Logically, if patriarchy is harmful to both sexes, white heterosexual men at large cannot be privileged. Psychologically, Barry's witticisms are feats of creativity facilitating his colleagues' job by bringing to conscious scrutiny shadow contents that, unwisely, they may have been projecting onto white heterosexual men—thus neglecting, *inter alia*, how intersectionality applies to them too, as well as to the deeper, fundamental clinical principle whereby each token of 'white heterosexual man' is actually and ultimately a unique living, thinking, and feeling *person* to be understood on her own terms (see also Chapter 1 of Part 2 and Jung 1958, 1–11).
[67] Barry (2019), par. 11. Following Penelas (2019, 324), we see Barry as offering a "redescription that may shed some light on cruelty in unpredicted areas" because of "lack of imagination" aka "hermeneutical injustice". Also, after focussing on female-specific suffering in *H&C1* and *H&C2*, it seemed fair to address male suffering too. Boys do cry. Life's cruelty, like death itself, is certainly capable of gender equality.
[68] Deleuze (1995), 6. At the same time, we are probably guilty of *unintentional* misinterpretations and errors. As stressed in *H&C1* and *H&C2*, perfection eludes us.
[69] See Jacobs and Allen (2005).
[70] In 1933, Polanyi accepted the Chair of Physical Chemistry at the University of Manchester that had belonged to Dalton himself, i.e., the founder of modern chemistry (Hargittai 2016).
[71] Polanyi (1962c), 99.

cially meaningful domains.⁷² Under this perspective, it should be no surprise that so many different renditions of both concepts have been encountered in our survey of the Western humanities and social sciences.⁷³ Given the personal *quid* of all knowledge, each researcher offers inevitably a more or less uniquely articulated rendition of each notion, of which s/he is not the exclusive creator, however. And this is where solipsism and relativism are countered, if not neutered.

Albeit entitled to their own unique take on any notion, all researchers could and cannot avoid operating within established socio-cultural traditions and, at times, in highly specific and specialistic professional circumstances calling for explicitly defined and agreed-upon terminologies. Thus, while a smudge of individual difference is important and unavoidable, so is a conspicuous degree of conformity, especially but not exclusively in expert contexts.⁷⁴ After all, in our own survey, we have encountered a plurality of meanings, rather than singular meaninglessness.⁷⁵ As the Catholic Chesterton quipped: "A man must be orthodox upon most things, or he will never even have time to preach his own heresy."⁷⁶ And as was noted by the atheist Bertrand Russell:

> To disbelieve what one is told is the method of the rebel and as a general practice has nothing to recommend it. Wisdom is not achieved by refusing to believe that 2 and 2 make 4, or that there is such a place as Vladivostok. When the authorities are unanimous, they are usually right; when they are not, the plain man does well to suspend judgement. A general habit of intellectual rebellion is more foolish than a general habit of intellectual acquiescence, and if it became common it would make civilisation impossible.⁷⁷

Even though it is far from infallible, invariable, immaculate, immune to incoherence, impervious to immorality and/or inherently impeccable, common sense is, at the end of the day, a sensible thing to have in common—not least should we happen to be in the mood to express vocal disagreement or launch into a heated argument with someone else. As also ordinary parlance entails, common sense is

---

72 How the structuring of subsidiary details into a focal object occurs lies beyond the scope of our present volume.
73 The stated polysemy of "humour" would have been even broader had we included its usages as a verb as well.
74 As known, while certain disciplines (e.g., physics) and social contexts (e.g., the army) generally discourage individualistic deviation and experimentation, others (e.g., poetry and consensual sex) are far more open to both.
75 Here lies the irony of all disputes and debates: we understand each other well enough to be able to disagree.
76 Chesterton (1910), par. 2. We believe the same to be true of women too.
77 Russell (1998), 127–128.

not yet, *per se*, good sense.[78] For the former to become the latter, an instructively 'Polanyian' element is needed, i.e., the qualitative reliability of a specific *person*'s characteristic judgement.[79]

4.2.2 Plurality and Viability

With regard to our readers, some of the surveyed conceptions are likely to come across as far more sensible than others, for they happen to be consistent with some of the received views that many or even most of our readers take tacitly for granted in their daily life, and by means of which they interpret and perhaps cope successfully with such a life.[80] Other conceptions, in contrast, are bound to read as confusing, weird, vague, odd, exasperating, erroneous, insincere, and/or even dangerous.[81] By supplying all of these conceptions to our readers, it was indirectly and, until now, *tacitly* suggested that the present book's two authors believe these conceptions to be worthy of note.[82]

Our belief is based upon four main reasoned considerations.

(1) Progress in all fields is attainable thanks also to the fact that "unexpected distortions of the semantic field" of any term, whether it is "cruelty" proper or some other consequential notion (e.g., energy, personhood, justice, patriarchy), can be effectively operated, first by an individual, and then by broader social circles.[83]

---

[78] More on 'common sense', including its ironies and cruelties, follows in Chapter 1 of Part 2. In any case, our views on this notion can be found in Baruchello (2019b), 140–154, where we followed G.B. Vico's classic take on it. Here, let us note instead how "intellectual passions" must be at work for the most aloof and professional debate to start, in line with Polanyi's (1962c, 103 *et passim*) study of the personal components at play in all scientific endeavours.

[79] Fittingly and squarely situated within a socio-cultural and historico-political context, Polanyi's (1962c) central notion of *personal responsibility* can thus be recovered from its trite, atomising use in right-wing circles. Even in a Marxist context, were a proletarian not to assent in earnest to the tenets of socialism, then s/he would not be gaining class consciousness but, at best, accepting unthinkingly a new ideology in *lieu* of an old one.

[80] We leave to each reader the determination of whether s/he is coping successfully with life.

[81] Deleuze and Guattari (1983, 13) argued that there are always historico-political roots behind the "perspectives ... of the culture [people] inhabit", which entail "powerful signs that massacre desire", i.e., the libidinal forces animating human agency, and thereby ensure conformism.

[82] We do not tackle here the thorny issue of what exactly is meant by the verb "believe" and the noun "belief".

[83] Penelas (2019), 328. Not all distortions are progressive. Their being so or not is a person's evaluation to make.

(2) The meanings of both "humour" and "cruelty" have varied enormously in our culture. Our embracing these terms ecumenically, rather than concentrating only on some of them, is likelier to help us understand the history of our culture, which is not one homogenous stream (i.e., a monolithic 'Western culture'), but a confluence of many different streams.[84]

(3) The same ecumenical embrace might well help us and, hopefully, our readers to detect subsidiary details of the concepts of 'humour' and/or 'cruelty' that were far from obvious before writing/reading our volume, and yet were also tacitly at work in our/their grasp of these two notions throughout the writing/reading experience.[85]

(4) Each of the many interpretative angles available in the diverse and even contradictory history of the Western humanities and the world's social sciences is, on its own, a plausible hermeneutical circle whereby to approach reality and revise, on the latter's basis, the premises and characteristics of the interpretative angle at issue. Taken together, these many hermeneutical circles form something akin to a chainmail or a net.

(4a) As a chainmail, they offer some protection from both hopeless ignorance and dogmatic single-mindedness.

(4b) As a net, they can allow for capturing a number of different aspects of reality, augmenting our knowledge of the same reality, and helping us find our bearings within it, whether epistemically, ethically, aesthetically or politically.[86]

---

[84] Far too often, when talking about "culture", whether Icelandic, Italian, Indigenous or else, there comes the assumption that, somehow, each of them is easily identifiable, stable, and internally homogenous. As far as *our* experience of native and acquired cultures is concerned, we must testify to the opposite conclusion: cultures are rather mixed bags, highly mutable and/or unstable and internally diverse, when not contradictory and conflictual.

[85] Our concepts too are normally such subsidiary details, which allow us to grasp focal aspects of reality. Tellingly, when learning to use a microscope in cellular biology, students are routinely told what to look *for* in order to become able to look *at* that which they see, lest the shapes and blots that they view through the lenses remain an incomprehensible blur. Concepts, including those about our technologies, contribute to producing the observed phenomenon, thus exemplifying the "phenomenotechnic studies" that the 20th-century French chemist and philosopher Gaston Bachelard (1965, 111) deemed most pronounced in atomic and subatomic physics.

[86] In any case, *even so rich a tapestry as the one resulting from the combination of many interpretative angles is but a partial one.* So much that we do not know remains unknown. So much that we cannot know remains unknowable. And so much that we think we know may beg to differ, much to our own dismay and chagrin.

Our pluralistic embrace explains as well why we do not try to come up with clever-sounding definitions of either humour or cruelty.

(1) Given Polanyi's theory of concepts, we suspect that there are far too many subsidiary details that cannot be fully grasped and, instead, must be tacitly relied upon for any person's conception of 'humour' and/or 'cruelty' to be possible in the first place. Any given concept of our ordinary language, when it is treated as the figure-element of a cognitive *Gestalt*, casts inexorably its net over a multitude of subsidiary details that, *qua* background-element of the same *Gestalt*, are bound to remain diversely "inarticulable", "unspecifiable", "inarticulate", "ineffable", "unfathomable", "undefined", "imprecise and ambiguous", or "undefinable".[87] Among these details are included also all those ordinary concepts and/or attendant personal conceptions *from* which we all, if epistemically functional, must attend in order to be able to attend *to* each studied concept at issue, such as 'humour' or 'cruelty'.[88]

(2) Above all, the more intensely a given concept of our ordinary language is examined, the fewer and more specific *particular* subsidiary details end up being identified and, subsequently, focussed upon by the researchers. At the same time, countless other such details, which are plausibly as legitimate aspects of the examined concept as the focussed-upon ones, progressively disappear into the *Gestalt*'s background.[89] As enlightening and informative as any such exercise in critical analysis may be, we do not want to risk pushing the process of selection too far, i.e., to the point at which the examined concept loses its relevance or even meaning in *lieu* of the relevance and/or meaning of its fewer, more specific, particular details that are being focussed upon.[90] Detailing, as useful and as clever as it may be and/or is believed to be in societies that are very keen on ideas such as 'precision' and/or 'objectivity', can also be epistemically destructive.[91] Polanyi himself had already warned his readers about this matter: "the more detailed knowledge

---

[87] Polanyi (1962c), 62, 64, 71, 84, 121, 263, 377, and 405. Stipulations contain this phenomenon.

[88] Polanyi's *from-to* phenomenology will come handy to explain a few philosophical issues in Chapters 1 and 3 of Part 2.

[89] We use "progressively" in a loose sense: in many cases, vast hosts of details may disappear rather suddenly.

[90] E.g., an insistent focus on verbal types of humour ends up dealing with jibes, sallies, ripostes, etc., and no longer with "humour" proper, which may also consist in mimes, grimaces, loud burps and modulated farts. Or, alternatively, an insistent focus on the humourist's intentions causes the audience's role and the apt wry medium to disappear, hence leading to a study of "intentions", i.e., not of "humour" as such—as essentially argued, recently, by Sills (2020, 73) with regard to the "cleverness theory" of humour developed by Gimbel (2017).

[91] Knowing which and how much detailing is due under each circumstance is yet another personal skill for which no exact explicit rule can be prescribed.

we acquire of such a thing, the more our attention is distracted from seeing what it is".[92]

(3) Writing about comedy, Voltaire had famously stated: "Humour when explained is no longer Humour."[93] This is not a sheer laughing matter, to which wits, comics, and tummlers must pay special heed. Rather, it too reminds us of the risk of losing sight of the forest when looking too intently at its trees—or mistaking a film for its frames, if you are unfamiliar with forests. This realisation may sound perplexing to contemporary ears which are accustomed to reacting positively to terms such as "accuracy", "measurement" or "analysis", especially in the academic environment. Yet, as Hillman pointedly wrote at the close of the last century:

> [O]lder cultures ... have a better sense of th[e] enigmatic force in human life than does our contemporary psychology, which tends to narrow understanding of complex phenomena to single-meaning definitions. We should not be afraid of ... big nouns; they are not hollow. They have merely been deserted and need rehabilitation. These many words and names do not tell us what "it" is, but they do confirm that it is. They also point to its mysteriousness. We cannot know what exactly we are referring to because its nature remains shadowy, revealing itself mainly in hints, intuitions, whispers, and the sudden urges and oddities that disturb your life and that we continue to call symptoms.[94]

Albeit focussing upon his own field of study, i.e., psychology, Hillman's deeper wisdom and broader lesson are not too hard to grasp, also with respect to the issue of "humour" proper. Even popular science fiction can get the gist of it: the logical Vulcans of *Star Trek* lore can be much more precise than humans and make better scientists than we do, but only few of them ever develop a sense of humour.[95] Ordinary concepts, the inherent semantic ambiguities of which can be revealed by sharp-eyed detailing, make nonetheless viable pragmatic sense at higher levels of generality.[96]

---

92 Polanyi (1962c), 348. The "it" in the sentence being the "thing" that is being studied.
93 Voltaire (2005), 22nd letter, par. 2.
94 Hillman (1996), 10. The emphasis on the idea of 'mystery' is most apropos with regard to "humour" proper, the full mastery of which is the prerogative of select individuals whose comic genius we typically celebrate in our communities and in the Western arts. Only these men and women are capable of such regular feats which can be shown and even studied, but not explained fully in explicit terms that others can understand in theory and replicate in practice.
95 "Viability" is probably yet another principle for which no single explicit rule can be given.
96 Ordinary concepts are imperfect yet useful tools, as stated in Eco's (1980, 405) take on Wittgenstein's (1989, par. 6.54) "steps" or "ladder".

(4) Long before the conclusions reached by *Gestalt* psychologists or Polanyi, Voltaire had already noted that the whole is more than the sum of its parts.[97] Hence, we ourselves decided not to perform here, by means of an academic sleight of hand, the expedient trick of retrieving an allegedly "philosophical" or "technical" definition that, whether intentionally or indirectly, denies the historically and theoretically grounded polysemy that is lexically constitutive of both "humour" and "cruelty". Such a polysemy, as we surmise, has been amply demonstrated in Chapters 2 and 3—not to mention the heftier intellectual histories of these two concepts presented in *H&C1*.

(5) This kind of expedient trick would also imply that the authors of the present volume should know better than, say, Seneca, Aquinas, Montaigne, Freud, Harlow, or Hallie what either of these concepts means, if not both of them. We do *not*. As concerns the concepts of 'humour' and 'cruelty', we do not believe that we have been able to outwit all these thinkers. Instead, we recall their studies, and discuss them eagerly, because we think that they are still plausible, profound, and pregnant with insights. As such, they can assist us in exploring and explicating the many thorny issues surrounding the two titular concepts of our volume, which is devoted to *their* inquiry, not to that of some of these two concepts' countless constituent details and/or cases thereof, e.g., the humourists' highly hypothetical intentions, semantic scripts of select verbal jokes in Old Norse or Urdu, or likeliest biochemical imbalances of notorious murderers such as Belle Gunness, Ian Brady, Myra Hindley, and Tracey Wigginton.[98]

4.3 Two Sets of Family Resemblances

4.3.1 Humour

Considering the immense panorama of socio-scientific and literary-philosophical views, reasonings, intuitions, illustrations, and conceptions that we have surveyed, we cannot but be humbly honest *vis-à-vis* the amazing and perhaps puzzling plurality of possible and variously plausible definitions and/or ingenious interpretations of "humour" proper. Novel, neat, and deep definitions, as appealing as they

---

[97] Gadamer (1996, 81) reached an analogous conclusion in the sombre field of bioethics as he tackled "the loss of personhood ... within medical science when the individual patient is objectified", i.e., reduced to sheer data sets.

[98] Do note that our volume is *not* intended to be a 'ground-breaking' attack against some theories and/or theorists.

may be—even solely *qua* allegedly "working" definitions streamlining the fastidious and, at times, plainly tedious job of the careful scholar—cannot be credibly produced, at least by the two of us. Even less likely is that any such definitions may be held and validated as effective syntheses of the enormous realm of subsidiary details upon which the focal object of humour casts its wide and flexible net in our culture's long and internally diverse history.[99]

Rather, we content ourselves here with mere "family resemblances" *à la* Wittgenstein which span across the numerous and, on occasion, contradictory conceptions of 'humour' that have been acknowledged and addressed in our volume, so that repeated, believable, telling connotations of this concept that "overlap and criss-cross" may also be catalogued and clarified.[100] Generously general, yet not gimmicky and generic, the reader is to find below those resemblances that we repute most noticeable and/or particularly useful in the present context. Some of them, definitely, indicate associative conceptual 'bridges' that can take us from 'humour' to 'cruelty'.

(1) *Laughability:* Regularly, reasonably, and repeatedly, humour has been associated with laughter, although not adamantly and always. Humour, for instance, can fail to make people laugh and/or smile. It can be too potently charged with pathos, as many scholars have repeatedly recognised. It can be expressed wrongly and/or under the wrong circumstances, as also amply acknowledged. And it can turn into sober intellectual and/or existential challenges, e.g., logical and Christian paradoxes, which may not be funny at all, at least for the person facing them in earnest. Moreover, laughter can be entirely disassociated from humour, e.g., gelastic seizures and gas-induced laughter.[101] However, these cases of mutual separation remain a minority. More often than not, humour and laughter walk hand-in-hand, whether in refined circumstances or in vulgar ones, which may involve cruel jokes and/or jests, as well as cruel rejoinders and crueller responses.[102]

(2) *Medietas:* Notions of balance, measure, and/or equilibrium are recurrently associated with "humour" proper, so as to avoid both extremes of paucity (e.g., being too weak, too timid, too sympathetic, too bland, too simple) and of overabundance (e.g., being too powerful, too rude, too clownish, too mordant, too cerebral). Distinctions among types of humour (e.g., 'true' humour) or between humour and

---

[99] E.g., we use words such as "Western" or "West", but mainly as terms of contrast. When they are attended *to* rather than *from*, the vastity and complexity of our heritage become immediately apparent and overwhelming.
[100] Wittgenstein (1953), par. 67.
[101] See, e.g., Borloz (2017). See also *H&C1*.
[102] See Chapters 1 and 3 of Part 2 and *H&C2*.

other forms of comicality are often predicated on the shifting emphases and/or marked presences of certain 'ingredients' rather than others. Thus, issues of in/comprehensibility and, above all, un/refinement, un/relief, in/sufficient empathy, im/moderate aggression, callousness/sadism can be explained in terms of un/due measure.[103]

(3) *Role-centredness:* The enjoyer of a joke and the butt of the joke may be occasionally the same individual/s or group of people, but the two roles are clearly and continually demarcated, even when the enjoyer may happen to be thoroughly sympathetic to the joke's butt or *vice versa*.[104] As sadomasochistic relationships exemplify, even when taking turns, master and slave have distinct roles, notwithstanding their mutual dependence, practical as well as psychical.[105] At the same time, however, children may display plenty of 'good humour' without any such roles playing a part in their joyful smiling and spontaneous laughing.[106]

(4) *Surprise:* The role of surprise in humorous matters is highlighted repetitively, whether it is understood: as a stimulus or a shock pushing the recipient out of complacent normality, a novelty catching the attention and striking the curiosity of the recipient, or both.[107] A person's expectations, psychological disposition, consumption of alcoholic beverages or drugs, and many other factors may influence whether an attempt at humour or even a mere event is perceived as surprising or not. Still, it is clear that not all surprises are humorous, whether for those who suffer them or for those who merely witness them. Some, in point of fact, can lead to very different reactions, e.g., tears, sorrow, worry, anguish, despair, rage, etc. Foul surprises may be dreadful for their victims, but eminently laughable for the observers, as *per* the trite lover-in-the-closet or the proverbial fall-on-the-ice.[108]

(5) *Sociality:* Humour requires social settings and institutions for the fundamental sakes of onto-logical presence (i.e., without a community of intelligent interacting linguistic beings, there could exist no humour), pragmatic productivity (i.e., societal conventions and expectations determine when, where, how, how

---

[103] Tellingly, in the art of comedy, experts and reviewers talk of going "too far" or "not far enough" See, e.g., Crowther's (2021, 53–62) analyses of Baron Cohen's 2016 *Grimsby* and Julia Davis' 2004–2005 *Nighty Night*.
[104] McCann, Plummer, and Minichiello (2010), 505.
[105] We assume our readers know enough about such erotic practices, whether they engage in them or not. See also Chapter 3 of Part 2.
[106] As discussed in *H&C2*, Hyers (1996) regarded this type of "humour" proper to be 'paradisiac'.
[107] See, e.g., K. Kenny (2009) in the context of so-called "docu-parodies".
[108] Living in Iceland, we do not find people's falls on the ice funny: they hurt. Having been married for a long time, we do not look inside the closet.

much, and what sort of humour can occur), and plausible purpose (i.e., the same conventions and expectations determine the aims of humour, e.g., improving people, keeping them in their place, gaining or losing status and related appeal, titillating people, defending or attacking individuals, groups, and/or their beliefs, etc.).[109] As to the solitary humorous behaviours and/or soliloquies that people enjoy privately, they should be regarded as an originally interpersonal activity turned into intrapersonal.[110] We cannot forget, however, that there may be simpletons incapable of any sensible social interaction exhibiting great cheerfulness and laughing frequently, if not incessantly.[111]

(6) *Malevolence:* More often than not, some evil is said to lie at the centre—or at the very least around the centre—of humour, e.g., unrefined vulgarity, public humiliation, scathing critique, merciless unmasking, intellectual and/or moral weakness, partial or total indifference to suffering, the nihilistic destruction of cherished meanings and values, implicit mechanisms of in- and outgroup social separation, vertical hierarchical positioning, merciless spite camouflaged as constructive criticism, etc. Were we to write "cruelty" pure and simple, that would be no *verborum bombus*.[112] Indeed, it would be no mere hyperbole either. Our own *H&C2* corroborates substantially this point with a copious wealth of examples. Nevertheless, all this manifest malevolence has never stopped scholars and scientists from saluting humour as a 'rough diamond' in our cruel world. Indeed, we ourselves are going to do something of the sort in Chapters 2 and 3 of Part 2.

(7) *Duality:* Incongruous pairings, i.e., unresolved combinations of different elements, typically in the number of two, are regularly mentioned in connection with "humour" proper. This is why, to simplify things, we use the term "duality".[113] We have encountered paradoxes, ambivalences, bisociations, inconsistencies, ambiguities, interferences, disruptions, violations, shifts, mismatches, conflicts, contradictions, etc.[114] Such dualities are reported incessantly when dealing with humour, however and wherever these combinations of dissonant elements happen to be described. Yet, paradoxes, ambivalences, bisociations, inconsistencies, ambi-

---

[109] Social customs and institutions can be self-reflexive and operate *via negativa*, i.e., they can set up totems and/or standards that may (e.g., lawful satire) or can be attacked, so as to parade their rejection (see, e.g., Teune 2007).
[110] See Fernyhough (2017) on how and why we talk so much to ourselves—more so than to other people.
[111] See Darwin (1872), 197, which we addressed in *H&C1*. No offense is meant by the use of "simpletons".
[112] This rhetorical figure suggesting wild exaggeration, superior to hyperbole, is also known as *bomphiologia*.
[113] See also G. Noonan (1988, 913), who explains humour at large in terms of "duality" proper.
[114] See also Krikmann (2006) for a synoptic overview of all such dualities.

guities, etc. are not amusing *per se*. Quite the opposite, they may be the source of practical preoccupations, religious crises, claims of hypocrisy and immorality, prosaic frustrations, and many other unpleasant reactions that are hardly relatable to humour *qua* something funny.[115]

4.3.2 Cruelty

Ranging from being a loathsome moral vice or a vicious mental malady to being a useful psychological and/or evolutionary instrument for self-protection, if not even a much-maligned primordial virtue, an incredible assortment of interpretations of "cruelty" can be found in the Western humanities and social sciences. Out of this myriad of learned voices, we can extract some timidly general if not, this time, actually generic connotations of "cruelty". Somehow, Wittgenstein's "family resemblances" are spread over an even larger 'population' than in the case of "humour" proper. We therefore list below and describe some of the most recurrent and, in our judgement, relevant ones, keeping in mind ways to mirror, to a degree, those that were retrieved in connection with the various conceptions of 'humour' reported in our study.

(1) *Painfulness:* Whether bodily or mental, severe or small, defensible or unpardonable, imagined or actual, cathartic or catastrophic, character-building or soul-destroying, expiatory or gratuitous, cruelty implies pain. At the same time, human morality may extend beyond effectual pain, e.g., in its addressing politically in/correct intentions, issues of third-party dis/respect, financial harm, and/or corporate rights. Plausible instances of painless cruelty can be encountered and/or conceived of, e.g., acts of necrophilia in a secluded morgue, gossiping about a dead person who had neither friends nor relatives, torturing an intensely algophilic individual, burning wantonly a beehive, smashing angrily a comely statue, etc. Typically, though, cruelty is tied to an algetic component, whether physical or psychological, if not both.[116]

---

[115] As explained in *H&C1*, the incongruity theory stresses *one* corner of the rhetorical triangle.
[116] The disfiguration of humanity can be so strong a component, that people may end up being called "cruel" for the wanton destruction of creatures that are incapable of experiencing pain (e.g., insects). As Taylor (1932, series I, lecture 8, par. 25) states: "it is the cruel man, rather than the suffering he causes, who is the direct object of our loathing". A person's display of violence and/or resentment, then, even when vented onto an inanimate being, can justify material predications of "cruelty", e.g., Achilles' ill-treatment of Hector's cadaver in Homer (2009), 22nd book. This conception of 'cruelty' stands in contrast with the one expressed by Lewis (1982, chap. 1, par. 7), where-

(2) *Excessiveness:* Whether concerning pain as such, its common uses for more or less acceptable social aims (e. g., penal reprisals), our personal hopes of a decent existence, or reliable interpersonal understanding, cruelty moves 'beyond' some set boundary, e.g., moral appropriateness, physical tolerability, intellectual clarity, mental soundness, established etiquette, social utility, etc. Even behaviours that, compared to immolations or crucifixions, are socially widespread and relatively mild, e.g., toying with romantic suitors and ordinary tittle-tattle, can constitute out-and-out cases of cruelty inasmuch as some crucial threshold has been stepped past (e. g., with respect to decency, honesty, politeness, civility or justice) and, oftentimes, such a stepping-past has been denounced and/or attacked as blameworthy, whether by cruelty's victims or watchful third parties.[117]

(3) *Role-centredness:* Whether caused directly or indirectly, cruelty entails victims and perpetrators, even when the latter are one and the same self-abusing person, a wider human collective, an institutional body, an impersonal force, and/or an unknown agent. God Himself has been accused of "cruelty", as famously instantiated by Job's lament in the Old Testament: "You have become cruel to me; with the might of Your hand You persecute me."[118] As to the personification of suprapersonal agency, Leopardi's Mother Nature is a clear example of it, to which we should add, for the sake of praising outstanding literary poignancy, Dostoyevsky's description of industrial pauperism and social tensions in mid-19th-century London and Paris *qua* the bloodthirsty Phoenician god "Baal".[119]

In the case of cruel mockeries, the recognised roles are those of the amusing card and the "laughee", which is an archaic yet telling English word.[120] Self-mockeries, for their part, remind us of the fact that these two roles can be played by one person alone, as also exemplified by the self-punishing asceticism criticised

---

by "we speak of cruelty to animals but not to pieces of wood or stone", which lack "an 'inner' experience".

[117] Conceivably, the perpetrator too may denounce and/or attack his/her own action, having realised its wrongness.

[118] Job, 30:21. For obvious reasons, we do not address the many theological issues arising from any talk of "God".

[119] Dostoyevsky (1997), chap. 5. Thomson (1920, vol. 2, lecture 18, par. 6), for one, opposed "the accusation of cruelty" in the face of nature's gruesome parade of "parasitism", "carnivorousness", "violent death", and other such "dark shadows", as "an irrelevant anthropomorphism" that has no place in serious scholarship.

[120] Other expressive English words for the joke's "butt" or "laughingstock" are, however rare today, "beho", "gag", "game", "gamestock", "japingstock", "jestingstock", "makemirth", and "object".

by Nietzsche and Collins.[121] The *super-ego* can be cruel to the *ego*, the *id* to the *super-ego*, the *persona* to the shadow, the shadow to the *ego*, etc.[122]

(4) *Power:* The roles of victim and perpetrator require some power differential, which is egregiously exemplified by the relationship between a tyrant and his/her subjects. Far more subtly, this differential is still present, however limited and delimited, in the opportunity and in the skill needed for some ancient slave to deride the silly, head-in-the-clouds, yet free and richer philosopher Thales of Miletus, who was walking by and, inadvertently, fell into a well.[123] Similarly, it endures in the age-old tale of the volatile young maid teasing and tempting the pious cleric.[124] As Hobbes wrote in the 17th century: "Form is power … because being a promise of good, it recommendeth men [or women] to the favour of women [or men]."[125]

As Baroncelli confirmed at the close of the 20th century, "power", in the layered social reality that flesh-and-blood persons actually inhabit, means not only political or legal clout, but also "wealth, prestige, intellectual charm", the physical prow-

---

[121] Self-directed cruelty does not have to be religiously inspired. In psychotherapy and academic research, for example, we may develop the cruel habit of recalling one's own and/or other people's past traumatically, painfully, and/or resentfully, at least *in primis*, rather than, say, aesthetically, mystically, or self-appraisingly. Life-enabling opportunities may thus be irrevocably lost (see, e.g., Hillman and Ventura 1992, 9–10, on the distinction between "mania" and "insanity" and the unimaginative pathologisation of potential artistic revelations, religious experiences, and existential epiphanies). Or we can cultivate through the arts and/or our pedagogies the cruel tendency to select and focus upon failures rather than accomplishments, e.g., the times when we made a *faux pas* rather than those when we did not. Informed with the wisdom of philosophical pessimism and existentialism, our own volumes tend to highlight the cruel side of felt being and lived experience, which refers to the inner workings of the psyche too.
[122] We are using terms belonging to the psychological studies by Freud and Jung. While the former offered a tripartition of the psyche (i.e., the *ego*, the *super-ego* and the *id*), the latter outlined a slightly more intricate picture, i.e., the self or personality as comprising an unconscious part (i.e., the personal and the collective unconscious, where most archetypes reside most of the time) and a conscious one (i.e., the *ego*, which normally presents a public face or *persona* comprising many masks, as well as a private and often partly suppressed face, i.e., the so-called "shadow"). More on Jung's analytic psychology follows in Chapter 3 of Part 2 (see also *H&C2*).
[123] Countless accounts of this episode have been made. See, e.g., Amir (2013), 7.
[124] For recent reiterations, see the BBC's 2016–2019 dramedy *Fleabag*. The age difference works in reverse too, as noted in Pirandello (1920). And joking about this matter, Susan Sontag jibed: "When you get older, 45 plus, men stop fancying you. Or put it another way, the men I fancy don't fancy me. I want a young man. I love beauty. So what's new?" (as cited in Mackenzie 2000, par. 22).
[125] Hobbes (1985), part 1, chap. 10, par. 13. See also today's studies on "lookism" (Tietje and Cresap 2005, 31).

ess of "youth" and good "health", sexual "appeal", and exterior "beaut[y]".[126] Sheer common parlance acknowledges this fact. Someone is said to be "blessed with good looks", which also implies, sadly, that someone else is *not* so favoured by the gods.[127] A true balance of interpersonal power and full social equality may then stand in cruelty's way.[128] At the same time, however, such power and equality are also extremely rare in lived reality, given the inevitable unequal distribution of bodily and mental talents among us.[129]

Another *cruel irony* hides behind all claims about "power". Determining who has more or less power, of which kind, when, for how long, and how exactly, are far trickier tasks than it is often thought to be and/or cared to admit in much academic literature. Acknowledging such nuances and complexities would cause passing judgement on any cherished moral, aesthetic, or socio-political issue to become an even thornier endeavour than it already is, not least with regard to making untroubled claims of equal status. Even some of the most commonly presumed socio-cultural and historical hierarchies can reveal themselves to be far more intricate and rather baffling at a sufficiently deeper level of psychological scrutiny. Wittily, the great Czech-born writer and Jerusalem-prize laureate, Milan Kundera, noted in his 1979 *Book of Laughter and Forgetting:*

> The male glance ... is commonly said to rest coldly on a woman, measuring, weighing, evaluating, selecting her—in other words, turning her into an object. What is less commonly

---

126 Baroncelli (2009), 137. More on the many extant forms of 'power' is said in Chapter 1 of Part 2.
127 The remarks made by Hobbes (1985) and Baroncelli (2009) pointed not only towards the fact that beauty is a non-negligible form of power, but also that its counterpart, ugliness, can be a significant hindrance in a person's existence, limiting her opportunities for life-enablement at many levels, e.g., making friends, finding lasting companionship, career chances, sexual gratification, or being taken seriously at face value. On some rarer occasion, however, being particularly handsome or distractingly attractive can cause trouble too (see, e.g., Mehng 2021).
128 *In foro interno*, each reader is invited to reflect not only on how cruel the *felt* awareness is of one's own inadequacy *vis-à-vis* someone else's superior power in any relevant dimension of human existence (e.g., age, beauty, intelligence, wealth, public recognition), but also on how cruel the *felt* resentment arising thereof is and, whether intentionally or not, it spills out into intra- as well as interpersonal agency (e.g., informal conversations, general attitudes, practical assumptions). Extant disparities can even become entrenched in institutional agency, e.g., when selection committees include or exclude candidates on the basis of the schools or programmes where they studied, i.e., based on long-unverified expectations about their *almae matres*' presumed 'quality', hence independently of the candidates' actual professional de/merits. Also, considering our life experiences, we believe most of our readers not to be strangers to jealousy, vanity, insecurity, competitiveness, arrogance, pride, envy, vengefulness, bias, partiality, rashness, prejudice, and/or pettiness. Perhaps, *you* alone are the exception.
129 This diversity should be obvious. Still, the curious reader may want to look up Taparelli (1851), 571, par. 46.

known is that a woman is not completely defenseless against that glance. If it turns her into an object, then she looks back at the man with the eyes of an object. It is as though a hammer had suddenly grown eyes and stared up at the worker pounding a nail with it. When the worker sees the evil eye of the hammer, he loses his self-assurance and slams it on his thumb. The worker may be the hammer's master, but the hammer still prevails.[130]

Equal power and/or equivalent social standing may not be enough anyhow. Whilst seeking a viable, humane, and nominally "restorative" alternative to the failing business-as-usual penal solutions of 20th-century Western societies, the chief Norwegian criminologist of his generation, Nils Christie, wrote as follows: "So little State as we dare. So small systems as we dare. So independent systems as we dare. So egalitarian systems as we dare. So vulnerable participants as we dare. In such cases they would be inhibited in using pain."[131] If Christie is correct, thorough parity of interpersonal power and/or social condition does not eliminate vulnerability.[132]

On the contrary, this parity makes it more widespread, insofar as anyone can reach and hurt anyone else, if that is what s/he wants to do, even if it implies becoming as vulnerable in reply. Christie, obviously, did not think this line of conduct probable, or he would have not written about and advocated passionately the alternative punitive methods at issue. However, our aggressiveness, prickly pride, ir-

---

[130] Kundera (1987), 209. The reader may sense a hint at Hegel's master-slave dialectic. In any case, considering how much effort, time, risk, and money many men (and far fewer women) are willing to spend to be allowed to set their eyes on an enticing female (or male; e.g., in movie theatres, glossy magazines, night clubs), one wonders whether Kundera did not hit the nail on the head instead. See, e.g., Jones (2018) on admittedly overweight webcam performers describing their experiences as empowering, and Melia (2006) on Western artists' sexual self-portraits. Apropos, two philosophers recently presented a phenomenological, ethical, and existential case for allowing one's own erotic objectification based upon "the insights of Simone de Beauvoir", i.e., the feminist thinker of reference in the Francophone world (Ward and Anderson 2022, 55). An even more complex picture arises, perplexingly, if we follow the US neuropsychologist David Deida (1997, 48) in acknowledging a deeper and older spiritual need, hence the attendant implicit power, that may be at play in such seemingly prosaic, possibly lewd, and obviously voyeuristic and irreligious contexts: "Men will even pay to watch a woman's body express ecstasy, even if she is only faking it, like in a porn movie. In our secular culture, most men are only familiar with sexual ecstasy, and so it is this form of free bodily expression that men pay to see, in movies, on the stage, and in private rooms around the world." Similarly, Phillips (1998, 148) offered a complementary female-centred account of sado-masochism *qua* secular erotic path to spiritual fulfilment akin to the one long known to "Christians" (see Chapter 3 of Part 2).

[131] Christie (1981), par 11.6. On Christie's accomplishments, see the obituary by David Cayley (2015).

[132] "Vulnerability" meaning here the possibility of suffering real harm because of someone else's intentional agency.

rational preferences, bad habits, capriciousness, and/or sheer stupidity may contradict his optimism.[133] As caustically noted by Chesterton: "Christianity ... says that [we] are all fools. This doctrine is sometimes called the doctrine of original sin. It may also be described as the doctrine of the equality of men... All men can be criminals, if tempted."[134]

(5) *Culpability:* Whether delighted in or indifferent to the inflicted pain, the perpetrator displays a meaningful amount of *mens rea*.[135] As Nell himself stated, there exist two "preconditions for cruelty", i.e., "an action, which is the deliberate infliction of physical or psychological pain on another living creature or on the self" and, opportunely, "a mental state, namely the intention to inflict pain, which in turn presupposes a theory of mind".[136] Most approaches and working definitions in the social sciences share this outlook, which many humanists have also espoused and whose roots lie in the fields of jurisprudence and theology.[137]

However, it is equally true that those social and/or medical studies focussing upon severe impairments, physical and/or psychical, of nominally "cruel" agents, exclude or reduce such a *mens rea*.[138] In parallel, the notion of 'cruelty' *qua* callousness or brutality reminds us of the fact that the intention to inflict pain can be subordinate to ulterior aims, which at times may be deemed paramount, sacred, noble, just, profitable, useful, and/or rational. Furthermore, it is interesting to notice that, when dealing with unknown, unfathomable, impersonal, or institutional perpetrators, some thinkers personify them as, say, Destiny, Fate, Mother Nature, Divine Will, the System, the Establishment, the Market, etc.[139]

---

[133] See Cipolla (2011) for a witty yet argute study of the staggering threat of stupidity in human life. As he argued, unlike evil people, stupid people do not realise that they are stupid; hence, there can be neither end to, nor control over, the harm that they cause. Note also that three quarters of Pareto (1935) dealt with non-logical human conduct. Basically, stupidity might be responsible for most social ills, rather than, say, greed, apathy, violence or envy.

[134] Chesterton (1919a), chap. 12, par. 14 (who also added: "all men can be heroes, if inspired".). "Men" meaning all human beings, not just males. Dostoyevsky is, as shown in *H&C2*, a major explorer of the many dark motives leading to prosaic interpersonal cruelty, e.g., envy, resentment, boredom, capriciousness, self-doubt, pettiness, etc.

[135] Determining whether and how much a person is responsible for a given cruelty is the hard job of, e.g., judges and priests.

[136] Nell (2006), 212.

[137] See, e.g., Lévitt (1922–1923).

[138] See, e.g., Hallevy (2015), exploring the complexities of psychiatric diagnoses and penal implications thereof.

[139] As discussed in *H&C1*, Deleuze and Guattari (2004) personalised the State as an "Anal Oedipus".

At the opposite end of the same implicit axiological scale stand, instead, lamb-like innocence and magnanimous beneficence. Hence, crueller are normally taken to be sheer indifference and/or utter delight *vis-à-vis* the sufferings of innocent victims and/or benefactors, as also vividly represented in the structure of Dante's *Inferno*, in which the worse a sin is, the closer is the sinner's collocation to Satan, who resides at the bottom of the hellish pit. Evil traitors of innocent benefactors, then, lie in Lucifer's immediate proximity.[140]

(6) *Malevolence:* Cruelty, normally, is seen as a species of evil [*malum*], ill, or malevolence (the Latin etymon being *malum volens*, i.e., "willing", "wanting", or "wishing evil"). In the rare cases in which cruelty is conceived of as good, it is either an instrumental evil (e.g., Machiavellianism, self-defence) or an apparent evil, the goodness of which is then 'unveiled' and justified (e.g., Sade's and Nietzsche's rediscovery of the 'natural' cruelty drive under the incrustations of alleged "civilisation").[141]

Ironically, since at least the age of the Enlightenment, most modern authors have been busy 'unveiling' or 'unmasking', i.e., exposing or revealing, the possibly real face of all sorts of recognised institutions, varying from Christianity and morality in the 18th century to paternal benevolence and human-resource development in our times.[142] Following this intellectual trend over the centuries, it is impossible not to notice how our institutions, once they are no longer believed to be what they were before the 'unmasking' took place, become something else and lose much of their earlier value. Meanwhile, anomie and disenchantment endure, when they do not grow.[143] Whether humankind benefits from this process of 'unmasking' or not is, overall, unobvious.[144] Perhaps, in yet another instance worthy of Hallie's 1969

---

[140] Many illustrations of Dante's hell have been produced since the 14th century, including a 1485 map by Botticelli.

[141] See also *H&C1*.

[142] See, on the last example, Garrick (1998).

[143] Faced with the ongoing relentless destruction and, more deeply, desecration of life on Earth by "globalised capitalism" and with the perverse ability of the "language of science and technology … to obfuscate th[e human] connection [to Earth]", the Dutch-Icelandic geographer Edward H. Huijbens (2021, 110–119) stated: "our current imagination and vocabulary betrays us. Therefore, we need to reinvent the shamans of old, killed by the Moderns."

[144] Jung (1989, 252), in the face of the Pueblo Indians' concomitant "dignity" and "naïveté", admitted: "Knowledge does not enrich us; it removes us more and more from the mythic world in which we were once at home by right of birth." We do not know whether the world can be re-enchanted. Cruelly, we only know that the old one is gone.

Paradox of Cruelty, there is some cruelty hidden also in all or part of this benevolent 'unmasking'.[145]

(7) *Paradoxicality:* Cruelty's baffling character has been highlighted repeatedly, whether directly (e. g., Shklar) or indirectly (e. g., Smith). Intrinsically, the most patent and potent expression of its paradoxicality has been its possible conceptualisation as a vice (e. g., Montaigne) and, at the same time, a virtue (e. g., Nietzsche).[146] Extrinsically, as outlined in Chapter 3, Hallie's list of exemplary ways in which cruel agency may be preferable to its avoidance is plausibly the strongest exposition of the same baffling character.[147] Even in the social sciences, as we have seen, the same feature emerges.[148] Thus, many scientists have tackled "cruelty" as obviously negative (e. g., Collins), whereas others remained neutral (e. g., Freud) or even dared acknowledge, if not emphasise, occasional positive functions for cruelty (e. g., Ainslie).[149]

---

[145] Each reader can pass judgement on this matter if s/he wishes to do so. We have no trenchant claim to make here. Still, we can suggest that LVOA may help us in distinguishing between good and bad progress (see the opening Chapter 1).
[146] See also *H&C1*.
[147] *Ditto.*
[148] *Ditto.*
[149] Cruelty's paradoxes often involve the nastiest evils, i.e., behaviours departing from ordinary conduct in the most striking manners, hence instantiating dualities that normally, to the horrified observers, are *not* funny at all.

Bibliography

"'We Are Not Afraid': France Rallies after Teacher Beheaded" (2020). *Aljazeera*, https://www.aljazeera.com/news/2020/10/19/we-are-not-afraid-france-rallies-after-teacher-beheaded [Accessed 26/08/2022].

"Arab League and Top Muslim Body Condemn Paris Attack" (2015). *AFP*, https://www.straitstimes.com/world/europe/paris-shooting-arab-league-and-top-muslim-body-al-azhar-condemn-attack [Accessed 26/08/2022].

"Attaque contre Charlie Hebdo: ce que l'on sait" (2015). *Radio France*, https://www.francetvinfo.fr/faits-divers/attaque-contre-charlie-hebdo-ce-que-l-on-sait_168 [Accessed 20/06/2021].

"Belgium: Apology for Lumumba Killing" (2002). *New York Times*, https://www.nytimes.com/2002/02/06/world/world-briefing-europe-belgium-apology-for-lumumba-killing.html [Accessed 26/08/2022].

"Berlusconi: A casa mia solo cene eleganti" (2012). *Giornale di Puglia*, https://www.giornaledipuglia.com/2012/04/berlusconi-casa-mia-solo-cene-eleganti.html [Accessed 22/08/2022].

"Fawlty Towers: John Cleese Attacks 'Cowardly' BBC over Episode's Removal" (2020). *BBC News*, https://www.bbc.com/news/entertainment-arts-53020335 [Accessed 26/08/2022].

"Groucho Marx Old Joke Not Funny for Family of Dead Mom: Ashes Moved by Cemetery?" *MyNewsLA.com*, https://mynewsla.com/hollywood/2018/06/05/groucho-marx-old-joke-not-funny-for-family-of-dead-mom-ashes-moved-by-cemetery/ [Accessed 10/06/2022].

"Inside the Shein Machine: UNTOLD" (2022). *Channel 4*, https://www.channel4.com/programmes/inside-the-shein-machine-untold [Accessed 25/10/2022].

"Les frères Kouachi, des hommes 'calmes, déterminés, professionnels'" (2015). *Europe 1*, https://www.europe1.fr/faits-divers/Les-freres-Kouachi-des-hommes-calmes-determines-professionnels-708420 [Accessed 25/10/2022].

"Les SDF du net" (2011). *Charlie Hebdo Le Blog*, https://charliehebdo.wordpress.com/2011/11/03/les-sdf-du-net/ [Accessed 26/08/2022].

"Nippon Killer Blandly Smiles. Japanese Caretaker of Moving Picture Studio, Who Killed Manager of Concern Because He 'Knew He Was Bad Man' Is Bound Over Charged" (1911). *Los Angeles Times*, https://web.archive.org/web/20121013163000/http://pqasb.pqarchiver.com/latimes/access/348208812.html?dids=348208812:348208812&FMT=ABS&FMTS=ABS:AI&date=Nov+09,+1911&author=&pub=Los+Angeles+Times&desc=NIPPON+KILLER+BLANDLY+SMILES.&pqatl=google [Accessed 11/11/2021].

"Paris Attacks: French Judges Order Trial for 20 Suspects" (2020). *BBC News*, https://www.bbc.com/news/world-europe-51915513 [Accessed 26/08/2022].

"Paris Attacks: Millions Rally for Unity in France" (2015). *BBC News*, https://www.bbc.com/news/world-europe-30765824 [Accessed 26/08/2022].

"Sanna Marin Denies Taking Drugs after Party Video Leak" (2019). *Newsarchive.com*, https://newsachieve.com/2022/08/19/sanna-marin-denies-taking-drugs-after-party-video-leak/ [Accessed 22/08/2022].

"Somali Comic Who Mocked al-Shabab Shot Dead" (2012). *Aljazeera*, https://www.aljazeera.com/news/africa/2012/10/201210301668923774.html [Accessed 14/04/2023].

"Taliban Accepts Killing Comedian Nazar Mohammad" (2021). *India Today*, https://www.indiatoday.in/programme/world-today/video/taiban-killing-comedian-nazar-mohammad-china-us-1835058-2021-07-31 [Accessed 26/08/2022].

"The Kennedy Center" (2023), https://www.kennedy-center.org/whats-on/marktwain/ [Accessed 21/03/2023].

"The Treaty of Westphalia" (2008), https://www.youtube.com/watch?v=c-WO73Dh7rY&ab_channel=Plymhistnet [Accessed 28/11/2022].

Abere, S.S. and Akinobobola, T.O. (2020). "External Shocks, Institutional Quality, and Macroeconomic Performance in Nigeria". *SAGE Open*, 10(2), https://doi.org/10.1177/2158244020919518 [Accessed 29/09/2022].

Abrahamson, Maria (2004). "Alcohol in Courtship Contexts: Focus-Group Interviews with Young Swedish Women". *Contemporary Drug Problems*, 31(1): 3 – 29.

Abrams v. United States (1919). 250 US 616. *Justia. US Supreme Court*, https://supreme.justia.com/cases/federal/us/250/616/#:~:text=United%20States%2C%20250%20U.S.%20616%20(1919)&text=The%20First%20Amendment%20does%20not,by%20fueling%20sedition%20and%20disorder [Accessed 17/11/2022].

Addison, Joseph *et al.* (1891). *The Spectator. A New Edition* (ed. Henry Morley). London: George Routledge, https://onlinebooks.library.upenn.edu/webbin/gutbook/lookup?num=12030 [Accessed 01/05/2022].

Adler, Alfred (1938) [1933]. *Social Interest: A Challenge to Mankind* (trans. John Linton and Richard Vaughan). London: Faber & Faber.

Adler, Alfred (1952) [1931]. *What Life Should Mean to You* (ed. Alan Porter). London: George Allen & Unwind.

Adler, Alfred (1955) [1908 – 1920]. *The Practice and Theory of Individual Psychology* (trans. P. Radin). London: Routledge & Kegan Paul.

Adorno, Theodor (1939). "On Kierkegaard's Doctrine of Love". *Zeitschrift für Sozialforschung*, 8(3): 413 – 429.

Adorno, Theodor (1988) [1967]. "Veblen's Attack on Culture". In *Prisms* (trans. Samuel and Shierry Weber), 73 – 94. Cambridge, MA: The MIT Press.

Adorno, Theodor (1994) [1946]. "Antisemitism and Fascist Propaganda". In *The Stars Down to Earth and Other Essays on the Irrational in Culture* (ed. Stephen Crook), 162 – 170. London: Routledge.

Adorno, Theodor (1996) [1930 and 1964]. "Chaplin Times Two" (trans. John MacKay). *The Yale Journal of Criticism*, 9(1): 57 – 61.

Adorno, Theodor (1997) [1970]. *Aesthetic Theory* (trans. Robert Hullot-Kentor). Minneapolis: University of Minnesota Press.

Adorno, Theodor (2005) [1945]. Minima Moralia: *Reflections on a Damaged Life* (trans. E.F.N. Jephcott). London: Verso.

Adorno, Theodor and Horkheimer, Max (2019) [1942 – 1961]. *Towards a New Manifesto* (trans. Rodney Livingstone, Iain Macdonald and Martin Shuster). London: Verso.

Agamben, Giorgio (1998) [1995]. *Homo Sacer: Sovereign Power and Bare Life* (trans. Daniel Heller-Roazen). Stanford: Stanford UP.

Agazzi, Evandro (2009). "The Infinite between the Inexhaustible and Negation". *Ontology Studies*, 9: 21 – 30.

Agazzi, Evandro (2014). *Scientific Objectivity and its Contexts*. Cham: Springer.

Ahmed, Ali, Granberg, Mark and Khanna, Shantanu (2021). "Gender Discrimination in Hiring: An Experimental Reexamination of the Swedish Case". *Plos One*, 16(1): e0245513 [Accessed 21/12/2022].

Ainslie, George (2006). "Cruelty May Be a Self-Control Device against Sympathy". *Behavioral and Brain Sciences*, 29(3): 224 – 225.

Bibliography

Alba, Antonella and Galimberti, Umberto (2021). "Galimberti: 'La libertà dei "No-vx" è schiava di convinzioni errate". *Rai News*, https://www.rainews.it/dl/rainews/articoli/intervista-umberto-galimberti-la-liberta-dei-novax-schiava-di-convinzioni-errate-494c246a-1310-46ec-9e8d-e95b416d53b7.html?fbclid=IwAR2ebhwFCRe_XdmhfZefLMG-RF1gCZuY9PPTlqqUzvZOOo0Q4XOedt52pFI [Accessed 21/09/2021].

Alexander, Julia (2019). "Saturday Night Live Fires Comedian Shane Gillis over Racist, Homophobic Comments". *The Verge*, https://www.theverge.com/2019/9/16/20869209/saturday-night-live-shane-gillis-racist-homophobic-remarks [Accessed 26/08/2022].

Al-Jibaly, Muhammad M. (2005) [2002]. *Closer than a Garment. Marital Intimacy According to the Pure Sunnah*, revised ed. Austin, TX: Al-Kitaab & As-Sunnah.

Allen, R.T. (2014). *Ethics as Scales of Forms*. Newcastle-upon-Tyne: Cambridge Scholars.

Allen, Valerie (2007). *On Farting. Language and Laughter in the Middle Ages*. New York: Palgrave Macmillan.

Allison, Anne (1996). *Permitted and Prohibited Desires. Mothers, Comics, and Censorship in Japan*. New York: Routledge.

Amir, Lydia B. (2013). "Philosophy's Attitude towards the Comic. A Re-Evaluation". *The European Journal of Humour Research*, 1(1): 6–21.

Amir, Lydia B. (2014). *Humor and the Good Life in Modern Philosophy: Shaftesbury, Hamann, Kierkegaard*. Albany: State University of New York Press.

Amir, Lydia B. (2019). *Philosophy, Humor, and the Human Condition. Taking Ridicule Seriously*. Cham: Palgrave Macmillan.

Amir, Lydia B. (forthcoming). *The Legacy of Nietzsche's Philosophy of Laughter: Bataille, Deleuze, Rosset*. New York: Routledge.

Amnesty International (2019). "Myanmar: Satire Performers Who Mocked Military Face Prison in 'Appalling' Conviction", https://www.amnesty.org.uk/press-releases/myanmar-satirical-poets-imprisoned-mocking-military-appalling-conviction [Accessed 26/08/2022].

Amnesty International (2020). "Myanmar: New Convictions for 'Peacock Generation' Members", https://www.amnesty.org.uk/resources/myanmar-new-convictions-peacock-generation-members [Accessed 26/08/2022].

Andreasen, Uffe (2008). "Reflections on Public Diplomacy after the Danish Cartoon Crises: From Crisis Management to Normal Public Diplomacy Work". *The Hague Journal of Diplomacy*, 3(2): 201–207.

Andreutti, Elena (2016). "Carnival and Puritanism in *Falstaff*". MA. Padua University.

Andrew, Edward G. (1995). *The Genealogy of Values: The Aesthetic Economy of Nietzsche and Proust*. Lanham: Rowman & Littlefield.

Andrews, Malcom (2013). *Dickensian Laughter: Essays on Dickens and Humour*. Oxford: Oxford UP.

Anonymous (1924). *History of Flagellation among Different Nations. A Narrative of the Strange Customs and Cruelties of the Romans, Greeks, Egyptians, Etc. With an Account of Its Practice among the Early Christians as a Religious Stimulant and Corrector of Morals. Also Anecdotes of Remarkable Cases of Flogging and of Celebrated Flagellants*. New York: Medical Publishing.

Anonymous (2003). "English-Word Information", https://wordinfo.info/unit/2533/page:5 [Accessed 20/05/2022].

Anonymous (2009). "Un'uniforme senza fascino. Considerazioni di un ex militare". *Machete. Aperiodico anarchico*, 7: 7–8.

Anscombe, G.E.M. (1963) [1957]. *Intention*, 2nd ed. Cambridge, MA: Harvard UP.

Antal, Adriana (2016). "Risus, Cucullatus, Venus, Divine Protectors and Protective Divinities of Childhood in Dacia and Pannonia". *Studia Universitatis Babeş-Bolyai*, 61(1): 1–16.

Antoniou, Laura (2012). "Defending Pornography". *The Gay and Lesbian Review Worldwide*, 19(6): 23–58.

Aoyama, Tomoko and Hartley, Barbara (Eds.) (2010). *Girl Reading Girl in Japan*. London: Routledge.

APPROACH (2017). *Ending Legalised Violence Against Children*, http://endcorporalpunishment.org/wp-content/uploads/global/Global-report-2017-spreads.pdf [Accessed 03/10/2022].

Aquinas, Thomas (1920) [ca. 1265]. *Summa Theologica* (trans. Fathers of the English Dominican Province), 2nd ed. Oxford: English Dominican Province.

Arendt, Hannah (1985) [1958]. *The Origins of Totalitarianism*, 2nd ed. London: Harvest.

Arendt, Hannah (1998). *Eichmann in Jerusalem: A Report on the Banality of Evil*. New York: Rowman & Littlefield.

Armstrong McKay, David I. *et al.* (2022). "Exceeding 1.5 °C Global Warming Could Trigger Multiple Climate Tipping Points". *Science*, 377(6611), doi: 10.1126/science.abn7950 [Accessed 13/01/2023].

Armstrong, Gary and Young, Malcom (2000). "Fanatical Football Chants: Creating and Controlling the Carnival". In Finn, Gerry P.T. and Giulianotti, Richard (Eds.), *Football Culture: Local Contests, Global Visions*, 173–211. London: Frank Cass.

Arnarsson, Ársæll Már (2010). "Compensating the Crashers". *Nordicum-Mediterraneum. Icelandic E-journal of Nordic and Mediterranean Studies*, 5(1), https://nome.unak.is/wordpress/05-1/reflection-on-the-economic-crisis/compensating-the-crashers/ [Accessed 04/02/2023].

Arnason, Johann P. (2020) *The Labyrinth of Modernity. Horizons, Pathways and Mutations*. Lanham: Rowan & Littlefield.

Artaud, Antonin (1958) [1938]. *The Theatre and Its Double* (trans. Mary C. Richards). New York: Grove.

Arvedlund, Erin (2009). *Too Good to Be True: The Rise and Fall of Bernie Madoff*. New York: Penguin.

Asheim, Lester (1974). Review of *The Anatomy of Censorship* by Jay E. Daily. *The Library Quarterly*, 44(3): 285–286.

Asim, Jabari (2007). *The N Word: Who Can Say It, Who Shouldn't, and Why*. New York: Houghton Mifflin.

Assereto, Giovanni (Ed.) (2016). "Tra I Palazzi di Via Balbi". *Atti della Società Ligure di Storia Patria*, 43(117/2): 5–666.

Astapova, Anastasiya (2021). *Humour and Rumour in the Post-Soviet Authoritarian State*. Lanham: Lexington.

Ataner, Attila (2006). "Kant on Capital Punishment and Suicide". *Kant-Studien*, 97(4): 452–482.

Attardo, Salvatore (2017). "Humor and Pragmatics". In Attardo, Salvatore (Ed.), *The Routledge Handbook of Language and Humor*, 174–188. New York: Routledge.

Attardo, Salvatore (2020). *The Linguistics of Humor. An Introduction*. Oxford: Oxford UP.

Attardo, Salvatore and Raskin, Victor (1991). "Script Theory Revis(it)ed: Joke Similarity and Joke Representation Model". *Humor: International Journal of Humor Research*, 4(3–4): 293–347.

Attardo, Salvatore and Raskin, Victor (2017). "Linguistics and Humour Theory". In Attardo, Salvatore (Ed.), *The Routledge Handbook of Language and Humor*, 49–63. New York: Routledge.

Auden, W.H. (1939). "September 1, 1939", https://poets.org/poem/september-1-1939 [Accessed 12/07/2022].

Augoustakis, Antony and Traill, Ariana (Eds.) (2013). *A Companion to Terence*. Maiden, MA: Wiley-Blackwell.

Augustine (1877) [ca. 426]. *De civitate Dei, libri XXII*. Leipzig: B.G. Teubner, https://www.thelatinlibrary.com/augustine/civ22.shtml [Accessed 01/05/2022].

Augustine (1898) [ca. 400]. *Confessiones*. Leipzig: B.G. Teubner, https://faculty.georgetown.edu/jod/lat inconf/latinconf.html [Accessed 31/01/2023].

Austin, John Langshaw (1962). *How to Do Things with Words: The William James Lectures Delivered at Harvard University in 1955* (ed. J.O. Urmson). London: Oxford UP.

Austin, Sue (2005). *Women's Aggressive Fantasies. A Post-Jungian Exploration of Self-Hatred, Love and Agency*. London: Routledge.

Avaliani, Sergi (2018). *The Philosophy of Pseudoabsolute*. Hauppauge, NY: Nova Science.

Bachelard, Gaston (1965) [1951]. *L'activité rationaliste de la physique contemporaine*, 2nd ed. Paris: PUF.

Baer, John W. (1984). "The Great Depression Humor of Galbraith, Leacock, and Mencken". *Studies in American Humor*, new series 2, 3(2–3): 220–227.

Baier, Annette C. (1993). "Moralism and Cruelty: Reflections on Hume and Kant". *Ethics*, 103(3): 436–457.

Baker, Jean-Claude and Chase, Chris (2001) [1993]. *Josephine. The Hungry Heart*. New York: Cooper Square.

Bakhtin, Mikhail (1976). "The Art of the Word and the Culture of Folk Humor (Rabelais and Gogol)". *Soviet Studies in Literature*, 12(2): 27–39.

Bakhtin, Mikhail (2014) [1940s]. "Bakhtin on Shakespeare: Excerpt from 'Additions and Changes to Rabelais'". *PMLA*, 129(3): 522–537.

Baldensperger, Fernand (1907) [1899–1900]. *Les définitions de l'humour. Leçon d'ouverture du cours public de littérature étrangère*. Paris: Hachette.

Balibar, Etienne (2001). "Outlines of a Topography of Cruelty: Citizenship and Civility in the Era of Global Violence". *Constellations*, 8(1): 15–29.

Balibar, Etienne (2008). "Violencia: idealidad y crueldad". *Polis. Revista Latinoamericana*, 19, http://polis.ulagos.cl/index.php/polis/article/view/570/1054 [Accessed 21/09/2021].

Ball, John Clement (2017). "Capital Offenses: Public Discourse on Satire after *Charlie Hebdo*". *Genre. Forms of Discourse and Culture*, 50(3): 297–317.

Baraz, Daniel (1998). "Seneca, Ethics, and the Body: The Treatment of Cruelty in Medieval Thought". *Journal of the History of Ideas*, 59(2): 195–215.

Baraz, Daniel (2003). *Medieval Cruelty: Changing Perceptions, Late Antiquity to the Early Modern Period*. Ithaca: Cornell UP.

Barden, Garrett (2014). "On the Range or Scope of [Moral] Action". *Nordicum-Mediterraneum. Icelandic E-journal of Nordic and Mediterranean Studies*, 9(2), https://skemman.is/bitstream/1946/18417/1/On%20the%20range.pdf [Accessed 21/09/2021].

Barden, Garrett and Baruchello, Giorgio (2019). *Why Believe? Approaches to Religion*. Akureyri: University of Akureyri.

Barden, Garrett and Murphy, Tim (2010). *Law and Justice in Community*. Oxford: Oxford UP.

Barendt, Eric (2005). *Freedom of Speech*. Oxford: Oxford UP.

Baroncelli, Flavio (1994). "Lettera aperta a un maestro della *Grunfphilosophie*". In Comanducci, Paolo (Ed.), *Analisi e diritto. Ricerche di Giurisprudenza analitica 1994*, 85–95. Turin: Giappichelli.

Baroncelli, Flavio (1996). *Il razzismo è una gaffe. Eccessi e virtù del "politically correct"*. Rome: Donzelli.

Baroncelli, Flavio (1997). "Etica e razionalità. Un finto divorzio?" *Materiali per una storia della cultura giuridica*, 27(1): 127–148.

Baroncelli, Flavio (1998). "Come scrivere sulla tolleranza. Michael Walzer e l'intolleranza delle teorie". *Materiali per una storia della cultura giuridica*, 28(1): 49–68.

Baroncelli, Flavio (1999). "Trent'anni dopo Marcuse, la tolleranza repressiva e gli *speech codes*". *Ragion pratica*, 12: 31–56.

Baroncelli, Flavio (2001). "Le quattro indegnità dei liberali irresoluti". *Teoria politica*, 17(3): 23–47.
Baroncelli, Flavio (2006). "Velo e Rispetto". *Flavio Baroncelli*, http://www.dif.unige.it/dot/baroncelli/VELO-E-RISPETTO.pdf [Accessed 26/07/2022].
Baroncelli, Flavio (2009). *Mi manda Platone*. Genoa: il melangolo.
Baroncelli, Flavio (2011). *Alfabeto. Con scritti e testimonianze sull'autore* (ed. Giosiana Carrara). Novara: Interlinea.
Baron-Cohen, Simon (2012). *The Science of Evil. On Empathy and the Origins of Cruelty*. New York: Basic Books.
Barrozo, Paulo D. (2008). "Punishing Cruelly: Punishment, Cruelty, and Mercy". *Criminal Law and Philosophy*, 2: 67–84.
Barrozo, Paulo D. (2015). "Cruelty in Criminal Law: Four Conceptions". *Criminal Law Bulletin*, 51(5): 1025–1073.
Barry, John (2019). "How the Social Sciences Can Benefit by Taking a Fresh Look at Men's Mental Health". *Social Science Matters*, https://www.palgrave.com/gp/blogs/social-sciences/john-barry [Accessed 18/05/2022].
Barry, Peter Brian (2022). "#MeToo and the Ethics of Doxing Sexual Transgressors". In Boonin, David (Ed.), *The Palgrave Handbook of Sexual Ethics*, 507–523. Cham: Palgrave Macmillan.
Bartels, Dennis (2001). "Wartime Mobilization to Counter Severe Global Climate Change". *Human Ecology*, 10: 229–232.
Barton, Charles K.B. (1999). *Getting Even: Revenge as a Form of Justice*. Chicago: Open Court.
Baruchello, Giorgio (2001). Book review of *The Cancer Stage of Capitalism* by John McMurtry. *Canadian Journal of Development Studies/Revue canadienne d'études du développement*, 22(1): 255–269.
Baruchello, Giorgio (2002). "Rorty's Painful Liberalism". *Bijdragen. International Journal for Philosophy and Theology*, 63(1): 22–45.
Baruchello, Giorgio (2011). "Western Philosophy and the Life Ground". In McMurtry, John (Ed.), *Philosophy and World Problems*, vol. 3: 1–79. Paris & Oxford: UNESCO/EOLSS.
Baruchello, Giorgio (2017a). *Mortals, Money, and Masters of Thought. Collected Philosophical Essays*. Gatineau: Northwest Passage Books.
Baruchello, Giorgio (2017b). *Philosophy of Cruelty. Collected Philosophical Essays*. Gatineau: Northwest Passage Books.
Baruchello, Giorgio (2018a). *The Business of Life and Death, Volume 1: Values and Economies*. Gatineau: Northwest Passage Books.
Baruchello, Giorgio (2018b). *The Business of Life and Death, Volume 2: Politics, Law, and Society*. Gatineau: Northwest Passage Books.
Baruchello, Giorgio (2019a). "Business Legitimacy from a Catholic Perspective: Thomas Aquinas, Papal Encyclicals and Human Rights". In Rendtorff, Jacob Dahl (Ed.), *Handbook of Business Legitimacy*, 179–202. Cham: Springer.
Baruchello, Giorgio (2019b). *Thinking and Talking. Collected Philosophical Essays*. Gatineau: Northwest Passage Books.
Baruchello, Giorgio (forthcoming). "Pareto and Jung: A Coincidence of Opposites". *European Journal of Social Sciences (Cahiers Vilfredo Pareto)*. Special November 2023 issue.
Baruchello, Giorgio and Arnarsson, Ársæll M. (2022). *Humour and Cruelty. Volume 1: A Philosophical Exploration of the Humanities and Social Sciences*. Berlin: De Gruyter.
Baruchello, Giorgio and Arnarsson, Ársæll M. (forthcoming). *Humour and Cruelty. Volume 2: Dangerous Liaisons*. Berlin: De Gruyter.

Baruchello, Giorgio and Hamblet, Wendy C. (2004). "What Is Cruelty?" *Appraisal*, 5(1): 33–38 and 56.
Baruchello, Giorgio and Johnstone, Rachael Lorna (2011). "Rights and Value: Construing the International Covenant on Economic, Social and Cultural Rights as Civil Commons". *Studies in Social Justice*, 5(1): 91–125.
Baruchello, Giorgio and Rorty, Richard (1998). "Una filosofia tra conversazione e politica. Intervista a Richard Rorty". *Iride*, 11(5): 457–484.
Basu, Sammy (2007). "'A Little Discourse Pro & Con': Levelling Laughter and Its Puritan Criticism". *International Review of Social History*, 52: 95–113.
Bataille, Georges (1962) [1957]. *Death and Sensuality. A Study of Eroticism and the Taboo* (trans. Mary Dalwood). New York: Walker.
Baudelaire, Charles (1988) [1857–1864]. "Le joueur généraux". *Le Spleen de Paris. Petits Poèmes en prose*. Paris: Club du livre.
Baum, Bruce (2001). "Freedom, Power and Public Opinion: J.S. Mill on the Public Sphere". *History of Political Thought*, 22(3): 501–524.
Beam, Craig (1996). "Hume and Nietzsche: Naturalists, Ethicists, Anti-Christian". *Hume Studies*, 22(2): 299–234.
Bearth, Thomas, Beck, Rose Marie and Döbel, Reunald (2014). *Communicative Sustainability: The Role of Language in Development*. Münster: LIT.
Beato, Giulia (2021). "The Human Right to Conscientious Objection to Military Service. A Case Study on Greece". MA. Padua University.
Beattie, James (1778) [1777]. *On Poetry and Music, as They Affect the Minds; on Laughter, and Ludicrous Composition; on the Utility of Classical Learning*. Edinburgh: William Creech, https://archive.org/details/essaysonpoetrymu00beat [Accessed 01/05/2022].
Beaumont, Peter (2017). "Unesco: Israel Joins US in Quitting UN Heritage Agency over 'Anti-Israel Bias'". *The Guardian*, https://www.theguardian.com/world/2017/oct/12/us-withdraw-unesco-december-united-nations [Accessed 26/08/2022].
Beccaria, Cesare (1880) [1764]. *Crimes and Punishments* (trans. James Anson Farrer). London: Chatto & Windus, https://www.gutenberg.org/files/58700/58700-h/58700-h.htm [Accessed 01/05/2022].
Beccaria, Cesare (1994) [1764]. *Dei delitti e delle pene e Commento di Voltaire*. Rome: Newton.
Becker, Kenneth L. (2001). *Unlikely Companions: C.G. Jung on the Spiritual Exercises of Ignatius of Loyola*. Leominster: Gracewing.
Beckett, Samuel (1957). *Endgame*, https://genius.com/Samuel-beckett-endgame-annotated [Accessed 10/06/2022].
Beddeleem, Martin (2019). "Michael Polanyi and Early Neoliberalism". *Tradition and Discovery*, 45(3): 31–44.
Beeching, Jack (1975). *The Chinese Opium Wars*. London: Mariner.
Behrendt, Marc (2020). "The Moral Case for Sexbots". *Paladyn, Journal of Behavioural Robots*, 11: 171–190.
Beilharz, Peter (1989). Review article of *Cornelius Castoriadis*. *Thesis Eleven*, 24(1): 132–141.
Beiser, Friedrick C. (2018). "Humor as Redemption in the Pessimistic Philosophy of Julius Bahnsen". In Moland, Lydia L. (Ed.), *All Too Human*, 105–114. Cham: Springer.
Bek-Thomsen, Jakob *et al.* (Eds.) (2017). *History of Economic Rationalities. Economic Reasoning as Knowledge and Practice Authority*. Cham: Springer.
Bell, Rudolph M. (2007). *Fate, Honor, Family and Village: Demographic and Cultural Change in Rural Italy since 1800*. London: Routledge.

Benesch, Susan (2015) "Charlie the Freethinker: Religion, Blasphemy, and Decent Controversy". *Religion and Human Rights*, 10: 244–254.

Benjamin, Walter (1998) [1963]. *The Origin of German Tragic Drama* (trans. John Osborne). London: Verso.

Benjamin, Walter (1999) [1972]. *The Arcades Project* (trans. Howard Eiland and Kevin McLaughlin). Cambridge, MA: Belknap.

Benjamin, Walter (2007a) [1955]. "Karl Kraus". In *Reflections: Essays, Aphorisms, Autobiographical Writings* (trans. Edmund Jephcott; ed. Peter Demetz), 239–275. New York: Schocken.

Benjamin, Walter (2007b) [1955]. *Illuminations* (ed. Hannah Arendt, trans. Harry Zohn). New York: Schocken.

Bennet, Scott H. (2003). *Radical Pacifism: The War Resisters and Gandhian Nonviolence in America, 1915–1963*. Syracuse: Syracuse UP.

Bentham, Jeremy (2000) [1781]. *An Introduction to the Principles of Morals and Legislation*. Kitchener: Batoche, https://historyofeconomicthought.mcmaster.ca/bentham/morals.pdf [Accessed 12/01/2023].

Bentley, Joseph (1967). "Satire and the Rhetoric of Sadism". *The Centennial Review*, 11(3): 387–404.

Berger, Adolf (1953). *Encyclopedic Dictionary of Roman Law*. Philadelphia: American Philosophical Society.

Berger, Peter L. (1969). *A Rumour of Angels: Modern Society and the Rediscovery of the Supernatural*. New York: Doubleday.

Bergson, Henri (1959) [1900 and 1924]. *Le rire. Essai sur la signification du comique*. In *Oeuvres de Bergson*, 391–485. Paris: Presses universitaires de France, http://classiques.uqac.ca/classiques/bergson_henri/le_rire/le_rire.html [Accessed 19/02/2022].

Berlant, Lauren (2010). "Cruel Optimism". In Gregg, Melissa and Seigworth, Gregory J. (Eds.), *The Affect Theory Reader*, 93–117. Durham: Duke UP.

Berlin v. EC Publications, Inc. (1964). 329 F. 2d 541 – Court of Appeals, 2nd Circuit, https://openjurist.org/329/f2d/541 [Accessed 14/04/2023].

Bernasconi, Robert (2003). "Will the Real Kant Please Stand Up?" *Radical Philosophy*, 117: 13–22.

Bernburg, Jón Gunnar (2016). *Economic Crisis and Mass Protest. The Pots and Pans Revolution in Iceland*. Abingdon: Routledge.

Bernhut, Stephen and Galbraith, John K. (2006) [2003]. "An Interview with John Kenneth Galbraith". *Ivey Business Journal*, https://iveybusinessjournal.com/publication/an-interview-with-john-kenneth-galbraith/ [Accessed 26/08/2022].

Besançon, Alain (2000). *The Forbidden Image: An Intellectual History of Iconoclasm* (trans. Jean Marie Todd). Chicago: University of Chicago Press.

Bhatia, Monish (2020). "The Permission to be Cruel: Street-Level Bureaucrats and Harm Against People Seeking Asylum". *Critical Criminology*, 28: 277–292.

Bhungalia, Lisa (2020). "Laughing at Power: Humor, Transgression, and the Politics of Refusal in Palestine". *Environment and Planning C: Politics and Space*, 38(3): 387–404.

Bidgoli, Mehrdad (2020). "Comedy and Humour: An Ethical Perspective". *The European Journal of Humour Research*, 8(1): 82–94.

Bienenfeld, David (2002). "History of Psychotherapy". In Hersen, Michel and Sledge, William (Eds.), *Encyclopaedia of Psychology*, vol. 1: 923–935. Amsterdam: Elsevier.

Bierce, Ambrose (1911) [1892–1903]. "Wit and Humor". In *The Collected Works of Ambrose Bierce*, vol. 10: 98–101. New York: Walter Neale.

Bierce, Ambrose (2000) [1911]. *The Unabridged Devil's Dictionary* (ed. David E. Shultz and S.T. Joshi). London: University of Georgia Press.
Biggar, Nigel (2015). "In Defence of War". *New Blackfriars*, 96(1062): 192–205.
Billig, Michael (2005). *Laughter and Ridicule. Towards a Social Critique of Humour.* London: Sage.
Blackwell, Kenneth (2011). "The Wit and Humour of *Principia Mathematica*". *Russell*, 31(1): 151–160.
Blake, Charlie and Christiansen, Steen (2011). "Transgression Now". *Akademisk Kvarter*, 3: 4–16.
Blanshard, Bran (1975). *Reason and Goodness.* Atlantic Highlands: Humanities Press.
Blinka Lukas *et al.* (2022). "Online Sex Addiction: A Qualitative Analysis of Symptoms in Treatment-Seeking Men". *Frontiers Psychiatry*, 13, doi: 10.3389/fpsyt.2022.907549 [Accessed 30/12/2022].
Blocian, Ilona and Kuzmicki, Andrew (2019). *Contemporary Influences of C.G. Jung's Thought.* Leiden: Brill.
Bluhm, Heinz (1950). "Nietzsche's Idea of Luther in *Menschliches, Allzumenschliches*". *PMLA*, 65(6): 1053–1068.
Blum, Deborah (2002). *Love at Goon Park. Harry Harlow and the Science of Affection.* New York: Basic Books.
Blumenthal, Stephen (2006). "Violence as Communication". *Criminal Justice Matters*, 66(1): 4–5.
Boadella, David (1973). *Wilhelm Reich. The Evolution of His Work.* Chicago: Henry Regnery.
Boccaccio, Giovanni (1886) [1350]. *The Decameron* (trans. John Payne). London: Villon Society, https://www.gutenberg.org/files/23700/23700-h/23700-h.htm [Accessed 20/09/2022].
Bodin, Jean (1955) [1576]. *Six Books of the Commonwealth* (trans. M.J. Tooley). Oxford: Blackwell.
Bodin, Jean (1995) [1580]. *On the Demon-Mania of Witches* (trans. Randy A. Scott). Toronto: Centre for Reformation and Renaissance Studies.
Boethius, Severinus (1999) [524]. *The Consolation of Philosophy* (trans. Victor Watts). London: Penguin.
Boghossian, Peter (2021). "My University Sacrificed Ideas for Ideology. So Today I Quit". *Common Sense*, https://bariweiss.substack.com/p/my-university-sacrificed-ideas-for [Accessed 26/08/2022].
Bolduc, Paula (2008). "The Cruelty of Mercy: Oxymoronic Paradoxes". *Mercy Illuminates*, 10: 35–40.
Boltanski, Luc and Thévenot, Laurent (1991). *De la justification. Les économies de la grandeur.* Paris: Gallimard.
Boonin, David (Ed.) (2022). *The Palgrave Handbook of Sexual Ethics.* Cham: Palgrave Macmillan.
Borgomeo, Vincenzo and Manara, Milo (2022). "Milo Manara: 'Non farò causa a Musk ma pongo il problema dei diritti d'autore'". *La Repubblica*, https://www.repubblica.it/tecnologia/2022/11/22/news/milo_manara_non_faro_causa_a_musk_ma_pongo_il_problema_dei_diritti_dautore-375650410/?ref=RHLM-BG-I375288850-P2-S5-T1 [Accessed 22/11/2022].
Borisova, Tanya (2019). "Linguistic Aspects of the Contemporary Theories of Humour". *Proceedings of University of Ruse*, 58(6.3): 47–53.
Borloz, Sophie-Valentine (2017). "Du 'gaz de paradis des poëtes anglais' au 'sourire de force'. Sur les traces du gaz hilarant dans la littérature du XIXe siècle (France et Angleterre)". In Caraion, Marta and Danguy, Laurence (Eds.), *Le rire: forms et fonctions du comique*, https://www.fabula.org/colloques/document4559.php [Accessed 21/09/2021].
Borràs Isnardo, Marina and Álvarez Giner, Natalia (2018). "Alternativa X". BA. Jaume I University.
Boryslawski, Rafael (2020). "The Monsters That Laugh Back: Humour as a Rhetorical Apophasis in Medieval Monstrology". In Derrin, Daniel and Burrows, Hannah (Eds.), *The Palgrave Handbook of Humour*, 239–256. Cham: Palgrave Macmillan.
Boskin, Joseph (1986). *Sambo. The Rise and Demise of an American Jester.* New York: Oxford UP.

Bouissac, Paul (2015). *The Semiotics of Clowns and Clowning: Ritual Transgression and the Theory of Laughter.* London: Bloomsbury.
Bouquet, Brigitte and Riffault, Jacques (2010). "L'humour dans les diverses formes du rire". *La vie sociale,* 2(2): 13 – 22.
Bourke, Joanna (2020). "Sadism: A History of Non-Consensual Sexual Cruelty". *The International Journal of Forensic Psychotherapy,* 2(1): 1 – 12.
Bourne, H.R. (1876). *Life of John Locke. In Two Volumes.* New York: Harper & Brothers, https://books.google.je/books?id=NOjWAAAAMAAJ&source=gbs_book_other_versions [Accessed 01/05/2022].
Bower, Carol (2015). "Evaluation of the Global Initiative to End All Corporal Punishment of Children". London: APPROACH.
Boyers, Robert, Bernstein, Maxime and Sontag, Susan (2015 – 2016) [1975]. "Women, The Arts, & The Politics of Culture: An Interview with Susan Sontag". *Salmagundi,* 188 – 189: 240 – 262.
Boyle, Gregory J. and Joss-Reid, Jeanne M. (2004). "Relationship of Humour to Health: A Psychometric Investigation". *British Journal of Health Psychology,* 9(1): 51 – 66.
Braavig, Jens (2009). "The Buddhist Hell: An Early Instance of the Idea?" *Numen,* 56(2 – 3): 254 – 281.
Brailsford, Henry N. (1961). *The Levellers and the English Revolution* (ed. Christopher Hill). Stanford: Stanford UP.
Bramon, B. and Leslie, J. (2012). "Slavery and Human Trafficking". In Chadwick, Ruth (Ed.), *Encyclopedia of Applied Ethics,* 2nd ed., vol. 4: 114 – 121. London: Academic Press.
Branca, Paolo, De Poli, Barbara and Zanelli, Patrizia (2011). *Il sorriso della mezzaluna. Umorismo, ironia e satira nella cultura araba.* Rome: Carocci.
Braudel, Fernand (2002) [1985]. *Il Mediterraneo* (trans. Elena De Angeli). Milan: Bompiani.
Breeden, Aurelien (2020). "Paris Attack Suspect Wanted to Target Charlie Hebdo with Arson". *The New York Times,* https://www.nytimes.com/2020/09/29/world/europe/france-attack-suspect-terrorism.html [Accessed 26/08/2022].
Bremmer, Jan and Roodenburg, Herman (Eds.) (1997). *A Cultural History of Humour: From Antiquity to the Present Day.* Cambridge: Polity.
Brogaard, Berit and Gatzia, Dimitria Electra (Eds.) (2021). *The Philosophy and Psychology of Ambivalence.* London: Routledge.
Bromell, David and Shanks, David (2021). "Censored! Developing a Framework for Making Sound Decisions Fast". *Policy Quarterly,* 17(1): 42 – 49.
Brooke, Henry (1792). "Redemption". In *The Poetical Works,* vol. 1: 383 – 405. Dublin: npa, https://catalog.hathitrust.org/Record/011922351 [Accessed 22/12/2022].
Brooks, David (2015). "I Am Not Charlie Hebdo". *New York Times,* https://www.nytimes.com/2015/01/09/opinion/david-brooks-i-am-not-charlie-hebdo.html [Accessed 26/08/2022].
Brown, Marvin (2010). "Free Enterprise and the Economics of Slavery". *Real-World Economics Review,* 52: 28 – 39.
Bruce, Lenny (1974) [1967]. *The Essential Lenny Bruce* (ed. John Cohen). New York: Ballantine.
Bruni, Pierfranco (2016). *Luigi Pirandello. Il tragico e la follia.* Alghero: Nemapress.
Brüntrup, Godehard and Jaskolla, Ludwig (Eds.) (2017). *Panpsychism. Contemporary Perspectives.* Oxford: Oxford UP.
Buccola, Gaetano Roberto (2019). *L'azione malata. Male universale e Bene individuale. Psicoanalisi del terrorismo.* Palermo: Carlo Saladino.
Buckley, Sarah-Anne (2013). *The Cruelty Man. Child Welfare, the NSPCC and the State of Ireland, 1889 – 1956.* Manchester: Manchester UP.

Budi, Didik R. and Widyaningsih, Rindha (2021). "Revealing Fanaticism of Football Supporters: Mass Psychology Perspective". *Annals of Tropical Medicine and Public Health*, 24(S03), https://doi.org/10.36295/ASRO.2021.24343 [Accessed 09/11/2022].

Buijzen, Moniek and Valkenburg, Patti M. (2004). "Developing a Typology of Humor in Audio-Visual Media". *Media Psychology*, 6(2): 147–167.

Bundtzen, Lynda K. (1990). "Bertolucci's Erotic Politics and the 'Auteur' Theory: From 'Last Tango in Paris' to 'The Last Emperor'". *Western Humanities Review*, 44(2): 198–215.

Burke, Edmund (1890) [1790]. *Reflections on the Revolution in France*. London: Macmillan, https://books.google.is/books/about/Reflections_on_the_Revolution_in_France.html?id=kFpaAAAAMAAJ&redir_esc=y [Accessed 5/12/2022].

Burris, Christopher T. and Leitch, Rebecca (2016). "Your Pain, My Gain: The Interpersonal Context of Sadism". In Aumer, Katherine (Ed.), *The Psychology of Love and Hate in Intimate Relationships*, 85–103. Cham: Springer.

Butler, Nick (2015). "Joking Aside: Theorizing Laughter in Organizations". *Culture and Organization*, 21(1): 42–58.

Byock, Jesse L. (1982). *Feud in the Icelandic Saga*. Berkeley: University of California Press.

Byrne, Emma (2017). *Swearing Is Good for You. The Amazing Science of Bad Language*. London: Profile.

Cahill, Lisa Sowle (1994). *Love Your Enemies: Discipleship, Pacifism, and Just War Theory*. Minneapolis: Augsburg Fortress.

Callamard, Agnes (2015). "Religion, Terrorism and Speech in a 'Post-Charlie Hebdo' World". *Religion and Human Rights*, 10: 207–228.

Callimachi, Rukmini and Yardley, Jim (2015). "From Amateur to Ruthless Jihadist in France". *The New York Times*, https://www.nytimes.com/2015/01/18/world/europe/paris-terrorism-brothers-said-cherif-kouachi-charlie-hebdo.html [Accessed 26/08/2022].

Calverley, Charles Stuart (1959) [1937]. "Sad Memories". In Slater, W.E. (Ed.), *Humour in Verse. An Anthology*, 65–69. Cambridge: Cambridge UP.

Camões, Luís de et al. (2022) [1500s–1935]. *Poeti di Lisbona* (trans. Paola D'Agostino and Andrea Ragusa). Lisbon: Shantarin.

Canetti, Elias (1966) [1960]. *Crowds and Power* (trans. Carol Stewart). New York: Viking.

Canetti, Elias (1999) [1977–1987]. *The Memoirs of Elias Canetti* (trans. Joachim Neugroschel). New York: Farrar, Straus & Giroux.

Cannon, Walter B. (1932). *The Wisdom of the Body*. New York: W.W. Norton.

Capaldi, Nicholas (2004). *John Stuart Mill: A Biography*. Cambridge: Cambridge UP.

Cappelli, Valerio and Vega, Paz (2021). "Paz Vega a Venezia: 'Oggi manca la trasgressione perché siamo meno coraggiosi". *Corriere della Sera*, https://www.corriere.it/spettacoli/cinema-serie-tv/21_settembre_06/manca-trasgressioneperche-meno-coraggiosi-d89bbac8-0f38-11ec-9614-5f4fa1f949f6.shtml. [Accessed 26/08/2022].

Caputo, Alicia A., Brodsky, Stanley and Kemp, Simon (1997). "How Cruel Is a Cat Playing with a Mouse? A Study of People's Assessment of Cruelty". *New Zealand Journal of Psychology*, 26(2): 19–24.

Caputo, Alicia A., Brodsky, Stanley and Kemp, Simon (2000). "Understanding and Experiences of Cruelty: An Exploratory Report". *The Journal of Social Psychology*, 140(5): 649–660.

Carabelli, Anna M. and Cedrini, Mario A. (2010). "Global Imbalances, Monetary Disorder, and Shrinking Policy Space: Keynes' Legacy for Our Troubled World". *Interventions*, 7(2): 315–335.

Carleton, Gregory (2005). *Sexual Revolution in Bolshevik Russia*. Pittsburgh: University of Pittsburgh Press.

Carlin, George (2004). *When Will Jesus Bring the Pork Chops?* Westport, CT: Hyperion.
Carlström, Charlotta (2019). "BDSM – The Antithesis of Good Swedish Sex?" *Sexualities*, 22(7–8): 1164–1181.
Carlyle, Thomas (1835) [1827]. "Jean Paul Friedrich Richter". In Cross, Maurice (Ed.). *Selections from the Edinburgh Review*, 2: 448–459. Paris: Baudry's European Library, https://books.google.bj/books?id=aD5BAAAAYAAJ [Accessed 12/12/2022].
Carlyle, Thomas (1850). *Latter-Day Pamphlets*. London: Cahpman and Hall.
Carroll, John (1973). "Pareto's Irrationalism". *Sociology*, 7(3): 327–340.
Carroll, Joshua and Diamond, Cape (2019). "Gagged: Performers Face Jail in Myanmar for Raucous Satire". *Aljazeera*, https://www.aljazeera.com/news/2019/10/gagged-performers-face-jail-myanmar-raucous-satire-191030013805556.html [Accessed 26/08/2022].
Carroll, Noël (2014). *Humour. A Very Short Introduction*. Oxford: Oxford UP.
Carroll, Noël (2020). "Timings: Notes on Stand-Up Comedy". In Amir, Lydia B. (Ed.), *Philosophy of Humor Yearbook*, 1: 3–15. Berlin: De Gruyter.
Carter, Angela (1978). *The Sadean Woman and the Ideology of Pornography*. New York: Pantheon Books.
Cassirer, Ernst (1953) [1932]. *The Platonic Renaissance in England* (trans. James P. Pettergrove). Edinburgh: Thomas Nelson.
Cassirer, Ernst (1980) [1923–1929]. *The Philosophy of Symbolic Forms* (trans. Ralph Manheim). New Haven: Yale UP.
Castañar Rubio, Guillem (2023). Review of *Danish Humour – Sink or Swim* by Lita Lundquist and Helen Dyrbye. *The European Journal of Humour Research*, 10(4): 241–244.
Castoriadis, Cornelius (1997a) [1989]. "Done and To Be Done". In *The Castoriadis Reader* (trans. David Ames Curtis), 361–417. Oxford: Blackwell.
Castoriadis, Cornelius (1997b) [1975]. *The Imaginary Institution of Society* (trans. Kathleen Blamey). Cambridge: Polity.
Castoriadis, Cornelius (2003). *The Rising Tide of Insignificancy (The Big Sleep)* (trans. anonymously). Costis.org – Lightning Archive, https://www.costis.org/x/castoriadis/Castoriadis-rising_tide.pdf [Accessed 11/11/2021].
Castoriadis, Cornelius (2005). *Figures of the Thinkable, Including Passion and Knowledge* (trans. anonymously). Costis.org – Lightning Archive, https://www.notbored.org/FTPK.pdf [Accessed 11/11/2021].
Castoriadis, Cornelius (2013) [1994]. *Democracy and Relativism* (trans. anonymously). Costis.org – Lightning Archive, https://www.notbored.org/DR.pdf [Accessed 11/11/2021].
Castoriadis, Cornelius (2015) [1979–1996]. *Window on the Chaos* (trans. anonymously), Beta version. Costis.org – Lightning Archive, https://www.notbored.org/WoC.pdf [Accessed 11/11/2021].
Castoriadis, Cornelius (2017) [1992]. "C.L.R. James and the Fate of Marxism". In *Postscript on Insignificance* (trans. anonymously), 280–309. Costis.org – Lightning Archive, https://www.notbored.org/PSRTI.pdf [Accessed 11/11/2021].
Castoriadis, Cornelius (2018) [2007]. *A Socialism ou Barbarie Anthology* (trans. anonymously). London: ERIS.
Cavanna, Georges F. *et al.* (2018). *Hara Kiri, Journal Bête et Méchant: Les belles images*. Paris: Hoëbeke.
Cayley, David (2015). "Nils Christie: In Memoriam". *davidcaley.com*, https://www.davidcayley.com/blog/2015/6/2/nils-christie-in-memoriam [Accessed 09/11/2021].
Cazamian, Louis (1930). *The Development of English Humour*. New York: MacMillan.
Ceccarelli, Fabio (1988). *Sorriso e riso: Saggio di antropologia biosociale*. Milan: Einaudi.

Çelik, Adem (2020). "Pastoral Power, Justice, Cruelty, Order and Rebellion in Islamic Political Thought: An Evaluation Based on Siyasatnamas (Mirror for Princes)". In Babacan, Hasan and Inan, Ruhi (Eds.), *Social and Humanities Sciences. Theory, Current Research and New Trends*, 115–135. Cetinje: IVPE.

Cerna, Christina (2002). "Bombing for Peace: Collateral Damage and Human Rights". *Proceedings of the Annual Meeting (American Society of International Law)*, 96: 95–108.

Chan, Anita and Xiaoyang, Zhu (2003). "Disciplinary Labor Regimes in Chinese Factories". *Critical Asian Studies*, 35(4): 559–594.

Chan, Wing-Tsit (1973). *A Source Book in Chinese Philosophy*. Princeton: Princeton UP.

Chang, Ha-Jung (2010). *23 Things They Don't Tell You About Capitalism*. London: Allen Lane.

Chapman, A.H. and Chapman-Santana, Miriam (1995). "The Influence of Nietzsche on Freud's Ideas". *The British Journal of Psychiatry*, 166(2): 251–253.

Chapman, Anthony J. and Foot, Hugh C. (Eds.) (1977). *It's a Funny Thing, Humour*. Oxford: Pergamon Press.

Chapple, Alison and Ziebland, Sue (2004). "The Role of Humor for Men with Testicular Cancer". *Qualitative Health Research*, 14(8): 1123–1139.

Charest, Maxime and Kleinplatz, Peggy J. (2021). "What Do Young Canadian, Straight and LGBTQ Men and Women Learn About Sex and From Whom?" Sexuality Research and Social Policy, https://doi.org/10.1007/s13178-021-00578-7 [Accessed 28/11/2021].

Chateau Canguilhem, Johann (2014). "La chair virtuelle du cybérérotisme". PhD. Michel de Montaigne University.

Chatterjee, Biswajit and Ray, Runa (2019). *Economics of Child Labour*. Singapore: Springer.

Chattoo, Caty Borum and Feldman, Lauren (2020). *A Comedian and an Activist Walk into a Bar: The Serious Role of Comedy in Social Justice*. Oakland: University of California Press.

Chesterton, G.K. (1904). "Christianity and Rationalism". In *The Blatchford Controversies*, 1st essay. London: Macmillan, http://www.gkc.org.uk/gkc/books/Christianity_and_Rationalism.html [Accessed 20/06/2021].

Chesterton, G.K. (1910) [1909]. *George Bernard Shaw*, 1st ed. New York: John Lane, http://www.gkc.org.uk/gkc/books/Shaw.html [Accessed 02/10/2022].

Chesterton, G.K. (1916). *The Crimes of England*. New York: John Lane, http://www.gkc.org.uk/gkc/books/Crimes_of_England.html#1_0_5 [Accessed 02/10/2022].

Chesterton, G.K. (1919a) [1905]. *Heretics*, 12th ed. New York: John Lane, http://www.gkc.org.uk/gkc/books/heret12.txt [Accessed 02/10/2022].

Chesterton, G.K. (1919b). *Irish Impressions*. London: W. Collins Sons, http://www.gkc.org.uk/gkc/books/Irish_Impressions.html [Accessed 02/10/2022].

Chesterton, G.K. (1922). *What I Saw in America*. London: Hodder and Stoughton, http://www.gkc.org.uk/gkc/books/27250-h.htm [Accessed 02/10/2022].

Chesterton, G.K. (1929–1973) [1929–1938]. "Humour". In Garvin, J.L. *et al.* (Eds.), *Encyclopædia Britannica*, 14th ed. Chicago: Encyclopædia Britannica, https://nonsenselit.com/g-k-chesterton-humour-1938/ [Accessed 19/04/2022].

Chesterton, G.K. (1931). *Come to Think of It*. New York: Dodd-Mead.

Chesterton, G.K. (1933). *All I Survey*, http://www.gkc.org.uk/gkc/books/All_I_Survey.txt [Accessed 26/08/2022].

Chesterton, G.K. (1950). *The Common Man*, http://www.gkc.org.uk/gkc/books/Common_Man.txt [Accessed 26/08/2022].

Chesterton, G.K. (1956) [1933]. *St. Thomas Aquinas. "The Dumb Ox"*. London: Image Books.

Chesterton, G.K. (1958) [1909]. *Lunacy and Letters* (ed. Dorothy Collins). New York: Sheed & Ward, http://www.gkc.org.uk/gkc/books/Lunacy_and_Letters.pdf [Accessed 26/08/2022].

Chesterton, G.K. (1975) [1911]. "The Return of Pageantry". In *The Apostle and the Wild Ducks and Other Essays* (ed. Dorothy Collins), 106–109. London: P. Elek.

Chesterton, G.K. (1987) [1923]. *Saint Francis.* London: Image Classics.

Chesterton, G.K. (1997) [1925]. *The Everlasting Man.* Leicester: De Montfort University, http://www.gkc.org.uk/gkc/books/everlasting_man.pdf [Accessed 19/02/2022].

Chesterton, G.K. (1998–1999) [1906]. *Charles Dickens. Part Two.* Leicester: De Montfort University, http://www.gkc.org.uk/gkc/books/CD-2.html [Accessed 19/02/2022].

Chesterton, G.K. (2000–2012) [1917]. *Utopia of Usurers and Other Essays.* Fairbanks: Project Gutenberg Literary Archive Foundation, http://www.gkc.org.uk/gkc/books/2134.txt.

Chesterton, G.K. (2015) [1905]. "Introduction". In Gorky, Maxim, *Creatures That Once Were Men and Other Stories* (trans. by J.M. Shirazi), 5–10. Erik Publications.

Chey, Jocelyn (2011). "*Youmo* and the Chinese Sense of Humour". In Chey, Jocelyn and Milner Davis, Jessica (Eds.), *Humour in Chinese Life and Letters: Classical and Traditional Approaches*, 1–29. Hong Kong: Hong Kong UP.

Chiarelli, Maria Vittoria (2016). "Pasolini – Il processo a 'La ricotta': La persecuzione nelle aule di un tribunale". *Videoteca Pasolini*, https://pasolinilepaginecorsare.blogspot.com/2016/10/pasolini-il-processo-la-ricotta-la_22.html?m=0 [Accessed 04/06/2022].

Chiaro, Delia (2010). "Laughing At or Laughing With? Italian Comic Stereotypes Viewed from Within the Peripheral Group". In Dunphy, Graeme and Emig, Rainer (Eds.), *Hybrid Humour. Comedy in Transcultural Perspectives*, 65–83. Leiden: Brill.

Chomsky, Noam (1980). "Some Elementary Comments on the Rights of Freedom of Expression". *Chomsky.Info*, https://chomsky.info/19801011/ [Accessed 27/01/2023].

Chomsky, Noam (1981). "His Right to Say It". *Chomsky.Info*, https://chomsky.info/19810228/ [Accessed 27/01/2023].

Chomsky, Noam (2003) [2002]. *Understanding Power* (ed. Peter R. Mitchell and John Schoeffel). London: Vintage.

Chomsky, Noam (2020). "Noam Chomsky on Jung, Wittgenstein, and Gödel (Ask Me Anything)", https://www.youtube.com/watch?v=pUWmTXkpHjE&ab_channel=TheoriesofEverythingwithCurtJaimungal [Accessed 25/11/2022].

Chrisafis, Angelique (2022). "Paris Olympic and Paralympic Games Mascots Likened to 'Clitoris in Trainers'". *The Guardian*, https://www.theguardian.com/sport/2022/nov/15/mascot-paris-olympic-games-2024-likened-to-clitoris-in-trainers-phryges?CMP=fb_gu&utm_medium=Social&utm_source=Facebook&fbclid=IwAR0whIcJvefcCHw0tY68y416dnVczrTmYFWdJEbm3mXjoeBjC4yMWLmtWeI#Echobox=1668516091 [Accessed 16/11/2022].

Christie, Nils (1981). *Limits to Pain.* Oslo: Universitetsforlaget.

Christie, Nils (2017) [1996]. *Crime Control as Industry. Towards Gulags, Western Style?* London: Routledge.

Chwe, Michael Suk-Young (1990). "Why Were Workers Whipped? Pain in a Principal-Agent Model". *The Economic Journal*, 100: 1109–1121.

Cioran, Emil (1970) [1964]. *The Fall into Time* (trans. Richard Howard). Chicago: Quadrangle.

Cipolla, Carlo M. (2005) [1993]. *Before the Industrial Revolution. European Society and Economy, 1000–1700*, 3rd ed. London: Routledge.

Cipolla, Carlo M. (2011) [1976]. *The Basic Laws of Human Stupidity.* Bologna: il Mulino.

Clark, Carol (1983). *Vulgar Rabelais*. Glasgow: Pressgang.
Clark, Gregory (1994). "Factory Discipline". *The Journal of Economic History*, 54(1): 128–163.
Clarkson, Jay and Kopaczewski, Shana (2013). "Pornography Addiction and the Medicalization of Free Speech". *Journal of Communication Inquiry*, 37(2): 128–148.
Classen, Albrecht (2010). "Sex on Stage (and in the Library) of an Early Medieval Convent: Hrotsvit of Gandersheim". *Orbis litterarum*, 65(3): 167–200.
Cleves, Rachel Hope (2020). "The Problem of Modern Pederasty in Queer History: A Case Study of Norman Douglas". *Historical Reflections/Réflexions Historiques*, 46(1): 47–62.
Clinton, Bill (1996). *Between Hope and History*. New York: Random House.
Cocei, Liviu Iulian (2015). "The Image of Socratic Irony from the Sophists to Nietzsche". *Hermeneia*, 15: 125–134.
Cocei, Liviu Iulian (2022). *Homo ironicus. O abordare antropologică a ironiei filosofice*. Bucharest: Eikon.
Coetsier, Rosanne (2020). "XXX – What Women Want. An Inductive Thematic Analysis of the Female Experience of Porno and Porna in a Patriarchal Society". MA. Gent University.
Cogan, Rosemary *et al.* (1987). "Effects of Laughter and Relaxation on Discomfort Thresholds". *Journal of Behavioral Medicine*, 10: 139–144.
Colafemmina, Cesare (2006). "Un medico ebreo di Oria alla corte dei Fatimidi". *Materia giudaica*, 11(1–2): 5–12.
Cole, Dagmar (2019). "Avoiding Ambiguity". *Business Rules Community*, 20(2), https://www.brcommunity.com/articles.php?id=b981 [Accessed 21/09/2021].
Coleridge, Samuel T. (1895). *Letters* (ed. Ernest Coleridge), vol. 1. Boston: Houghton Mifflin.
Coleridge, Stephen (1918). *Great Testimony against Scientific Cruelty*. London: John Lane, Bodley Head.
Collins, Randall (1974). "Three Faces of Cruelty: Towards a Comparative Sociology of Violence". *Theory and Society*, 1(4): 415–440.
Committee on the Judiciary (1997). "A Review of the Global Tobacco Settlement". Serial No. J-105–28. Washington: US Government Printing Office.
Condorcet (1998) [1793–1794]. *Esquisse d'un tableau historique des progrès de l'esprit humain*. Florence: Eliohs.
Connolly, Angela (2008). "Jung in the Twilight Zone: The Psychological Functions of Horror Film". In Rowland, Susan (Ed.), *Psyche and the Arts*, 128–138. London, New York: Routledge.
Connolly, Billy (2009). "On Swearing", https://www.youtube.com/watch?v=h68CfIUkPKs&ab_channel=Gareth%26JoanneForbes [Accessed 17/12/2022].
Conze, Edward (1980) [1958]. *A Short History of Buddhism*. London: Allen & Unwin.
Cooke-Cornell, Beth Anne (2018). "Rape Jokes in the Era of #MeToo". *Response – The Journal of Popular and American Culture*, 3(2), https://responsejournal.net/issue/2018-11/article/rape-jokes-era-metoo#fnref:fn18 [Accessed 26/08/2022].
Cooper, William M. (1910). *A History of the Rod. In All Countries. From the Earliest Period to the Present Time*. London: William Reeves.
Cope, Theo A. (2006). *Fear of Jung: The Complex Doctrine and Emotional Science*. London: Karnac.
Cora, N. İpek Hüner (2022). "Serial Murder and Honor: Rereading the Story of an Ottoman Murderess". *International Journal of Middle East Studies*, 54: 135–140.
Corbett, Lionel (2015). *The Soul in Anguish: Psychotherapeutic Approaches to Suffering*. Asheville: Chiron.
Corvino, John (2022). "Naughty Fantasies (With a New Postscript Including Sex Robots)". In Boonin, David (Ed.), *The Palgrave Handbook of Sexual Ethics*, 525–533. Cham: Palgrave Macmillan.

Cosenza, Giovanna (2016). "Umberto Eco su Internet e i media digitali: Un anticipatore lungimirante, altro che apocalittico". *Dis.Amb.Iguando*, https://giovannacosenza.wordpress.com/2016/12/12/umberto-eco-su-internet-e-i-media-digitali-un-anticipatore-lungimirante-altro-che-apocalittico/ [Accessed 06/10/2022].

Costea, Bogdan and Amiridis, Kostas (2017). "Ernst Jünger, Total Mobilisation and the Work of War". *Organization*, 24(4): 475–490.

Cowen, Nick (2016). "Millian Liberalism and Extreme Pornography". *American Journal of Political Science*, 60(2): 509–520.

Cox, Harvey (1987). "God's Last Laugh". *Christianity and Crisis*, 47(5), http://www.religion-online.org/article/gods-last-laugh/ [Accessed 21/09/2021].

Cox, Lara (2015). "Standing Up against the Rape Joke: Irony and Its Vicissitudes". *Signs: Journal of Women in Culture and Society*, 40(4): 963–984.

Cram, Ian (2006). *Restrictions on Freedom of Speech in Liberal Democracies*. Aldershot: Ashgate.

Craun, Sarah W. and Bourke, Michael L. (2015). "Is Laughing at the Expense of Victims and Offenders a Red Flag? Humor and Secondary Traumatic Stress". *Journal of Child Sexual Abuse*, 24(5): 592–602.

Cristaudo, Wayne (2021). Review of *Why Believe? Approaches to Religion* by Garrett Barden and Giorgio Baruchello. *The European Legacy*, 26(5): 554–556

Critchley, Simon (2000). "De l'humour". *Les papiers du Collège International de Philosophie*, 52: 1–53.

Critchley, Simon (2002a). "Did You Hear the One about the Philosopher Writing a Book on Humour?" *Richmond Journal of Philosophy*, 2: 40–45.

Critchley, Simon (2002b). *On Humour*. London: Routledge.

Crowther, Sarah (2021). "Bloody Disgusting! Abjection, Excess and Absurdity: The Carnivalesque Cohesion Between Horror and Comedy in Film and Television". PhD. Swansea University.

Csapo, Eric and Miller, Margaret C. (2007). "General Introduction". In Csapo, Eric and Miller, Margaret C. (Eds.), *The Origins of Theater in Ancient Greece and Beyond: From Ritual to Drama*, 1–38. Cambridge: Cambridge UP.

Curtis, J.A.E. (1991). *Manuscripts Don't Burn: A Life in Letters and Diaries*. London: Bloomsbury.

Cusick, Daniel (2020). "Climate Helped Turn These 5 Places into Ghost Towns". *Scientific American*, https://www.scientificamerican.com/article/climate-helped-turn-these-5-places-into-ghost-towns/ [Accessed 17/07/2022].

Czech, Brian (2022). "Herman Daly (1938–2022): Up to the Steady State Economy". *Mother Pelican. A Journal of Solidarity and Sustainability*, 18(12), http://www.pelicanweb.org/solisustv18n12page6.html [Accessed 01/12/2022].

D'Ancona, Alessandro (1880). *Studi di Critica e Storia Letteraria*. Bologna: Zanichelli.

Dahlkvist, Tobias (2007). *Nietzsche and the Philosophy of Pessimism*. Uppsala: Acta Universitatis Upsaliensis.

Daily, Jay E. (1973). *The Anatomy of Censorship*. New York: Marcel Dekker.

Damasso, Maddalena (2017). "Pulcinella tra Maschera e Persona: Un'esperienza di psicoterapia". *Babel*, 35: 259–267.

Dante (1903) [1308]. *The Convivio of Dante Alighieri*. London: J.M. Dent.

Dante (n.d.a) [1314]. "Canto XXI", *Inferno* https://divinacommedia.weebly.com/inferno-canto-xxi.html [Accessed 02/06/2022].

Darwin, Charles (1872). *The Expression of the Emotions in Man and Animals*. New York: D. Appleton.

Daskalopoulou, Athanasia and Zanette, Maria Carolina (2020). "Women's Consumption of Pornography: Pleasure, Contestation, and Empowerment". *Sociology*, 54(5): 969–986.

Dastagir, Hussain Ghulam *et al.* (2020). "The Criminalization of Cruelty within the Malaysian and Pakistani Family Laws: A Comparative Analysis". *Proceedings of the International Law Conference "Law, Technology and the Imperative of Change in the 21st Century"*, 281–286. Setúbal: Science and Technology Publications.

Dave, Aashka, Ndulue, Emily Boardman and Schwartz-Henderson, Laura (2020). "Targeting Greta Thunberg: A Case Study in Online Mis/Disinformation". *German Marshall Fund of the United States*, 11: 5–20.

Davies, Christie (1998). *Jokes and their Relations to Society*. Berlin: De Gruyter.

Davis, Chelsea (2020). "Sicko Doctors. Suffering and Sadism in 19th-Century America". *The Public Domain Review*, https://publicdomainreview.org/essay/sicko-doctors [Accessed 26/08/2022].

Dayal, Gyaneshwar (2021). "Freedom of Speech Is a Joke". *The Pioneer*, https://www.dailypioneer.com/2021/columnists/freedom-of-speech-is-a-joke.html [Accessed 12/07/2022].

De Alarcón, Rubén *et al.* (2019). "Online Porn Addiction: What We Know and What We Don't— A Systematic Review". *Journal of Clinical Medicine*, 8(1), https://doi.org/10.3390/jcm8010091 [Accessed 25/06/2022].

De Armey, Michael H. (2020). *Cosmopolitanism and the Evils of the World*. Cham: Palgrave Macmillan.

De Beauvoir, Simone (1956) [1949]. *The Second Sex* (ed. and trans. H.M. Parshley). London: Jonathan Cape.

De Beauvoir, Simone (1966) [1951–1952]. *Must We Burn Sade?* (trans. Annette Michelson). New York: Grove.

De la Boétie, Étienne (1942) [1574]. *The Discourse of Voluntary Servitude* (trans. Harry Kurz). Indianapolis: Liberty Fund.

De Paz González, Isaac, Bernal Ballestreros, María José and Murillo Ortiz, Alejandro (2019). "Vertientes de reformas constitucionales en constituciones europeas y americanas: ¿Renovación en torno al derecho internacional de los derechos humanos?" In Sandoval Figueroa, Luis, Bernal Ballestreros, Maria José, De Paz González, Isaac and Camarillo Govea, Laura Alicia (Eds.), *Estudios de derecho internacional de los derechos humanos*, 149–186. Tijuana: Universidad Autónoma de Baja California.

De Unamuno, Miguel (1967) [1905]. *Our Lord Don Quixote. The Life of Don Quixote and Sancho with Related Essays* (trans. Anthony Kerrigan). New York: Bollingen/Princeton UP.

De Unamuno, Miguel (2018) [1921]. *Tragic Sense of Life* (trans. J.E. Crawford Flitch). Pantianos Classics.

De Vries, Bouke (2019). "The Right to be Publicly Naked: A Defence of Nudism". *Res Publica*, 25: 407–424.

Dearden, Lizzie (2015). "Isis 'Crucifies Children for Not Fasting During Ramadan' in Syria". *The Independent*, https://www.independent.co.uk/news/world/middle-east/isis-crucifies-children-not-fasting-during-ramadan-syria-10338215.html [Accessed 26/08/2022].

Dědečková, Eva and Charlesworth, Simon J. (2022). "Anthropocene, Technocene and the Problem of Philosophy of Education". *Anthropocenica*, 3: 95–110.

Deida, David (1997). *The Way of the Superior Man*. Austin, TX: Plexus.

Dekimpe, Arthuria (2020). "La diffusion de la culture populaire japonaise en Belgique francophone, des origines à nos jours". MA. Catholic University of Louvain.

Del Rocío Bello-Urrego, Alejandra (2020). "Entre a zona do ser e do nao-ser: a economia moderna da crueldade". *Tabula Rasa*, 33: 335–355.

Deleuze, Gilles (1989) [1967]. *Masochism* (trans. Jean McNeil). New York: Zone Books.

Deleuze, Gilles (1990) [1969]. *The Logic of Sense* (trans. Mark Lester and Charles Stivale). New York: Columbia UP.
Deleuze, Gilles (1994) [1968]. *Difference and Repetition* (trans. Paul Patton). New York: Columbia UP.
Deleuze, Gilles (1995) [1990]. *Negotiations* (trans. Martin Joughin). New York: Columbia UP.
Deleuze, Gilles and Guattari, Félix (1983) [1975]. "What Is a Minor Literature?" (ed. and trans. Robert Brinkley). *Mississippi Review*, 11(3): 13 – 33.
Deleuze, Gilles and Guattari, Félix (1987) [1980]. *A Thousand Plateaus: Capitalism and Schizophrenia* (trans. Brian Massumi). Minneapolis: Minnesota UP.
Deleuze, Gilles and Guattari, Félix (2004) [1972]. *Anti-Oedipus: Capitalism and Schizophrenia* (trans. Robert Hurley, Mark Seem and Helen R. Lane). London: Continuum.
Delfino, Jessica (2019). "Writing Comedy Means Sometimes Pissing People Off and Facing the Awful Repercussions". *The Writing Cooperative*, https://writingcooperative.com/writing-comedy-means-sometimes-pissing-people-off-e264a3bb4c95.
Delon, Michel (1997). *Dictionnaire européen des Lumières*. Paris: Presses universitaires de France.
Demont, François (2017). "Morale et humour chez Emil Cioran". *Le rire: Forms et fonctions du comique*, https://www.fabula.org/colloques/document4565.php [Accessed 21/09/2021].
Denis, Lara (1999). "Kant on the Wrongness of 'Unnatural' Sex". *History of Philosophy Quarterly*, 16(2): 225 – 248.
Dentith, Simon (2000). *Parody*. London: Routledge.
Deotto, Francesco (2021). "Letteratura e rifiuti: Bataille, DeLillo, Gordon, Pusterla". *L'Ulisse*, 24: 367 – 380.
Derrida, Jacques (2002) [2000]. *Without Alibi* (trans. Peggy Kamuf). Stanford: Stanford UP.
Detert, James R. and Edmondson, Amy C. (2011). "Implicit Voice Theories: Taken-for-Granted Rules of Self-Censorship at Work". *The Academy of Management Journal*, 54(3): 461 – 488.
Díaz-Bild, Aída (2012). "Paula Spencer or the Miraculous Transformation of Misery into Joy". *Estudios Irlandeses*, 7: 19 – 32.
Dickie, Simon (2003). "Hilarity and Pitilessness in the Mid-Eighteenth Century: English Jestbook Humor". *Eighteenth-Century Studies*, 37(1): 1 – 22.
Dickie, Simon (2011). *Cruelty and Laughter. Forgotten Comic Literature and the Unsentimental Eighteenth Century*. Chicago: Chicago UP.
Diderot, Denis (1883) [1773]. *The Paradox of Acting* (trans. Walter Harries Pollock). London: Chatto & Windus, https://ia802606.us.archive.org/22/items/cu31924027175961/cu31924027175961.pdf [Accessed 11/02/2022].
Diderot, Denis (1994) [1773]. "Paradoxe sur le comédien". In *Œuvres*, vol. 4: 1367 – 1426. Paris: Robert Laffont.
Dines, Gail (2010). *Pornland. How Porn Has Hijacked Our Sexuality*. Boston: Beacon.
Diogo de Sousa, Ana Matilde (2020). "Cutencyclopedia. A Theoretical-Practical Investigation on the *Kawaii* as an Aesthetic Category in Art and Pop Culture". PhD. Lisbon University.
Dionigi, Alberto *et al.* (2023). "Humor and Attachment: Exploring the Relationships between Insecure Attachment and the Comic Styles". *European Journal of Investigation in Health, Psychology and Education*, 13, https://doi.org/10.3390/ejihpe13010012 [Accessed 27/01/2023].
Do Go On (2017). "The Last Japanese Soldiers", https://www.youtube.com/watch?v=hoBtGdEAUew&ab_channel=DoGoOn [Accessed 20/10/2022].
Domenici, Gaia (2019). *Jung's Nietzsche: Zarathustra, The Red Book, and 'Visionary' Works*. Cham: Palgrave-Macmillan.

Donner, Wendy (1991). *The Liberal Self: John Stuart Mill's Moral and Political Philosophy*, Ithaca, NY: Cornell UP.

Dooley, Ben and Ueno, Hisako (2022). "This Man Married a Fictional Character. He'd Like You to Hear Him Out". *The New York Times*, https://www.nytimes.com/2022/04/24/business/akihiko-kondo-fictional-character-relationships.html [Accessed 18/05/2022].

Dostoyevsky, Fyodor M. (1997) [1863]. *Winter Notes on Summer Impressions* (trans. David Patterson). Evanston: Northwestern UP.

Doughty, Howard A. (2017). Review of *The Cancer Stage of Capitalism* by John McMurtry. *The Innovation Journal: The Public Sector Innovation Journal*, 22(1), article 6, https://www.innovation.cc/book-reviews/2017_22_1_6_doughty_bk-rev_%20mc-murtry.pdf [Accessed 26/08/2022].

Downing, Joseph, Jackson-Preece, Jennifer and Werdine-Norris, Marie (2015). "*The Security Threat Posed by 'Outsiders' is Becoming a Central Theme of French Politics in the Aftermath of Charlie Hebdo*". *LSE European Politics and Policy (EUROPP) Blog*, http://eprints.lse.ac.uk/62775/ [Accessed 26/08/2022].

Downs, Donald A. and Surprenant, Chris W. (Eds.) (2018). *The Value and Limits of Academic Speech. Philosophical, Political, and Legal Perspectives*. London: Routledge.

Dozio, Cristina (2021). *Laugh like an Egyptian. Humour in the Contemporary Egyptian Novel*. Berlin: De Gruyter.

Dribbusch, Heiner and Birke, Peter (2012). "Trade Unions in Germany. Organisation, Environment, Challenges". *Friedrich Ebert Stiftung*, https://library.fes.de/pdf-files/id-moe/09113-20120828.pdf [Accessed 31/10/2022].

DuBois, W.E. Burghardt (1897). "Strivings of the Negro People". *The Atlantic*, https://www.theatlantic.com/magazine/archive/1897/08/strivings-of-the-negro-people/305446/ [Accessed 18/05/2022].

Dudro, Vivian (2018). "Camille Paglia, Plato, and the Paradox of Freedom". *The Catholic World Report*, https://www.catholicworldreport.com/2018/12/13/camille-paglia-plato-and-the-paradox-of-freedom/ [Accessed 26/08/2022].

Duffy, Bobby et al. (2021). "Culture Wars in the UK: Political Correctness and Free Speech". *The Policy Institute*, https://www.kcl.ac.uk/policy-institute/assets/culture-wars-in-the-uk-political-correctness-and-free-speech.pdf [Accessed 29/01/2023].

Dugger, William M. (1984). "Veblen and Kropotkin on Human Evolution". *Journal of Economic Issues*, 18: 971–985.

Dukore, Bernard F. (2014). "To Laugh or Nor to Laugh: Shaw's Comedy on Stage". *English Literature in Transition, 1880–1920*, 57(3): 324–334.

Dumas, Felicia (2020). "Les discours religieux orthodoxe et l'humour. Les pères spirituels et les fols-en-Christ". *Anadiss*, 30(2): 65–74.

Dunn, Stephen P. and Pressman, Steven (2005). "The Economic Contributions of John Kenneth Galbraith". *Review of Political Economy*, 17(2): 161–209.

Dworkin, Andrea (1976). *Our Blood. Prophecies and Discourses on Sexual Politics*. New York: Perigee.

Dworkin, Andrea (1981). *Pornography: Men Possessing Women*. New York: Putnam.

Dyck, Arnold (1985–1990) [1948–1972]. *Collected Works – Werke*, 4 vols. Winnipeg: Manitoba Mennonite Historical Society.

Dyer, Gwyne (2020). "Save the Old or Save the Economy?" *Bangkok Post*, https://www.bangkokpost.com/opinion/opinion/1890595/save-the-old-or-save-the-economy [Accessed 26/08/2022].

Dynel, Marta (2018). *Irony, Deception and Humour: Seeking the Truth about Overt and Covert Untruthfulness*. Berlin: De Gruyter.

Eagleton, Terry (2019). *Humour*. New Haven: Yale UP.

Eagleton, Terry (2022). "Vladimir Putin's War on Chaos". *The Post*, https://unherd.com/2022/03/vladimir-putins-war-on-chaos/?fbclid=IwAR2E-umhj_wGPjosUAg6c4aWGWiHBIzqXBJ42W1iNe3xJhxgAnjxV54Yx8A [Accessed 23/03/2022].

Earle, John, Moran, Cahal and Ward-Perkins, Zach (2016). *The Econocracy: The Perils of Leaving Economics to the Experts*. Manchester: Manchester UP.

Eco, Umberto (1980). *Il Nome della Rosa*. Sonzogno: Fabbri-Bompiani.

Eco, Umberto (1983) [1981]. "Il comico e la regola". *Sette anni di desiderio*, 253–261. Milan: Bompiani.

Eco, Umberto (1988). "Intentio lectoris". *Differentia: Review of Italian Thought*, 2: 147–168.

Eco, Umberto (1995). "Ur-Fascism". *The New York Review of Books*, https://www.pegc.us/archive/Articles/eco_ur-fascism.pdf [Accessed 14/07/2022].

Eco, Umberto, Scalfari, Eugenio and Gnoli, Antonio (2015). "Numero Zero", https://www.youtube.com/watch?v=b9UAHyyIDV4 [Accessed 15/07/2022].

Edelheim, Johan, Joppe, Marion and Flaherty, Joan (Eds.) (2022). *Teaching Tourism. Innovative Values-Based Learning Experiences for Transformative Practices*. Cheltenham: Edward Elgar.

Edinger, Edward F. (1996). *The New God-Image. A Study of Jung's Key Letters Concerning the Evolution of the Western God-Image*. Wilmette, IL: Chiron.

Eker, Gülin Öğüt (2017). "Is Humor a Gift from God or a Way of Punishment from Satan?" *Folklor/Edebiyat*, 23(92): 49–62.

Ekman, Paul *et al.* (1990). "The Duchenne Smile: Emotional Expression and Brain Physiology 2". *Journal of Personality and Social Psychology*, 58(2): 342–353.

Ellapen, Jordache A. (2021). "Performing Blackness as Transgressive Erotics: African Futurities and Black Queer Sex in South African Live Art". *Feminist Formations*, 33(2): 52–78.

Eller, Jack David (2010). *Cruel Creeds, Virtuous Violence: Religious Violence across Culture and History*. Amherst: Prometheus Books.

Eltis, David (Ed.) (2016). *The Cambridge World History of Slavery*, volume 4. Cambridge: Cambridge UP.

Emerson, Ralph Waldo (1904) [1875]. "The Comic". *Complete Works*, vol. 8: 158–174. Boston: Houghton, Mifflin.

Emmerich, Stuart (2007). "Today's Phnom Penh: A City of Contrasts". *The New York Times*, https://www.nytimes.com/2007/02/13/travel/13iht-trcambo.html [Accessed 01/10/2022].

Enkelmann, Wolf Dieter (2013). "Hegel and the French: Economical Philosophy Instead of Ethics". In Luetge, Christoph (Ed.), *Handbook of the Philosophical Foundations of Business Ethics*, 2: 431–459. Dordrecht: Springer.

Ercoli, Lucrezia (2013a). *Filosofia della crudeltà. Etica ed estetica di un enigma*. Milan: Mimesis.

Ercoli, Lucrezia (2013b). *Filosofia dell'umorismo*. Rome: Inschibboleth.

Ergen, Fulden (2018). "An Analysis on the Impact of Ethical Porn Discourse on the Communication of Pornographic Content Online". MA. Uppsala University.

Erikson, Emily (2014). *Between Monopoly and Free Trade: The English East India Company, 1600–1757*. Princeton: Princeton UP.

Ernst, Edzard (2018). "Alternative Practitioners Amuse the Patient, While Medics Cure the Disease". *Journal of Clinical Medicine*, 7(6): 137.

Esar, Evan (1954) [1952]. *The Humor of Humor. The Art and Techniques of Popular Comedy Illustrated by Comic Sayings, Funny Stories and Jocular Traditions through the Centuries*. London: Phoenix.

Espinoza Ariza, Jelmut (2015). "El derecho a la libertad de expresión contra el derecho a la libertad religiosa ¿Existe un derecho a blasfemar? A propósito del caso de la revista Charlie Hebdo". *Lex*, 15(1): 85–110.

Esposito, Roberto (2008) [2004]. *Bios: Biopolitics and Philosophy* (trans. Timothy Campbell). Minneapolis: University of Minnesota Press.
Etienne, Bruno (2007). "Islam and Violence". *History and Anthropology*, 18(3): 237–248.
Evans, Kelly Kate (2021). "Sex Robots and Views from Nowhere: A Commentary on Jecker, Howard and Sparrow, and Wang". In Fa, Ruiping and Cherry, Mark J. (Eds.), *Sex Robots. Social Impact and the Future of Human Relations*, 161–178. Cherry. Cham: Springer.
Evans, Mel and Cleese, John (2020). "John Cleese Hits Out at 'Stifling' Political Correctness: 'Can You Tell Me a Woke Joke?'" *Metro*, https://metro.co.uk/2020/09/03/john-cleese-criticises-stifling-political-correctness-13217733/) [Accessed 21/09/2021].
Ezzo, David A. (2008). *Cannibalism in Cross-Cultural Perspective*. Indianapolis: Dog Ear.
Fairfield, Paul (2000). *Moral Selfhood in the Liberal Tradition: The Politics of Individuality*. Toronto: University of Toronto Press.
Fambrini, Alessandro and Muzzi, Nino (2006). "A mezzanotte dormono i borghesi. Anarchia e cabaret nella Germania del primo Novecento". *Labirinti*, 96: 7–218.
Farmsworth-Alvear, Ann (1997). "Orthodox Virginity/Heterodox Memories: Understanding Women's Stories of Mill Discipline in Medellin, Colombia". *Signs. Journal of Women in Culture and Society*, 23(1): 71–101.
Farrell, Warren (1993). *The Myth of Male Power. Why Men Are the Disposable Sex*. New York: Simon & Schuster.
Febos, Melissa (2020). "Mind Fuck: Writing Better Sex". *Sewanee Review*, 128(3): 547–578.
Feinberg, Leonard (1978). *The Secret of Humor*. Amsterdam: Rodopi.
Feldbæk, Ole (1986). "The Danish Trading Companies of the Seventeenth and Eighteenth Centuries". *Scandinavian Economic History Review*, 34(3): 204–218.
Felsen, Liam Ethan (2008). "Medieval Monks: Funnier Than You Thought". In Harris, Stephen and Grisby, Byron L. (Eds.), *Misconceptions About the Middle Ages*, 70–76. London: Routledge.
Femia, Joseph (1998). "Pareto and the Critique of Justice". In Boucher, David and Kelly, Paul (Eds.), *Perspectives on Social Justice: From Hume to Walzer*, 69–81. London: Routledge.
Feng, Yen-Ju *et al.* (2014). "Specialization of Neural Mechanisms Underlying the Three-Stage Model in Humor Processing: An ERP Study". *Journal of Neurolinguistics*, 32: 59–70.
Fenoglio, Irène and Georgeon, François (Eds.) (1995). "L'humour en Orient". *Revue du monde musulman et de la Méditerranée*, 77–78: 1–308.
Fernyhough, Charles (2017). *The Voices Within: The History and Science of How We Talk to Ourselves*. London: Profile.
Feros Ruys, Juanita (2017). *Demons in the Middle Ages*. Kalamazoo: Arc Humanities Press.
Ferrero Camoletto, Raffaella and Todesco, Lorenzo (2019). "From Sexual Objectification to Sexual Subjectification? Pornography Consumption and Italian Women's Sexual Empowerment". *About Gender. International Journal of Gender Studies*, 8(16): 129–157.
Fiala, Andrew (Ed.) (2018). *The Routledge Handbook of Pacifism and Nonviolence*. New York: Routledge.
Fieschi Adorno, Caterina (1858) [1551]. *Treatise on Purgatory* (trans. anonymously). London: Burns & Lambert, https://ia600200.us.archive.org/3/items/TheTreatiseOnPurgatory/TheTreatiseOnPurgatory.pdf [Accessed 11/11/2022].
Figueroa-Dorrego, Jorge (2018). "The Fear of Laughter in Restoration Prose Fiction". *English Literature*, 5: 113–130.
Figueroa-Dorrego, Jorge and Larkin-Galiñanes, Cristina (Eds.) (2009). *A Source Book of Literary and Philosophical Writings about Humour and Laughter*. Lewiston: Edwin Mellen.

Fish, Stanley (1994). *There's No Such Thing as Free Speech... And It's a Good Thing Too.* New York: Oxford UP.
Flandreau, Marc and Zumer, Frédéric (2004). *The Making of Global Finance 1880–1913.* Paris: OECD.
Florêncio, João (2020). *Bareback Porn, Porous Masculinities, Queer Futures. The Ethics of Becoming-Pig.* London: Routledge.
Follain, Antoine (2022). "*Décartèlment* or Quartering: An Edifying Penalty in Modern Age". *Hal Open Science*, paper #03648856 (preprint), https://hal.archives-ouvertes.fr/hal-03648856/document [Accessed 7/12/2022].
Foroohar, Rana (2019). "Old Economists Can Teach Us New Tricks. It Is Time for US Business and Government to Embrace Galbraith's Pragmatic Approach". *Financial Times*, https://www.ft.com/content/ece567f4-83c1-11e9-b592-5fe435b57a3b [Accessed 26/08/2022].
Forrest, Amy E. (2013). "'Leave No Normative Code Intact': Subverting Socio-Cultural Norms in Post-Porn". MA. University of Manchester.
Foucault, Michel (1975). *Surveiller et punir.* Paris: Gallimard.
Foucault, Michel (1978) [1976]. *The History of Sexuality, Volume 1: An Introduction* (trans. Robert Hurley). New York: Pantheon.
Foucault, Michel (1990) [1984]. *The History of Sexuality. Volume 2: The Use of Pleasure* (trans. Robert Hurley). New York: Vintage.
Foucault, Michel (2006) [1961]. *History of Madness* (trans. Jean Khalfa). London: Routledge.
Foucault, Michel (2007) [1977–1978]. *Security, Territory, Population: Lectures at the College de France, 1977–1978* (trans. Graham Burchell; ed. Michel Senellart). Basingstoke: Palgrave Macmillan.
Foucault, Michel (2008) [1978–1979]. *The Birth of Biopolitics: Lectures at the College de France, 1978–1979* (trans. Graham Burchell; ed. Michel Senellart) Basingstoke: Palgrave Macmillan.
Fozooni, Babak (2020). *Psychology, Humour and Class. A Critique of Contemporary Psychology.* London: Routledge.
Fraiman, Susan (1995). "Re: Catharine MacKinnon and the Feminist Porn Debates". *American Quarterly*, 47(4): 743–749.
Francis, Pope (2020). Encyclical Letter *Fratelli Tutti*, https://www.vatican.va/content/francesco/en/encyclicals/documents/papa-francesco_20201003_enciclica-fratelli-tutti.html?fbclid=IwAR1RRSMXXWL71krhh784rArJmIJ2xECxj4mbdjF_xHHg-Ee12b2fRkIcGWQ [Accessed 27/08/2022].
Franco, Zeno E. *et al.* (2016). "Heroism Research: A Review of Theories, Methods, Challenges, and Trends". *Journal of Humanistic Psychology*, 58(4): 382–396.
Frankl, Viktor E. (1972) [1952]. *The Doctor and the Soul* (trans. Richard and Clara Winston), 2nd ed. New York: Alfred A. Knopf.
Frankl, Viktor E. (1978) [1947–1977]. *The Unheard Cry for Meaning: Psychotherapy and Humanism* (trans. Richard and Clara Winston). New York: Simon & Schuster.
Frankl, Viktor E. (1984) [1946]. *Man's Search for Meaning. An Introduction to Logotherapy* (trans. Ilse Lansch), 2nd ed. New York: Washington Square Press.
Frappier-Mazur, Lucienne (1996) [1991]. *Writing the Orgy: Power and Parody in Sade* (trans. Gillian C. Gill.). Philadelphia: University of Pennsylvania Press.
Frederick, Danny (2011). "Pornography and Freedom". *Kritike*, 5(2): 84–95.
Fredrickson, Barbara L. (1998). "What Good are Positive Emotions?" *Review of General Psychology*, 2(3): 300–319.
Freeman, Gillian P. and Ventis, W. Larry (2010). "Does Humor Benefit Health in Retirement? Exploring Humor as a Moderator". *Europe's Journal of Psychology*, 6(3): 122–148.

Freese, Barbara (2020). *Industrial-Strength Denial. Eight Stories of Corporations Defending the Indefensible, From the Slave Trade to Climate Change*. Oakland: University of California Press.

Frege, Gottlob (1892). "Über Sinn und Bedeutung". *Zeitschrift für Philosophie und philosophische Kritik*, 100(1): 25–50, https://www.philosophie.uni-konstanz.de/typo3temp/secure_downloads/67505/0/c99ff447dfc9c50553da291d1a1dfdbb95eb983d/Frege_Sinn_Bedeutung.pdf [Accessed 01/05/2022].

Frege, Gottlob (1956) [1919]. "The Thought: A Logical Inquiry" (trans. M.P. Geach and M. Black). *Mind*, 65(259): 289–311.

Freiherr von Aretin, Karl Otmar (Ed.) (1974). *Der Aufgeklärte Absolutismus*. Cologne: Neue Wissenschaftliche Bibliothek.

Freud, Sigmund (1928) [1927]. "Humour" (trans. J. Riviere). *The International Journal of Psychoanalysis*, 9: 1–6.

Freud, Sigmund (1957a) [1915]. "Instincts and Their Vicissitudes". In Freud, Sigmund and Anna, and Strachey, James (Eds.), *The Standard Edition of the Complete Psychological Works of Sigmund Freud*, vol. 14: *1914–1916*, 109–140. London: Hogarth Press.

Freud, Sigmund (1957b) [1915]. "Thoughts for the Times on War and Death". In Freud, Sigmund and Anna, and Strachey, James (Eds.), *The Standard Edition of the Complete Psychological Works of Sigmund Freud*, vol. 14: *1914–1916*, 275–301. London: Hogarth Press.

Freud, Sigmund (1960) [1905]. *Jokes and their Relation to the Unconscious* (trans. James Strachey). New York: Norton (Kindle version).

Freud, Sigmund (1995) [1924]. "The Economic Problem of Masochism". In Fitzpatrick Hanly, Margaret A. (Ed.), *Essential Papers on Masochism*, 274–285. New York: New York UP.

Freud, Sigmund (2018) [1905]. *Three Essays on the Theory of Sexuality* (trans. A.A. Brill). London: Global Grey.

Friedman, Hershey H. (2004). "Talmudic Humor and the Establishment of Legal Principles". *Thalia: Studies in Literary Humor*, 21(1): 14–28.

Friedman, Howard Steven (2020). *Ultimate Price. The Value We Place on Life*. Oakland: University of California Press.

Friedman, Jonathan (2019). *PC Worlds. Political Correctness and Rising Elites at the End of Hegemony*. New York: Berghahn Books.

Fritz, Heidi L. et al. (2017). "Humor Use Moderates the Relation of Stressful Life Events with Psychological Distress". *Personality and Social Psychology Bulletin*, 43(6): 845–859.

Fromm, Erich (1967) [1947]. *Man for Himself. An Inquiry into the Psychology of Ethics*. New York: Fawcett.

Fromm, Erich (1985) [1976]. *To Have or to Be?* London: Abacus.

Fromm, Erich (1992) [1973]. *The Anatomy of Human Destructiveness*. New York: Owl Books.

Fry, W.F. Jr. and Salameh, W.A. (Eds.) (1987). *Handbook of Humor and Psychotherapy: Advances in the Clinical Use of Humor*. Sarasota, FL: Professional Resource Exchange.

Funk, Albrecht (2003). "The Monopoly of Legitimate Violence and Criminal Policy". In Heitmeyer, W. and Hagan, J. (Eds.), *International Handbook of Violence Research*, 1057–1077. Dordrecht: Springer.

Gadamer, Hans-Georg (1996) [1993]. *The Enigma of Health. The Art of Healing in a Scientific Age* (trans. Jason Gaiger and Nicholas Walker). Oxford: Polity.

Galbraith, John Kenneth (1952). *American Capitalism. The Concept of Countervailing Power*. Boston: Houghton Mifflin.

Galbraith, John Kenneth (1958). *The Affluent Society*. New York: Houghton Mifflin.

Galbraith, John Kenneth (1973). *Economics and the Public Purpose*. Boston: Houghton Mifflin.

Galbraith, John Kenneth (1975) [1971]. *A Contemporary Guide to Economics, Peace and Laughter.* London: Penguin.
Galbraith, John Kenneth (1980) [1979]. *The Nature of Mass Poverty.* Harmondsworth: Penguin.
Galbraith, John Kenneth (1982) [1979]. *A Life in Our Times: Memoirs.* New York: Ballantine.
Galbraith, John Kenneth (1983). *The Anatomy of Power.* New York: Houghton Mifflin.
Galbraith, John Kenneth (1991) [1967]. *The New Industrial State.* London: Penguin.
Galbraith, John Kenneth (1994) [1990]. *A Short History of Financial Euphoria.* New York: Penguin.
Galbraith, John Kenneth (1996). *The Good Society: The Humane Agenda.* Boston: Houghton Mifflin.
Galbraith, John Kenneth (1997) [1954]. *The Great Crash 1929,* 7th ed. Boston: Houghton Mifflin.
Galbraith, John Kenneth (2004). *The Economics of Innocent Fraud: Truth for Our Time.* London: Penguin.
Galbraith, John Kenneth (2007) [1967]. *The New Industrial State. With a New Foreword by James K. Galbraith.* Princeton: Princeton UP.
Galbraith, John Kenneth and Salinger, Nicole (1979) [1978]. *Almost Everyone's Guide to Economics.* London: Clarion.
Galbraith, Patrick W. (2011). "Lolicon: The Reality of 'Virtual Child Pornography' in Japan". *Image & Narrative,* 12(1): 82–119.
Galdon, Maria José *et al.* (2006). "Multidimensional Approach to the Differences between Muscular and Articular Temporomandibular Patients: Coping, Distress, and Pain Characteristics". *Oral Surgery, Oral Medicine, Oral Pathology, Oral Radiology, and Endodontics,* 102(1): 40–46.
Galeano, Eduardo (2001) [1998]. *Upside Down: A Primer for the Looking-Glass World* (trans. Mark Fried). New York: Picador.
Gamble, Andrew (2018) [1996]. *Hayek: The Iron Cage of Liberty.* New York: Routledge.
Gamboriko, Elias Rinaldo (2012). *The Funny Risen Jesus. Elias Christology Now!* Bloomington: iUniverse.
Garavaglia, Susanna (2007). *Diario di psicosomatica.* Milan: Tecniche nuove.
García Villena, Belén (2012). "Análisis de Hentai desde una perspectiva feminista: grietas en una reproducción patriarcal". MA. University of Granada.
Gardiner, Gwendolyn *et al.* (2023). "The Economic Well-Being of Nations is Associated with Positive Daily Situational Experiences". *Current Research in Ecological and Social Psychology,* https://doi.org/10.1016/j.cresp.2023.100088 [Accessed 27/01/2023].
Gardner, Richard A. (2020). "Humour and Religion: New Directions?" In Derrin, Daniel and Burrows, Hannah (Eds.), *The Palgrave Handbook of Humour,* 151–172: Palgrave Macmillan.
Garrard, Eve (2006). "Violence, Cruelty and Evil". In Ó Murchadha, Felix (Ed.), *Violence, Victims, Justifications: Philosophical Approaches,* 115–130. Basel: Peter Lang.
Garrick, John (1998). *Informal Learning in the Workplace. Unmasking Human Resource Development.* London: Routledge.
Gasché, Rodolphe (2020). "Violence, Brutality, Cruelty. On Differentiation (and Its Refusal)". *The New Centennial Review,* 20(2): 1–24.
Gaspar, Augusta, Esteves, Francisco and Arriaga, Patrícia (2014). "On Prototypical Facial Expressions Versus Variation in Facial Behavior: What Have We Learned on the 'Visibility' of Emotions from Measuring Facial Actions in Humans and Apes". In Pina, Marco and Gontier, Nathalie (Eds.), *The Evolution of Social Communication in Primates: A Multidisciplinary Approach,* 101–126. Cham: Springer.
Gatzia, Dimitria Electra and Arnaud, Sarah (2022). "Loving Objects: Can Autism Explain Objectophilia?" Archives of Sexual Behavior, 51: 2117–2133.

Genovesi, Antonio (1765). *Delle lezioni di commercio o sia d'economia civile*, vol. 1. Naples: Simone Bros, https://archive.org/details/dellelezionidico01geno [Accessed 01/02/2022].
George, Timothy (1984). "War and Peace in the Puritan Tradition". *Church History*, 53(4): 492–503.
Gerber, Paula (Ed.) (2021). *Worldwide Perspectives on Lesbians, Gays, and Bisexuals*, 3 vols. Santa Barbara: Praeger.
Gerlach, Joel C. (1966). "Is There a Relationship Between Confessional Lutheranism and Political Conservatism?" *Wisconsin Lutheran Seminary Essay*, http://wlsessays.net/handle/123456789/1813 [Accessed 08/06/2021].
Getty, J. Arch and Naumov, Oleg V. (1999). *The Road to Terror. Stalin and the Self-Destruction of the Bolsheviks, 1932–1939*. New Haven: Yale UP.
Giaccardi, Giorgio (2014). "Defenses". In Leeming, David A. (Ed.), *Encyclopedia of Psychology and Religion*, 2nd ed., 468–472. New York: Springer.
Gidal, Eric (2003). "Civic Melancholy: English Gloom and French Enlightenment". *Eighteenth-Century Studies*, 37(1): 23–45.
Gifford, Paul (1981). "Humor and the French Mind: Towards a Reciprocal Definition". *Modern Languages Review*, 76(3): 534–548.
Giglietto, Fabio and Lee, Yenn (2015). "To Be or Not to Be Charlie: Twitter Hashtags as a Discourse and Counter-Discourse in the Aftermath of the 2015 Charlie Hebdo Shooting in France". In Rowe, Matthew, Stankovic, Milan and Dadzie. Aba-Sah (Eds.), *#Microposts 2015 – 5th Workshop on Making Sense of Microposts: Big Things Come in Small Packages*, 33–37. Florence: WWW.
Gilbert, Christopher J. (2015). "If This Statue Could Talk: Statuary Satire in the Pasquinade Tradition". *Rhetoric and Public Affairs*, 18(1): 79–112.
Gilhus, Ingvild Sælid (1997). *Laughing Gods, Weeping Virgins. Laughter in the History of Religion*. London: Routledge.
Gilliam, Terry (2015). *Gilliamesque. A Pre-Posthumous Memoir*. New York: Harper.
Gilyazova, Olga S., Zamoshchanskii, Ivan I. and Zamoshchanskaya, A.N. (2020). "A Liberal Arts and Sciences Education at the Russian Higher School: Concepts, Formats, Benefits and Limitations". *Perspectives of Science and Education*, 46(4): 10–22.
Gimbel, Steven (2017). *Isn't That Clever? A Philosophical Account of Humor and Comedy*. London: Routledge.
Gimbel, Steven (2021). Review of *Christianity and the Triumph of Humor: From Dante to David Javerbaum* by Bernard Schweizer. *The European Journal of Humour Research*, 9(1): 196–199.
Gini, Al and Singer, Abraham (2020). "Why'd You Have to Choose Us? On Jews and Their Jokes". In Amir, Lydia B. (Ed.), *Philosophy of Humor Yearbook*, 1: 17–31. Berlin: De Gruyter.
Giovannelli, Raffaele (2014). "L'Architettura prima del decostruttivismo". In *Tornare all'Architettura. Antologia di scritti sull'Architettura*, 1: 64–96. Nca: Lacrimae rerum.
Giovannini, Paolo (2017). "Re-Reading Pareto: A Guide to Power Studies". *Cambio. Rivista sulle trasformazioni sociali*, 8(13): 185–195.
Giroux, Henry A. (2012). *Disposable Youth: Racialized Memories, and the Culture of Cruelty*. New York: Routledge.
Gissurarson, Hannes H. (2004). "Miracle on Iceland". *The Wall Street Journal*, https://www.wsj.com/articles/SB107533182153814498 [Accessed 6/12/2022].
Glacier, Osire (2009). "Droits de la personne et Islam. Les droits fondamentaux des femmes marocaines: entre la loi islamique et le droit international des droits de la personne". *Thémis*, 43: 205–217.

Glacier, Osire (2013). *Universal Rights, Systemic Violations, and Cultural Relativism in Morocco*. New York: Palgrave MacMillan.
Glenn, Phillip and Holt, Elizabeth (2017). "Conversation Analysis of Humor". In Attardo, Salvatore (Ed.), *The Routledge Handbook of Language and Humor*, 295–308. New York: Routledge.
Glyn, Andrew (1990). "Contradictions of Capitalism". In *Marxian Economics*, 104–109. London: Palgrave.
Gobineau, Arthur de (1915) [1853]. *The Inequality of Human Races* (trans. Adrian Collins). London: Heinmann.
Goel, Ambika and Sahni, Rajni (2014). "Sanity and the Insane". *The Journal of Positive Psychology*, 3(2): 225–229.
Goethals, George R. and Allison, Scott T. (2012). "Making Heroes: The Construction of Courage, Competence, and Virtue". In Olson, J.M. and Zanna, M.P. (Eds.), *Advances in Experimental Social Psychology*, 46: 183–235. San Diego: Elsevier.
Góis, Alan Diógenes, Franco de Lima, Gerlando Augusto Sampaio and Mendes De Luca, Marcia Martins (2020). "Everyday Sadism in the Business Area". *RAUSP*, 55(3): 393–408.
Goldberg, Brenda (1999). "A Genealogy of the Ridiculous: From 'Humours' to Humour". *Outlines. Critical Social Studies*, 1: 59–71.
Golozubov, Oleksandr (2015). "Interpretations of St. Francis of Assisi in the 20th Century: Philosophical-Anthropological Perspective". *History Research*, 5(1): 12–27.
Gomez, Luis (2017). "7 Famous Comedians Who Said Political Correctness Is Killing Comedy". *The San Diego Union-Tribune*, https://www.sandiegouniontribune.com/opinion/the-conversation/sd-mel-brooks-comedians-say-political-correctness-killing-comedy-20170922-htmlstory.html [Accessed 21/09/2021].
Gonzales, Philippe and Kaufmann, Laurence (2016). "La Caricature sans Blasphème? Sémantique et Pragmatiques du Prophète en une de *Charlie Hebdo*". *Communication et langages*, 187(1): 47–68.
Goodenough, Belinda and Ford, Jennifer (2005). "Self-Reported Use of Humor by Hospitalized Pre-Adolescent Children to Cope with Pain-Related Distress from Medical Intervention". *Humor: International Journal of Humor Research*, 18(3): 279–298.
Gottfried, Jeffrey and Barthel, Michael (2015). "After Charlie Hebdo, Balancing Press Freedom and Respect for Religion". *Journalism and Media*, https://www.journalism.org/2015/01/28/after-charlie-hebdo-balancing-press-freedom-and-respect-for-religion/ [Accessed 26/08/2022].
Goulson, Dave (2019). "The Insect Apocalypse, and Why It Matters". *Current Biology Magazine*, 29: R942–R995.
Graf, Fritz (1997). "Cicero, Plautus and Roman Laughter". In Bremmer, Jan and Roodenburg, Herman (Eds.), *A Cultural History of Humour: From Antiquity to the Present Day*, 29–39. Cambridge: Polity.
Gramsci, Antonio (1977) [1929–1935]. *Quaderni del carcere* (ed. Valentino Gerratana), 4 vols. Milan: Einaudi.
Grana, Francesco Antonio (2021). "Papa Francesco in Iraq". *Il Fatto Quotidiano*, https://www.ilfattoquotidiano.it/2021/03/06/papa-francesco-in-iraq-il-terrorismo-e-un-abuso-della-religione-lestremismo-e-la-violenza-sono-il-tradimento/6124242/ [Accessed 26/08/2022].
Grandi, Annalisa *et al.* (2021). "I Nearly Died Laughing: Humor in Funeral Industry Operators". *Current Psychology*, 40: 6098–6109, https://doi.org/10.1007/s12144-019-00547-9 [Accessed 26/08/2022].
Graves, Robert (1927). *Lars Porsena. Or, the Future of Swearing and Improper Language*. London: Kegan Paul, Trench, Trubner, https://ia601808.us.archive.org/19/items/dli.ministry.16038/E09633_

Lars_Porsena_Or_The_Future_Of_Swearing_And_Improper_Language_text.pdf [Accessed 18/01/ 2023].

Gray, Justin (2013). "That's Not Funny, That's Sexist: The Controversial Legacy of Benny Hill". *Vulture*, https://www.vulture.com/2013/05/thats-not-funny-thats-sexist-the-controversial-legacy-of-benny-hill.html. [Accessed 04/06/2022].

Greengross, Gill and Miller, Geoffrey (2011). "Humor Ability Reveals Intelligence, Predicts Mating Success, and Is Higher in Males". *Intelligence*, 39(4): 188–192.

Greenspan, Alan (2005). "Remarks by Chairman Alan Greenspan. Economic Flexibility. Before the National Italian American Foundation, Washington, D.C.". *The Federal Reserve Board*, https://www.federalreserve.gov/boarddocs/speeches/2005/20051012/ [Accessed 6/12/2022].

Griffin, James (2008). *On Human Rights*. Oxford: Oxford UP.

Gritsch, Eric W. (2012). "Martin Luther's Humor". *Word and World*, 32(2): 132–140.

Grove, Laurence (2015). "*Charlie Hebdo* is Nothing New". *Jewish Quarterly*, 62(1): 4–5.

Grubbs, Joshua B. and Perry, Samuel L. (2019). "Moral Incongruence and Pornography Use: A Critical Review and Integration". *The Journal of Sex Research*, 56(1): 29–37.

Grubbs, Joshua B., Grant, Jennifer T. and Engelman, Joel (2019). "Self-Identification as a Pornography Addict: Examining the Roles of Pornography Use, Religiousness, and Moral Incongruence". *Sexual Addiction and Compulsivity*, https://doi.org/10.1080/10720162.2019.1565848 [Accessed 18/10/ 2021].

Gruber, Ada (2020). *The Feminist War on Crime: The Unexpected Role of Women's Liberation in Mass Incarceration*. Oakland, CA: University of California Press.

Guidère, Mathieu (2012). *Historical Dictionary of Islamic Fundamentalism*. Lanham: Scarecrow.

Gulliver, Robyn et al. (2022). *The Psychology of Effective Activism*. Newcastle-upon-Tyne: Cambridge Scholars Publishing.

Gunawan, F. and Rini, J.E. (2013). "Translation Errors in English-Indonesian Humor Text Produced by Students of Basic Translation Class". *Kata Kita*, 1(1): 154–165.

Gupta, R.K. (1975). "Freud and Schopenhauer". *Journal of the History of Ideas*, 36(4): 721–728.

Gutiérrez, Luis T. (2022). "From *Homo economicus* to *Homo ecologicus* ~ Sequel 12 ~ Degrowth Dynamics". *Mother Pelican. A Journal of Solidarity and Sustainability*, 18(12), http://www.pelicanweb.org/solisustv18n12page24.html [Accessed 01/12/2022].

Gutting, Gary (2020). "Rorty and Analytic Philosophy". In Malachowski, Alan (Ed.), *A Companion to Rorty*, 211–228. Chichester: Wiley Blackwell.

Hallevy, Gabriel (2015). *The Matrix of Insanity in Modern Criminal Law*. Cham: Springer.

Hallie, Philip P. (1969). *The Paradox of Cruelty*. Middletown: Wesleyan University.

Hallie, Philip P. (1971a). "Justification and Rebellion". In Sanford, Nevitt and Comstock, Craig (Eds.), *Sanctions for Evil. Sources of Social Destructiveness*, 247–263. Boston: Beacon.

Hallie, Philip P. (1971b). "Raskolnikov, the SCHOLAR, and Fresh Air". *The American Scholar*, 40(4): 579–582.

Hallie, Philip P. (1985a) [1981]. "From Cruelty to Goodness". In Sommers, C. (Ed.), *Vice and Virtue in Everyday Life*, 9–24. San Diego: Harcourt College.

Hallie, Philip P. (1985b) [1979]. *Lest Innocent Blood Be Shed: The Story of the Village of Le Chambon, and How Goodness Happened There*. New York: Harper & Row.

Hallie, Philip P. (1985c). "The Evil That Men Think—And Do". Review of *Wickedness: A Philosophical Essay*, by Mary Midgley, *Ordinary Vices*, by Judith Shklar, and *Immorality*, by Ronald D. Milo. *Hastings Center Report*, 15(6): 42–45.

Hallie, Philip P. (1988). "Cruelty: The Empirical Evil". In Woodruff, Paul and Wilmer, Harry A. (Eds.), *Facing Evil: Confronting the Dreadful Power behind Genocide, Terrorism, and Cruelty*, 119–137. Chicago: Open Court.

Hallie, Philip P. (1992). "Cruelty". In Becker, Lawrence C. [1981] (Eds.), *Encyclopaedia of Ethics*, 229–231. New York: Garland.

Hallie, Philip P. (2001) [1997]. *In the Eye of the Hurricane: Tales of Good and Evil, Help and Harm*. Middleton: Wesleyan UP.

Hanek, Bailey A. (2015). "Clinical Use of Sexually Explicit Media in the Treatment of Sexual Concerns". PhD. Massachusetts School of Professional Psychology.

Hanna, Nathan (2009). "The Passions of Punishment". *Pacific Philosophical Quarterly*, 90: 232–250.

Hansen, Kristine (1983). "The Anals of History: Unintentional Humor from Freshman Compositions". *The English Journals*, 72(7): 44–48.

Hansen, Miriam (1993). "Of Mice and Ducks: Benjamin and Adorno on Disney". *The South Atlantic Quarterly*, 92(1): 27–61.

Hanson, Philip (2010). "Alexander Zinoviev and the Russian Tragedy". *Baltic Worlds*, 3(2): 19–25.

Hargittai, Istvan (2016). "Michael Polanyi—Pupils and Crossroads—On the 125th Anniversary of His Birth". *Structural Chemistry*, 27: 1327–1344.

Häring, Norbert and Douglas, Niall (2012). *Economists and the Powerful: Convenient Theories, Distorted Facts, Ample Rewards*. London: Anthem Press.

Harlow, Harry (1969). "The Anatomy of Humour". *Impact of Science on Society*, 19(3): 225–240.

Harper, Douglas (2001–2021). *Online Etymology Dictionary*, https://www.etymonline.com/ [Accessed 23/03/2022].

Hartley, David (1801) [1749]. *Observations on Man, His Frame, His Duty, and His Expectations. In Two Parts*. Warrington: J. Johnson, https://archive.org/details/dli.granth.71827 [Accessed 01/05/2022].

Hartley, Nina (2018) [1994]. "Confessions of a Feminist Porno Star". In Jagger, Alison M. (Ed.), *Living with Contradictions*, 176–178. New York: Routledge.

Hartman, Edwin (2013). "Aristotle and Character Formation". In Luetge, Christoph (Ed.), *Handbook of the Philosophical Foundations of Business Ethics*, vol. 2: 67–88. Dordrecht: Springer.

Harvey, Jean (1999). *Civilized Oppression*. Lanham: Rowman & Littlefield.

Haslam, S. Alexander et al. (2019). "Rethinking the Nature of Cruelty: The Role of Identity Leadership in the Stanford Prison Experiment". *American Psychologist*, 74(7): 809–822.

Hassapopoulou, Marina (2007). "It's All Greek to Me: Misappropriations of Greekness in American Mass Media". *Journal of Hellenic Diaspora*, 33(5): 59–80.

Hatherley, Owen (2016). *The Chaplin Machine: Slapstick, Fordism and the International Communist Avant-Garde*. London: Pluto Press.

Haugh, Michael (2017). "Teasing". In Attardo, Salvatore (Ed.), *The Routledge Handbook of Language and Humor*, 204–218. New York: Routledge.

Hayek, Friedrich A. (1944). *The Road to Serfdom*. London: Routledge.

Hayek, Friedrich A. (1987) [1985]. "Individual and Collective Aims". In Mendus, Susan and Edwards, David (Eds.), *On Toleration*, 35–47. Oxford: Clarendon.

Hazlitt, William (1845) [1819]. *Lectures on the English Comic Writers*. New York: Wiley & Putnam, https://archive.org/details/lecturesonengli01unkngoog [Accessed 01/05/2022].

Hazlitt, William (1912) [1830]. "On Prejudice". In *Sketches and Essays*, 56–60. Oxford: H. Frowde.

Heard, Gerald (1930). Review of *The History of the Devil: The Horned God of the West* by R. Lowe Thompson. *Antiquity*, 4(14): 260–261.

Heckhausen, Jutta and Heinz (Eds.) (2018). *Motivation and Action*. Cham: Springer.

Heinberg, Richard (2022). "The Final Doubling ~ Dedicated to the Memory of Herman Daly, the Father of Ecological Economics". *Mother Pelican. A Journal of Solidarity and Sustainability*, 18(12), http://www.pelicanweb.org/solisustv18n12page5.html [Accessed 01/12/2022].
Heller, Agnes (2005). *Immortal Comedy: The Comic Phenomenon in Art, Literature, and Life*. Lanham: Lexington.
Heller, Joseph (1961). *Catch 22*. New York: Simon & Schuster.
Heltzel, Virgil B. (1928). "Chesterfield and the Anti-Laughter Tradition". *Modern Philology*, 26(1): 73–90.
Hemmat, Amrollah (2021). "Hermeneutical Translation of Classics and Cultures: The Case of the *I Ching* and China's Intercivilizational Dialogue". *Comparative Literature: East and West*, 5(1): 1–14.
Hemmer, Nicole (2021). "The Man Who Created President Donald Trump". *CNN*, https://edition.cnn.com/2021/02/17/opinions/trump-is-the-rush-limbaugh-legacy-hemmer/index.html [Accessed 21/09/2021].
Henberg, Marvin (1990). *Retribution. Evil for Evil in Ethics, Law, and Literature*. Philadelphia: Temple UP.
Hennig-Thurau, Thorsten and Houston, Mark. B. (2019). *Entertainment Science. Data Analytics and Practical Theory for Movies, Games, Books, and Music*. Cham: Springer.
Herdt, Gilbert H. (Ed.) (1984). *Ritualised Homosexuality in Melanesia*. Berkeley: University of California Press.
Hermand, Pierre (1972) [1923]. *Les idées morales de Diderot*. Hildesheim: Georg Holms.
Hietalahti, Jarno (2015). "Laughing at Oneself: On the New Social Character". *Studies in Social and Political Thought*, 25: 116–131.
Hietalahti, Jarno (2019). "Carl Jung and the Role of Shadow and Trickster in Political Humor: Social Philosophical Analysis". In Martins, C.P. (Ed.), *Comedy for Dinner and Other Dishes*, 20–41. Coimbra: Instituto de Estudos Filosóficos, http://www.uc.pt/fluc/uidief/ebooks/Comedy_for_dinner [Accessed 14/08/2022].
Hillebrand, Hans J. (Ed.) (1996). *The Oxford Encyclopedia of the Reformation*. Oxford: Oxford UP.
Hillman, James (1964) [1961]. *Emotion. A Comprehensive Phenomenology of Theories and Their Meanings for Therapy*. Evanston: Northwestern UP.
Hillman, James (1975). *Re-Visioning Psychology*. New York: Harper & Row.
Hillman, James (1981). "Alchemical Blue and the *Unio Mentalis*". In Eshleman, C. (Ed.), *Sulfur I*, 33–50. Pasadena: California Institute of Technology.
Hillman, James (1983). *Healing Fictions*. New York: Station Hill.
Hillman, James (1985) [1981]. *Archetypal Psychology. A Brief Account*. Dallas: Spring.
Hillman, James (1989) [1975]. *Loose Ends. Primary Papers in Archetypal Psychology*. Dallas: Spring.
Hillman, James (1991) [1989]. *A Blue Fire* (ed. Thomas More). New York: Harper.
Hillman, James (1995a). *Kinds of Power. A Guide to Its Intelligent Uses*. New York: Currency Doubleday.
Hillman, James (1995b). "Pink Madness or Why Does Aphrodite Drive Men Crazy with Pornography?" *Spring*, 57(1): 37–67.
Hillman, James (1996). *The Soul's Code. In Search of Character and Calling*. New York: Ballantine.
Hillman, James (1999). *The Force of Character – And the Lasting Life*. New York: Ballantine. Electronic version.
Hillman, James (2004). *A Terrible Love of War*. New York: Penguin Press.
Hillman, James (2010). "Carl Gustav Jung and the Red Book". *Library of Congress*, https://studylib.net/doc/7013535/from-the-library-of-congress-in-washington–d.c.-%5Em00-00-05 [Accessed 11/07/2022].

Hillman, James (2011). "On Archetypal Psychotherapy and the Soulless Society", https://www.youtube.com/watch?v=VFng0WCJ8X8 [Accessed 27/06/2022].

Hillman, James (2015). "Changing the Object of Our Desire", https://www.youtube.com/watch?v=rFa0X06hLOU [Accessed 17/07/2022].

Hillman, James (2018). "The Roots of Imagination", https://www.youtube.com/watch?v=cuYg3QKj2K4 [Accessed 04/06/2022].

Hillman, James and Ventura, Michael (1992). "We've Had a Hundred Years of Psychotherapy and the World's Getting Worse", http://michaelventura.org/wp-content/uploads/2013/11/from-We%E2%80%99ve-Had-a-Hundred-Years-of-Psychotherapy-and-the-World%E2%80%99s-Getting-Worse.pdf [Accessed 04/06/2022].

Hinton, Elizabeth (2021). *America on Fire: The Untold History of Police Violence and Black Rebellion Since the 1960s.* London: Liveright.

Hobbes, Thomas (1985) [1651]. *Leviathan.* London: Penguin Classics.

Hobsbawm, Eric (1994). *The Age of Extremes: The Short Twentieth Century.* London: Michael Joseph

Hochschild, Adam (1999). *King Leopold's Ghost: A Story of Greed, Terror and Heroism in Colonial Africa.* Boston: Houghton Mifflin.

Hoffmann, Lara Wilhelmine and Baruchello, Giorgio (2020). "History and Philosophy". In Meckl, Markus et al. (Eds.), *REMix: The University as an Advocate for Responsible Education about Migration in Europe: Inclusive Societies: A Textbook for Interdisciplinary Migration,* 15–32. Akureyri: University of Akureyri, https://opinvisindi.is/handle/20.500.11815/1906 [Accessed 09/06/2022].

Holberg, Amelia S. (1999). "Betty Boop: Yiddish Film Star". *American Jewish History,* 87(4): 291–312.

Holmes, (Oliver Wendell) Mr. Justice and Laski, Harold J. (1953) [1916–1935]. *Holmes Laski Letters,* vol. 2 (ed. Mark DeWolfe). Cambridge, MA: Harvard UP.

Homer (2009) [n.d.a.]. *The Iliad* (trans. A.S. Kline). Manchester: Poetry in Translation.

Hongladarom, Soraj (2013). "Language, Reality, Emptiness and Laughter". *Prajna Vihara,* 14(1–2): 236–256.

Hood, Edwin P. (1865) [1852]. *The Mental and Moral Philosophy of Laughter. A Vista on the Ludicrous Side of Life.* London: Partridge & Oakey.

Horace (n.d.a.) [1st century BC]. *Carmina,* http://www.thelatinlibrary.com/horace/carm4.shtml [Accessed 23/03/2022].

Horberg, E.J. et al. (2009). "Disgust and the Moralization of Purity". *Journal of Personality and Social Psychology,* 97(6): 963–976.

Horkheimer, Max (1947). *Eclipse of Reason.* New York: Oxford UP.

Horkheimer, Max and Adorno, Theodor (1989) [1944]. *Dialectic of Enlightenment* (trans. John Cummings). New York: Continuum.

Horney, Karen (1939). *New Ways in Psychoanalysis.* New York: Norton, https://archive.org/details/newwaysinpsychoa00hornrich [Accessed 12/12/2022].

Horney, Karen (1945). *Our Inner Conflicts. A Constructive Theory of Neurosis.* New York: Norton, https://archive.org/details/ourinnerconflict0000unse [Accessed 12/12/2022].

Horney, Karen (1993) [1967]. *Feminine Psychology* (ed. Harold Kelman). New York: Norton.

Horney, Karen (2000) [1927–1952]. *The Unknown Karen Horney: Essays on Gender, Culture, and Psychoanalysis* (ed. Bernard J. Paris). New Haven: Yale UP.

Hösle, Vittorio (2013) [2006]. *The Philosophical Dialogue. A Poetics and a Hermeneutic* (trans. Steven Rendall). Notre Dame: Notre Dame Press.

Hoy, Mikita (1994). "Joyful Mayhem: Bakhtin, Football Songs, and the Carnivalesque". *Text and Performance Quarterly,* 14(4): 289–304.

Hughes, David A. (2020). "9/11 Truth and the Silence of the IR Discipline". *Alternatives: Global, Local, Political*, doi: 10.1177/0304375419898334 [Accessed 26/08/2022].

Hughes, Sophia C. (2009). "Addressing Terror Through Group Psyche". In Vardalos, M. *et al.* (Eds.), *Engaging Terror. A Critical and Interdisciplinary Approach*, 245–252. Boca Raton: Brown Walker.

Huijbens, Edward H. (2021). *Developing Earthly Attachments in the Anthropocene*. London: Routledge.

Human Rights Watch (2019). *World Report 2019*. New York: Human Rights Watch.

Hund, Wulf Dietmar (2011). "'It Must Come from Europe'. The Racisms of Immanuel Kant". In Hund, Wulf Dietmar *et al.* (Eds.), *Racisms Made in Germany*, 69–98. Zurich: LIT.

Hunt, Lynn (Ed.) (1993). *The Invention of Pornography. Obscenity and the Origins of Modernity, 1500–1800*. New York: Zone Books.

Hunt, Tristram (2001). "Britain's Very Own Taliban". *New Statesman*, https://www.newstatesman.com/node/194286 [Accessed 02/02/2022].

Huntington, Samuel (2007) [1996]. *The Clash of Civilizations and the Remaking of World Order*. New York: Simon & Schuster.

Hurley, Matthew M. *et al.* (2011). *Inside Jokes: Using Humor to Reverse-Engineer the Mind*. Cambridge, MA: MIT Press.

Hutcheson, Francis (1973) [1725]. *Reflections upon Laughter*. Reprinted as the Appendix to *An Inquiry Concerning Beauty, Order, Harmony, Design*, 102–119. The Hague: Martin Nijhoff.

Hutcheson, Francis (2002) [1742]. *Essay on the Nature and Conduct of the Passions and Affections, with Illustrations on the Moral Sense*. Indianapolis: Liberty Fund, https://oll.libertyfund.org/title/garrett-an-essay-on-the-nature-and-conduct-of-the-passions-and-affections-1742-2002 [Accessed 25/02/2022].

Hutcheson, Francis (2007) [1747]. *A Short Introduction to Moral Philosophy*. Indianapolis: Liberty Fund, https://oll.libertyfund.org/title/hutcheson-philosophiae-moralis-institutio-compendiaria-1747-2007 [Accessed 26/02/2022].

Huxley, Aldous (2006) [1932]. *Brave New World*. New York: Harper Perennial.

Hyers, Conrad (1996). *The Spirituality of Comedy. Comic Heroism in a Tragic World*. New Brunswick: Transaction.

Hylton, Kevin (2018). "I'm Not Joking! The Strategic Use of Humour in Stories of Racism". *Ethnicities*, 18(3): 327–343.

Iaccino, James F. (1998). *Jungian Reflections within the Cinema. A Psychological Analysis of Sci-Fi and Fantasy Archetypes*. Westport, CT: Praeger.

Ibeas-Altamira, Juan Manuel (2018). "Le *Bijou Rocaille* de Diderot, Un Exemple d'Humour Rococo". *Romanica Olomucensia*, 30(2): 287–298.

Il Corano (1993) [7th century AD] (trans. Angelo Terenzoni). La Spezia: I Dioscuri.

Illinois State Board of Education (1983). "Corporal Punishment: An Overview". Springfield: Illinois State Board of Education.

International Movie Database (1990–2020). IMDb.com Inc.

Ingarden, Roman (1983) [1970]. *Man and Value* (trans. Arthur Szylewicz). Washington, DC: Catholic University of America.

Irigaray, Luce (1994) [1986–1989]. *Thinking the Difference. For a Peaceful Revolution* (trans. Karin Montin). New York: Routledge.

Isenberg, Nancy (2017). *White Trash. The 400-Year Untold History of Class in America*. New York: Penguin.

Ishay, Micheline R. (2004). *The History of Human Rights. From Ancient Times to the Globalization Era*. Berkeley: University of California Press.

Islamic Networks Group (2020). "Global Condemnations of ISIS/ISIL". San Jose: Odyssey, https://ing.org/global-condemnations-of-isis-isil/ [Accessed 26/08/2022].
Jackson, Danielle (2017). "Persona of Anime: A Depth Psychological Approach to the Persona and Individuation". PhD. Pacifica Graduate Institute.
Jacobs, Struan and Allen, R.T. (Eds.) (2005). *Emotion, Reason and Tradition: Essays on the Social, Political and Economic Thought of Michael Polanyi*. Aldershot: Ashgate.
James, C.L.R. (1962) [1938]. *The Black Jacobins: Touissant L'Overture and the San Domingo Revolution*, 2nd ed. New York: Vintage.
James, C.L.R. (1979) [1978]. "Fanon and the Caribbean". In *International Tribute to Frantz Fanon: Record of the Special Meeting of the United Nations Special Committee Against Apartheid, 3 November 1978*, 43–46. New York: United Nations Centre Against Apartheid.
Jamin, Jürgen (2022). "III Domenica di Quaresima, C". Manuscript.
Jane, Emma A. (2022). "Rise Up in Mirth: On Angry Feminist Humor and Why Taking It Personally Is Political". *Signs*, 47(3): 561–587.
Jarvie, Ian (2015). "Pornography Stumps Analytic Philosophers of Art". Book review of *Art and Pornography: Philosophical Essays* edited by Hans Maes and Jerrold Levinson. *Philosophy of the Social Sciences*, 45(1): 122–140.
Jauregui, Eduardo S. (1998). "Situating Laughter: Amusement, Laughter, and Humour in Everyday Life". PhD. European University Institute.
Jespersen, Jesper (2016a). "Can Macroeconomics and Ideology Be Separated? Some Experiences from Europe and the Nordic Countries". *Nordicum-Mediterraneum. Icelandic E-Journal of Nordic and Mediterranean Studies*, 10(3), https://nome.unak.is/wordpress/volume-10-no-3-2016/conference-paper-10-3/can-macroeconomics-and-ideology-be-separated-some-experiences-from-europe-and-the-nordic-countries/ [Accessed 06/12/2022].
Jespersen, Jesper (2016b). "When the Treasury and its Models Seize Power". *Nordicum-Mediterraneum. Icelandic E-Journal of Nordic and Mediterranean Studies*, 11(1), https://nome.unak.is/wordpress/volume-11-no-1-2016/01_double-blind-peer-reviewed-article/treasury-models-seize-power/ [Accessed 06/12/2022].
Johansson, W. (1990). "Pederasty". In Dynes, Wayne R. (Ed.), *Encyclopedia of Homosexuality*, 1: 964–970. London: Routledge.
Jonas, Hans (1984) [1979]. *The Imperative of Responsibility. In Search for an Ethics for the Technological Age*. Chicago: University of Chicago Press.
Jonas, Silvia (2019). "Mathematical and Moral Disagreement". *The Philosophical Quarterly*, 70(279): 302–327.
Jones, Angela (2018). "The Pleasures of Fetishization: BBW Erotic Webcam Performers, Empowerment, and Pleasure". *Fat Studies. An Interdisciplinary Journal of Body Weight and Society*, 8(3): 279–298.
Jones, Derek (Ed.) (2001). *Censorship: A World Encyclopedia*. London: Routledge.
Jones, Pete (2015). "Preaching Laughter in the Thirteenth Century: The *Exempla* of Arnold of Liège (d.c.1308) and His Dominican Milieu". *Journal of Medieval History*, 41(2): 169–183.
Jones, Virgil L. (1922). "Methods of Satire in the Political Drama of the Restoration". *The Journal of English and Germanic Philology*, 21(4): 662–669.
Joselit, David (2007). *Feedback: Television against Democracy*. Cambridge, MA: MIT Press.
Joshua, Anthony M. *et al.* (2005). "Humor and Oncology". *Journal of Clinical Oncology*, 23(3): 645–648.

Jospehy-Hernández, Daniel E. (2017). "Fansubbing Hentai Anime: Users, Distribution, Censorship and Ethics". In Orrego-Carmona, David, and Lee, Yvonne (Eds.), *Non-Professional Subtitling*, 171–197. Newcastle-upon-Tyne: Cambridge Scholars Publishing.

Jouanna, Jacques (2012). *Greek Medicine from Hippocrates to Galen*. Leiden: Brill.

Joy, Francis (2018). *Sámi Shamanism, Cosmology and Art as Systems of Embedded Knowledge*. Rovaniemi: Lapin Yliopisto.

Judges, Donald P. (1995). "When Silence Speaks Louder Than Words: Authoritarianism and the Feminist Antipornography Movement". *Psychology, Public Policy, and Law*, 1(3): 643–713.

Jung, Carl Gustav (1910). "The Association Method". *The American Journal of Psychology*, 21(2): 219–269.

Jung, Carl Gustav (1916) [1912]. *The Psychology of the Unconscious. A Study of the Transformations and Symbolisms of the Libido* (trans. Beatrice M. Hinkle). New York: Moffat, Yard.

Jung, Carl Gustav (1923) [1921]. *Psychological Types: Or, the Psychology of Individuation* (trans. H. Godwin Baynes). London: Kegan Paul, Trench, Trubner.

Jung, Carl Gustav (1958) [1957]. *The Undiscovered Self* (trans. R.F.C. Hull). Boston: Little, Brown.

Jung, Carl Gustav (1960–1990). *Collected Writings* (ed. Herbert Read, Michael Fordham and Gerard Adler; trans. R.F.C. Hull), 20 vols, 2nd ed. Princeton: Bollingen/Princeton UP.

Jung, Carl Gustav (1973). *Letters* (trans. by R.F.C. Hull), 2 vols. New York: Routledge.

Jung, Carl Gustav (1989) [1961]. *Memories, Dreams, Reflections* (ed. Aniela Jaffé; trans. Richard and Clara Winston). New York: Vintage.

Jung, Carl Gustav (2009) [1915–1930]. *The Red Book. Liber Novus* (ed. Sonu Shamdasani; trans. Mark Kyburs, John Peck and Sonu Shamdasani). New York: Norton.

Kahn, Robert (2010). "Tragedy, Farce or Legal Mobilization? The Danish Cartoons in Court in France and Canada". *University of Saint Thomas Legal Studies*, research paper no. 10–21, https://papers.ssrn.com/sol3/papers.cfm?abstract_id=1666980 [Accessed 10/01/2023].

Kahneman, Daniel (2012). *Thinking, Fast and Slow*. London: Penguin.

Kant, Immanuel (1887) [1796]. *Philosophy of Law. An Exposition of the Fundamental Principles of Jurisprudence as Science of Right* (trans. W. Hastie). Edinburgh: T. & T. Clark, https://oll.libertyfund.org/title/hastie-the-philosophy-of-law [Accessed 01/05/2022].

Kant, Immanuel (1956) [1788]. *Critique of Practical Reason* (trans. Lewis White Beck). Indianapolis: Bobbs-Merrill.

Kant, Immanuel (1977) [1795]. *Zum ewigen Frieden. Ein philosophischer Entwurf*. In *Werke in zwölf Bänden* (ed. Wilhelm Weischedel), vol. 11: 195–252. Frankfurt am Main: Suhrkamp.

Kant, Immanuel (1987) [1790]. *Critique of Judgment* (trans. Werner S. Pluhar). Indianapolis: Hackett.

Karhulahti, Veli-Matti and Välisalo, Tanja (2021). "Fictosexuality, Fictoromance, and Fictophilia: A Qualitative Study of Love and Desire for Fictional Characters". *Frontiers Psychology*, 11, https://doi.org/10.3389/fpsyg.2020.575427 [Accessed 02/02/2023].

Karlsson, Mikael M. (2019). "Flavio Baroncelli: A Personal Recollection". *Nordicum-Mediterraneum. Icelandic E-Journal of Nordic and Mediterranean Studies*, 14(2), https://doi.org/10.33112/nm.14.2.9 [Accessed 21/09/2021].

Karp, David R. (1998). "The Judicial and Judicious Use of Shame Penalties". *Crime and Delinquency*, 44(2): 277–294.

Kasunic, Anna and Kaufman, Geoff (2018). "'At Least the Pizzas You Make Are Hot': Norms, Values, and Abrasive Humor on the Subreddit r/RoastMe". *Proceedings of the Twelfth International AAAI Conference on Web and Social Media*, 161–170.

Kaufmann, Walter (1961). *Religion from Tolstoy to Camus*. New York: Harper.

Kaufmann, Eric (2021). "Academic Freedom in Crisis: Punishment, Political Discrimination, and Self-Censorship". *Center for the Study of Partisanship and Ideology*, report no. 2, https://cspicenter.org/wp-content/uploads/2021/03/AcademicFreedom.pdf [Accessed 20/10/2022].

Keen, Steve (2001). *Debunking Economics. The Naked Emperor of the Social Sciences*. London: Zed.

Kekes, John (1990). *Facing Evil*. Princeton: Princeton UP.

Kekes, John (1996). "Cruelty and Liberalism". *Ethics*, 106(4): 841–843.

Kekes, John (1997). *Against Liberalism*. Ithaca, NY: Cornell UP.

Kelly, Michael J. (2016). *Prosecuting Corporations for Genocide*. Oxford: Oxford UP.

Kemp, Peter (2012). "The Idea of University in a Cosmopolitan Perspective". *Ethics and Global Politics*, 5(2): 119–128.

Kennedy, Gavin (2009). "Adam Smith and the Invisible Hand: From Metaphor to Myth". *Economic Journal Watch*, 6(2): 239–263.

Kenny, Anthony (1995). *Frege. An Introduction to the Founder of Modern Analytic Philosophy*. London: Penguin.

Kenny, Kate (2009). "'The Performative Surprise': Parody, Documentary and Critique". *Culture and Organization*, 15(2): 221–235.

Kepel, Gilles (2003). "The Origins and Development of the Jihadist Movement: From Anti-Communism to Terrorism". *Asian Affairs*, 34(2): 91–108.

Kepel, Gilles and Jardin, Antoine (2017). *Terror in France: The Rise of Jihad in the West*. Princeton: Princeton UP.

Kerkkanen, Paavo *et al.* (2004). "Sense of Humor, Physical Health, and Well-Being at Work: A Three-Year Longitudinal Study of Finnish Police Officers". *Humor: International Journal of Humor Research*, 17(1–2): 21–35.

Kerras, Nassima and Serhani, Meriem (2019). "Audiovisual Translation of Humour into Arabic". In Faiq, Said (Ed.), *Arabic Translation Across Discourses*, 95–114. London: Routledge.

Kerstein, Samuel J. (2008). "Treating Oneself Merely as a Means". In Betzler, Monika (Ed.), *Kant's Ethics of Virtue*, 201–218. Berlin: De Gruyter.

Kesting, Stefen (2010). "John Kenneth Galbraith: A Radical Economist?" *International Journal of Social Economics*, 37(3): 179–196.

Khader, Jamil (2015). "Repeating Fundamentalism and the Politics of the Commons: The Charlie Hebdo Tragedy and the Contradictions of Global Capitalism". *Islamophobia Studies Journal*, 3(1): 12–28.

Khan, M. Masud R. (1979). *Alienation in Perversions*. London: Routledge.

Khomeini, Imam (1981). *Islam and Revolution* (trans. by Hamid Algar). Berkeley: Mizan Press.

Khroul, Victor (2015). "From *Charlie Hebdo* to *Stade de France*: The Mediatization of Religion as a Challenge for Journalism". *Global Media Journal*, 3(1): 6–17.

Kiblansky, Raymond, Panofsky, Erwin and Saxl, Fritz (1964). *Saturn and Melancholy: Studies in the History of Natural Philosophy, Religion, and Art*. London: Nelson.

Kierkegaard, Søren A. (1992) [1841–1861]. *The Concept of Irony. With Continual References to Socrates. Notes on Schelling's Lectures* (ed. and trans. Howard V. Hong and Edna H. Hong). Princeton: Princeton UP.

Kierkegaard, Søren A. (2009) [1864]. *Concluding Unscientific Postscript* (trans. Alastair Hannay). Cambridge: Cambridge UP.

Kinsella, Sharon (2014). *Schoolgirls, Money and Rebellion in Japan*. London: Routledge.

Kinsman Dean, Ruth Ann and Gregory, David M. (2004). "Humour and Laughter in Palliative Care: An Ethnographic Investigation". *Palliative and Supportive Care*, 2: 139–148.

Kipnis, Laura (1998). *Bound and Gagged. Pornography and the Politics of Fantasy in America*. Durham: Duke UP.

Kipnis, Laura (2006). "How to Look at Pornography". In Lehman, Peter (Ed.), *Pornography. Film and Culture*, 118–129. New Brunswick: Rutgers.

Kipnis, Laura (2017). *Unwanted Advances: Sexual Paranoia Comes to Campus*. New York: Harper.

Kipnis, Laura (2018). "A Man Lost His Job to a Rape Joke. Are You Cheering?" *The Guardian*, https://www.theguardian.com/commentisfree/2018/dec/22/rape-joke-metoo-movement-career-repercussions [Accessed 04/06/2022].

Kirby, Mike (2021). "Pornography and Its Impact on the Sexual Health of Men". *Trends in Urology and Men's Health*, 12(2): 6–10.

Kivistö, Sari Anneli (2008). "Sour Faces, Happy Lives? On Laughter, Joy and Happiness of the Agelasts". *COLLeGIUM*, 3: 79–100.

Kiwan, Nadia (2016). "Freedom of Thought in the Aftermath of the *Charlie Hebdo* Attacks". *French Cultural Studies*, 27(3): 233–244.

Klar, Elisabeth (2013). "Tentacles, Lolitas, and Pencil Strokes. The Parodist Body in European and Japanese Erotic Comics". In Berndt, Jacqueline and Kümmerling-Meibauer, Bettina (Eds.), *Manga's Cultural Crossroads*, 121–142. London: Routledge.

Klein, Melanie (1948) [1928]. "Early Stages of the Oedipus Conflict". In *Contributions to Psycho-Analysis 1921–1945*, 202–214. London: Hogarth.

Klepec, Peter (2021). "Sadizem, Schadenfreude in krutost". *Filozofski vestnik*, 42(3): 155–201.

Klintip, Worranan *et al.* (2022). "First Study on Stress Evaluation and Reduction in Hospitalized Cats after Neutering Surgery". *Veterinary World*, 15(9): 2111–2118.

Knudsen, Are (2004). "License to Kill: Honour killings in Pakistan". *Christian Michelsen Institutt*, working paper 2004/1, http://hdl.handle.net/11250/2435896. [Accessed 26/08/2022].

Koestler, Arthur (1964). *The Act of Creation*. London: Hutchinson.

Kohn, Eric (2021). "What Will It Take to Stop Woody Allen's Career? Why 'Allen v. Farrow' Isn't Enough". *IndieWire*, https://www.indiewire.com/2021/03/woody-allen-career-allen-v-farrow-new-movies-1234623181/ [Accessed 09/05/2022].

Kohnle, Uli (1994). *Paul Scheerbart : eine Bibliographie*. Bellheim: Phantasia

Kolirin, Lianne (2023) "Changes to Roald Dahl's Classic Children's Books Spark Censorship Spat". *CNN*, https://edition.cnn.com/style/article/roald-dahl-censored-gbr-scli-intl/index.html [Accessed 22/02/2023].

Kolnai, Aurel (1938). *War Against the West*. London: V. Gollancz, https://archive.org/details/in.ernet.dli.2015.46524 [Accessed 09(02/2023].

Kolnai, Aurel (1978). *Ethics, Value and Reality. Selected Papers*. Indianapolis: Hackett.

Korfmacher, Anne (2020). "Reviewing Pornography: Asserting Sexual Agency on Girls on Porn". *Gender Forum*, 77: 13–33.

Kors, Alan Charles and Peters, Edward (2001). *Witchcraft in Europe 400–1700. A Documentary History*, 2nd ed. Philadelphia: University of Pennsylvania Press.

Kozain, Rustum (2013). "A Brief History of Throwing Shit". *The Chronic*, http://chimurengachronic.co.za/shit-throwing/ [Accessed 26/08/2022].

Kozintsev, Alexander (2010). *The Mirror of Laughter* (trans. Richard P. Martin). New Brunswick: Transaction.

Kraidy, Marwan M. and Khalil, Joe F. (2018) [2009]. *Arab Television Industries*. London: The British Film Institute.

Krichtafovitch, Igor (2006) [2005]. *Humor Theory: Formula of Laughter* (trans. Anna Tonkonogui). Denver: Outskirts.

Krikmann, Arvo (2006). "Contemporary Linguistic Theories of Humour". *Folklore*, 33: 27–58.

Kristeva, Julia (1984) [1974]. *Revolution in Poetic Language* (trans. Margaret Waller). New York: Columbia UP.

Kristeva, Julia (1993). *Les nouvelles maladies de l'âme*. Paris: Fayard.

Kristeva, Julia (1997) [1977]. "Women's Time". In Oliber, Kelly (Ed.), *The Portable Kristeva*, 349–368. New York: Columbia UP.

Krugman, Paul (1996). "Review of John Kenneth Galbraith's 'The Good Society: The Humane Agenda'", http://www.pkarchive.org/cranks/GalbraithGoodSociety.html [Accessed 26/08/2022].

Krugman, Paul (2009). "A Dark Age of Macroeconomics". *The Conscience of a Liberal*, 27 January 2009 at 9:40am, https://archive.nytimes.com/krugman.blogs.nytimes.com/2009/01/27/a-dark-age-of-macroeconomics-wonkish/ [Accessed 6/12/2022].

Kuhn, Thomas (1970) [1962]. *The Structure of Scientific Revolutions*. Chicago: Chicago UP.

Kuiper, Nicholas A. and Martin, Rod A. (1998). "Is Sense of Humor a Positive Personality Characteristic?" In Ruch, Willibald (Ed.), *The Sense of Humor. Explorations of a Personality Characteristic*, 159–178. Berlin: De Gruyter.

Kuipers, Giselinde (2006). *Good Humor, Bad Taste. A Sociology of the Joke*. Berlin: De Gruyter.

Kumar, Ashutosh (2017). *Coolies of the Empire. Indentured Indians in the Sugar Colonies, 1830–1920*. Cambridge: Cambridge UP.

Kümper, Hiram (2020). *Der Traum vom Ehrbaren Kaufmann. Die Deutschen und die Hanse*. Berlin: Propyläen.

Kundera, Milan (1987) [1979]. *The Book of Laughter and Forgetting* (trans. Michael Henry Heim). London: Penguin.

Kushner, Irving (2013). "The 4 Humors and Erythrocyte Sedimentation: The Most Influential Observation in Medical History". *The American Journal of Medical Science*, 346(2): 154–157.

L'Estrange, Alfred Guy (1877–1878). *History of English Humour*, 2 vols. London: Hurst & Blackett, https://www.gutenberg.org/ebooks/18300 [Accessed 01/05/2022].

Laffranchi, Andrea and Guccini, Francesco (2021). "Francesco Guccini il più amato dai teenager 'Io, un cialtrone di 80 anni'". *Corriere della Sera*, https://www.corriere.it/sette/incontri/21_gennaio_15/francesco-guccini-piu-amato-teenager-io-cialtrone-80-anni-0d5de25e-575b-11eb-8f51-2cbbf1c2346f.shtml [Accessed 26/08/2022].

Lamont, David (2001). "The Empathy of God: A Biblical and Theological Study of the Christological Implications of John 11:35". MTh. McMaster University.

Lançon, Philippe (2018). *Le Lambeau*. Paris: Gallimard.

Landert, Daniela (2021). "The Spontaneous Co-Creation of Comedy: Humour in Improvised Theatrical Fiction". *Journal of Pragmatics*, 173: 68–87.

Lankoski, Petri *et al.* (2023). "Platform-Produced Heteronormativity: A Content Analysis of Adult Videogames on Patreon". *Games and Culture*, 18(1), 102–123.

Lantos, John (2010). "Cruel Calculus: Why Saving Premature Babies Is Better Business Than Helping Them Thrive". *Health Affairs*, 29(11): 2114–2117.

Laperche, Blandine and Uzunidis, Dimitri (Eds.) (2005). *John Kenneth Galbraith and the Future of Economics*. London: Palgrave Macmillan.

Laqueur, Thomas W. (2003). *Solitary Sex: A Cultural History of Masturbation*. New York: Zone Books.

Larsen, Egon (1980). *Wit as a Weapon: Political Joke in History*. London: F. Muller.

Larsen, Øjvind (2011). *"Die Versprachlichung des Sakralen:* The Transformation of the Authority of the Sacred into Secular Political Deliberation in Habermas' Theory of Communicative Action". *Nordicum-Mediterraneum. Icelandic E-journal of Nordic and Mediterranean Studies*, 6(1), https://nome.unak.is/wordpress/06-1/articles61/die-versprachlichung-des-sakralen-the-transformation-of-the-authority-of-the-sacred-into-secular-political-deliberation-in-habermas-theory-of-communicative-action/ [Accessed 26/08/2022].

Lashley, Conrad (2018a). "Neo-Liberalism and Neo-Slavery". *Research in Hospitality Management*, 8(1): 17–22.

Lashley, Conrad (2018b). "Slavery, Neo-Slavery and Business Ethics". *Research in Hospitality Management*, 8(1): 5–10.

Lauchlan, Iain (2010). "Laughter in the Dark: Humour under Stalin". In Duncan, Alastair and Chamayou, Anne (Eds.), *Le rire européen*, 257–274. Perpignan: Perpignan UP.

Lawrence, C.H. (2015) [1999]. *Medieval Monasticism. Forms of Religious Life in Western Europe in the Middle Ages*, 4th ed. London: Routledge.

Le Goff, Jacques (1997). "Laughter in the Middle Ages". In Bremmer, Jan and Roodenburg, Herman (Eds.), *A Cultural History of Humour: From Antiquity to the Present Day*, 40–53. Cambridge: Polity.

Le Goff, Jacques (2004) [1999]. *Saint Francis of Assisi* (trans. Christine Rhone). London: Routledge.

Leacock, Stephen (1913). "Making a Magazine (The Dream of a Contributor)". In *Behind the Beyond, and Other Contributions to Human Knowledge*, 167–181. London: John Lane, The Bodley Head, https://www.gutenberg.org/ebooks/23449 [Accessed 22/12/2022].

Leacock, Stephen (1922). *My Discovery of England*. New York: Dodd, Mead, https://www.fadedpage.com/showbook.php?pid=20160136 [Accessed 13/02/2023].

Leacock, Stephen (1934). *Lincoln Frees the Slaves*. New York: G.P. Putnam's Sons, https://www.fadedpage.com/showbook.php?pid=20171138 [Accessed 22/12/2022].

Leacock, Stephen (1935). *Humor: Its Theory and Technique*. London: Bodley Head, https://www.fadedpage.com/showbook.php?pid=20160929 [Accessed 22/12/2022].

Leacock, Stephen (1938). *Humor and Humanity: An Introduction to the Study of Humor*. New York: Henry Holt, https://www.fadedpage.com/showbook.php?pid=20160617 [Accessed 22/12/2022].

Leacock, Stephen (1942). *Our Heritage of Liberty*. London: Bodley Head, https://www.fadedpage.com/showbook.php?pid=201410A3 [Accessed 22/12/2022].

Leacock, Stephen (1945). *While There Is Time: The Case Against Social Catastrophe*. Toronto: McClelland & Stewart, https://www.fadedpage.com/showbook.php?pid=20171142 [Accessed 22/12/2022].

Leborgne, Erik (2018). *L'Humour noir des Lumières*. Paris: Garnier.

Lecky, William E.H. (1890) [1865]. *History of European Morals from Augustus to Charlemagne*. London: Longmans and Green, https://www.gutenberg.org/files/39273/39273-pdf.pdf [Accessed 19/02/2022].

Leeming, David A. (Ed.) (2014). *Encyclopedia of Psychology and Religion*, 2nd ed. New York: Springer.

Leo XIII, Pope (1891). *Rerum Novarum*, https://www.vatican.va/content/leo-xiii/en/encyclicals/documents/hf_l-xiii_enc_15051891_rerum-novarum.html [Accessed 19/03/2022].

Leopardi, Giacomo (n.d.a) [1835]. *Operette morali*. Milan: Einaudi, http://www.letteraturaitaliana.net/pdf/Volume_8/t345.pdf [Accessed 21/09/2021].

Leopardi, Giacomo (n.d.a) [1898]. *Zibaldone di pensieri*. Milan: Einaudi, http://www.letteraturaitaliana.net/pdf/Volume_8/t226.pdf [Accessed 21/09/2021].

Leskosky, Richard J. (2022). "Shapeshifting in Anime. Form and Meaning". In Desser, David (Ed.), *A Companion to Japanese Cinema*, 247 268. Chichester: Wiley.

Levi, Ken (1980). "Homicide as Conflict Resolution". *Deviant Behavior*, 1: 281–307.

Levin, Abigail (2010). *The Cost of Free Speech: Pornography, Hate Speech, and Their Challenge to Liberalism.* Basingstoke: Palgrave MacMillan.
Lévitt, Albert (1922–1923). "Extent and Function of the Doctrine of *Mens Rea*". *Illinois Law Review*, 17(117): 578–583.
Levy, Neil (2011). *Hard Luck: How Luck Undermines Free Will and Moral Responsibility.* Oxford: Oxford UP.
Lewis, C.S. (2016) [1941]. *The Screwtape Letters.* Quebec City: Samizdat.
Lewis, Hywel (1982). *The Elusive Self.* London: Macmillan, https://www.giffordlectures.org/books/elusive-self [Accessed 13/02/2023].
Ley, David J. (2012). *The Myth of Sex Addiction.* Lanham: Rowman & Littlefield.
Lezard, Nicholas (2000). "Don't You Just Hate Comedians?" *Index on Censorship*, 6: 90–92.
Li, Huihui and Wen, Guihua (2019). "Sample Awareness-Based Personalized Facial Expression Recognition". *Applied Intelligence*, 49: 2956–2969.
Lilti, Ayelet (2018). "Caricature as Desacralization of the Image: The *Charlie Hebdo* Case". In Sover, Arie (Ed.), *The Languages of Humor. Verbal, Visual, and Physical Humor*, 188–201. London: Bloomsbury.
Lilti, Ayelet (2021). "Charlie Hebdo: 6 Years On. An Ongoing Struggle against the Sacralization of the Image". Paper presented on 15 January 2021 at the IAPH conference, 117th annual meeting of APA's Eastern Division.
Lincoln, Abraham (1932) [1861]. "3 December 1861 Message to the Fellow-Citizens of the Senate and House of Representatives". Washington: National Archives.
Lippi, Chiara, Gutiérrez, Ortiz Montasterio and Luis, Enrique (2021). "Odio a los Putos Mexicanos". *PopMeC Research Blog*, https://popmec.hypotheses.org/4658 [Accessed 08/05/2022].
Lippitt, John (1992). "Nietzsche, Zarathustra and the Status of Laughter". *British Journal of Aesthetics*, 32(1): 39–49.
Lippitt, John (2009). "True Self-Love and True Self-Sacrifice". *International Journal for Philosophy of Religion*, 66(3): 125–138.
Lippitt, John (2015). "Giving 'The Dear Self' Its Due: Kierkegaard, Frankfurt and Self-Love". In Davenport, John J. and Rudd, Anthony (Eds.), *Love, Reason and Will: Kierkegaard after Frankfurt*, 137–154. London: Bloomsbury.
Lippitt, John (2016). "What Can Therapists Learn from Kierkegaard?" In Bazzano, Manu and Webb, Julie (Eds.), *Therapy and the Counter-Tradition: The Edge of Philosophy*, 23–33. London: Routledge.
Lippitt, John (2017). "Kierkegaard's Virtues? Humility and Gratitude as the Grounds of Contentment, Patience and Hope in Kierkegaard's Moral Psychology". In Minister, Stephen, *et al.* (Eds.), *Kierkegaard's God and the Good Life*, 95–113. Bloomington: Indiana UP.
Lippitt, John (2019). "Beyond Worry: On Learning Humility from the Lilies and the Birds". In Buben, Adam, *et al.* (Eds.), *The Kierkegaardian Mind*, 89–99. New York: Routledge.
Lippmann, Walter (2005) [1938]. *The Good Society.* New Brunswick: Transaction.
Lipps, Theodor (1898). *Komik und Humor, eine psychologisch-ästhetische Untersuchung.* Hamburg: Voss.
List, Christian, Caruso, Greg and Clark, Cory (2020). "Free Will: Real or Illusion?" *The Philosopher*, 108(1): 41–80.
Lock, Grahame, Maiolo, Francesco and Zinoviev, Alexander (n.d.a). "Conversation with Alexander Zinoviev", http://www.zinoviev.ru/en/writings/zinoviev-interview-nijmegen.html [Accessed 09/06/2022].

Locke, John (1824) [1693]. *Some Thoughts Concerning Education*. In *The Works of John Locke in Nine Volumes*, 12th ed., vol. 8: 1–210. London: Rivington, https://oll.libertyfund.org/title/locke-the-works-of-john-locke-in-nine-volumes [Accessed 01/05/2022].
Lockwood, Samuel (1876). "Animal Humor". *American Naturalist*, 10(5): 257–270.
Lomas, Gabriel I. (2008). "Stop the Insanity". *JADARA*, 41(2): 69–71.
Long, Robyn (2018). "Sexual Subjectivities within Neoliberalism: Can Queer and Crip Engagements Offer an Alternative Praxis?" *Journal of International Women's Studies*, 19(1): 78–93.
Lorenz, Konrad (1962) [1959]. "Gestalt Perception as Fundamental to Scientific Knowledge". *General Systems*, 7: 37–56.
Lorenz, Konrad (2002) [1949]. *King Solomon's Ring. New Light on Animal Ways* (trans. Marjorie Kerr Wilson). London: Routledge.
Lothane, Zvi (1999). "The Perennial Freud: Method versus Myth and the Mischief of Freud Bashers". *International Forum of Psychoanalysis*, 8(3–4): 151–171.
Lovelock, James (2009). *The Vanishing Face of Gaia. A Final Warning*. New York: Basic Books.
Lunacek, Tilen Izar (2016). "Juicily Juxtaposed: Pleasure Tropes in the History of Erotic Comics". *Teorija in Praksa*, 53(4): 875–890.
Lunardi, Antonio (2015). "Scritture Separate: Autocensura testuale e imposizione visuale del bondage in Dino Buzzati". *Between*, 5(9), https://doi.org/10.13125/2039-6597/1416 [Accessed 29/03/2022].
Lundquist, Lita and Dyrbye, Helen (2022). *Danish Humour – Sink or Swim*. Friedriksberg: Samfundslitteratur.
Luxmoore, Matthew (2018). "In Russia, 'The Death of Stalin' Is No Laughing Matter". *The New York Times*, https://www.nytimes.com/2018/01/24/movies/death-of-stalin-banned-russia.html [Accessed 04/06/2022].
Lynch, Caitrin (1999). "Good Girls or Juki Girls? Learning and Identity in Garment Factories". *Anthropology of Work Review*, 19(3): 18–22.
Maalej, Zouhair (2008). "The Heart and Cultural Embodiment in Tunisian Arabic". In Sharifian, Farzad, Dirven, René, Yu, Ning and Niemeier, Susanne (Eds.), *Culture, Body, and Language. Conceptualizations of Internal Body Organs across Cultures and Languages*, 395–428. Berlin: De Gruyter.
Maasen, Thijs (2010). "Man-Boy Friendships on Trial: On the Shift in the Discourse on Boy Love in the Early Twentieth Century". *Journal of Homosexuality*, 20(1–2): 47–70.
MacCulloch, Diarmaid (2018). *Thomas Cromwell: A Life*. London: Allen Lane.
Machiavelli, Niccolò (1908) [1515]. *The Prince* (trans. W.K. Marriott). London: J.M. Dent, https://onlinebooks.library.upenn.edu/webbin/gutbook/lookup?num=1232 [Accessed 02/05/2022].
Mackenzie, Suzie (2000). "Finding Fact from Fiction". *The Guardian*, https://www.theguardian.com/books/2000/may/27/fiction.features [Accessed 04/05/2022].
MacKinnon, Catharine A. (1993). *Only Words*. Cambridge, MA: Harvard UP.
Macleod, Patricia Jean (2018). "Conscionable Consumption: A Feminist Grounded Theory of Porn Consumer Ethics". PhD. Middlesex University.
Macleod, Patricia Jean (2020). "Conscionable Consumption: A Theoretical Model of Consumer Ethics in Pornography". *Porn Studies*, 8(1), https://www.researchgate.net/publication/337482960 [Accessed 28/11/2021].
Maerz, Mary (2020). "Corporate Cruelty: Holding Factory Farms Accountable for Animal Cruelty Crimes to Encourage Systemic Reform". *Journal of Animal Law*, 16: 137–170.
Maes, Hans (2013). *Pornographic Art and the Aesthetics of Pornography*. Houndmills: Palgrave Macmillan.

Maes, Hans (2019). *What is Sexy? Een oefening in feministische filosofie*. Antwerp: Vrijdag.
Maes, Hans R.V. and Levinson, Jerrold (Eds.) (2012). *Art and Pornography: Philosophical Essays*. Oxford: Oxford UP.
Mahon, Alyce (2020). *The Marquis de Sade and the Avant-Garde*. Princeton: Princeton UP.
Mahony, Diana L. et al. (2001). "The Effects of Laughter on Discomfort Thresholds: Does Expectation Become Reality?" *The Journal of General Psychology*, 128(2): 217–226.
Maiti, Abhik and Deep Naskar (2016). "A Critical Evaluation of the Lawless Utopia Proposed by Golding's The Lord of the Flies and the Gta Games". *International Journal of English Language, Literature and Humanities*, 4(12): 230–248.
Maletz, Donald J. (2002). "Tocqueville's Tyranny of the Majority Reconsidered". *The Journal of Politics*, 64(3): 741–763.
Mantoux, Paul (1935) [1928]. *The Industrial Revolution in the Eighteenth Century* (trans. Marjorie Vernon). London: Jonathan Cape.
Maraschi, Andrea (2018). "When Banquets Were Dangerous for the Soul: Church Opposition to Wedding Feasts in Early Medieval Times". *Proceedings of the Dublin Gastronomy Symposium*, 2018, 1–7.
Marazzi, Christian (2002). *Capitale & Linguaggio. Dalla new economy all'economia di Guerra*. Rome: DeriveApprodi.
Marcuse, Herbert (1966) [1955]. *Eros and Civilization. A Philosophical Inquiry into Freud*. Boston: Beacon.
Marcuse, Herbert and Magee, Bryan (1977). "Herbert Marcuse and the Frankfurt School", https://www.youtube.com/watch?v=vm3euZS5nLo&ab_channel=mehranshargh [Accessed 19/01/2023].
Maritain, Jacques (1941) [1914–1939]. *Ransoming the Time* (trans. Harry Lorin Binsse). New York: Charles Scribner's Sons.
Maritain, Jacques (1943) [1942]. *Education at the Crossroads*. New Haven: Yale UP.
Maritain, Jacques (1952) [1942]. *The Range of Reason*. New York: Charles Scribner's Sons.
Maritain, Jacques (1957) [1947]. *Existence and Existent* (trans. Lewis Galantiere and Gerald B. Phelon). New York: Image.
Maritain, Jacques (1958). *Reflections on America*. New York: Charles Scribner's Sons.
Maritain, Jacques (1959) [1932]. *Distinguish to Unite. Or the Degrees of Knowledge* (trans. Gerald B. Phelan). New York: Charles Scribner's Sons.
Maritain, Jacques (1960) [1952]. *Creative Intuition in Art and Poetry*. New York: Bollingen/Princeton UP.
Maritain, Jacques (1964) [1960]. *Moral Philosophy. An Historical and Critical Survey of the Great Systems*. New York: Charles Scribner's Sons.
Maritain, Jacques (1973a) [1936]. *Integral Humanism. Temporal and Spiritual Problems of a New Christendom* (trans. Joseph W. Evans). Notre Dame, IN: University of Notre Dame Press.
Maritain, Jacques (1973b) [1970]. *On the Church of Christ. The Person of the Church and Her Personnel* (trans. Joseph W. Evans). Notre Dame, IN: University of Notre Dame Press.
Maritsas, Kostantinos (Costas) (2016). "Ancient Ritual Places and Pornography". Paper delivered at the 2nd International Symposium 'Megalithic Monuments and Cult Practices', South-West University 'Neofit Rilski', Blagoevgrad, Bulgaria, https://www.academia.edu/29358835/ANCIENT_RITUAL_PLACES_AND_PORNOGRAPHY [Accessed 10/11/2022].
Markey, Patrick M. and Ferguson, Christopher J. (2017). *Moral Combat. The War on Violent Video Games Is Wrong*. Dallas, TX: BenBella.
Markowitz, Gerald (2000). "'Cater to the Children': The Role of the Lead Industry in a Public Health Tragedy, 1900–1955". *American Journal of Public Health*, 90(1): 36–46.

Marmysz, John (2003). *Laughing at Nothing: Humor as a Response to Nihilism*. Albany: SUNY Press.
Marmysz, John (2020). "That's Not Funny. The Humor of Diogenes". In Amir, Lydia B. (Ed.), *Philosophy of Humor Yearbook*, 1: 97–115. Berlin: De Gruyter.
Marsonet, Michele (2023). "Politically Correct: L'autrice di Harry Potter colpita dalla censura". *Per Sempre News*, https://www.persemprenews.it/cultura/politically-correct-lautrice-di-harry-potter-col pita-dalla-censura/?fbclid=IwAR0cSUtS1TBsRpIQvSXbSxJZyhlei0MBC6iuBW1I_bsr_o-m2wqokDiuSJ8 [Accessed 17/01/2023].
Martin, Rod A. (2001). "Humor, Laughter, and Physical Health: Methodological Issues and Research Findings". *Psychological Bulletin*, 127(4): 504–519.
Martin, Rod A. (2004). "Sense of Humor and Physical Health: Theoretical Issues, Recent Findings, and Future Directions". *Humor: International Journal of Humor Research*, 17: 1–19.
Martin, Rod A. and Lefcourt, Herbet M. (1983). "Sense of Humor as a Moderator of the Relation between Stressors and Moods". *Journal of Personality and Social Psychology*, 45: 1313–1324.
Martin, Rod A. and Lefcourt, Herbet M. (1984). "Situational Humor Response Questionnaire: Quantitative Measure of the Sense of Humor". *Journal of Personality and Social Psychology*, 47: 145–155.
Martin, Rod A. *et al.* (2003). "Individual Differences in Uses of Humor and Their Relation to Psychological Well-Being: Development of the Humor Styles Questionnaire". *Journal of Research in Personality*, 37(1): 48–75.
Marwah, Sanjay and Joplin, Jerry W. (2020). "Modernizing and Activating Beccaria's Proportionality". *Journal of Theoretical and Philosophical Criminology*, 12: 37–51.
Marx, Karl and Engels, Friedrich (1967) [1848]. *The Communist Manifesto* (trans. Samuel Moore). London: Penguin.
Maslow, Abraham H. (1954). *Motivation and Personality*. New York: Harper & Row.
Mastrantonio, Luca and Becker, Emma (2021). "Ho lavorato in due case: racconto una prostituzione onesta". *Corriere della Sera*, https://www.corriere.it/sette/attualita/21_ottobre_02/emma-becker-ho-lavorato-due-case-racconto-prostituzione-onesta-a3695f2e-1f9e-11ec-b908-b44816b61f2f.shtml [Accessed 26/08/2022].
Mathews, Basil (2007) [1926]. *Young Islam on Trek*. Whitefish: Kessinger.
Mavridis, Symeon (2018). "Greece's Economic and Social Transformation 2008–2017". *Social Sciences*, 7(1): 1–14.
Max Ehrlich Association (2000–2012). "Max Ehrlich", http://www.max-ehrlich.org/max.htm [Accessed 14/04/2023].
Maxfield, Megan (2022). "Sadism, Sontag, and Snuff in The Act of Killing". *Masthead 2021*, https://wp.nyu.edu/mercerstreet/2021-2022/sadism-sontag-and-snuff-in-the-act-of-killing/ [Accessed 15/12/2022].
Maxwell, Lida (2019). *Insurgent Truth: Chelsea Manning and the Politics of Outsider Truth-Telling*. Oxford: Oxford UP.
McCann, Pol D., Plummer, Dave and Minichiello, Victor (2010). "Being the Butt of the Joke: Homophobic Humour, Male Identity, and Its Connection to Emotional and Physical Violence for Men". *Health Sociology Review*, 19(4): 505–521.
McCarthy, Arlie H. *et al.* (2019). "Antarctica: The Final Frontier for Marine Biological Invasions". *Global Change Biology*, 25: 2221–2241.
McCloskey, Deirdre N. (1998) [1985]. *The Rhetoric of Economics*. Madison: University of Wisconsin Press.
McDougall, William (1926). *An Introduction to Social Psychology*, revised ed. Boston: John W. Luce.

McElroy, Wendy (1995). *XXX – A Woman's Right to Pornography.* New York: St. Martin's.
McElroy, Wendy (1997). "A Feminist Defense of Pornography". *Free Inquiry,* 17(4), https://secularhumanism.org/1997/09/a-feminist-defense-of-pornography/ [Accessed 28/11/2021].
McElroy, Wendy (2001) [1996]. *Sexual Correctness. The Gender-Feminist Attack on Women.* Jefferson, NC: McFarland.
McGhee, Paul E. (1979). *Humor: Its Origin and Development.* San Francisco: W.H. Freeman.
McKee, Alan, et al. (2020). "An Interdisciplinary Definition of Pornography: Results from a Global Delphi Panel". *Archives of Sexual Behavior,* 49: 1085–1091.
McLuhan, Marshall and Powers, Bruce R. (1989) [1964]. *The Global Village. Transformations in World Life and Media in the 21st Century.* Oxford: Oxford UP.
McManus, Curtis R. (2016). *Clio's Bastards: Or, the Wrecking of History and the Perversion of Our Historical Consciousness.* Victoria, BC: Friesen.
McMillan, Graeme (2012). "Iranian Cartoonist Mahmoud Shokraye Sentenced to 25 Lashes for Satirical Cartoon". *Comics Alliance,* https://comicsalliance.com/iranian-cartoonist-sentenced-to-25-lashes [Accessed 26/08/2022].
McMurtry, John (1972). "Monogamy: A Critique". *The Monist,* 56(4): 587–599.
McMurtry, John (1979). "How to Tell the Left from the Right". *Canadian Journal of Philosophy,* 9(3): 387–412.
McMurtry, John (1984). "Fascism and Neo-Conservatism: Is there a Difference?" *Praxis International,* 4(1): 86–102.
McMurtry, John (1989). *Understanding War.* Toronto: Science for Peace.
McMurtry, John (1997). "The Contradictions of the Free Market: Is There a Solution?" *Journal of Business Ethics,* 16(7): 645–662.
McMurtry, John (1998). *Unequal Freedoms. The Global Market as an Ethical System.* Toronto: Garamond.
McMurtry, John (1999). *The Cancer Stage of Capitalism,* 1st ed. London: Pluto.
McMurtry, John (2002). *Value Wars: The Global Market versus the Life Economy.* London: Pluto.
McMurtry, John (2008). "The Human Vocation: An Autobiography of Higher Education". *Nordicum-Mediterraneum. Icelandic E-Journal of Nordic and Mediterranean Studies,* 3(2), https://nome.unak.is/previous-issues/issues/vol3_2/mcmurtry.html [Accessed 20/05/2022].
McMurtry, John (2012). "Economic Globalization and Ethico-Political Rights". In Chadwick, Ruth (Ed.), *Encyclopedia of Applied Ethics,* 2nd ed., vol. 2: 20–27. London: Academic Press.
McMurtry, John (2013). *The Cancer Stage of Capitalism: From Crisis to Cure,* 2nd ed. London: Pluto.
McMurtry, John (2020). Review of *Embodiment and the Meaning of Life* by Jeff Noonan. *University of Toronto Quarterly,* 89(3): 531–533.
McMurtry, John (2021). Message to the Global Unity Network mailing list. 28 May 2021, 02:46.
McMurtry, John (Ed.) (2011). *Philosophy and World Problems,* vols. 1–3. Paris and Oxford: UNESCO/EOLSS.
McNair, Brian (2013). *Porno? Chic! How Pornography Changed the World and Made It a Better Place.* London: Routledge.
Meadows, Donella H. et al. (1972). *The Limits to Growth.* New York: Universe.
Meckl, Markus (2014). Review of *The Cost of Free Speech: Pornography, Hate Speech, and Their Challenge to Liberalism* by Abigail Levin. *The European Legacy,* 19(5): 662–663.
Meerloo, Joost A.M. (2015) [1956]. *The Rape of the Mind. The Psychology of Thought Control, Menticide, and Brainwashing.* Joshua Tree, CA: Progressive. Electronic version.

Mehng, Si Ahn (2021). "When Physical Attractiveness Does Not Benefit: Focusing on Interpersonal Relationship, Target Employee Personality, and Career Success". *2021 North American Management Society Conference Proceedings*, 130–145.

Meinecke, Friedrich (1998) [1924]. *Machiavellism: The Doctrine of the Raison d'État and Its Place in Modern History* (trans. Douglas Scott). New Brunswick: Transaction.

Meister, Robert (2011). *After Evil. A Politics of Human Rights*. New York: Columbia UP.

Melia, Juliette (2006). "Empowerment through Pornography? The Sexual Self-Portraits of Jeff Koons and Natacha Merritt". *E-CRINI*, 8, https://www.academia.edu/download/53664220/Juliette_MELIA_5.pdf [Accessed 28/112021].

Melossi, Dario and Pavarini, Massimo (1977). *Carcere e fabbrica. Alle origini del sistema penitenziario*. Bologna: il Mulino.

Melzack, Ronald and Wall, Patrick D. (1965). "Pain Mechanisms: A New Theory". *Science*, 150(3699): 971–979.

Menatti, Laura, and Casado da Rocha, Antonio (2016). "Landscape and Health: Connecting Psychology, Aesthetics, and Philosophy Through the Concept of *Affordance*". *Hypothesis and Theory*, 7, article 571: 1–17.

Merleau-Ponty, Maurice (1964a) [1960]. *Signs* (trans. Richard C. McCleary). Evanston: Northwestern UP.

Merleau-Ponty, Maurice (1964b) [1951]. "The Child's Relations with Others". In *The Primacy of Perception and Other Essays on Phenomenological Psychology, the Philosophy of Art, History, and Politics* (ed. James M. Edie; trans. William Cobb), 96–155. Evanston: Northwestern UP.

Merz, Erin L. *et al.* (2009) "A Longitudinal Analysis of Humor Coping and Quality of Life in Systemic Sclerosis". *Psychology, Health and Medicine*, 14(5): 553–566.

Meyer, John C. (2000). "Humour as a Double-Edged Sword: Four Functions of Humor in Communication". *Communication Theory*, 10(3): 310–331.

Meynell, Everard (1913). *The Life of Francis Thompson*. New York: C. Scribners' Sons, https://www.gutenberg.org/ebooks/45106 [Accessed 11/11/2022].

Miesel, Sandra (2001). "Who Burned the Witches?" *Crisis*, 19(9): 21–26.

Miethe, Terance D. (2019). *Whistleblowing at Work. Tough Choices in Exposing Fraud, Waste, and Abuse on the Job*. London: Routledge.

Migliardi, Dario (2015). ""Haeret in vultu trucis imago facti". Il personaggio tragico di Seneca come specchio distorto dell'animo umano". *Mantichora*, 5: 2–37.

Mill, John Stuart (1920) [1848]. *Principles of Political Economy. With Some of Their Applications to Social Philosophy*. London: Longmans, Green.

Mill, John Stuart (2001) [1863]. *Utilitarianism*. Kitchener: Batoche, https://socialsciences.mcmaster.ca/econ/ugcm/3ll3/mill/utilitarianism.pdf [Accessed 11/11/2022].

Miller, Geoffrey (2000). *The Mating Mind*. New York: Anchor.

Miller, Harold W. (1945). "Aristophanes and Medical Language". *Transactions and Proceedings of the American Philological Association*, 76: 74–84.

Miller-Young, Mireille (2016). "Confessions of a Black Feminist Academic Performer". *Nka Journal of Contemporary African Art*, 38–39: 90–95.

Milner Davis, Jessica (2013). "Humour and Its Cultural Context". In Milner Davis, Jessica and Chey, Jocelyn (Eds.), *Humour in Chinese Life and Culture: Resistance and Control in Modern Times*, 1–22. Oxford: Oxford UP.

Mini, Piero V. (1974). *Philosophy and Economics: The Origins and Development of Economic Theory*. Gainesville: UP of Florida.

Ministry of Foreign Affairs of the People's Republic of China (2022). "20th CPC National Congress Concludes in Beijing, Xi Jinping Presides over Closing Session and Delivers Important Speech", https://www.fmprc.gov.cn/eng/zxxx_662805/202210/t20221024_10790661.html?fbclid=IwAR3KFhPcDFeDr_MOkHQ5URyICWwa9IY_XoYE11eDZ9axGrM_NIGL_SpbCk [Accessed 25/10/2022].

Minois, Georges (2000). *Histoire du rire et de la dérision*. Paris: Fayard.

Mitchell, Laura A. *et al.* (2006). "A Comparison of the Effects of Preferred Music, Arithmetic and Humour on Cold Pressor Pain". *European Journal of Pain*, 10(4): 343–351.

Moio, Jené A. (2006). "Torture". *Journal of Ethnic and Cultural Diversity in Social Work*, 15(3–4): 1–30, doi: 10.1300/J051v15n03_01 [Accessed 21/09/2021].

Molina Gayà, Enric (2021). "L'Humor com a Eina de Comunicació Corporativa. Com minimizar-ne els riscos". BA. Universitat Oberta de Catalunya.

Monk, Ray (1996). *Bertrand Russell: The Spirit of Solitude, 1872–1921*. New York: Free Press.

Montaigne, Michel de (1877) [1595]. *Essays* (trans. Charles Cotton). London: Reeves & Turne, https://www.gutenberg.org/files/3600/3600-h/3600-h.htm [Accessed 19/02/2022].

Montesquieu (2001) [1748]. *The Spirit of the Laws* (trans. Thomas Nugent). Kitchener: Batoche, https://socialsciences.mcmaster.ca/econ/ugcm/3ll3/montesquieu/spiritoflaws.pdf [Accessed 10/11/2022].

Montgomery, Yavanna Meghann (2013). "A Burlesque". PhD. Griffith University.

Moosa, Imad A. (2019). *The Economics of War: Profiteering, Militarism and Imperialism*. Cheltenham: Edward Elgar.

More, Thomas (1750) [1515]. *De optimo statu reipublicae deque nova insula utopia*. Glasgow: R. & A. Foulis, https://archive.org/details/deoptimoreipubli00more [Accessed 01/05/2022].

More, Thomas (1973) [1532–1533]. *The Confutation of Tyndale's Answer*. In *The Complete Works of St. Thomas More*, vol. 8. New Haven: Yale UP.

Morel, Olivier (2016). "The Weight of a Portrait: *Caricatura* and Industrial Violence after the *Charlie Hebdo* Attack". *French Cultural Studies*, 27(3): 256–267.

Moretti, Felice (2001). *La ragione del sorriso e del riso nel Medioevo*. Bari: Edipuglia, 2001.

Mornati, Fiorenzo (2018). *Una biografia intellettuale di Vilfredo Pareto. II. Illusioni e delusioni della libertà (1891–1898)*. Rome: Edizioni Storia e Letteratura.

Mornati, Fiorenzo (2020). *Vilfredo Pareto: An Intellectual Biography: III. From Liberty to Science (1898–1923)*. Cham: Palgrave Macmillan.

Morreall, John (1983) *Taking Laughter Seriously*. Albany: State University of New York Press.

Morreall, John (1999). *Comedy, Tragedy, and Religion*. Albany: State University of New York Press.

Morreall, John (2008). "Philosophy and Religion". In Raskin, Victor (Ed.), *The Primer of Humor Research*, 211–242. Berlin: De Gruyter.

Morreall, John (2016). "Philosophy of Humor". In Zalta, Edward N. (Ed.), *Stanford Encyclopedia of Philosophy*. Stanford: Stanford University, https://plato.stanford.edu/entries/humor/ [Accessed 21/02/2022].

Morreall, John (2020). "It's a Funny Thing, Humor". In Amir, Lydia B. (Ed.), *Philosophy of Humor Yearbook*, 1: 33–48. Berlin: De Gruyter.

Morreall, John (Ed.) (1987). *The Philosophy of Laughter and Humor*. Albany: State University of New York Press.

Morrell, Robert (2001). "Corporal Punishment in South African Schools: A Neglected Explanation for its Persistence". *South African Journal of Education*, 21(4): 292–299.

Morricone, Ennio and Valentina (2020). "I Salmi di Morricone: ponte tra Dio e l'umanità". *Corriere della Sera*, https://www.pressreader.com/italy/corriere-della-sera-la-lettura/20200920/281483573811023 [Accessed 08/11/2022].

Morrison, Alan D. and Wilhelm, William J., Jr. (2007). *Investment Banking: Institutions, Law and Politics*. Oxford: Oxford UP.

Moxnes, Halvor (2010) [1996]. "Honor and Shame". In Rohrbaugh, Richard L. (Ed.), *The Social Sciences and New Testament Interpretation*, 19–40. Grand Rapids, MI: Baker Academics.

Murphy, Scott Patrick (2017). "Humor Orgies as Ritual Insult: Putdowns and Solidarity Maintenance in a Corner Donut Shop". *Journal of Contemporary Ethnography*, 46(1): 108–132.

Murray, James A.H. et al. (Eds.) (1989). *The Oxford English Dictionary*, 2nd ed. Oxford: Clarendon.

Nadler, Steven (2002). *Spinoza's Heresy: Immortality and the Jewish Mind*. Oxford: Oxford UP.

Nandar, Win (2019). "A Year in Jail for Satirists Who Mocked Military in Street Performance". *Myanmar Now*, https://myanmar-now.org/en/news/a-year-in-jail-for-satirists-who-mocked-military-in-street-performance [Accessed 26/08/2022].

Napier, Susan J. (2007). *From Impressionism to Anime: Japan as Fantasy and Fan Cult in the Mind of the West*. Hampshire: Palgrave Macmillan.

Nardin, Terry (2001). *The Philosophy of Michael Oakeshott*. University Park: Pennsylvania State UP.

Nardinelli, Clark (1982). "Corporal Punishment and Children's Wages in Nineteenth Century Britain". *Explorations in Economic History*, 19: 283–295.

Nash, David (2007). *Blasphemy in the Christian World: A History*. Oxford: Oxford UP.

Nell, Victor (2006). "Cruelty and the Psychology of History". *Behavioral and Brain Sciences*, 29(3): 211–257.

Nelson, Maggie (2011). *The Art of Cruelty: A Reckoning*. New York: W.W. Norton.

Nessa, Shumirun (2022). "Men Be Like 'It's Not All Men'". *The Female Lead*, https://www.facebook.com/thefemalelead/videos/534368868104907 [Accessed 25/04/ 2022].

Nevo, Ofra et al. (1993). "Humor and Pain Tolerance". *Humor: International Journal of Humor Research*, 6(1): 71–88.

Nicholls, Roderick (2002). "Voltaire and the Paradoxes of Fanaticism". *The Dalhousie Review*, 82(3): 441–467.

Nicolacopulos, Toula and Vassilacopoulos, George (2020). "Castoriadis, Racist and Anti-Racist Ontologies". *Thesis Eleven*, 16(1): 76–88.

Nietzsche, Friedrich (1911a) [1871]. "The Greek State. Preface to an Unwritten Book". In *The Complete Works of Friedrich Nietzsche*, 13 vols. (trans. Oscar Levy), vol. 2: 1–18. New York: MacMillan, https://www.gutenberg.org/files/51548/51548-h/51548-h.htm [Accessed 10/01/2022].

Nietzsche, Friedrich (1911b) [1883–1891]. *Thus Spake Zarathustra* (trans. Thomas Common). Edinburgh: T.N. Foulis, https://www.gutenberg.org/files/1998/1998-h/1998-h.htm [Accessed 11/01/2022].

Nietzsche, Friedrich (1968) [1901]. *The Will to Power* (trans. Walter Kaufmann and M.J. Hollingdale). New York: Random House.

Nietzsche, Friedrich (1997a) [1881]. *Daybreak* (trans. R.J. Hollingdale). Cambridge: Cambridge UP.

Nietzsche, Friedrich (1997b) [1889]. *Twilight of the Idols* (trans. Richard Polt). Indianapolis: Hackett.

Nietzsche, Friedrich (2002) [1886]. *Beyond Good and Evil* (trans. Judith Norman). Cambridge: Cambridge UP.

Nietzsche, Friedrich (2004) [1888 and 1895]. *Ecce Homo and The Antichrist* (trans. Thomas Wayne). New York: Algora.

Nietzsche, Friedrich (2005) [1878–1880]. *Human, All Too Human. A Book for Free Spirits* (trans. R.J. Hollingdale). Cambridge: Cambridge UP.

Nietzsche, Friedrich (2006) [1887]. *On the Genealogy of Morals* (trans. Carol Diethe). Cambridge: Cambridge UP.

Nilsen, Håvard (2008). "Gestalt and Totality. The Case of Merleau-Ponty and Gestalt Psychology". *Nordicum-Mediterraneum. Icelandic E-journal of Nordic and Mediterranean Studies*, 3(2) https://nome.unak.is/previous-issues/issues/vol3_2/nilsen.html [Accessed 07/06/2022].

Noelle-Neumann, Elisabeth (1991) [1973]. "The Theory of Public Opinion: The Concept of the Spiral of Silence". In Anderson, James A. (Ed.), *Communication Yearbook*, 14: 256–287. Newbury Park: Sage.

Noonan, Gerald (1988). "Canadian Duality and the Colonization of Humour". *College English*, 50(8): 912–919.

Noonan, Jeff (2018). *Embodiment and the Meaning of Life*. Ottawa & Kingston: McGill-Queen's UP.

Noonan, Will (2011). "Reflecting Back, or What Can the French Tell the English about Humour?" *Sydney Studies in English*, 37: 92–115.

Nordhoff, Charles (1965) [1875]. *The Communistic Societies of the United States*. New York: Shocken.

Norlock, Kate (2014). "Jean Harvey, 1947–2014". *Feminist Philosophers. News Feminist Philosophers Can Use*, https://feministphilosophers.wordpress.com/2014/04/22/jean-harvey-1955-2014/ [Accessed 26/08/2022].

Nors, Sofie R. (2018). "How I, A Single Gal, Became More Attracted to Dildos Than Real Dick". *Fizzy Mag*, https://fizzymag.com/articles/dildos-do-it-better-than-dick [Accessed 18/05/2022].

North, David (2015). "Le discours hypocrite de la 'liberté d'expression' au lendemain de l'attaque contre Charlie Hebdo". *Global Research*, http://www.mondialisation.ca/le-discours-hypocrite-de-la-liberte-dexpression-au-lendemain-de-lattaque-contre-charlie-hebdo/5424215.

Nosov, N.R. Ganelin and Likhacëv, D. (Eds.) (1980). *Lineamenti di storia dell'URSS* (trans. Libreria italiana). Moscow: Progress.

Nussbaum, Martha (2010). *Not for Profit. Why Democracy Needs the Humanities*. Princeton: Princeton UP.

O'Neil, Cathy (2022). *The Shame Machine. Who Profits in the New Age of Humiliation*. New York: Penguin Random House.

O'Pray, Michael (1984). "Censoring Video?" *Art Monthly*, 80: 36.

O'Rourke, Shane (2016). "The Emancipation of the Serfs in Europe". In Eltis, David *et al.* (Eds.), *The Cambridge World History of Slavery*, vol. 4: 422–440. Cambridge: Cambridge UP.

Oakeshott, Michael (2004) [1948]. "The Voice of Conversation in the Education of Mankind". In *What Is History? And Other Essays* (ed. Luke O'Sullivan), 187–199. Exeter: Imprint Academic.

Oboler, Andre (2015). "After the Charlie Hebdo Attack: The Line between Freedom of Expression and Hate Speech". *Kantor Center Position Papers*, https://ohpi.org.au/line-between-freedom-of-expression-and-hate-speech/ [Accessed 26/08/2022].

OECD (2018). "Is the Last Mile the Longest? Economic Gains from Gender Equality in Nordic Countries", https://www.oecd.org/els/is-the-last-mile-the-longest-economic-gains-from-gender-equality-in-nordic-countries-9789264300040-en.htm [Accessed 02/10/2022].

Ogien, Ruwen (2003). "Libéraux et Pornographes". *Raisons Politiques*, 3(11): 5–28.

Ogien, Ruwen (2005). *La panique morale*. Paris: Grasset.

Ogien, Ruwen (2007). *La liberté d'offenser. Le sexe, l'art et la morale*. Paris: La Musardine.

Ogien, Ruwen (2008) [2003]. *Penser la pornographie*, 2nd ed. Paris: PUF.

Ojala, Martta Karolina (2019). "More Than Just Pleasure: A Study on Finnish Women's Use of Pornography". MA. University of Oslo.

Okabe, Tsugumi and Pelletier-Gagnon, Jérémie (2019). "Playing with Pain: The Politics of *Asobigokoro* in *Enzai Falsely Accused*". *Journal of the Japanese Association for Digital Humanities*, 4(1): 37–53.

Okwoli Ogba, Martin (2022). "Bizarre Masculinity. Female Responses to Rape Jokes on Social Media in Nigeria". In Chukwumah, Ignatius (Ed.), *Sexual Humour in Africa. Gender, Jokes, and Societal Change*, 243–256. London: Routledge.

Olin, Lauren (2020). "The Comic Stance". In Amir, Lydia B. (Ed.), *Philosophy of Humor Yearbook*, 1: 49–71. Berlin: De Gruyter.

Oliver, Sharma (2001). "Claims of Satanic Ritual Abuse Are Unsubstantiated". In Roleff, Tamara L. (Ed.), *Satanism*, 49–66. San Diego: Greenhaven.

Omar, Qais Omar Darwesh and Biçeroğlu, Ekrem (2021). "UNESCO Adopts Pro-Palestinian Resolutions". *AA*, https://www.aa.com.tr/en/middle-east/unesco-adopts-pro-palestinian-resolutions/2391474 [Accessed 17/05/2022].

Onion, Amanda et al. (2020) "Satirical Writer, Voltaire, Is Imprisoned in the Bastille". *History*, https://www.history.com/this-day-in-history/voltaire-is-imprisoned-in-the-bastille [Accessed 26/08/2022].

Onyanga-Omara, Jane (2015). "Video Shows Paris Gunman Pledging Allegiance to Islamic State". *USA Today*, https://eu.usatoday.com/story/news/world/2015/01/11/video-gunman-islamic-state/21589723/ [Accessed 26/08/2022].

Orrell, David (2017). *Economyths: 11 Ways That Economics Gets It Wrong*, 2nd ed. London: Icon.

Ortega y Gasset, José (1964) [1929]. *What Is Philosophy?* (trans Mildred Adams). New York: Norton.

Orwell, George (2014) [1944]. *Animal Farm*. Adelaide: eBooks, https://ia800905.us.archive.org/25/items/AnimalFarmByGeorgeOrwell/Animal%20Farm%20by%20George%20Orwell.pdf [Accessed 28/01/2023].

Orwell, George (1949). *1984*. Australia: Planet Ebook, https://rauterberg.employee.id.tue.nl/lecturenotes/DDM110%20CAS/Orwell-1949%201984.pdf [Accessed 17/05/2022].

Ostrower, Chaya (2015). "Humor as a Defense Mechanism During the Holocaust". *Interpretation*, 69(2): 183–195.

Otto, Beatrice K. (2001). *Fools Are Everywhere. The Court Jester around the World*. Chicago: University of Chicago Press.

Ovadia, Moni (1998). *L'ebreo che ride. L'umorismo ebraico in otto lezioni e duecento storielle*. Turin: Einaudi.

Ovidio, Publio Nasone (2013) [8 AD]. *Metamorfosi*. Novara: UTET.

Özveren, Eyüp (2012). "Veblen's 'Higher Learning': The Scientist as Sisyphus in the Iron Cage of a University". In Reinert, Erik S. and Viano, Francesca (Eds.), *Thorstein Veblen. Economics for an Age of Crises*, 257–280. Viano. London: Anthem.

Paasonen, Susanna (2010). "Good Amateurs: Erotica Writing and Notions of Quality". In Attwood, Feona (Ed.), *Porn.com: Making Sense of Online Pornography*, 138–154. New York: Peter Lang.

Paasonen, Susanna (2019). "Monstrous Resonance: Affect and Animated Pornography". In van Alphen, Ernst and Jirsa, Tomáš (Eds.), *How to Do Things with Affects: Affective Triggers in Aesthetic Forms and Cultural Practices*, 143–162. Amsterdam: Brill.

Paasonen, Susanna (2021). "'We Watch Porn for the Fucking, Not for the Romantic Tiptoeing': Extremity, Fantasy and Women's Porn Use". *Porn Studies*, https://doi.org/10.1080/23268743.2021.1956366 [Accessed 28/11/2021].

Paasonen, Susanna, Nikunen, Kaarina and Saarenmaa, Laura (Eds.) (2007). *Pornification: Sex and Sexuality in Media Culture*. Oxford: Berg.

Pagani, Marco, George, Whaley and Czerwinski, David (2022). "Frameworks for Assessing Financial Censorships and Its Implications". *Journal of Accounting and Finance*, 22(1): 79–90.

Paglia, Camille (2008). "Fresh Blood for the Vampire". *Salon*, https://www.salon.com/2008/09/10/palin_10/ [Accessed 26/08/2022].

Paglia, Camille (2017). *Free Women, Free Men. Sex, Gender, Feminism*. New York: Pantheon.
Pal, Amitbah and Galbraith, John Kenneth (2000). "John Kenneth Galbraith Interview". *The Progressive Magazine*, https://progressive.org/magazine/john-kenneth-galbraith-interview/ [Accessed 07/06/2022].
Pandita, Venerable (2017). "Who Are the *Chabbaggiya* Monks and Nuns?" *Journal of Buddhist Ethics*, 24: 102–18.
Panksepp, Jaak (2007). "Neuroevolutionary Sources of Laughter and Social Joy: Modelling Primal Human Laughter in Rats". *Behavioural Brain Research*, 182(2): 231–244.
Pareto, Vilfredo (1914). *Il mito virtuista e la letteratura immorale*, 2nd ed. Rome: Lux.
Pareto, Vilfredo (1935) [1916]. *The Mind and Society* (trans. Andrew Bongiorno and Arthur Livingston), 4 vols. New York: Harcourt, Brace.
Pareyson, Luigi (2013) [2005]. *Truth and Interpretation* (trans. Robert T. Valgenti). Albany: SUNY Press.
Park, Sihyun and Sin-Hyang, Kim (2019). "Who Are the Victims and Who Are the Perpetrators in Dating Violence? Sharing the Role of Victim and Perpetrator". *Trauma, Violence and Abuse*, 20(5): 732–741.
Parker, Richard (2005). *John Kenneth Galbraith. His Life, His Politics, His Economics*. New York: Farrar, Straus & Giroux.
Parsons, Talcott (1991) [1937]. *The Social System*. London: Routledge.
Part, Kai *et al*. (2011). "Gender Differences in Factors Associated with Sexual Intercourse among Estonian Adolescents". *Scandinavian Journal of Public Health*, 39: 389–395.
Partito comunista internazionale (2015). "Giornate capitalistiche: Schiavitù, rivolta, repressione", https://sinistracomunistainternazionale.files.wordpress.com/2015/06/giornate-capitalistiche-schiavitc3b9-rivolta-repressione.pdf [Accessed 26/08/2022].
Pascal, Blaise (1993) [1670]. *Pensieri* (trans. Marco Magni). Milan: Rusconi.
Pasolini, Pier Paolo (2008) [1975]. *Scritti Corsari*. Milan: Garzanti.
Patrinou, Sonia (2017). "Pornohealing: Pornography as a Healing Process for Individuals with a History of Sexual Violence". *Kohl: A Journal for Body and Gender Research*, 3(2): 216–231.
Pearson, Geoff (2012). *An Ethnography of English Football Fans. Cans, Cops and Carnivals*. Manchester: Manchester UP.
Peksen Yakar, Azime and Demirtepe Saygili, Dilek (2018). "'Oh, Cruelty, To Steal My Basil-Pot Away from Me!': The Reflection of Bereavement in John Keats' Isabella, or The Pot of Basil". *DTCF Dergisi*, 58(1): 732–741.
Pelletier-Gagnon, Jérémie (2011). "Video Games and Japaneseness: An Analysis of Localization and Circulation of Japanese Video Games in North America". MA. McGill University.
Penelas, Federico (2019). "Rorty on Hermeneutical Injustice, Liberal Redescription and Utopian Imagination". *Éndoxa*, 43: 313–333.
Pereira Portes, Gustavo and Haig, Edward (2013). "Seeking a Methodology for the Analysis of the Influence of Anime on Brazilian Youth – A Post-Jungian Approach". *Matrizes*, 7(1): 247–262.
Perelman, Chaïm and Olbrechts-Tyteca, Lucie (1969) [1958]. *The New Rhetoric. A Treatise on Argumentation* (trans. John Wilkinson and Purcell Weaver). Notre Dame: Notre Dame UP.
Perera, Sasanka and Pathak, Dev Nath (Eds.) (2022). *Humour and the Performance of Power in South Asia: Anxiety, Laughter and Politics in Unstable Times*. London: Routledge.
Peresin, Anita and Cervone, Alberto (2015). "The Western *Muhjirat* of ISIS". *Studies in Conflict and Terrorism*, 38(7): 495–509.
Pérez-Aranda, Adrian *et al*. (2019). "Laughing Away the Pain: A Narrative Review of Humour, Sense of Humour and Pain". *European Journal of Pain*, 23: 220–233.

Perlmutter, Daniel D. (2002). "On Incongruities and Logical Inconsistencies in Humor: The Delicate Balance". *Humor: International Journal of Humor Research*, 15: 155–168.
Pernecky, Tomas (2016). *Epistemology and Metaphysics for Qualitative Research*. Los Angeles: Sage.
Perrault, Gilles (Ed.) (1998). *Livre noir du capitalisme*. Pantin: Le Temps des Cerises.
Perry, John (2016). "Putting Hell First: Cruelty, Historicism, and the Missing Moral Theory of Damnation". *Scottish Journal of Theology*, 69(1): 1–19.
Perry, Lucy and Schwarz, Alexander (Eds.) (2011). *Behaving Like Fools: Voice, Gesture, and Laughter in Texts, Manuscripts, and Early Books*. Turnhout: Brepols.
Petersen, Corinne (2020). "Comedy as a Form of Cathartic Life Writing". *TCNJ Journal of Student Scholarship*, 22, https://joss.tcnj.edu/wp-content/uploads/sites/176/2020/04/2020-Petersen-Comedy-.pdf [Accessed 10/06/2022].
Peterson, Jordan (1999). *Maps of Meaning: The Architecture of Belief*. New York: Routledge.
Pezzuto, Sophie and Comella, Lynn (2020). "Trans Pornography. Mapping an Emerging Field". *Transgender Studies Quarterly*, 7(2): 152–171.
Phillips, Anita (1998). *A Defence of Masochism*. London: Faber & Faber.
Pianigiani, Pietro O. (1907). *Vocabolario etimologico della lingua italiana*. Rome: Società editrice Dante Alighieri.
Piazza, Jared, Landy, Justin F. and Goodwin, Geoffrey P. (2014). "Cruel Nature: Harmfulness as an Important, Overlooked Dimension in Judgments of Moral Standing". *Cognition*, 131: 108–124.
Picart, Caroline Joan and Frank, David A. (2006). *Frames of Evil. The Holocaust as Horror in American Film*. Carbondale: Southern Illinois UP.
Picheta, Rob (2021). "Laughed Off for Years as Gaffes, Prince Philip's Outbursts Complicate His Legacy". *CNN*, https://edition.cnn.com/2021/04/09/uk/prince-philip-outbursts-legacy-intl-gbr-cmd/index.html [Accessed 26/08/2022].
Piemonte, Nicole M. (2015). "Last Laughs: Gallows Humor and Medical Education". *Journal of Medical Humanities*, 36: 375–390.
Piketty, Thomas (2014) [2013]. *Capital in Twenty-First Century* (trans. Arthur Goldhammer). Cambridge, MA: Belknap. Electronic version.
Pinto, Caterina (2015). "I vignettisti arabi stanno con *Charlie Hebdo*". *Arab Media Report*, http://arabmediareport.it/i-vignettisti-arabi-stanno-con-charlie-hebdo/ [Accessed 26/08/2022].
Pirandello, Luigi (1920) [1908]. *L'umorismo. Saggio*, 2nd ed. Florence: Luigi Battistelli.
Pirandello, Luigi (1982) [ca. 1890]. "'Elegie' non comprese nella raccolta del 1895". In *Tutte le poesie* (ed. Manlio Lo Vecchio-Musti), 195–201. Milan: Mondadori, https://www.liberliber.it/online/autori/autori-p/luigi-pirandello/tutte-le-poesie/ [Accessed 29/11/2022].
Pirandello, Luigi (1992) [1926]. *One, No One and One Hundred Thousand* (trans. William Weaver). Venice: Marsilio.
Pirandello, Luigi (1994) [1901]. *L'esclusa*, https://www.academia.edu/34682402/Luigi_Pirandello_Lesclusa_pdf [Accessed 13/10/2022].
Pius X, Pope (1907). "Pascendi Dominici Gregis", https://www.vatican.va/content/pius-x/en/encyclicals/documents/hf_p-x_enc_19070908_pascendi-dominici-gregis.html [Accessed 04/06/2022].
Plato (1903) [4th century BC]. *Cratylus*. In *Platonis Opera* (ed. E.A. Duke *et al.*), vol. 1. Oxford: Oxford UP, http://www.perseus.tufts.edu/hopper/text?doc=Perseus%3Atext%3A1999.01.0171%3Atext%3DCrat.%3Apage%3D402 [Accessed 17/05/2022].
Pluchino, Alessandro *et al.* (2018). "Talent Versus Luck: The Role of Randomness in Success and Failure". *Advances in Complex Systems*, 21(3–4), https://www.worldscientific.com/doi/epdf/10.1142/S0219525918500145 [Accessed 07/06/2022].

Plumptre, Andrew J. *et al.* (2021). "Where Might We Find Ecologically Intact Communities?" *Frontiers in Forests and Global Change* 4, article 626635: 1–13.

Polanyi, Karl (2001) [1944]. *The Great Transformation. The Political and Economic Origins of Our Time*, 2nd ed. Boston: Beacon.

Polanyi, Michael (1962a). "History and Hope: An Analysis of Our Age". *McEnerney Lectures*, https://youtu.be/5FT-NxvE7NQ [Accessed 21/09/2021].

Polanyi, Michael (1962b). "The Unaccountable Element in Science". *Philosophy Today*, 6(3): 171–182.

Polanyi, Michael (1962c) [1958]. *Personal Knowledge: Towards a Post-Critical Philosophy*, reprint. London: Routledge.

Polanyi, Michael (1969a). *Knowing and Being: Essays*. London: Routledge & Kegan Paul.

Polanyi, Michael (1969b) [1959]. *The Study of Man*. Chicago: Chicago UP.

Polanyi, Michael (2009) [1966]. *The Tacit Dimension*. London: Routledge.

Polanyi, Michael (2023) [1954]. "Rules of Rightness". *Tradition and Discovery*, 49(1): 4–13.

Pope, Nicole (2012). *Honor Killings in the Twenty First Century*. New York: Palgrave Macmillan.

Popper, Karl (1987) [1981]. "Toleration and Intellectual Responsibility". In Mendus, Susan and Edwards, David (Eds.), *On Toleration*, 17–34. Oxford: Clarendon.

Popper, Karl (1994). *Cattiva maestra televisione* (trans. Francesco Erbani). Milan: Reset.

Popper, Karl (1997). *Lessons of this Century: With Talks on Freedom and the Democratic State*. London: Routledge.

Poullain de la Barre, François (1677) [1673]. *The Woman as Good as the Man; Or, the Equality of Both Sexes* (trans. A.L. [sic]). London: N. Brooks, https://quod.lib.umich.edu/cgi/t/text/text-idx?c=eebo;idno=A55529.0001.001 [Accessed 25/04/2022].

Priestley, J.B. (1929). *English Humour*. London: Longmans, Green, https://ia801700.us.archive.org/10/items/dli.ernet.475665/475665-English%20Humour%281929%29_text.pdf [Accessed 07/02/2023].

Prusa, Igor (2016). "Heroes Beyond Good and Evil. Theorising Transgressivity in Japanese and Western Fiction". *Electronic Journal of Contemporary Japanese Studies*, 16(1), https://www.researchgate.net/profile/Igor-Prusa/publication/350787604_Heroes_Beyond_Good_and_Evil_Theorizing_Transgressivity_in_Japanese_and_Western_Fiction/links/6071c85ba6fdcc5f77982250/Heroes-Beyond-Good-and-Evil-Theorizing-Transgressivity-in-Japanese-and-Western-Fiction.pdf [Accessed 07/07/2022].

Prust, Richard and Geller, Jeffrey (2019). *Personal Identity in Moral and Legal Reasoning*. Wilmington: Vernon.

Psarras, Dimitris and Karidas, Dimitris (2019). "A Revolutionary from the OECD – The Castoriadis/Poulantzas Debate". *Verso / Blog*, https://www.versobooks.com/blogs/4427-a-revolutionary-from-the-oecd-the-castoriadis-poulantzas-debate [Accessed 26/08/2022].

Putnam, Hilary (1992). *Renewing Philosophy*. Cambridge, MA: Harvard UP.

Quek, Natasha and Huzaifah Bin Othman Alkaff, Syed (2019). "Analysis of the Tunisian Foreign Terrorist Fighters Phenomenon". *Counter-Terrorist Trends and Analyses*, 11(5): 1–5.

Quiggin, John (2010). *Zombie Economics. How Dead Ideas Still Walk Among Us*. Princeton: Princeton UP.

Quintilian (1920) [1st century AD]. *Institutio oratoria* (trans. Harold E. Butler). London: William Heinemann, http://www.perseus.tufts.edu/hopper/searchresults?q=quintilian [Accessed 22/10/2022].

Räikkä, Juha and Weyermann, Daniel (2011). "Cultural Diversity and the Shared Premises Requirement". *Nordicum-Mediterraneum. Icelandic E-journal of Nordic and Mediterranean Studies*, 6(1), https://nome.unak.is/wordpress/06-1/conference-paper/cultural-diversity-and-the-shared-premises-requirement/ [Accessed 26/08/2022].

Ralkovski, Mark (Ed.) (2021). *Dave Chappelle and Philosophy. When Keeping It Wrong Gets Real.* Chicago: Open Universe.
Ramachandran, V.S. (1998). "The Neurology and Evolution of Humor, Laughter, and Smiling: The False Alarm Theory". *Medical Hypotheses*, 51(4): 351–354.
Ramos Sarment, Érica and Baltar, Mariana (2021). "Redes de deboche e excess. Práticas performáticas no pós-pornó de América Latina". *Ecopos*, 24(1): 75–98.
Rand, Ayn (1997). *Journals of Ayn Rand* (ed. Daniel Harriamn). New York: Penguin.
Randall, Richard S. (1989). *Freedom and Taboo. Pornography and the Politics of a Self Divided.* Berkeley: University of California Press.
Rankin, Jennifer (2018). "Paris Attacks Suspect Salah Abdeslam Gets 20-Year Sentence in Belgium". *The Guardian*, https://www.theguardian.com/world/2018/apr/23/paris-attacks-suspect-salah-abdeslam-gets-20-year-sentence-in-belgium [Accessed 26/08/2022].
Ranstorp, Magnus (1998). "Interpreting the Broader Context and Meaning of Bin-Laden's *Fatwa*". *Studies in Conflict and Terrorism*, 21(4): 321–330.
Raphael, D.D. (Ed.) (1991). *British Moralists 1650–1800*, 2 vols. Indianapolis: Hackett.
Raskin, Victor (1979). "Semantic Mechanisms of Humor". *Proceedings of the Fifth Annual Meeting of the Berkeley Linguistics Society*, 325–335.
Raskin, Victor (1985). *Semantic Mechanisms of Humor.* Dordrecht: Reidel.
Redwine, Jr., James D. (1961). "Beyond Psychology: The Moral Basis of Jonson's Theory of Humour Characterization". *ELH*, 28(4): 316–334.
Rees, Stuart (2020). *Cruelty or Humanity: Challenges, Opportunities and Responsibilities.* Bristol: Bristol UP.
Regan, Tom (1975). "The Moral Basis of Vegetarianism". *Canadian Journal of Philosophy*, 5(2): 181–214.
Regan, Tom (1983). *The Case for Animal Rights.* Berkeley: California UP.
Reich, Wilhelm (1953). *The Murder of Christ.* New York: Simon & Schuster.
Reich, Wilhelm (1968) [1947]. *The Discovery of the Orgone. Volume 1: The Function of the Orgasm*, 2nd ed. New York: Farrar, Straus & Giroux.
Reinert, Erik S. (2006). "Institutionalism Ancient, Old and New. A Historical Perspective on Institutions and Uneven Development". *UNU-WIDER*, research paper no. 1006/77, http://hdl.handle.net/10419/63562 [Accessed 13/01/2023].
Rendtorff, Jacob Dahl (2004). "Det fælles gode og samfundsansvar i det økonomiske liv: er virksomheden andet og mere end et instrument til egoistisk profitmaksimering?" In Harbo, Niels Jakob et al. (Eds.), *Det gode liv : Mere end dig selv*, 187–213. Aarhus: Forlaget Philosophia.
Rendtorff, Jacob Dahl (2010). "Philosophy of Management: Concepts of Management from the Perspectives of Systems Theory, Phenomenological Hermeneutics, Corporate Religion, and Existentialism". In Koslowski, Peter (Ed.), *Elements of a Philosophy of Management and Organization*, 19–44. Berlin: Springer.
Rendtorff, Jacob Dahl (2020). *Moral Blindness in Business. A Social Theory of Evil in Organizations and Institutions.* London: Palgrave Macmillan.
Rhonheimer, Martin (2012). "Capitalism, Free Market Economy, and the Common Good: The Role of State Authorities in the Economic Sector". In Schlag, M. and Mercado, J.A. (Eds.), *Free Markets and the Culture of Common Good*, 3–40. Dordrecht, Springer.
Rican, Pavel (1999). "Cruelty as Experience and as Motive". *Ceskoslovenska Psychologie*, 43(6): 543–555.

Rich, Frank (2001). "Naked Capitalists". *The New York Times Magazine*, https://www.nytimes.com/2001/05/20/magazine/naked-capitalists.html [Accessed 26/08/2022].

Richards, Ivor Armstrong (1965) [1936]. *The Philosophy of Rhetoric*. Oxford: Oxford UP.

Richards, Kirsten and Kruger, Gert (2017). "Humor Styles as Moderators in the Relationship between Perceived Stress and Physical Health". *SAGE Open*, 7(2): 1–8.

Richlin, Amy (Ed.) (1992). *Pornography and Representation in Greece and Rome*. Oxford: Oxford UP.

Ringer, Beat (2015). "Neoliberalismus und Neokonservatismus: Eine historische Skizze". In *Denknetz Jahrbuch 2015*, 8–30. Zurich: Denknetz.

Roberts, Alan (2019). *A Philosophy of Humour*. Cham: Palgrave Macmillan.

Roberts, Stephen G.H. (2016). "Clowning and Tragic Clowning: Miguel de Unamuno as a Funny Writer". *Romance Quarterly*, 63(2/2): 53–62.

Robertson, J.G. (1939). *Lessing's Dramatic Theory. Being an Introduction to & Commentary on His Hamburgische Dramaturgie*. Cambridge: Cambridge UP.

Robinson, Majied (2022). "The Population Size of Muhammad's Mecca and the Creation of the Quraysh". *Der Islam*, 99(1): 10–37.

Rochefoucauld, François Duc de la (1871) [1693]. *Reflections; Or, Sentences and Moral Maxims* (trans. J.W. Willis Bund and J. Hain Friswell). London: Simpson Low, Son, and Marston, https://www.gutenberg.org/files/9105/9105-h/9105-h.htm [Accessed 11/07/2022].

Roesler, Christian (2012). "Are Archetypes Transmitted More by Culture than Biology? Questions Arising from Conceptualizations of the Archetype". *The Journal of Analytical Psychology*, 57(2): 223–246.

Roesler, Christian (Ed.) (2018). *Research in Analytical Psychology. Empirical Research*. London: Routledge.

Roldán, Concha, Brauerb, Daniel and Rohbeck, Johannes (Eds.) (2018). *Philosophy of Globalization*. Berlin: De Gruyter.

Rorty, Richard (1989). *Contingency, Irony, and Solidarity*. Cambridge, MA: Cambridge UP.

Rorty, Richard (1993). "Taking Time Seriously", https://www.youtube.com/watch?v=c1BlCjVFFLk [Accessed 21/09/2021].

Rorty, Richard (2001). "The Decline of Redemptive Truth and the Rise of a Literary Culture". *The John M. Olin Center for Inquiry into the Theory and Practice of Democracy*, http://olincenter.uchicago.edu/pdf/rorty.pdf [Accessed 21/09/2021].

Rose, Nikolas and Novas, Carlos (2005) "Biological Citizenship". In Ong, Ahiwa and Collier, Stephen (Eds.), *Global Assemblages: Technology, Politics and Ethics as Anthropological Problems*, 439–463. Maiden: Blackwell.

Rosen, Ralph M. (2005). "Galen, Satire and the Compulsion to Instruct". In Horstmanshoff, Manfred (Ed.), *Hippocrates and Medical Education*, 323–342. Leiden: Brill.

Rosenberg, Clifford D. (2006). *Policing Paris: The Origins of Modern Immigration Control Between the Wars*. Ithaca, NY: Cornell UP.

Rosenblatt, Helena (2018). *The Lost History of Liberalism. From Ancient Rome to the Twenty-First Century*. Princeton: Princeton UP.

Rosenthal, Fran (2011) [1956]. *Humor in Early Islam*. Leiden: Brill.

Roshwald, Mordechai (1973a). "Marginal Jewish Sects in Israel (I)". *International Journal of Middle East Studies*, 4(2): 219–237.

Roshwald, Mordechai (1973b). "Marginal Jewish Sects in Israel (II)". *International Journal of Middle East Studies*, 4(3): 328–354.

Ross, Alison (1998). *The Language of Humour*. London: Routledge.

Rosset, Clément (1993) [1983–1988]. *Joyful Cruelty* (trans. David F. Bell). Oxford: Oxford UP.
Roszak, Piotr (2013). "Anatomy of Ludic Pleasure in Thomas Aquinas". *Pensamiento y Cultura*, 16(2): 50–71.
Rotton, James and Shats, Mark (1996). "Effects of State Humor, Expectancies, and Choice on Postsurgical Mood and Self-Medication: A Field Experiment". *Journal of Applied Social Psychology*, 26: 1775–1794.
Rousseau, Jean-Jacques (1889) [1782–1789]. *Les confessions*. Paris: Librérie artistique Launette.
Rousseau, Jean-Jacques (1997) [1755]. "Discourse on the Origin and Foundation of Inequality among Mankind". In *The Discourses, and Other Early Political Writings* (trans. Victor Gourevitch), 111–222. Cambridge: Cambridge UP.
Rowe, Alison and Regehr, Cheryl (2010). "Whatever Gets You Through Today: An Examination of Cynical Humor Among Emergency Service Professionals". *Journal of Loss and Trauma*, 15(5): 448–464.
Rowland, Susan (2016). *Remembering Dionysus. Revisioning Psychology and Literature in C.G. Jung and James Hillman*. London: Routledge.
Rubin, Miri (Ed.) (1997). *The Work of Jacques Le Goff and the Challenges of Medieval History*. Woodbridge: Boydell.
Rubin, Roger H. (2001). "Alternative Lifestyles Revisited, or Whatever Happened to Swingers, Group Marriages, and Communes?" *Journal of Family Issues*, 22(6): 711–726.
Rubinson, Gregory J. (2000). "'On the Beach of Elsewhere': Angela Carter's Moral Pornography and the Critique of Gender Archetypes". *Women's Studies*, 29(6): 717–740.
Ruch, Willibald and Köhler, Gabriele (1998). "A Temperament Approach to Humor". In Ruch, Willibald (Ed.), *The Sense of Humor. Explorations of a Personality Characteristic*, 203–228. Berlin: De Gruyter.
Ruch, Willibald et al. (1993). "Toward an Empirical Verification of the General Theory of Verbal Humor". *Humor: International Journal of Humor Research*, 6(2): 123–136.
Rundell, John (2012). "Violence, Cruelty, Power: Reflections on Heteronomy". *Cosmos and History: The Journal of Natural and Social Philosophy*, 8(2): 3–20.
Russell, Bertrand (1920). *The Practice and Theory of Bolshevism*. London: George Allen & Unwin.
Russell, Bertrand (1998) [1934]. "What to Believe". In *Mortals and Others, Volume II. American Essays 1931–1935*, 127–128. (ed. Harry Ruja). London: Routledge.
Russell, Bertrand (2009). *Basic Writings*. London: Routledge.
Russell, Bertrand (2016) [1962]. 22 January 1962 Letter to Sir Oswald Mosley, https://lettersofnote.com/2016/02/02/every-ounce-of-my-energy/ [Accessed 24/08/2022].
Sade, Marquis de (1999) [1801]. *Histoire de Juliette ou les prospérités du vice*. In Selva, T. and Franval, J. (Eds.), *Oeuvres du Marquis de Sade*. Sade-ecrivain, http://www.sade-ecrivain.com/juliette/juliette.htm [Accessed 18/05/2001].
Sade, Marquis de (2010) [1795]. *La philosophie dans le boudoir*. Chicoutimi: University of Quebec http://classiques.uqac.ca/classiques/sade_marquis_de/sade_philo_dans_le_boudoir/sade_philo_dans_le_boudoir.html [Accessed 19/02/2022].
Salem, Harry, Ternay Jr., Andrew L. and Smart, Jeffrey K. (2019). "Brief History and Use of Chemical Warfare Agents in Warfare and Terrorism". In Lukey, Brian J., Romano Jr., James A. and Salem, Harry (Eds.), *Chemical Warfare Agents. Biomedical and Psychological Effects, Medical Countermeasures, and Emergency Response*, 3rd ed., 3–16. Boca Raton: CRC.
Santayana, George (1896). *The Sense of Beauty. Being the Outlines of Aesthetic Theory*. New York: C. Scribner's Sons, https://www.gutenberg.org/ebooks/26842 [Accessed 01/05/2022].

Santayana, George (1998) [1912]. *The Genteel Tradition* (ed. Douglas L. Wilson). Lincoln: University of Nebraska Press.

Santoro-Brienza, Liberato (2004). "On Laughter, Comicality, Humour". *Literature and Aesthetics*, 14(1): 71–87.

Sarink, Federico S.M. and García-Montes, José (2023). "Humor Interventions in Psychotherapy and Their Effect on Levels of Depression and Anxiety in Adult Clients, a Systematic Review". *Frontiers Psychiatry*, doi: 10.3389/fpsyt.2022.1049476 [Accessed 27/01/2023].

Sartre, Jean-Paul (1973) [1945]. *The Age of Reason* (trans. Eric Sutton). London: Penguin.

Saunders, David (2009). "France on the Knife-Edge of Religion: Commemorating the Centenary of the Law of 9 December 1905 on the Separation of Church and State". In Levey, Geoffrey Brahm and Modood, Tariq (Eds.), *Secularism, Religion and Multicultural Citizenship*, 56–82. Cambridge: Cambridge UP.

Scammell, Michael (2009). *Koestler: The Literary and Political Odyssey of a Twentieth-Century Skeptic*. New York: Random House.

Schlefer, Jonathan (2012). *The Assumptions Economists Make*. Cambridge, MA: Belknap.

Schmidt, Rich (2008). "Censor This Essay". In Jopp, Jenny (Ed.), *Campus Conversations. The Role of Freedom of Expression in a Multicultural and Democratic Society. Volume One: 2007–2008*, 195–214. Salem: Willamette University.

Schopenhauer, Arthur (1909) [1859]. *The World as Will and Idea* (trans. R.B. Haldane and J. Kemp), 3 vols, 3rd ed. London: Kegan Paul, https://www.gutenberg.org/files/38427/38427-h/38427-h.html [Accessed 19/02/2022].

Schritt, Jannik (2015). "'The Protests against Charlie Hebdo' in Niger: A Background Analysis". *Africa Spectrum*, 50(1): 49–64.

Schurman, Bart, Grol, Peter and Flower, Scott (2016). "Converts and Islamist Terrorism: An Introduction". *International Centre for Counter-Terrorism*, 7(3), doi: 10.19165/2016.2.03 [Accessed 26/08/2022].

Schwartz, Joseph (2001). "Commentary on David Black: Beyond the Death Drive Detour – How Can We Deepen Our Understanding of Cruelty, Malice, Hatred, Envy and Violence?" *British Journal of Clinical Psychotherapy*, 18(2): 199–203.

Schwartz, Stephen P. (2012). *A Brief History of Analytic Philosophy: From Russell to Rawls*. Chichester: Wiley & Sons.

Scott, George Riley (1996) [1960]. *History of Corporal Punishment*. London: Senate.

Scott, Joseph E. (1988). Review of *Attorney General's Commission on Pornography: Final Report July 1986*, *United States of America vs Sex: How the Meese Commission Lied About Pornography* by Phillip Nobile and Eric Nadler, and *Polluting the Censorship Debate: A Summary and Critique of the Final Report of the Attorney General's Commission on Pornography* by American Civil Liberties Union. *The Journal of Criminal Law and Criminology*, 78(4): 1145–1165.

Scott, Karly-Lynne (2016). "Performing Labour: Ethical Spectatorship and the Communication of Labour Conditions in Pornography". *Porn Studies*, 3(2): 120–132.

Scott, Tricia (2007). "Expression of Humour by Emergency Personnel Involved in Sudden Deathwork". *Mortality*, 12(4): 350–364.

Screech, Michael A. (2015). *Laughter at the Foot of the Cross*. Chicago: University of Chicago Press.

Seelow, Soren (2015). "Attentat à 'Charlie Hebdo': 'Vous allez payer car vous avez insulté le Prophète'". *Le Monde*, https://www.lemonde.fr/societe/article/2015/01/08/vous-allez-payer-car-vous-avez-insulte-le-prophete_4551820_3224.html [Accessed 26/08/2022].

Segal, Robert A. (2012). Review of *Fear of Jung: The Complex Doctrine and Emotional Science* by Theo A. Cope. *Religion*, 42(2): 351–354.
Senatore, Mauro (2018). "'This Obscure and Enigmatic Concept'. Philosophy of Cruelty in Nietzsche, Freud, and Beyond". *Itinera*, 15: 57–76.
Seneca (1900) [56 AD]. *De clementia* (ed. Carl Hosius), http://www.thelatinlibrary.com/sen/sen.clem.shtml [Accessed 4/01/2022].
Serrano Ruano, Delfina (Ed.) (2011). *Crueldad y compasión en la literatura árabe e islámica*. Cordoba: Servicio de Publicaciones de la Universidad de Córdoba.
Serumaga, Kalundi (2020). "It Ends How It Started". *The Elephant*, 1–6, https://www.theelephant.info/features/2020/10/09/it-ends-how-it-started/ [Accessed 26/08/2022].
Setia, Adi (2019). "Islam, the West and Human Rights Discourse: Towards a Mutually Protective Engagement". *Tafhim. IKIM Journal of Islam and the Contemporary World*, 12(1): 39–58.
Shaftesbury (1732) [1709]. "*Sensus communis*, an Essay on the Freedom of Wit and Humour in a Letter to a Friend". In *Characteristics of Men, Manners, Opinions, Times*, 5th edition, 59–150. London: Egbert Sanger, https://babel.hathitrust.org/cgi/pt?id=uc2.ark:/13960/t8nc5vm4x&view=1up&seq=361 [Accessed 01/05/2022].
Shaftesbury (1999) [1711]. "A Letter Concerning Enthusiasm to Lord ****". In *Characteristics of Men, Manners, Opinions, Times*, 4–28. Cambridge: Cambridge UP.
Shahak, Israel and Mezvinsky, Norton (1999). *Jewish Fundamentalism in Israel*. London: Pluto.
Shamloo, Sheida (2021). "Self-Censorship and Political Oppression". MA. Concordia University.
Shapiro-Phim, Toni (2020). "Embodying the Pain and Cruelty of Others". *International Journal of Transitional Justice*, 14: 209–219.
Sharifov, Mehmonsho (2006–2007). "The Self Between Political Chaos and the New Political 'Order' in Tajikistan". *Transcultural Studies*, 2–3: 315–326.
Shaw, Beau (2015). "Nietzsche, Humor and Masochism". *Israeli Journal for Humor Research*, 4(2): 31–50.
Shaw, George Bernard (2006) [1910]. *A Treatise on Parents and Children*. Fairbanks: Project Gutenberg Literary Archive Foundation, https://www.gutenberg.org/files/908/908-h/908-h.htm [Accessed 03/10/2022].
Shaw, Tom (2011). "Time to Be Heard: A Pilot Forum". Edinburgh: The Scottish Government.
Sheinerman, Marie-Rose and Limestahl, Caitlin (2019). "Finkelstein GS '87 Delivers Anti-Semitic Remarks at Panel on Black and Palestinian Solidarity". *The Daily Princetonian*, https://www.dailyprincetonian.com/article/2019/10/finkelstein-anti-semitic-remarks [Accessed 26/08/2022].
Shestov, Leo (1920) [1905]. *All Things Are Possible* (trans. S.S. Koteliansky). London: Martin Secker, https://www.gutenberg.org/ebooks/57369 [Accessed 19/02/2022].
Shklar, Judith (1984). *Ordinary Vices*. Oxford: Belknap.
Shklar, Judith (1989). "The Liberalism of Fear". In Rosenbaum, Nancy (Ed.), *Liberalism and the Moral Life*, 21–38. Harvard: Harvard UP.
Short, Philip (2004). *Pol Pot*. Paris: Denoël.
Shrage, Laurie (2022). "A Solution to the Problem of Rape by Fraud". In Boonin, David (Ed.), *The Palgrave Handbook of Sexual Ethics*, 387–403. Cham: Palgrave Macmillan.
Sidgwick, Henry (1907) [1874]. *The Methods of Ethics*, 7th ed. London: Macmillan.
Sigurðsson, Geir (2010). "In Praise of Illusions: Giacomo Leopardi's Ultraphilosophy". *Nordicum-Mediterraneum. Icelandic E-Journal of Nordic and Mediterranean Studies*, 5(1), https://nome.unak.is/wordpress/05-1/articles51/in-praise-of-illusions-giacomo-leopardis-ultraphilosophy/#_ftn33 [Accessed 21/09/2021].

Sills, Liz (2020). "The Evolution of the Funny: American Folk Hunmor and Gimbel's Cleverness Theory". In Amir, Lydia B. (Ed.), *Philosophy of Humor Yearbook*, 1: 73–96. Berlin: De Gruyter.
Silva Correia, Marco Paulo (2022). "O Humor no Ensino da Geografia", https://repositorio-aberto.up.pt/bitstream/10216/143093/2/573884.pdf [Accessed 7/12/2022].
Silvestri, Paolo and Walraevens, Benoît (2022). "The Wealth of Humans: Core, Periphery and Frontiers of Humanomics". *Journal of Economic Methodology*, doi: 10.1080/1350178X.2022.2160003 [Accessed 13/01/2023].
Simon, Alice (2019). "Les attentats de Charlie Hebdo du point de vue d'élèves dits 'musulmans'. Étude sur l'action politique de l'école". *Agora débats*, hal-02297500.
Simon, Elliott M. (2012). "Thomas More's Humor in his Religious Polemics". *Moreana*, 53(1–2): 7–50.
Simpson, James A. (1998). *The Laugh Shall be First*. Edinburgh: Saint Andrew Press.
Siswanto, Dwi Joko et al. (2023). "Islamic Economy, Maqashid Sharia Happiness Index and Islamic City Index". *Jurnal Cafetaria* 4(1): 87–97.
Shaktini, Namascar (Ed.) (2005). *On Monique Wittig. Theoretical, Political, and Literary Essays*. Urbana: University of Illinois Press.
Skinner, Quentin (2008). "Political Rhetoric and the Role of Ridicule". In Pulkkinen, Tujia (Ed.), *The Ashgate Research Companion to the Politics of Democratization in Europe: Concepts and Histories*, 137–150. Abingdon: Ashgate.
Skúlason, Páll (2015). *A Critique of Universities*, Reykjavik: University of Iceland Press.
Smart, Ninian (1981). *Beyond Ideology: Religion and the Future of Western Civilization*. San Francisco: Harper & Row, https://www.giffordlectures.org/books/beyond-ideology-religion-and-future-western-civilization [Accessed 22/09/2022].
Smith, Adam (1790) [1759]. *The Theory of Moral Sentiments*. London: A. Millar, https://quod.lib.umich.edu/cgi/t/text/text-idx?c=ecco;idno=004894986.0001.000 [Accessed 19/02/2022].
Smith, Adam (1904) [1776]. *An Inquiry into the Nature and Causes of the Wealth of Nations*. London: Methuen, https://oll.libertyfund.org/title/smith-an-inquiry-into-the-nature-and-causes-of-the-wealth-of-nations-cannan-ed-in-2-vols [Accessed 19/02/2022].
Smith, David (2012). "Somali Comedian Who Mocked Islamists is Shot Dead". *The Guardian*, https://www.theguardian.com/world/2012/aug/01/somali-comedian-islamists-shot-dead [Accessed 26/08/2022].
Smith, Vernon L. and Wilson, Bart J. (2019). *Humanomics. Moral Sentiments and the Wealth of Nations for the Twenty-first Century*. Cambridge: Cambridge UP.
Smits, Anne-May (2020). "The Invisibility of Female Masturbation: How Young Dutch Women Relate to Masturbation". MA. Utrecht University.
Smythe, Arthur J. (2010) [1898]. *The Life of William Terriss, Actor*. Whitefish: Kessinger.
Snarey, John R. (1985). "Cross-Cultural Universality of Social-Moral Development: A Critical Review of Kohlbergian Research". *Psychological Bulletin*, 97(2): 202–232.
Snow, Edward (1989). "Theorizing the Male Gaze: Some Problems". *Representations*, 25: 30–41.
Snyder, Edward D. (1920). "The Wild Irish: A Study of Some English Satires against the Irish, Scots, and Welsh". *Modern Philology*, 17(12): 147–185.
Soble, Alan (1986). *Pornography: Marxism, Feminism, and the Future of Sexuality*. New Haven: Yale UP.
Sontag, Susan (1977). *On Photography*. New York: Farrar, Straus & Giroux.
Sontag, Susan (1978). *Illness as Metaphor*. New York: Farrar, Straus & Giroux.
Sorensen, Ted (2008). *Counselor: A Life at the Edge of History*. New York: Harper Collins.

Soucy-Humphreys, Jade, Judd, Karina and Jürgens, Anna-Sophie (2023). "Challenging the Stereotype through Humor? Comic Female Scientists in Animated TV series for Young Audiences". *Frontiers Communication.* 7, doi: 10.3389/fcomm.2022.1024602 [Accessed 27/01/2023].

Sousa, Ana Matilde (2020). "She's Not Your *Waifu*; She's an Eldritch Abomination: *Saya no uta* and Queer Antisociality in Japanese Visual Novels". *Mechademia*, 13(1): 72–100.

Spierenburg, Petrus C. (2008). *A History of Murder: Personal Violence in Europe from the Middle Ages to the Present.* Cambridge: Polity.

Spinoza, Baruch (1985) [1677]. *Ethics.* In *The Collected Works* (trans. Edwin Curley), vol. 1: 408–620. Princeton: Princeton UP.

Srdarov, Suzanne and Bourgault du Coudray, Chantal (2016). "Still Reading the Romance: Gothic Sexuality and the Remembrance of Feminism through *Twilight* and *Fifty Shades of Grey*". *Continuum,* 30(3): 347–354.

St. Clare, Kameron Johnston (2018). "Linguistic Disarmament: On How Hate Speech Functions, The Way Hate Words Can Be Reclaimed, and Why We Must Pursue Their Reclamation". *Linguistic and Philosophical Investigations,* 17: 79–109.

Stade, Ronald (2016). "Cruelty". *Conflict and Society,* 2: 6–8.

Stafford, William (1998). "How Can a Paradigmatic Liberal Call Himself a Socialist? The Case of John Stuart Mill". *Journal of Political Ideology,* 3(3): 325–345,

Stambusky, Alan A. (1977). "Roman Comedy on Trial in the Republic: The Case of Censorship Against Gnaeus Naevius the Playwright". *Educational Theatre Journal,* 29(1): 29–36.

Stardust, Zahra Zsuzsanna (2014). "'Fisting Is Not Permitted'; Criminal Intimacies, Queer Sexualities and Feminist Porn in the Australian Legal Context". *Porn Studies,* 1(3): 258–275.

Stardust, Zahra Zsuzsanna (2019). "Alternative Pornographies, Regulatory Fantasies and Resistance Politics". PhD. University of New South Wales.

Staub, Ervin (1999). "The Roots of Evil: Social Conditions, Culture, Personality, and Basic Human Needs". *Personality and Social Psychology Review,* 3(3): 179–192.

Steele, Brent J. (2021). "'The Cruelty of Righteous People': Niebuhr on the Urgency of Cruelty". *Journal of International Political Theory,* 17(2): 1–18, https://journals.sagepub.com/doi/full/10.1177/1755088221989745 [Accessed 05/01/2023].

Stelling, Lieke (2020). "'By God's Arse': Genre, Humour and Religion in William Wager's Moral Interludes". In Derrin, Daniel and Burrows, Hannah (Eds.), *The Palgrave Handbook of Humour, History and Methodology,* 325–339. Cham: Palgrave Macmillan.

Stephens, Carolyn *et al.* (2006). "Disappearing, Displaced, and Undervalued: A Call to Action for Indigenous Health Worldwide". *The Lancet,* 367: 2019–2028.

Stevenson, Rebekah and Hiebert, Dennis (2021). "Silenced Desire: Personal Effects of the Evangelical Construction of Female Sexuality". *Journal of Sociology and Christianity,* 11(2): 59–83.

Stewart, Jack F. (1968). "Romantic Theories of Humor Relating to Sterne". *The Personalist,* 49(4): 459–473.

Steyer, Rolf *et al.* (2015). "A Theory of States and Traits – Revised". *Annual Review of Clinical Psychology,* 11: 7189.

Stone, Margaret (2002) [1995]. *The Corporal Punishment of Schoolgirls: A Documentary Survey,* 2nd ed. London: Wildfire.

Storey, Robert (2003). "Humor and Sexual Selection". *Human Nature,* 14(4): 319–336.

Strauss, Leo (1988) [1952]. *Persecution and the Art of Writing.* Chicago: University of Chicago Press.

Strossen, Nadine (1993). "A Feminist Critique of 'the' Feminist Critique of Pornography". *Virginia Law Review,* 79(5): 1099–1190.

Strossen, Nadine (1995). *Defending Pornography: Free Speech, Sex and the Fight for Women's Rights*. New York: Scribner.
Sugunasiri, Surwanda H.J. (2005). "Ādiyāna: An Alternative to Hīnayāna, Śrāvakayāna and Theravāda". *Canadian Journal of Buddhist Studies*, 1: 127.
Sullivan, Corrinne T. (2018). "Indigenous Australian Women's Colonial Sexual Intimacies: Positioning Indigenous Women's Agency". *Culture, Health and Sexuality*, 20(4): 397–410.
Sullivan, Corrinne T. (2021). "Pussy Power: A Contemporaneous View of Indigenous Women and Their Role in Sex Work". *Genealogy*, 5(3)/65, https://doi.org/10.3390/genealogy5030065 [Accessed 25/11/ 2021].
Sullivan, Corrinne T. (2022). "'People Pay Me for Sex': Contemporary Lived Experiences of Indigenous Australian Sex Workers". *Journal of Intercultural Studies*, 43(1): 23–38.
Sullivan, Dylan and Hickel, Jason (2023). "Capitalism and Extreme Poverty: A Global Analysis of Real Wages, Human Height, and Mortality since the Long 16th Century". *World Development*, 161, https://doi.org/10.1016/j.worlddev.2022.106026 [Accessed 20/09/2022].
Suls, Jerry M. (1972). "A Two-Stage Model for the Appreciation of Jokes and Cartoons". In Goldstein, Jeffrey H. and McGhee, Paul E. (Eds.), *The Psychology of Humor. Theoretical Perspectives and Empirical Issues*, 81–100. New York: Academic Press.
Svebak, Sven (1996). "The Development of the Sense of Humor Questionnaire: From SHQ to SHQ-6". *Humor: International Journal of Humor Research*, 9: 341–361.
Swabey, Marie Collins (1958). "The Comic as Nonsense, Sadism, or Incongruity". *The Journal of Philosophy*, 55(19): 819–833.
Swabey, Marie Collins (1961). *Comic Laughter: A Philosophical Essay*. New Haven: Yale UP.
Swords, Jon (2020). "Interpenetration and Intermediation of Crowd-Patronage Platforms". *Information Communication and Society*, 23(4): 523–538.
Symington, Neville (2018) [2004]. *The Blind Man Sees: Freud's Awakening and Other Essays*. New York: Routledge.
Symonds, John Addington (2004) [1896]. *A Problem in Modern Ethics*. London, https://www.sacred-texts.com/lgbt/pme/index.htm [accessed 13/10/2022].
Tacitus (1900) [98 AD]. In *De Vita Iulii Agricolae* (ed. Henry Furneaux). Oxford: Clarendon, http://www.perseus.tufts.edu/hopper/text?doc=Perseus%3Atext%3A1999.02.0084%3Achapter%3D30%3Asection%3D6 [Accessed 22/06/2022].
Tagore, Rabindranath (1918). *Nationalism*. London: Macmillan.
Takase, Fumiko (1983–1984). "The Function of Disguise in Ben Jonson's Comedies". *Ronshu*, 30: 1–14.
Tallentyre, Stephen G. (1906). *The Friends of Voltaire*. London: John Murray, https://www.gutenberg.org/files/56618/56618-h/56618-h.htm [accessed 12/10/2022].
Tamer, Georges (Ed.) (2009). *Humor in der arabischen Kultur*. Berlin: De Gruyter.
Tanitoc (2009) [2007]. "Cabu Reporter". *European Comic Art*, 2(1): 130–151.
Tanner, Julia (2015). "Clarifying the Concept of Cruelty: What Makes Cruelty to Animals Cruel". *The Heythrop Journal*, 56(5): 818–835.
Taparelli, Luigi (1851). *Saggio teoretico di diritto naturale appoggiato sul fatto*, 2nd ed. Livorno: V. Mansi.
Tarachow, Sidney (1949). "Remarks on the Comic Process and Beauty". *The Psychoanalytic Quarterly*, 18(2): 215–226.
Tate, John William (2016). "Toleration, Skepticism, and Blasphemy: John Locke, Jonas Proast, and Charlie Hebdo". *American Journal of Political Science*, 60(3): 664–675.

Tauler, Johannes (1958) [1498]. *Signposts to Perfection: A Selection from the Sermons of Johannes Tauler* (ed. and trans. Elizabeth Strakosch). St. Louis: Herder.

Taylor, Alan (2014). "The Soviet War in Afghanistan, 1979–1989". *The Atlantic*, https://www.theatlantic.com/photo/2014/08/the-soviet-war-in-afghanistan-1979-1989/100786/ [Accessed 26/08/2022].

Taylor, Alfred Edward (1932). *The Faith of a Moralist*. London: Macmillan, https://www.giffordlectures.org/lecturers/alfred-edward-taylor [Accessed 03/03/2022].

Temple, William (1934). *Nature, Man and God*. London: Macmillan, https://www.giffordlectures.org/lectures/nature-man-and-god [Accessed 04/03/2022].

Terence (n.d.a.) [163 BC]. *Heauton Timorumenos*, https://www.thelatinlibrary.com/ter.heauton.html [Accessed 31/01/2023].

Testerman, John K. *et al.* (1996). "The Natural History of Cynicism in Physicians". *Academic Medicine*, 71(10): 43–45.

Teune, Simon (2007). "Humour as a Guerrilla Tactic: The West German Student Movement's Mockery of the Establishment". *International Review of Social History*, 52(S15): 115–132.

TheBroJose (2019). "Anime Girl Says N Word", https://www.youtube.com/watch?v=qGeUG8FG2_c [Accessed 26/06/2022].

Thomas, Leah and Egan, Vincent (2022). "Subclinical Sadism: Examining Temperamental Predispositions and Emotional Processing". *Personality and Individual Differences*, 196, https://doi.org/10.1016/j.paid.2022.111756 [Accessed 15/12/2022].

Thompson, Francis (1912). "Ex Ore Infantium". In Quiller-Couch, Arthur (Ed.), *The Oxford Book of Victorian Verse*, 807–808. Oxford: Clarendon, https://library.um.edu.mo/ebooks/b34390339.pdf [Accessed 10/11/2022].

Thomson, John Arthur (1920). *The System of Animate Nature*. New York: Henry Holt, https://www.giffordlectures.org/lecturers/john-arthur-thomson [Accessed 08/06/2022].

Tietje, Louis and Cresap, Steven (2005). "Is Lookism Unjust? The Ethics of Aesthetics and Public Policy Implications". *Journal of Libertarian Studies*, 19(2): 31–50.

Tillman, Melvin and Wells, Brooke E. (2022). "An Intersectional Feminist Analysis of Women's Experiences of Authenticity in Pornography". *The Journal of Sex Research*, https://doi.org/10.1080/00224499.2021.2024489 [Accessed 03/10/2022].

Tiso, Giovanni (2011). "Da James Joyce a John Assurbanipal Smith. La (de)legittimazione del comico nell'opera di Umberto Eco". *Italian Studies in Southern Africa*, 24(1): 83–102.

Todaro, Joseph and Miller, J. Mitchell (2014). "Beccaria, Cesare". In Miller, J. Mitchell (Ed.), *The Encyclopedia of Theoretical Criminology*, vol. 1: 43–45. Chichester: Wiley-Blackwell.

Tolstoy, Lev N. (1900). *The Slavery of Our Time* (trans. Aylmer Maude). Maldon: Free Age, https://ia904509.us.archive.org/11/items/slaveryourtimes00tolsiala/slaveryourtimes00tolsiala.pdf [Accessed 11/06/2022].

Tooley, Michael (2022). "Masturbation and the Problem of Irrational and Immoral Sexual Activity". In Boonin, David (Ed.), *The Palgrave Handbook of Sexual Ethics*, 129–151. Cham: Palgrave Macmillan.

Torretta, Gabriel (2015). "Preaching on Laughter: The Theology of Laughter in Augustine's Sermons". *Theological Studies*, 76(4): 742–764.

Tosi, Renzo (2013). "Sulla genesi di alcuni proverbi". In Pino Campos, Luis Miguel and Santana, Germán (Eds.). *Καλὸς καὶ ἀγαθὸς ἀνήρ· διδασκάλου παράδειγμα. Homenaje al Profesor Juan Antonio López Férez*, 813–819. Madrid: Ediciones Clásicas.

Tran-Gervat, Yen-Mai (2014). "Pastiche". In Attardo, Salvatore (Ed.), *Encyclopedia of Humor Studies*, vol. 2. Thousand Oaks, CA: Sage, https://hal-univ-paris3.archives-ouvertes.fr/hal-01419472/document [Accessed 07/02/2023].

Trimbull, Roberrt (2018). "Freud Beyond Foucault: Thinking Pleasure as a Site of Resistance". *Journal of Speculative Philosophy*, 32(3): 522–532.

Trivedi, Lisa (2007). *Clothing Gandhi's Nation: Homespun and Modern India*. Bloomington: Indiana UP.

Trubacheva, O.N. (Ed.) (1981). ЭТИМОЛОГИЧЕСКИЙ СЛОВАРЬ СЛАВЯНСКИХ ЯЗЫКОВ. ПРАСЛАВЯНСКИЙ ЛЕКСИЧЕСКИЙ ФОНД. Moscow: НАУКА.

Turner, Christopher (2011). "Wilhelm Reich: The Man Who Invented Free Love". *The Guardian*, https://www.theguardian.com/books/2011/jul/08/wilhelm-reich-free-love-orgasmatron [Accessed 02/11/2022].

Twenge, Jean M., Sherman, Ryne A. and Wells, Brooke E. (2017). "Declines in Sexual Frequency among American Adults, 1989–2014". *Archives of Sexual Behavior*, 46: 2389–2401.

Twenge, Jean M., VanLandingham, Hannah and Campbell, W. Keith (2017). "The Seven Words You Can Never Say on Television: Increases in the Use of Swear Words in American Books, 1950–2008". *SAGE Open*, 7(3), https://doi.org/10.1177/2158244017723689 [Accessed 11/02/2023].

Uddin, Asma T. (2015). "Provocative Speech in French Law: A Closer Look at Charlie Hebdo". *FIU Law Review*, 11(1): 189–199.

United Nations (1966a). *International Covenant on Civil and Political Rights*, https://www.ohchr.org/en/instruments-mechanisms/instruments/international-covenant-civil-and-political-rights [Accessed 03/08/2021].

United Nations (1966b). *International Covenant on Economic, Social and Cultural Rights*, https://www.ohchr.org/en/instruments-mechanisms/instruments/international-covenant-economic-social-and-cultural-rights [Accessed 05/07/2021].

Uribe, Juan Guillermo (2010). "El Hombre es un Hombre para el Hombre". *Affectio Societatis*, 12, http://antares.udea.edu.co/~psicoan/affectio12.htm [Accessed 28/03/2022].

Utz, Arthur F. (1994). *Wirtschaftsethik*. Bonn: Scientia Humana Institut.

Valgenti, Robert T. (2018). "Go Bleep Yourself!" In Ford, Russell (Ed.), *Why So Serious: On Philosophy and Comedy*, 103–114. London: Routledge.

Van Heyningen, Elizabeth (2009). "The Concentration Camps of the South African (Anglo-Boer) War, 1900–1902". *History Compass*, 7(1): 22–43.

Van Ree, Erik (1988). "The Quest for Purity in Communism". In van Beek, W.E.A. (Ed.), *The Quest for Purity. Dynamics of Puritan Movements*, 245–62. Berlin: Mouton de Gruyter.

Vanderheiden, Elisabeth and Mayer, Claude-Hélène (Eds.) (2021). *The Palgrave Handbook of Humour Research*. New York: Springer.

Vanek Smith, Stacey (2021). *Machiavelli for Women. Defend Your Worth, Grow Your Ambition, and Win the Workplace*. New York: Gallery Books.

Varoufakis, Yanis (2017). *Adults in the Room. My Battle with Europe's Deep Establishment*. London: The Bodley Head.

Vasey, George (1877) [1874]. *The Philosophy of Laughter and Smiling*, 2nd ed. London: J. Burns, https://books.google.is/books?id=g6jnKnyyJS0C&printsec=frontcover&redir_esc=y#v=onepage&q&f=false [Accessed 09/07/2023].

Vasic, Milica N. (2013). "Categorization of Pornographic Video Clips on the Internet: A Cognitive Anthropological Approach". PhD. University of Belgrade.

Veblen, Thorstein (1923). *Absentee Ownership and Business Enterprise in Recent Times: The Case of America*. New York: Huebsch, https://archive.org/details/absenteeownershi0000thor [Accessed 01/06/2022].

Veblen, Thorstein (1931) [1899]. *The Theory of the Leisure Class; An Economic Study of Institutions*. London: George Allen & Unwin, https://archive.org/details/in.ernet.dli.2015.59315 [Accessed 01/07/2022].

Veblen, Thorstein (2001) [1921]. *The Engineers and the Price System*. Kitchener: Batoche, https://socialsciences.mcmaster.ca/~econ/ugcm/3ll3/veblen/Engineers.pdf [Accessed 22/12/2022].

Venet, Gisèle (2002). "Shakespeare – des humeurs aux passions". *Etudes Epistémè*, 1(1), https://doi.org/10.4000/episteme.8441 [Accessed 29/03/2022].

Verdon, Jean (2001). *Rire au Moyen Age*. Paris: Perrin.

Verri, Pietro (1994) [1777]. *Osservazioni sulla tortura*. Rome: Newton.

Vick, Jason (2015). "'Putting Cruelty First': Liberal Penal Reform and the Rise of the Carceral State". *Social Justice*, 42(1): 35–52.

Vick, Karl (2015). "Al-Qaeda Group Claims Responsibility for Paris Terror Attack". *Time*, https://time.com/3661650/charlie-hebdo-paris-terror-attack-al-qaeda/ [Accessed 26/08/2022].

Vico, Giambattista (1948) [1744]. *The New Science* (trans. Thomas Goddard Bergin and Max Harold Fisch). Ithaca: Cornell UP.

Vidal, Gore (2002). *Perpetual War for Perpetual Peace. How We Got to Be So Hated*. New York: Thunder's Mouth.

Vidino, Lorenzo (Ed.) (2018). *De-Radicalization in the Mediterranean. Comparing Challenges and Approaches*. Milan: Ledi Publishing.

Vilaythong, Alexander P. et al. (2003). "Humor and Hope: Can Humor Increase Hope?" *Humor: International Journal of Humor Research*, 16(1): 79–89.

Viljamaa, Toivo (1994). "Quintilian's Theory of Wit". *Laughter down the Centuries*, 1: 85–95.

Vitali, Stefania, Glattfelder, James B. and Battiston, Stefano (2011). "The Network of Global Corporate Control". *Plos ONE*, 6(10): e25995, https://journals.plos.org/plosone/article?id=10.1371/journal.pone.0025995 [Accessed 03/02/2021].

Vivona, Brian Daniel (2014). "Humor Functions Within Crime Scene Investigations: Group Dynamics, Stress, and the Negotiation of Emotions". *Police Quarterly*, 17(2): 127–149.

Volokh, Eugene (2000). "Freedom of Speech and Information Privacy: The Troubling Implications of a Right to Stop People from Speaking about You". *Stanford Law Review*, 52(5): 1049–1124.

Voltaire (1912) [1755]. *On Toleration and Other Essays* (trans. Joseph McCabe). New York: G.P. Putnam's Sons, https://www.gutenberg.org/files/64858/64858-h/64858-h.htm [Accessed 07/03/2023].

Voltaire (1918) [1759]. *Candide* (trans. Philip Littell). New York: Boni & Liverlight, https://www.gutenberg.org/files/19942/19942-h/19942-h.htm [Accessed 19/02/2022].

Voltaire (2005) [1733]. *Letters on England*. London: Cassell, https://www.gutenberg.org/files/2445/2445-h/2445-h.htm [Accessed 07/03/2023].

Von Franz, Marie-Louise (1997). *Archetypal Dimensions of the Psyche*. Boulder: Shambhala.

Von Kraft-Ebing, Richard (1892) [1886]. *Psychopathia Sexualis* (trans. Charles G. Chaddock). London: F.A. Davis.

Von Mises, Ludwig (1978) [1927]. *Liberalism: A Socio-Economic Exposition* (trans. Ralph Raico). Kansas City: Sheed Andrews and McMeel.

Von Mises, Ludwig (1998) [1949]. *Human Action. A Treatise on Economics*. Auburn: Mises Institute.

Von Mises, Ludwig (2012) [1920]. *Economic Calculation in the Socialist Commonwealth* (trans. S. Adler). Auburn: Mises Institute.

Von Sacher-Masoch, Leopold (1989) [1870]. *Venus in Furs*. In Deleuze, Gilles, *Masochism*, 143–271. New York: Zone Books.

Vorkachev, Sergey G. (2021). "Dirty Hands: Bribery in Russian Anecdotes". Жанры речи, 30(2): 118–125.

Vosmer, Susanne (2022). "The Matrices of Black Humor and Death". *The Israeli Journal of Humor Research*, 11(2): 6–28.

Voss, Georgina (2015). *Stigma and the Shaping of the Pornography Industry*. London: Routledge.

Wagner, Ann (1997). *Adversaries of Dance. From the Puritans to the Present*. Urbana: University of Illinois Press.

Waligorski, Conrad P. (2006). *John Kenneth Galbraith. The Economist as Political Theorist*. Lanham: Rowman & Littlefield.

Wallace, Mike and Huxley, Aldous (1958). "Aldous Huxley Interviewed by Mike Wallace", https://www.youtube.com/watch?v=alasBxZsb40 [Accessed 26/08/2022].

Walters, Kerry (2021). "Mother Teresa: A Saint Who Conquered Darkness". *Franciscan Spirit*, https://www.franciscanmedia.org/franciscan-spirit-blog/mother-teresa-a-saint-who-conquered-darkness [Accessed 06/10/2022].

Walzer, Michael (1965). *The Revolution of the Saints*. Cambridge, MA: Harvard UP.

Wang, Rubin and Wang, Ziyin (2015). "Research on the Neural Energy Coding". In Liljenström, H. (Ed.), *Advances in Cognitive Neurodynamics (IV)*, 367–372. Dordrecht: Springer.

Wang, Yow-Jiun (2021). "Tabloid Female Sex Confessions and Everyday Pro-Sex Feminism: The Case of the *Apple Daily* Taiwan". *Sexualities*, 24 (1–2): 208–225.

Ward, Caleb and Anderson, Ellie (2022). "The Ethical Significance of Being an Erotic Object". In Boonin, David (Ed.), *The Palgrave Handbook of Sexual Ethics*, 55–71. Cham: Palgrave Macmillan.

Ward, Victoria (2015). "Charlie Hebdo Cartoonist Murdered in Paris Terrorist Attack Was on al-Qaeda Wanted List". *The Telegraph*, https://www.telegraph.co.uk/news/worldnews/europe/france/11330505/Murdered-Charlie-Hebdo-cartoonist-was-on-al-Qaeda-wanted-list.html [Accessed 03/10/2022].

Warren, Caleb and McGraw, Peter A. (2015). "Benign Violation Theory". *Mays Business School Research*, paper 1: 75–77.

Warren, Caleb and McGraw, Peter A. (2016). "Differentiating What is Humorous from What Is Not". *Journal of Personality and Social Psychology*, 110(3): 407–430.

Watson, Katie (2011). "Gallows Humor in Medicine". *The Hastings Center Report*, 41(5): 37–45.

Watts, Alan (2014) [1961]. "Alan Watts on Carl Jung", https://www.youtube.com/watch?v=Jr_20uEVOiE&ab_channel=MindPodNetwork [Accessed 11/12/2022].

Wear, Delese *et al.* (2009). "Derogatory and Cynical Humour Directed towards Patients: Views of Residents and Attending Doctors". *Medical Education*, 43: 34–41.

Webber, Julie A. (Ed.) (2018). *The Joke Is on Us. Political Comedy in (Late) Neoliberal Times*. London: Lexington.

Weber, Karl Julius (1838). *Democritos oder hinterlassene Papiere eines lachenden Philosophen*. Stuttgart: Hallberger'sche Verlagshandlung, https://books.google.com.na/books?id=66vXJtuJAEkC&printsec=frontcover&source=gbs_atb#v=onepage&q&f=false [Accessed 11/11/2022].

Weeks, Mark (2012). "Comic Theory and Perceptions of a Disappearing Self". *Language and Culture Studies*, 34(1): 19–29.

Weinberg, Martin S. et al. (2010). "Pornography, Normalization, and Empowerment". *Archives of Sexual Behaviour*, 39: 1389–1401.

Weir, Charlene R. et al. (2021). "Feeling and Thinking: Can Theories of Human Motivation Explain How HER Design Impacts Clinical Burnout?" *JAMIA*, 28(5): 1042–1046.

Weisenberg, Matisyohu et al. (1998). "The Influence of Film-Induced Mood on Pain Perception". *Pain*, 76(3): 365–375.

Weiss, Rebecca (2014). "Japan's Imaginary Obsession: How the Unreal Engendered a Subculture". *Proceedings of the National Conference on Undergraduate Research 2014*, http://citeseerx.ist.psu.edu/viewdoc/download?doi=10.1.1.1014.4425&rep=rep1&type=pdf [Accessed 28/11/2021].

Weltz, Eric (2017). "Online and Internet Humor". In Attardo, Salvatore (Ed.), *The Routledge Handbook of Language and Humor*, 504–518. New York: Routledge.

Weston Vauclair, Jane (2015). "Local Laughter, Global Polemics. Understanding *Charlie Hebdo*". *European Comic Art*, 8(1): 6–14.

Weston, Jane (2009). "*Bête et méchant:* Politics, Editorial Cartoons and *Bande dessinée* in the French Satirical Newspaper *Charlie hebdo*". *European Comic Art*, 2(1): 109–129.

White, Alan Richard (1958). "The Language of Motives". *Mind*, 67(266): 258–263.

White, Amy (2013). "Liberty and Pornography: An Examination of the Use of John Stuart Mill in Pro-Censorship Feminist Arguments". *Journal of Applied Ethics and Philosophy*, 5: 18–24.

Wiebe, Donald (2001). "Ninian Smart: A Tribute". *Religion*, 31: 379–383.

Wilkinson, Damon (2021). "Lad Who Got an England Euro 2020 Winners Tattoo". *Manchester Evening News*, https://www.manchestereveningnews.co.uk/news/greater-manchester-news/lad-who-england-euro-2020-21029896 [Accessed 17/05/2022].

Williams, Bernard (1976) [1972]. *Morality: An Introduction to Ethics*. Cambridge: Cambridge UP.

Williams, David and Young, Tom (1994). "Governance, the World Bank and Liberal Theory". *Political Studies*, 42: 84–100.

Williams, John (2012) [1965]. *Stoner*. London: Vintage.

Williams, Susan H. and David C. (1996). "A Feminist Theory of Malebashing". *Michigan Journal of Gender and Law*, 4(1): 35–127.

Williams, Zoe and Leigh, Mike (2021). "'You Have to Be a Control Freak': Mike Leigh on 50 Years of Film-Making". *The Guardian*, https://www.theguardian.com/film/2021/sep/27/you-have-to-be-a-control-freak-mike-leigh-on-50-years-of-film-making [Accessed 26/08/2022].

Willinger, Ulrike et al. (2017). "Cognitive and Emotional Demands of Black Humour Processing: The Role of Intelligence, Aggressiveness and Mood". *Cognitive Processing*, 18: 159–167.

Willis, Ellen (1981). "Nature's Revenge". *The New York Times*, https://www.nytimes.com/1981/07/12/books/nature-s-revenge.html [Accessed 25/08/2022].

Willis, Ellen (1994). "Porn Free: MacKinnon's Neo-Statism and the Politics of Speech". *Transition*, 63: 4–23.

Willis, Ellen (2012) [1992]. *No More Nice Girls. Countercultural Essays*. Minneapolis: University of Minnesota Press.

Willsher, Kim (2018). "Charlie Hebdo Suspect Arrested in Djibouti". *The Guardian*, https://www.theguardian.com/world/2018/dec/21/charlie-hebdo-suspect-arrested-in-djibouti [Accessed 26/08/2022].

Wilmhurst, Peter (2002). "Institutional Corruption in Medicine". *British Medical Journal*, 325: 1232–1235.

Wisler, J.C. (2018). "U.S. CEOs of SBUs in Luxury Goods Organizations: A Mixed Methods Comparison of Ethical Decision-Making Profiles". *Journal of Business Ethics*, 149: 443–518.

Wittgenstein, Ludwig (1953). *Philosophical Investigations* (trans. G.E.M. Anscombe). London: Macmillan.
Wittgenstein, Ludwig (1975) [1969]. *On Certainty* (ed. G.E.M. Anscombe and Georg Henrik von Wright; trans. Denis Paul and G.E.M. Anscombe). Oxford: Blackwell.
Wittgenstein, Ludwig (1984) [1977]. *Culture and Value* (ed. Georg Henrik von Wright and Heikki Nyman; trans. Peter Winch). Chicago: Chicago UP.
Wittgenstein, Ludwig (1989) [1921]. *Tractatus logico-philosophicus.* Milan: Einaudi.
Wolfers, Solvejg, File, Kieran A. and Schnurr, Stephanie (2017). "'Just Because He's Black': Identity Construction and Racial Humour in a German U-19 Football Team". *Journal of Pragmatics*, 112: 83–96.
Woode Amissah-Arthur, Hannah (2022). In Chukwumah, Ignatius (Ed.), *Sexual Humour in Africa. Gender, Jokes, and Societal Change*, 215–239. London: Routledge.
Woodward, Aylin (2021). "There Are Very Solid Engineering Reasons Why Jeff Bezos' Rocket Looks Exactly Like, You Know, That". *Business Insider*, https://www.businessinsider.com/jeff-bezos-rocket-resembles-penis-engineering-blue-origin-2021-7?r=US&IR=T [Accessed 16/11/2022].
Wright, Rebecca *et al.* (2006). "Child Abuse Investigation: An In-Depth Analysis of How Police Officers Perceive and Cope with Daily Work Challenges". *Policing: An International Journal of Police Strategies and Management*, 29(3): 498–512.
Wright, Susan (2018). "De-Pathologization of Consensual BDSM". *The Journal of Sexual Medicine*, 15(5): 622–624.
Yakhlef, Sophia (2022). "Humour, Trust, and Tacit Knowledge of Police and Border Officers in International Police Collaboration". *Journal of Policing, Intelligence and Counter Terrorism*, https://doi.org/10.1080/18335330.2022.2069474 [Accessed 15/12/2022].
Yamane, Hiroaki, Mori, Yusuke and Harada, Tatsuya (2021). "Humor Meets Morality: Joke Generation Based on Moral Judgement". *Information Processing and Management*, 58: 1–15.
Ying, Zheng (2006). "John Kenneth Galbraith: A Legend of a Towering Giant". *Open Times*, 5: 26–37.
Young, Dannagal Goldthwaite (2020). *Irony and Outrage: The Polarised Landscape of Rage, Fear, and Laughter in the United States.* New York: Oxford UP.
Zakaria, Rafia (2021). *Against White Feminism: Notes on Disruption.* New York: Norton.
Zara, Giorgia, Veggi, Sara and Farrington, David P. (2021). "Sexbots as Synthetic Companions: Comparing Attitudes of Official Sex Offenders and Non-Offenders". *International Journal of Social Robotics*, https://doi.org/10.1007/s12369-021-00797-3 [Accessed 28/11/2021].
Zeigler-Hill, Virgil and Marcus, David K. (Eds.) (2016). *The Dark Side of Personality. Science and Practice in Social, Personality, and Clinical Psychology.* Washington: American Psychological Association.
Zerhouni, Oulmann (2016). "'Qui est (Vraiment) Charlie?' Les Villes Françaises à plus Faible niveau de Préjugés Implicites envers les Maghrébins ont davantage Participé aux rassemblements de Charlie Hebdo". *International Review of Social Psychology*, 29(1): 69–76.
Zetkin, Clara (1926) [1919]. *Through Dictatorship to Democracy* (trans. Eden and Cedar Paul). Glasgow: Socialist Labour Press, https://www.marxists.org/archive/zetkin/1919/xx/dictdem.htm [Accessed 04/05/2022].
Zhang, Jundan (2019). "Tourism and Environmental Subjectivities in the Anthropocene: Observations from Niru Village, Southwest China". *Journal of Sustainable Tourism*, 27(4): 488–502.
Zillmann, Dolf (1998). *Connections Between Sexuality and Aggression*, 2nd ed. Mahwah, NJ: Lawrence Erlbaum.
Zolo, Danilo (1989) [1986]. *Reflexive Epistemology: The Philosophical Legacy of Otto Neurath* (trans. David McKie). Dordrecht: Kluwer.

Zorthian, Julia (2016). "Archbishop Says ISIS Crucified a Priest on Good Friday". *Time*, https://time.com/4273645/isis-crucified-priest-good-friday/ [Accessed 26/08/2022].

Zuboff, Shoashana (2019). *The Age of Surveillance Capitalism*. London: Profile.

Zucchelli, Alessandro (2009). *Il riso fa buon sangue. Fondamenti scientifici del riso*. Seattle: Amazon, https://books.google.com.do/books?id=-LT1nfKdmOcC&pg=PA1&source=gbs_selected_pages&cad=2#v=onepage&q&f=false [Accessed 17/05/2022].

Zweyer, Karen *et al.* (2004). "Do Cheerfulness, Exhilaration, and Humor Production Moderate Pain Tolerance? A FACS Study". *Humor: International Journal of Humor Research*, 17(1–2): 85–119.

Index

Addison, Joseph   34, 37, 40–42, 48, 51
Adorno, Theodor   46–48, 116f., 121, 140
aggression, aggressiveness   23, 76f., 87, 129, 137, 140, 166
Ainslie, George   142–144, 175
alcohol   120, 166
Amir, Lydia   36, 40, 51f., 170
anaesthesia of the heart   50, 79
anthropology, anthropological   156
Aquinas, Thomas   47, 64, 68, 89f., 93, 164
Aristotle   62, 74, 136, 152, 156
Artaud, Antonin   116f.
Attardo, Salvatore   2, 65, 71f.
Augustine, Saint   90

Bakhtin, Mikhail   32, 65f.
Baroncelli, Flavio   4, 7, 12, 24, 139, 157, 170f.
Barry, John   157f.
Beattie, James   40, 44, 63
Beccaria, Cesare   97f., 108f., 121, 134
Benign Violation Theory   73
Benjamin, Walter   46, 69
Bergson, Henri   49f., 89
Bierce, Ambrose   53
bisociation   77f., 167

Canetti, Elias   59
capitalism, capitalist   21, 97, 121, 174
carnival, carnivalesque   66f., 119, 134
Carroll, Lewis   54, 64, 152
Carroll, Noël   54, 64, 152
Cassirer, Ernst   51–54, 84
Castoriadis, Cornelius   7f., 97, 115, 130
Cazamian, Louis   37
censorship, censoriousness   8, 27, 34, 65, 73
Chaplin, Charlie   46
Chesterton, G.K.   7f., 53f., 83f., 92, 104f., 118, 142, 159, 173
Christianity, Christian   122, 124, 126, 173f.
Christie, Nils   172
Cioran, Emil   99, 116
Collins, Randall   133–135, 170, 175
colonialism, colonial   97, 110

communism, communist   7
Congreve, William   39
corporal punishment   97, 111
Critchley, Simon   33, 43f.

dancing   34, 112
Darwin, Charles   68f., 79, 167
De Beauvoir, Simone   88, 172
Deleuze, Gilles   47, 54–59, 115, 158, 160, 173
Derrida, Jacques   114f.
De Unamuno, Miguel   38
Dickens, Charles   53f.
Dickensian   32
Diderot, Denis   1, 8, 33, 118
Dostoyevsky, Fyodor M.   169, 173
Duchenne, Guillaume   69
Dworkin, Andrea   12, 139

Eagleton, Terry   8, 64f., 67
economics   58, 97
Eco, Umberto   2, 11, 28, 151, 163
epistemology, epistemological   12, 62, 149, 156
Erasmus, Desiderius   8, 52
Esar, Evan   36
ethics, ethical   3f., 7, 98, 124, 154
ethology, ethological   82–83

feminism, feminist   27, 32, 93, 119
focal point   22, 148
football   62, 66, 155f.
Foucault, Michel   11
Frege, Gottlob   54, 154f.
Freud, Sigmund   4, 55f., 64f., 67, 70, 75–79, 115, 129–133, 142, 164, 170, 175

Galbraith, John Kenneth   7f., 21, 44, 102, 111
Galen, Aelius   29f., 57
Galenic   30f.
gender   2, 6, 22, 119, 138, 158
Gestalt   10, 22, 38, 45, 62, 64, 147–149, 151, 158, 162, 164
Guattari, Félix   56, 115, 160, 173

Hallie, Philip   5 f., 110–113, 124, 127, 139, 157, 164, 174 f.
Harlow, Harry   60 f., 63, 67 f., 70 f., 73, 164
Hartley, David   43, 68, 119
Harvey, Jean   152
Hazlitt, William   44 f., 47, 50, 63, 97
hermeneutics, hermeneutical   106, 146
Hillman, James   8, 27, 87, 118, 131, 147, 163, 170
Hippocrates   29 f., 57
Hippocratic   30 f.
Hobbes, Thomas   62, 95 f., 170 f.
Homer   118, 125, 168
Hood, Edwin   41, 44, 83
Horkheimer, Max   121, 140
Hugo, Victor   33, 35
Hume, David   96, 118, 156
Hurley, Matthew   80–82
Hutcheson, Francis   94 f.
Hyers, Conrad   166

incongruity theory   63, 65, 168
Ingarden, Roman   137
irony, ironic   4, 8, 13, 24 f., 27, 36, 44, 48–50, 52 f., 55–57, 125, 128, 133, 146, 159, 171

Jesus Christ   47, 123, 138
Jews   24, 98, 106, 138
Jonson, Ben   30 f.
Jung, Carl Gustav   4, 8, 27, 47, 54, 56, 66, 76, 78, 103, 117, 127–129, 154 f., 158, 170, 174
jurisprudence   90, 173

Kant, Immanuel   11, 93, 98, 156
Kekes, John   104 f., 107, 127
Khomeini, Imam   7
Kierkegaard, Søren A.   46–49
Kipnis, Laura   19, 24, 28, 32, 155
Koestler, Arthur   77–79
Kolnai, Aurel   118, 139
Kozintsev, Alexander   60
Krichtafovitch, Igor   154

Leacock, Stephen   7 f., 12, 36, 40, 42, 63, 83, 106 f., 134
Lecky, William   100–103, 127
Lenin, Vladimir   112
Leopardi, Giacomo   47, 98 f., 118, 169

libido, libidinal   23, 55, 129–131, 133
Lipps, Theodor   51
Locke, John   84, 93 f., 103 f.
Lorenz, Konrad   152
Lutheran   46
Luther, Martin   39, 138

Machiavelli, Niccolò   113 f., 144
Maritain, Jacques   1, 19 f., 114, 117, 136
Martin, Rod   74 f.
Marxist, Marxism   46, 133, 160
Marx, Karl   103
Maslow, Abraham   85
masochism, masochist, masochistic   56 f., 59, 113, 118, 129, 131, 133, 139, 172
McMurtry, John   7, 9–11, 26, 110
Merleau-Ponty, Marcel   118, 144, 149, 155
Milgram, Stanley   128
Mill, John Stuart   7, 30, 79–81, 97, 119, 156
Montaigne, Michel de   91–97, 103, 107, 110, 124, 164, 175
More, Thomas   1 f., 4 f., 8–10, 12–19, 21, 23–25, 27 f., 32, 34, 38–40, 42–54, 56–58, 62–68, 70–73, 81–89, 91–93, 95, 98 f., 101 f., 107–109, 111, 114 f., 117–122, 125, 127–130, 137–139, 141, 144 f., 147, 149–151, 153–156, 158–160, 162–165, 167, 169–172, 174
Morreall, John   34, 63, 74
Mother Nature   98, 120, 169, 173
mutilation   4, 70, 93, 97, 134 f.
myth, mythic, mythology, mythological   18, 60, 87, 131

Nell, Victor   127, 131, 139–143, 173
neurotic, neurosis   1, 67, 111, 130 f.
Nietzsche, Friedrich   4, 8, 47, 84, 115, 117 f., 122–127, 132, 135, 137, 139, 170, 174 f.
nonsense, nonsensical   54 f., 63, 122

objectivism, objective, objectivity   77, 154, 162
Orwell, George   103

Pareto, Vilfredo   3, 7 f., 38, 66, 173
Pasolini, Pier Paolo   20
penal, penology   97, 102, 108 f., 113, 169, 172 f.
phenomenology   10, 12, 62, 149 f., 162
Phillips, Anita   56, 70, 172

physiology, physiological   64, 83
Pirandello, Luigi   42, 50–53, 170
Plato   29, 62, 118
poetry, poetic   54, 159
Polanyi, Michael   4, 10, 12, 16f., 20, 22, 47, 58, 62, 72, 84, 112, 145, 147–158, 160, 162–164
political economy   35, 109
politics, political   6, 28, 50, 114, 144, 156
polysemy, polysemic   3, 16, 39, 145f., 153, 159, 164
predation, predatory   95, 139f., 143
private property   6f., 102, 109
Protestant, Protestantism   22, 31, 93, 98
psychiatry   57, 129
psychoanalysis, psychoanalytical   56, 64, 75f., 78, 84, 129–131
psychology, psychological   4, 22f., 51, 54, 56, 63, 67f., 73, 76, 80f., 83–85, 106, 111, 113, 122f., 128f., 132, 138, 141, 147, 150, 155, 157, 163, 170
punishment   56, 87–90, 92, 97–100, 107f., 131, 134, 136, 142
Puritanism, Puritans   33f.

Quintilian, Marcus   38, 63f.

Ramachandran, Vilayanur   82f.
Rand, Ayn   121f.
Raskin, Victor   2, 71
Regan, Tom   103f., 127
relief theory   64, 67
Renaissance   30, 56, 91, 144
rhetoric, rhetorical   3, 39, 150
Roberts, Alan   36–38, 63
Rorty, Richard   13, 57, 102f., 105, 107
Rosset, Clément   115–117
Rousseau, Jean-Jacques   98, 131
Russell, Bertrand   7, 19, 32, 91, 107, 120, 133, 147f., 159

Sacher-Masoch, Leopold von   56f.
Sade, Marquis de   57, 84, 88, 118–122, 125, 129, 132, 137, 139, 174
sadism, sadistic   46, 55, 57, 95, 113, 117, 126f., 129, 131–133, 138, 166
sadomasochism, sadomasochistic   56
Santayana, George   45, 50
Satan, satanic, satanism   174

satire, satirical   5, 8, 27, 35f., 45f., 50, 52, 58, 67, 167
scepticism, sceptical   52, 96, 156
Schadenfreude   82, 143
Schopenhauer, Arthur   42, 47–49, 51, 99f., 115
script-based semantic theory of humour   71
self-censorship   viii
Seneca, Lucius A.   88–91, 93, 96, 109, 136, 164
Shaftesbury, Earl of   39f., 43, 51f., 64
Shakespearean   52
Shakespeare, William   24, 31, 83
Shestov, Leo   99
Shklar, Judith   3, 102f., 105, 107, 127, 175
Simpson, James A.   42, 60
Smith, Adam   21, 109f., 114, 133, 175
socialism, socialist   4, 8, 93, 160
sociology, sociological   133
Socratic   23
Sontag, Susan   104, 170
Spencer, Herbert   64
Spinoza, Baruch   106
Stanford Prison Experiment   128
Steele, Richard   34, 40
subjectivity, subjective   113
subsidiary details   22, 72, 148f., 151, 159, 161f., 165
superiority theory   64f.
Swabey, Marie Collins   46, 55
Swift, Jonathan   33, 50, 83, 97

tacit knowing, tacit knowledge   151
terrorism, terrorist   22
theatre   30f., 34, 116f., 128, 144, 172
theology, theological   150, 173
The Spectator   34, 40–42
tickling   68f., 80
Tolstoy, Lev N.   103
torture   66, 70, 89, 94, 97, 115, 123, 125, 128, 134–137, 141f.
transposition   49, 133
true humour   5, 41f., 48, 51, 53, 85

Vico, Giambattista   160
Voltaire   11, 34f., 52, 58, 97, 118, 163f.

Wittgenstein, Ludwig   4f., 85f., 146, 163, 165, 168

Zimbardo, Philip   128

www.ingramcontent.com/pod-product-compliance
Lightning Source LLC
Chambersburg PA
CBHW020227170426
43201CB00007B/342